Free Speech for Me But Not for Thee

Also by Nat Hentoff

Free Speech for Me— But Not for Thee

How the American Left and Right Relentlessly Censor Each Other

NAT HENTOFF

Aaron Asher Books
HarperCollins*Publishers*

HarperCollins books may be purchased for educational, business, or sales promotional use. For information, please write: Special Markets Department, HarperCollins Publishers, Inc., 10 East 53rd Street, New York, NY 10022.

FIRST EDITION

Designed by Alma Hochhauser Orenstein

Library of Congress Cataloging-in-Publication Data

Hentoff, Nat.
    Free speech for me—but not for thee: how the American left and right relentlessly censor each other/Nat Hentoff.—1st ed.
            p.   cm.
    Includes index.
    ISBN 0-06-019006-X
    1. Freedom of speech—United States.   2. Censorship—United States.
I. Title.
KF4772.H46   1992
342.73'0853—dc20
[347.302853]   92-52550

92 93 94 95 96 ❖/GL 10 9 8 7 6 5 4 3 2 1

*For Margot, who never lets my right to free speech get in the
way of her skeptical assessment of each word, and then some.*

*And for Alan Dershowitz, who never flinches from defending
the most unpopular speech.*

Driven from every other corner of the earth, freedom of thought and the right of private judgement in matters of conscience, direct their course to this happy country as their last asylum.

—SAMUEL ADAMS

We began well. No inquisition here. No kings, no nobles. No dominant church here, heresy has lost its terror.

—RALPH WALDO EMERSON

If large numbers of people believe in freedom of speech, there will be freedom of speech, even if the law forbids it. But if public opinion is sluggish, inconvenient minorities will be persecuted, even if laws exist to protect them.

—GEORGE ORWELL

Every time I criticize what I consider to be excesses or faults in the news business, I am accused of repression, and the leaders of the various media professional groups wave the First Amendment as they denounce me.

That happens to be my amendment, too. It guarantees my free speech as it does their freedom of the press. ... There is room for all of us—and for our divergent views—under the First Amendment.

—SPIRO AGNEW

Liberty wasn't guaranteed by the Constitution. It was only given a chance.

—STEPHEN CHAPMAN, *CHICAGO TRIBUNE*

Contents

Prologue

I had been writing a series of columns in the *Village Voice* about certain thought police at that very paper. I had found out that on Monday nights, when the paper went to bed, some editors and copy editors—without telling the writers—were cutting out certain words, sometimes sentences and paragraphs, that might offend the *Voice*'s constituencies.

Those constituencies are considered to be liberals, radicals, blacks, Hispanics, gays, and lesbians. The censors within the paper wanted to make sure that the feelings of our primary readers were not hurt.

As my columns exposing the thought police continued, I said, among other things, that some of my colleagues were mirror images of Phyllis Schlafly and Jerry Falwell, whom they regularly excoriated. A postcard came. It was from Phil Kerby, then an editorial writer for the *Los Angeles Times*. He advised me to look at my paper's thought police in perspective: "Censorship," he wrote, "is the strongest drive in human nature; sex is a weak second."

And the lust to suppress can come from any direction. In 1981, Frank P. L. Somerville, religion editor of the *Baltimore Sun*, reported on a historic Sunday morning service at the First Unitarian Church at which "centuries of Jewish, Christian, Islamic and Hindu writings were 'expurgated' because of sections described as 'sexist.'

"Touched off by a candle and consumed in a pot on a table in front of the altar were slips of paper containing 'patriarchal' excerpts from Martin Luther, Thomas Aquinas, the Koran, St. Augustine, St. John Chrysostom, the Hindu Code of Manu V, an anonymous Chinese author and the Old Testament. Also included were references from the writings of such... theologians as Kierkegaard and Karl Barth....

"As the last flame died in the pot and the organ pealed, there was applause.... From the pulpit, First Unitarian's minister, the Reverend Robert L. Zoerheide, inquired: 'Do you ever have the feeling you are making history in this ... liberal church?'" He hoped that no one would "undervalue" the significance of this purifying service.

A few weeks after that purging event, I was speaking to members of the Northern California affiliate of the American Civil Liberties Union. In mentioning the exorcism of sexist speech at the Unitarian church, I noted that the children present at that Sunday morning service were likely to have learned a powerful lesson. When speech offends, burn it.

An angry woman, a card-carrying civil libertarian, stood up, and said, "There was nothing wrong with what those women did. We did the same thing at our church two Sundays ago. And long past time too. Don't you understand it's just symbolic?"

I reminded her that in 1973, when the school board in Drake, North Dakota, threw thirty-four copies of Kurt Vonnegut's *Slaughterhouse Five* into the public school's furnace, it wasn't because the school was getting low on fuel. They, too, were engaging in a symbolic act of protest against what they considered harmful speech. Of the thirty-four students to whom the book had been assigned, thirty-two had asked the board for clemency for the book. They too learned a lesson about the vulnerability of the First Amendment. (I do not know if the kids ever found out that none of the members of the school board had read *Slaughterhouse Five*.)

There is another kind of censorship. Legally, censorship in violation of the First Amendment can only take place when an agent or agency of the state—a public school principal, a congressman, a President—suppresses speech. But the spirit of censorship, as Phil

Kerby observed, is pervasive in private institutions and among non-governmental individuals and groups throughout the society.

In the fall of 1991, I learned a lesson about that kind of censorship of which I was found guilty. It came from a preacher, Dan Martin, who presides over a ninety-one-member congregation near the Blue Ridge Parkway in western North Carolina. He and I were to be on a panel, "Censorship, Obscenity and the Arts," at Converse College in Spartanburg, South Carolina. Another panel member was to be Laura Hudson, executive director of C.A.D.R.E. (Citizens Advocating Decency and a Revival of Ethics).

I knew where she was coming from. And I figured I knew where this smoothly articulate, sweepingly self-confident Southern Baptist preacher was coming from. Before we went on, I teased him about what his flock might think if he were to appear one day wearing an ACLU button. He looked at me, smiled, and said, "You might be surprised."

During the panel discussion, Laura Hudson sounded like a fusion of Jesse Helms and law professor Catharine MacKinnon with regard to relentlessly ridding the nation of obscenity and pornography—as they so generously define those terms.

The Baptist minister, however, his voice a trombone of freedom, sounded like a cross between William O. Douglas and William Brennan. He was opposed to all censorship. Suppressing speech went against the convictions and hopes of the Framers of the Constitution. Americans were meant to think for themselves, not to have the authorities think for them.

Afterward, he just barely chastised me for what I had thought he was. "There is a censorship," said preacher Dan Martin, "of stereotype, of caricature. You know someone is a Baptist minister, let's say, so, unless you're forced to listen to him, you don't have to. You already know what he's going to say. So you shut him off. He doesn't get into the exchange of ideas. A lot of that kind of censorship goes on—on all sides." He was kind enough not to look at me.

I learned something else from another preacher who did want to suppress speech—in this case, a series of reading textbooks that had been ordered by a public school system. It was in the northern Idaho town of Coeur d'Alene (population twenty thousand). There was a civil war going on over the "Impressions" series of texts that included a number of well-written imaginative stories and poems by a wide range of reputable authors.

Opponents of the texts claimed that the books proselytized for witchcraft, satanism, and the occult. Some of those stories did involve such subjects, but hardly as propaganda. And some of the critics ingeniously charged that the schoolboard, by bringing in the "Impressions" texts, had violated the Establishment Clause of the First Amendment (the state shall not support or prefer any or all religions). The public school authorities in Coeur d'Alene—the critics claimed—were establishing the religions of satanism, occultism and humanism through adopting these books.

I had come to Coeur d'Alene to give a talk on the First Amendment at a local college. That afternoon, a young bearded, part-time minister (he worked as a carpenter during the day) came to see me, along with several members of his congregation who had children in the public schools.

The minister was the unyielding leader of the opposition to the new reading series. We went over a couple of volumes, and he pointed out what he saw as the satanism, the violence, the subliminal preaching of witchcraft.

I told him that as a child, I had read every one of the Lang books of fairy tales (*The Yellow Fairy Book, The Red Fairy Book,* etc.) and had even come upon an unexpurgated Brothers Grimm. By contrast, what he had shown me was quite mild and was far less likely to turn a young mind into rubble than any day's television program, and particularly the Saturday morning cartoons.

Neither of us convinced the other, but it became clear that something besides witches lurking in textbooks was disturbing him. His neighbors, he told me—including some of the professors at the nearby college where I was to lecture—were spreading the word that he and his followers were not only censors but kooks, zealots, obviously unable to take part in any meaningful dialogue on school curriculum. They were not only censors, they were cracked.

Indeed, I had heard that contemptuous evaluation from some of the professors at the college and a number of the other townspeople who were fighting to keep the reading texts. "These are the people," I was told again and again by the antagonists of the minister and his followers, "who are trying to impose *their* values on us."

"Surely," the minister said to me, "we have a right to protest, a right to fight for our beliefs."

On that we agreed.

Throughout our history, one group or another, right and left, has been labeled as unworthy of being heard. Or worse, too dangerous to be heard. Toward the end of his last term as President, Ronald Reagan, whose sense of history has been formed by clips from feature films, told the *Washington Times:*

"Remember, there once was a Congress in which they had a committee that would investigate even one of their own members if it was believed that person has Communist involvement or Communist leanings. Well, they've done away with those committees. That shows the success of what the Soviets were able to do in this country with making it unfashionable to be anti-Communist."

The President immediately brought to mind a book I use in talking to middle-school and high school students. It was given to me by Fred Bass, owner of Strand Books in New York, a huge source of secondhand books. He often buys private libraries, and this book came from one of them.

There is no author's or publisher's name on the cover or spine of the book. Those areas are covered with tape. The only printing on the cover is *The Civil War.* The reason for all this caution becomes clear when the book is opened to the title page:

The Civil War in the United States, by Karl Marx and Friedrich Engels.

There were other books in that library whose authors were also covered over. At some point in the heyday of the committees whose passing is mourned by Ronald Reagan, the collector had decided to make preparations in the event an informer happened to be in his home.

The school kids gape at the book and look puzzled when I tell them of the days and years when people were afraid of signing petitions for anything at all in fear of maybe being hauled before a congressional or a state committee hunting for Reds.

I tell them of buoyant Judy Holliday—whom some have seen on cable television "movie classics." After being grilled before a congressional committee so that she might shrive herself for having supported Henry Wallace in the 1948 presidential campaign, she later emphasized: "I don't say 'yes' to anything now except cancer and cerebral palsy."

The kids sometimes ask me if I ever had to testify before one of those committees. No, but in 1970, without asking me a word, the House Internal Security Committee—successor to the House Un-American Activities Committee—placed me on a list. Its indefatigable staff had put together the names of speakers who, they said, appeared at college campuses around the country "promoting violence and encouraging the destruction of our system of government." In our wake, the committee reported, there were often fires and uprisings.

The committee's list of incendiaries appeared, among many other places, in *The New York Times*. Alongside my name in the *Times* were three organizations to which—the committee had charged—I belonged. Before it printed the list, *The New York Times* did not call me to see if I did indeed belong to those revolutionary-sounding groups. *The New York Times* had faith in the House Internal Security Committee's research division. Actually, I belonged to none of the three, and never had.

As for my promoting violence, years before, the indomitable pacifist, A. J. Muste, had convinced me of the saving logic of nonviolence. During the period covered by the committee's list of people trying to destroy our system of government, I had been speaking against the war in Vietnam at various colleges while also speaking against the use of violence by antiwar activists on speakers who supported the war. Engaging in such violence, I would say, transmogrified opponents of the war into mirror images of Lyndon Johnson, Dean Rusk, General Westmoreland, and the other true believers that Vietnam had to be destroyed in order to save it.

At one college, I was drowned out by opponents of the war for uttering this heresy.

For years afterward, I would meet people who said they had been surprised to find out that I belonged to the three dangerous groups listed by the House Internal Security Committee. After all, if a congressional committee had said so, with the further imprimatur of *The New York Times*, it must all be true.

An epiphany of the years of the Great Fear concerned David

Susskind, a prolific producer of television programs. For a dramatic show, he had been looking for an eight-year-old girl. After a long search, he found the right one. Like those of all the actors, her name had to be sent to the Young & Rubicam advertising agency, which in turn delivered her name to Vincent Hartnett, who provided political clearance. Hartnett—head of Aware, Inc.—described himself as "a professional consultant on the Communist Front records of persons working in the entertainment industry."

The name of the eight-year-old girl did not clear. Susskind called the Young & Rubicam executive in charge of the program and said, "You've ordered me never to protest because it would be hopeless. But this is insane. I beg you to tell me what you have on this child."

The agency apparatchik said he'd check. He called Susskind back. "This is not to be taken as precedent," he told Susskind, "but in this one case, I will tell you that it is the child's father we regard as suspect, and therefore we will not permit the use of the child on the program."

In those years, anyone even remotely suspected of being a Communist sympathizer—or, in this case, the child of what used to be called a Comsymp—could quickly become a pariah. But in these years, so can members of quite different groups whose views are so hated that they are not considered worthy of any protection at all.

West Hartford, Connecticut, is a largely liberal community. In 1990, an anti-abortion protest in that city was broken up by unusually vicious police methods. Among those terrorized were protestors who had invaded the clinic and blocked its entrance. Obviously, they had committed illegal acts, and the police were entirely justified in arresting them—but not in torturing them. Others swept up in the police dragnet were pro-lifers picketing peaceably outside of the clinic. Many of them were also arrested and brutalized.

The West Hartford police, like a number of police forces in the country, were using what they call "pain compliance" techniques on the antiabortionists. The aim is to inflict so much pain on someone who has gone limp in noncooperation—as did all of these arrested pro-lifers—that they will "cooperate." (Going limp is a standard historic practice of many different kinds of nonviolent demonstrators, including civil rights and antiwar protesters.)

By bending arms, wrists, and fingers way back, as well as applying intense pressure to particularly sensitive parts of the body, police can cause such agony that the screams are frightening.

The extent of the torture—and that's exactly what it was—had been documented by the *Hartford Courant*, hardly an antiabortion newspaper, and also by the United States Civil Rights Commission, as well as by a videotape of what happened. I saw the videotape. The police riot in West Hartford was at least on the level of the official violence in Selma, Alabama, and other southern cities during the civil rights marches.

A friend of mine, a psychologist, lives and practices in West Hartford. A woman of considerable compassion, she has nonetheless been reluctant to talk about the savagery inflicted on the pro-lifers. Still, I asked her if it was true that not a single minister, priest, or rabbi in the town had protested against the police torture—either directly to the authorities or at least in their sermons.

"Not one," she said. What about some of the residents of West Hartford? A sizable number of professors, psychiatrists, physicians, and other professionals live in the town. No, she said, there had been no individual protests, and no committees had been formed to look into the matter. (I had heard that one person did criticize the police at a town meeting, but I was told by residents that he was a well-known eccentric. A kook.)

Why, then, in such a civilized place as West Hartford, most of whose residents deplore and are repelled by prejudice—let alone violence—against blacks or Jews, had there been such pervasive silence about the vicious police attacks on the pro-lifers? Indeed, during an arraignment in one courtroom the police, in the back of the courtroom, had continued beating others in custody. Everyone in the courtroom, including the judge, could hear what was going on, but nothing was done to stop it.

Anyone, moreover, who read the Hartford and West Hartford papers knew what was happening. Not everyone heard the screams, but they knew that the police had been out of control. So why, I again asked my friend, the silence?

"Well," she said, "it's a pro-choice community." And so is she.

Just as pro-choicers seldom defend the free-speech rights of those with a contrary choice (and the same is true of pro-lifers), so people who abhor racism do not believe that racists have a right to speak freely.

In the 1980s, I got to know a reporter for a pro-apartheid South African daily. He was stationed in New York and particularly enjoyed covering stories that illustrated, as he pointed out, Americans' unbounded hypocrisy concerning free speech. He was bright, nasty, and challenging.

There was one story we both knew about. At the State University of New York at New Paltz, a political science professor, opposed to apartheid, decided that it would be useful for his class to hear and debate an actual member of the South African government rather than get all their information about that government's attitudes and priorities secondhand. He invited a representative of the South African diplomatic corps to come to New Paltz.

The South African never got a chance to say a word to the class. Some fifty students, white and black, roared and screamed at the visitor as he entered the Humanities Building. In the lecture room, although a clear majority of the students wanted to hear and argue with him, the others made so much sustained noise that his only choice was to leave.

As the South African left the campus of this, one of the jewels of the New York State University System, a black student yelled, "Let the story go out that students would not allow a racist to speak on this campus!"

The reporter for the South African daily gleefully sent the story back home—just as it happened, capped by the self-congratulatory declaration of the black student. It ran in other South African newspapers as well.

And the students who would not let the South African speak were exhilarated at their silencing of this representative of a government that had devoted so much of its energy to silencing its opponents.

Throughout our own history, Americans have been silenced by patriots who considered themselves true sons of liberty. Only a small percentage of these assaults on speech and assembly are covered by the press, for it has only so much space. These small silencings in places remote from the big cities are known only to the natives and the victims.

For instance, in the summer of 1982, fifty-four women from various parts of the United States started a walk for peace in west central New York. They were headed for Seneca Falls, site of the first women's rights convention in 1848. Theirs was to be a nonviolent witness—in the tradition of Gandhi and Martin Luther King—to the accelerating dangers of the nuclear arms competition.

To avoid any misunderstanding as to the purpose and nature of their witnessing, they gave advance notice to the police chiefs of every town on their route. When the women arrived at the village of Waterloo, a hundred or so townspeople would not let them pass. Some of the citizens threatened the marchers with physical harm. Brandishing American flags, they thrust two-foot flagpoles at the women. Others in the welcoming crowd threw flowers at the women—flowers that had been sprayed with mace.

Blocked by the mob, the women sat down. The police arrested them all. None of their tormenters were arrested. The women, charged with disorderly conduct, spent five days in jail. Fortunately or not, the South African reporters based in New York and Washington did not hear of American constitutional democracy at work in Waterloo.

The urge—indeed, lust—to interfere with the "wrong" thoughts and speech of others is often manifested in anti-religious zealotry. The Establishment Clause of the First Amendment does indeed say that no agency of the state may support or prefer any religion or all religions, but this command is taken by some fierce secularists to justify assaults on certain religious expression that is not prohibited by the Establishment Clause.

For instance, some years ago, the president of the American Civil Liberties Union's Pierce County chapter in Washington State sent a stern warning to the superintendent of the Bethel School District in Spanaway. The superintendent was charged with permitting the production at Bethel High School of the rock opera *Jesus Christ, Superstar.*

The letter declared: "As you should be aware, the Establishment Clause of the First Amendment prohibits the use of public school facilities for religious purposes. The production of *Jesus Christ, Superstar* violates that prohibition. The opera is religious in nature, as is clearly demonstrated by the furor it has caused among the many religious residents of our community....

"The ACLU does not oppose religion, or the free exercise thereof." However, "the production of a religious work at a public high school with the approval of the school board impermissibly tends to place the imprimatur of the state on a particular religious statement. In short, Bethel High is engaging in religious instruction. Such instruction has no place in a public school....

"Further violations of this nature may result in more direct and more drastic action by the ACLU.... Recognizing that these decisions are not always easy, the ACLU stands ready to provide assistance in the future, if requested. Please do not hesitate to call on us."

The ACLU in Pierce County had actually proposed that it would screen musicals and other works being considered for production by high school students to determine if they should be censored for being "religious in nature." As time went on, an ACLU *Index Librorum Prohibitorum* would be established comprising plays, musicals, film strips, films, videocassettes, etc. With "Banned in Boston" no longer an active impetus to sales, "Banned by the ACLU" might well be a much more effective way to advertise controversial works.

I called the president of that civil liberties watchdog chapter and asked him if the ban would also apply to Verdi's *Requiem* and Duke Ellington's *Concert of Sacred Music.* I was accused of making light of a serious constitutional issue.

Although tempted to see how far this exceedingly expansive view of the Establishment Clause would go, and whether it might spread to other ACLU chapters and affiliates, I could not resist telling Ira Glasser, the executive director of the national ACLU, about this crusade to purify the Pierce County public schools of every bit of expression that might be interpreted as endorsing religion. He in turn persuaded that chapter in Washington that *Jesus Christ, Superstar* could be performed in a public high school without shattering the wall of separation between church and state.

Harder to persuade were officials of the Spring Lake Elementary School in Omaha, Nebraska, seven years later, in 1989. Leslie Halbleib, teacher of a fifth-grade reading class, has a rule of reward for her pupils. Anyone finishing all the assignments, including long-term assignments, can read a book of his or her choice during the rest of the period.

One day, ten-year-old James Gierke, having finished all his work, including a long-term assignment, picked up his Bible and started to read it. Silently. Observing what the boy had in his hands, the teacher came over and told him he was breaking the law. He must forthwith remove his Bible from the classroom and put it in his locker.

A week later, James Gierke tried again to read his Bible, silently, after all his work was done. Once more, the teacher ordered the boy to place the controversial book in his locker. Undaunted, the ten-year-old asked, after lunch, if his Bible might be paroled. The teacher solemnly informed him that the principal, Darline Blotzer, had let it be known that no Bibles were allowed in the school. Not even the child's locker could be a sanctuary anymore for the infectious book. James was ordered to take his Bible home, and leave it there.

On the same day, James's father, Robert Gierke, called the principal and asked why on earth his boy not only couldn't read his Bible in class but also had to remove it entirely from the premises. The principal said that either a federal law or a state law, she wasn't sure which, commanded her to act as she had.

The father was puzzled. He had been informed that there was a Bible, in plain view, in the school library. He asked what would have been wrong with James's checking out *that* Bible and reading it in class during his free time.

The principal was not stumped. She told Mr. Gierke that the Bible in the library was only for reference, and it could be checked out only by the adults in that elementary school.

By now there was a question as to whether even Thomas Jefferson had envisioned the wall between church and state growing quite this high. Nebraska attorney Douglas Veith, with the support of the National Legal Foundation—a Christian organization that litigates religious liberty cases—brought suit against Darline Blotzer and Leslie Halbleib.

The lawyers for James Gierke claimed in Federal District Court that snatching the Bible away from James—while the other kids could read what they liked—violated his First Amendment rights to free speech and free exercise of religion as well as his Fourteenth Amendment right to equal protection under the laws. Not to be ignored, they added, were provisions of the Nebraska constitution guaranteeing religious freedom and equal rights.

Meanwhile, while James Gierke's Bible was being treated as contraband by the Spring Lake Elementary School, fifth-grade students in another course were, in the normal course of curricular events, studying the First Amendment.

The federal case never came to trial, and James Gierke lost a chance to be a citation in constitutional law books. The parties settled. Henceforth, it is, and will be, the practice of the Omaha public schools "to permit students to read religious literature of the student's choice during a student's free time." The school district "agrees to appropriately publicize the existence of this practice in all of its schools."

The school also agreed to pay James and his parents $1,900.

According to the *Oklahoma World Herald*, Darline Blotzer and Leslie Halbleib were in the courtroom when the settlement became final. After it was approved by the judge, the fifth-grader "went to his teacher and hugged her."

It was not reported whether she hugged him back.

In any case, the principal and the teacher learned something of First Amendment value. A child silently reading the Bible on his own time in public school has no relationship to school authorities mandating that all children pray from the Bible at a given time. The latter is state action. What James Gierke did was kid action—with no imprimatur of the state.

James Gierke was no danger to the Constitution, and thanks to him, neither, any longer, are his principal and his reading teacher.

When the state is not involved—as in private schools and colleges, workplaces, corporations—those in charge cannot be sued under the First Amendment. In these situations, free speech can be secured—up to a point—by union contract or by pressuring the private authorities to respect the spirit of the First Amendment. This is hard to accomplish, but it sometimes happens, and a notable illustration of free speech at play is what happened at Bette's Ocean View Diner in Berkeley, California, in the summer and fall of 1991.

I first heard of the free-speech war at Bette's when someone sent me a copy of part of a column by Herb Caen in the *San Francisco Chronicle*:

"East Bay journalist Mike Hughes was breakfasting yesterday at Bette's Ocean View Diner ... and reading the new *Playboy* when the manager and a waitress confronted him to say that other customers were 'highly offended. Either put that away or leave.'

"Mike departed, leaving a tip in the form of a note saying, 'Read the First Amendment....'

"P.S. Mike was reading a Nat Hentoff column on freedom of the press."

I found out that it had been the waitress who had been much more than "highly offended." When Barbara, the waitress (the only name she gives), saw the magazine—she told Janet Weeks of the *Contra Costa Times*—"I was so appalled and shocked, I felt as if I had been struck."

There was an opposite reaction among some Bay Area residents who were appalled and shocked that a peaceful customer in a diner could have his reading material censored. They organized a read-in at Bette's Ocean View Diner on September 22 of that year.

About fifty paladins of the freedom to read showed up. The same number were also present to condemn the magazine and its readers as enemies of women. Or, as Gloria Steinem had said years ago, "A woman reading *Playboy* feels a little like a Jew reading a Nazi manual."

As Dara Tom reported the confrontation in the *San Jose Mercury News*, "While some clutched copies of the magazine and spoke of the First Amendment, others chanted anti-pornography slogans, mostly unprintable."

The waitress, Barbara, was there, unmoved by any invocations of the First Amendment. "I think pornography is offensive," she said, "and I feel pornography in my workplace is sexual harassment."

One of her supporters added: "This *is* an issue of sexual harassment in the workplace. Pornography subjugates women by its very existence. It's not a question of what someone is reading."

Some of the women protesting the magazine and its readers called *Playboy* "hate literature."

Asked for a definition of pornography, Joanna Masakowski of Bay Area Citizens Against Pornography explained that pornography is any "material designed to sexually arouse."

A San Francisco writer, Bill Redican, who organized the read-in, said he did it because he had "felt violated" when he heard of the ultimatum that had been given to Mike Hughes. (Put the magazine down or leave.)

Not all the women there that Sunday felt violated by *Playboy.* "If I want to come here and eat my breakfast, and read any kind of magazine," said Moira O'Brien, "I should be able to."

But one of the organizers of the counterdemonstration, Alissa Reuddmann, emphasized that "women's health is affected by *Playboy* being in a restaurant."

And a supporter of that counterdemonstration tried to sum it all up:

"The 'read-in' at Bette's Ocean View Diner had nothing to do with free speech; it had to do with power. Power of white men to impose their standards on anyone, no matter how humiliating."

Meanwhile, Bette Kroening, a former clinical social worker at Children's Hospital in San Francisco and co-owner of the diner, was embarrassed. She is a devout believer in freedom of speech, she told me. She is also an egalitarian, and so believes that all her employees have equal rights to be themselves.

Surprised by all the unwanted publicity that had followed the encounter between Barbara and her *Playboy*-reading customer, Bette had eventually decided, as she told the *Chicago Tribune:* "Barbara had strong opinions, but by expressing her opinions, she was saying to someone else that they didn't have the right to think and read."

On the day of the read-in—and the counterdemonstration—Bette set up tables outside the diner and presented free scones, pancakes, and coffee to everyone on all sides of the issue.

Meanwhile, the vigorous exchange of views continued. In her report for Californians Against Censorship Together, Bobby Lilly wrote: "Few of the men present had any understanding of the anger most women feel over the pain and humiliation we have felt because of overt sexual harassment in our lives." On the other hand, she pointed out, "No one challenged Barbara's assumption that the mere presence of a magazine like *Playboy* was sexual harassment or her assertion that she felt harassed because she might catch a glimpse of an image of a naked female body while serving her customer.

"No one commented that perhaps her reaction might be due to prudery on her part. No one asked whether she could conceivably understand that her asking the customer to be more 'discreet' could be in itself insulting, an attempt to shame, and a form of sexual harassment."

While Bobby Lilly was taking notes, some of the antiporn feminists were tearing copies of *Playboy* apart, and one threw a *Playboy* high in the air. It landed on Bobby Lilly's head. "This is violence against women," Lilly said. The woman came over and apologized.

As for the future of the right to read at Bette's Diner, nobody's reading material will be restricted in the diner, said Bette, nor will any of the employees comment on what any customer is reading. (At least not to the customer.)

In a press release distributed on the day of the verbal combat, Bette stipulated: "Bette's Diner does not nor will ever have a policy regarding the appropriateness of anyone's reading material.... Today Bette's Diner celebrates the expansive freedom we all share to explore and illuminate the issues of free speech and individual expression."

But what about Barbara—or any employee who is offended by a magazine she sees a customer avidly reading? The new policy is: if a waitress feels offended by what a customer is reading, she will ask the manager to wait on that table.

And if the manager is offended? Presumably, that is one of the perils and burdens of management.

There were shouting matches in front of Bette's Ocean View Diner on the day of the read-in, and although none said so, the cacophony was particularly appropriate in the year of the Bicentennial of the Bill of Rights.

Up north, in the state of Washington, Paul Lawrence, a Seattle lawyer who is president of the ACLU of Washington's board of directors, was talking about attempts at censorship there during the bicentennial year—and what lay ahead. Reporter Don Carter of the *Seattle Post-Intelligencer* summarized what Lawrence had to say:

"In the past year, the ACLU has taken a number of actions to stop censorship of school and library books," Lawrence said. And although far-right factions often are associated with censorship, "now there are people on the left, women and people of color, who seek to suppress what they find distasteful."

As you will see in the chapters ahead, censorship—throughout this sweet land of liberty—remains the strongest drive in human nature, with sex a weak second. In that respect, men and women, white and of color, liberals and Jesse Helms, are brothers and sisters under the skin.

I

The Right to Read a Book with "Niggers" in It

"Every time the teacher, reading it aloud, mentioned the word 'nigger,' I flinched."

> We have not abrogated anybody's First Amendment rights. We've just said we don't want any kid to be forced to read this racist trash.... The book is poison.... It is anti-American.... It works against the idea that all men are created equal.... Anybody who teaches this book is racist.—JOHN H. WALLACE, ADMINISTRATIVE AIDE, MARK TWAIN INTERMEDIATE SCHOOL, FAIRFAX COUNTY, VIRGINIA, 1982

> The last damn thing blacks should do is get into the vanguard of banning books. The next step is banning blacks.—DR. KENNETH B. CLARK, 1982

> The rush for racism-free literature is not a call for censorship, but rather a push for responsibility on the part of educators, librarians and authors.—DOROTHY GILLIAM, COLUMNIST, *WASHINGTON POST*, APRIL 12, 1982

The attempt in 1982 by black administrator John Wallace to roust the perennially troublesome *Huckleberry Finn* from his school's curriculum made the network newscasts, wire services, and most papers around the country. A teacher in Houston told me that when it came over the radio, she had to stop her car, she was so agitated. On the other hand, a group of black parents in Houston who are also trying to get this white trash out of *their* schools were pleased to hear they had an ally up there in Fairfax, Virginia.

My guess is that this wouldn't have been such a widely played story if the name of the school where Mr. Wallace works were not the Mark Twain Intermediate School. Mr. Clemens would have whooped long and loud over that one. Maybe even longer and louder over the name of the racially integrated six-member faculty committee that *unanimously* voted to protect the kids from his book. It's called the Human Relations Committee of the Mark Twain Intermediate School.

Dr. Kenneth Clark of *Brown* v. *Board of Education* and *Dark Ghetto* told me that he first came upon Huck Finn in the public library at 135th Street and Lenox Avenue when he was about twelve years old. No one was around at the time to protect Kenneth from certain books, and he got all caught up in *Huckleberry Finn.*

"I loved the book," Dr. Clark says. "I just loved it. Especially the relationship between Huck and Jim. It was such an easy, *understanding* relationship. The kind a boy wishes he could have."

Then, as now, the book was full of the word "nigger." Why, John Martin, the principal of the Mark Twain Intermediate School in Fairfax County—who agreed with the Human Relations Committee that *Huckleberry Finn* is racist—told National Public Radio that the word is repeated some 160 times in the book. How come Kenneth Clark, when he was just twelve years old, didn't recoil from this "racist" book?

Because he read it, he really read it. Without some adult exercising prior restraint on the books he read to make sure it did him no harm. Someone like John Wallace, who told me, "It's books like *Huckleberry Finn* that are screwing up black children—books that make black children feel bad about themselves. How can a black child, reading that racist trash, be proud of being black?"

Maybe Kenneth Clark didn't get the book's true message. Or maybe it's John Wallace, who has read *Huckleberry Finn* eight times in the last five months, as he tells me, who can't see past that word. Just as the whites in pre–Civil War Missouri whom Twain was writing about couldn't see past that word. They had no idea who "Miss Watson's big nigger, named Jim" actually was. Though Huck came to know Jim, underneath that word. And being able to do that changed his whole life.

My interest in the ceaseless assault on Huck Finn, this well-known drifter, has to do with my own ceaseless delight in the book. I keep going back to it, as I do to certain jazz recordings. When I feel tempted to agree with Mr. Twain's gloomy assessment, in his last years, of our species' prospects. "Why *was* the human race created?" he wrote William Dean Howells in 1900. "Or at least why wasn't something creditable created in place of it? God had his opportunity. He could have made a reputation. But no, He must commit this grotesque folly.…"

But then I become again a believer in the perfectibility of us all when I listen to Huck remembering what it was like being on the raft with Jim on the river: "It was kind of solemn, drifting down the big still river, laying on our backs, looking up at the stars, and we didn't ever feel like talking loud, and it warn't often that we laughed—only a little kind of low chuckle."

Although *Catcher in the Rye* and the works of Kurt Vonnegut and Judy Blume are among the most frequently censored books in school libraries, no novel has been on the firing line so long and so continuously as *Huckleberry Finn*. What is there about this book that manages to infuriate, differently, each generation of Americans? What does it tell us that we don't want to hear?

As for the history of Huck-the-fugitive, I noticed that none of the New York papers, covering the attempt to get the book thrown out of the Mark Twain Intermediate School in Virginia, mentioned their own city's involvement in the censorship of Huck. In September 1957, under pressure from the NAACP and the Urban League—which called the novel "racially offensive"—the New York City Board of Education removed Huck from the approved textbook reading lists in all elementary and junior high schools.

Herewith a brief chronicle of the ways in which *Huckleberry Finn* has been 'buked and scorned, and loved. At first, it was not *that* word, but rather the uncivilized, unsocialized nature of the wandering boy himself that kept getting him into trouble with decent citizens.

A year after the book was published, the *Boston Transcript* reported on March 17, 1885:

"The Concord [Massachusetts] Public Library committee has decided to exclude Mark Twain's latest book from the library. One member of the committee says that, while he does not wish to call it immoral, he thinks it contains but little humor, and that of a very coarse type. He regards it as the veriest trash. The librarian and other members of the committee entertain similar views, characterizing it as rough, coarse, and inelegant, dealing with a series of experiences not elevating, the whole book being more suited to the slums than to intelligent, respectable people."

Concord, where Emerson and Thoreau had lived! Where Louisa May Alcott still lived. And she—as quoted in Michael Patrick Hearn's invaluable *The Annotated Huckleberry Finn* (Clarkson N. Potter, 1981)—said derisively, "If Mr. Clemens cannot think of something better to tell our pure-minded lads and lasses, he had best stop writing for them."

Mr. Twain refused to be chastened: "Those idiots in Concord are not a court of last resort, and I am not disturbed by their moral gymnastics. No other book of mine has sold so many copies within 2 months after issue as this one...." Actually, the "idiots" in Concord had done him a good turn: "[They] have given us a rattling tip-top puff which will go into every paper in the country.... That will sell 25,000 copies for us sure."

In 1902, *Huck* was thrown out of the Denver Public Library ("immoral and sacrilegious"); and three years later, he was taken by the scruff of his neck and booted out of the children's room of the Brooklyn Public Library as "a bad example for ingenuous youth."

And so it went. By 1907, it was reported that at the time, Huck had been "turned out of some library every year." Not only did he lie his way out of danger, and steal—if only to stay alive—but his grammar was terrible. So was everybody else's in the book. Worse yet, said an editorial in the *Springfield Republican*, Mr. Clemens indulges in "a gross trifling with every fine feeling ... he has no reliable sense of propriety." And his "moral level is low."

Over the decades, however, the direction and nature of the

attacks on *Huckleberry Finn* changed. From the 1950s on, groups of black parents—with some white sympathizers among school faculties and administrators—have been concentrating on the 160 appearances of "nigger" in the book. In 1976, at New Trier High School in Winnetka, Illinois, for instance, after a five-year struggle, black parents succeeded in getting the novel taken off all required-reading lists on the charge that it is "morally insensitive" and "degrading and destructive to black humanity."

Four years earlier, *Huck* had also been stricken from required reading lists in Indianapolis. Said the curriculum director: "There's simply no reason to use books that offend minorities if other books may be used instead."

Said a protesting letter from a bunch of Indianapolis students—self-described as white, black, Catholics, Jews, and agnostics—"This is a pointless withdrawal from reality."

But black parents I have spoken to in Texas could not be more convinced that *Huck Finn* is, in reality, a clear and present danger to *their* children.

The easy way to think you're dealing effectively with censors is to see them as indistinguishable. On one side of the deep, clear Manichaean line, wearing white hats, are us—the forces of light, the boon companions of Madison and Jefferson. On the other side, shrouded in ignorance, pinched in spirit, are the dark hordes ready to start the bonfires. And whatever particular book each of these censors wants to toss into the flames, all of the censors are alike. They're all Yahoos. Barely literate.

I used to think that way until some of my own books started to get into trouble, and I tried to find out why. For instance, a novel for young readers, *This School Is Driving Me Crazy,* has been tossed out of a school in Maryland and is on permanent probation in Mobile. I couldn't figure it out. There's not even *implicit* sex in the book. It's what might be called a moral adventure story. As for the language, there are a few "damns" and "hells." And that's it. Not one of George Carlin's seven dirty words. Even more puzzling is that a lot of teachers and—more to the point—kids dig the book, without anybody at all getting upset. It only gets busted in a few places, but the parents in those places are very angry indeed at the book and at me.

One of those places is a small town in southern Illinois. At a librarians' conference in Chicago, I met the librarian from that town. She is as stubborn a free-speech fighter as any member of The International Workers of the World before the First World War, but she doesn't think of her opponents as if they were in cartoons.

"There are kids in my town," she told me, "who come from very religious families. What they see on television, what movies they go to, are controlled. They are taught at home that certain words, used in certain ways, are blasphemous. Sure, they hear other kids say them, but when they see those words in a *book*—and 'damn' and 'hell' are among them—these children are really stunned. And their parents go up the wall. And so would I—if I were them.

"I fight for your book," the librarian went on. "I tell the parents who want it ridden out of town that they cannot decide what *all* the children in my library are going to read. But I do tell these very religious parents that I will give *their* children alternative books to read."

That is standard American Library Association policy, with which the American Civil Liberties Union concurs. An individual parent should have some say in what the state does with his or her child's mind. Education up to a certain age is compulsory.

But this standard answer—"We'll give *your* kids alternative books where *Huckleberry Finn* is under intense attack"—is not acceptable, the black parents say, because the book—by its incessant use of the word "nigger," and by the way it portrays blacks—incites racism. So no child, white or black, should be required to read it. And some of these parents, who really believe *no child* should read *Huckleberry Finn*, point to the black eighth-grader in Warrington, Pennsylvania, who, his father says, was verbally and physically abused by his white classmates after they had all read *Huckleberry Finn* in class. In Warrington, the novel was required reading in the eighth grade then. It no longer is.

From Texas to Virginia, I've talked to black objectors to *Huckleberry Finn*, as I've talked to Jewish objectors to the *Merchant of Venice*. They're not Yahoos. I think they were wrong in wanting to throw out or hide these works, but they do raise questions about how to teach certain books. Questions that go even more deeply into the very nature of teaching itself.

But first, it's useful to understand the depth of these protesters' feelings. Consider John Wallace, the black administrator at the Mark Twain Intermediate School who led the fight to remove *Huckleberry Finn* from that school's curriculum.

"The press has cut me down something terrible," Wallace told me. Yes, it has, if only by quoting him. ("Anybody who teaches this book is racist," he has said. But where's he coming from? There wasn't much in the press about that. "I grew up in Aurora, Illinois," Wallace told me, "and there were very few black kids there. When I was a kid, I had to study *Huckleberry Finn* in that school; and every time the teacher, reading it aloud, mentioned the word 'nigger,' I flinched. There was only one other black kid in the room, and every time he heard the teacher say that word, he put his head down on the desk."

Wallace's mother was dead by the time he was twelve, but he remembers how an aunt, and the minister of his church, led the battle to kick *Huckleberry Finn* out of that school. They failed. But Wallace, who has worked in schools for twenty-eight years, has never stopped trying to save black kids from this book which, as he sees it, will make them feel unworthy. It's become a family mission, he tells me, as he looks at a photograph of his two heroes, Malcolm X and Martin Luther King, shaking hands. His son in Chicago, Wallace adds, is also involved in the jihad against *Huck Finn*.

"You want to know why it's so important to get rid of this book?" Wallace says. "We are always lamenting that black students don't learn or progress as well as whites. Well, if you give them this kind of crap about themselves, how are they going to feel good about themselves?"

I tried to tell Wallace what Twain was saying in the book. Russell Baker put it pretty good in the *Times* on April 14, 1982, when he wrote about Huck and Jim on the Mississippi:

"The people they encounter are drunkards, murderers, bullies, swindlers, lynchers, thieves, liars, frauds, child abusers, numbskulls, hypocrites, windbags and traders in human flesh. All are white. The one man of honor in this phantasmagoria is black Jim, the runaway slave. 'Nigger Jim,' as Twain called him to emphasize the irony of a society in which the only true gentleman was held beneath contempt."

I didn't get anywhere with Mr. Wallace about what the book is saying. I didn't get anywhere with Mrs. Dora Durden, mother of an eleventh-grade student at Westfield High School in the Spring Independent School District of Houston. She was one of the leaders of a black parent "Sensitivity Committee" that had been trying for months to get *Huckleberry Finn* off the required-reading list there. The committee claims that the book is degrading to blacks, that no book is worth the humiliation of their children, and that to compound the harm, the book has been taught insensitively.

Dora Durden is no Yahoo either. Crisply articulate, she points out how difficult it is for black kids in a school district where they make up only about 4.4 percent of the student body. "When a child, like my daughter, is the only black in her class, teachers have to be more sensitive about what and how they teach. But they're not, and they make some of our kids feel like dogs."

If *Huckleberry Finn* has to be taught, Mrs. Durden said, "then at least don't mention the word 'nigger.' But actually, why does it have to be taught? Surely there are other good American novels without that word in it? I myself would just as soon have *Huckleberry Finn* removed not only from the reading list, but taken out of the school entirely. And that may not be the only book that should go. I have asked the curriculum director for a list of all the books used in all the courses so that we can examine them and determine which are good for our children and which are harmful to them. And that means any book that degrades *any* race."

Mrs. Durden and her allies failed to get *Huck Finn* taken off the required-reading list. A Westfield High School review committee (two teachers and a librarian), set up to deal with the complaint, reported: "... no other literary selection illustrates the mid-nineteenth century and its evils of slavery as well as this novel, Mark Twain's satirical masterpiece."

In Fairfax County, Virginia, John Wallace reacted with derision to the notion that Mark Twain's satire can get through to kids. "It's asinine to think that," says Wallace. "How many children understand satire?"

And back in Texas, Mrs. Durden tells me that eight black youngsters at Westfield High School took the option of not reading *Huckleberry Finn,* and instead chose another book. One of those students was her daughter. I asked which book she had chosen.

"*Fahrenheit 451,*" Mrs. Durden said. "I read it, too, and I think it's a fine book."

That Ray Bradbury novel—about official arsonists of the future torching subversive books—was taken off the required-reading list at another Texas high school in 1981. The school principal decided it gave students "too negative" an outlook. Since then, it has been banished from other schools—for the same reason.

The way it used to be in Warrington—about twenty-five miles north of Philadelphia—most junior high school students were required to pick their class reading assignments from a small list of books, and from only those books. *Huck* was on that list, and was often chosen because, as Mr. Hemingway once said, "All modern American literature comes from one book by Mark Twain called *Huckleberry Finn.*"

Then came the complaint. The parents of a black eighth-grader asked that Mr. Twain's book be removed from junior high school reading lists and from the school libraries. Their son, they said, had been harassed verbally and physically by white kids in his class because of the infectious use of the word "nigger" in the novel.

These parents agreed that Mr. Twain himself was not a racist. Why, *Huckleberry Finn,* they said, is strongly anti-slavery and anti-racist. But the book is too subtle, too difficult, for eighth-graders to understand in terms of Mr. Twain's intentions. All that the kids, white and black, see is "nigger."

I was unable to find out the nature and extent of the abuse of the black eighth-grader by his classmates. School officials told me they just don't know. They had heard the charges, but they had no specifics, nor had they gone after any. The black parents involved did not wish to speak to the press. Since they are not public officials or public figures, I did not try to crack their unlisted phone number. The right to say "No" to the press is—or should be—one of the most fundamental American liberties.

But, for the sake of argument, let me stipulate that a very bad scene did occur—the actual beating of the black child. (Though if that had happened, I would think his parents would have insisted the white hooligans be at least suspended.) And let me stipulate that, in fact, there was constant taunting of the boy as a "nigger."

Should you keep *Huckleberry Finn* on a required-reading list when it leads to such palpably harmful results?

I have asked this question of a good many citizens, black and white, including teachers. The overwhelming consensus has been that what happened in that eighth-grade classroom in Warrington is a boon to any reasonably awake teacher. What a way to get Huck and Jim, on the one hand, and all those white racists they meet, on the other hand, off the pages of the book and into that very class-room. Talk about a book coming alive!

Look at that Huck Finn. Reared in racism, like all the white kids in his town. And then, on the river, on the raft with Jim, shuck-ing off that blind ignorance because this runaway slave is the most honest, perceptive, fair-minded man this white boy has ever known. What a book for the children, all the children, in Warrington, Pennsylvania, in 1982!

"To miss that teaching opportunity, to not confront what hap-pened to that black kid in Warrington head-on by really exploring this book," Dr. Kenneth Clark told me, "is to underestimate every child in that classroom. And by underestimating them—while also 'protecting' the black child from this book—you deprive them all of what they should know. And what they can especially learn from *Huckleberry Finn*."

Ah, but the book is too difficult for eighth-grade kids! But keep this in mind: *Huckleberry Finn* is not *The Magic Mountain* or *The Cas-tle* or *Remembrance of Things Past*. It is a novel by a writer who, as he put it, "never cared what became of the cultured classes; they could go to the theater and the opera, they had no use for me and the melodeon." Instead, Mr. Twain, in his words, "always hunted for the bigger game—the masses."

All the more so in 1884, when *Huckleberry Finn* was published, because Twain was in need of money and wanted to attract as many book buyers as he could that year. He even went on a three-and-a-half-month reading tour of seventy cities to advertise *Huckleberry Finn*. In every way, this was intended to be a popular novel.

And surely, kids in 1982—after all the television programs and movies they've seen—were at least as able as children were in 1884 to fathom what Mr. Twain is saying in this novel. Kids have not grown dumber. I will grant you that reading it again as an adult, I found more in *Huckleberry Finn* than when I first read it the summer I was fourteen. Or, as Lionel Trilling wrote:

"One can read it at ten and then annually ever after, and each year find that it is as fresh as the year before, that it has changed only in becoming somewhat larger. To read it young is like planting a tree young—each year adds a new growth ring of meaning, and the book is as little likely as the tree to become dull. So, we may imagine, an Athenian boy grew up together with the *Odyssey*. There are few other books which we can know so young and love so long."

But at ten, or twelve, or fourteen, even with only the beginning ring of meaning, any child who can read will not miss the doltishness and sheer meanness and great foolishness of most of the whites in the book, particularly in their attitudes toward blacks. Nor will the child miss the courage and invincible decency of the white boy and the black man on the river.

And if any child, black or white, does miss—through being blocked in one way or another—these points as big as barn doors, then what is the teacher for?

Well, what *did* happen in Warrington after the pain inflicted on the black youngster in connection with *Huckleberry Finn*? Were the teachers told that now is the time to really get inside that novel? No, they were not. The novel was removed from the required-reading list at Tamamend Junior High School, where the incident took place. And by the following September, it was gone from the reading lists in all junior high schools in the Central Bucks County School District. But Huck still had shelf room in all school libraries for voluntary reading, and he was to be taught in high school. Sort of.

Although the black parents had started by urging that *Huckleberry Finn* be taken off all reading lists, and from all school libraries, they were pleased by the compromise. So were the white school officials. They had shown themselves to be sensitive to the feelings of this very small minority in the district (about two hundred black kids out of eleven thousand students). One of the school officials told me, by the way, that "it's unfortunate that most of our kids don't have experiences with people of other races."

In years past, many of those white kids had gotten to know Jim, though, but he was now being told to make himself scarce.

I don't know how many Jewish kids there are in the Central Bucks County schools; but the educators there are so nice, so eager to insulate youngsters from having to think beyond Hallmark greeting cards, that they've removed *The Merchant of Venice* from all the junior high schools. It'll be optional in high school. No one had even complained about Shylock, but as one administrator told me, "We had become concerned with the way the Jewish people are presented in that play."

As for Huck, now that the junior high kids have been protected from him, what was to take his place? Well, three books replaced Mr. Twain's misguided novel on that small required reading list from which teachers choose what the junior high kids can absorb without harm, and without their imaginations being unduly stimulated. The winners were: William H. Armstrong's *Sounder;* Allen Eckert's *Incident at Hawk's Hill;* and Chaim Potok's *The Chosen.*

With all respect to fans of any or all of the above, ain't none of them *Huckleberry Finn.* It's like removing Duke Ellington from a music course, and substituting Oscar Peterson, Dave Brubeck, and Chick Corea.

But anyway, it was decided after the incident with the black child that the kids will be able to get on that raft with Huck and Jim when they reach the safety zone, the tenth grade. There, *Huckleberry Finn* will be one of eight titles from which teachers must choose. Kind of long odds against Huck, and all the longer when you realize that the book now had a stigma attached to it in Central Bucks County. After all, Huck had to be bodily removed from junior high, so how many tenth-grade teachers were going to take a chance on maybe getting into trouble with this book, even though it's permitted by that grade? Who needs a grim visit from black parents when you can teach something that minds its manners and never gets anybody into trouble?

Such victories for niceness in the Central Bucks County School District—and in other districts around the county—are more insidiously harmful to kids than the Armageddons of censorship that get widespread press play. In most of the latter battles, the enemy is clear. There are folks out there who want to censor, ban, burn (if they can) certain books.

But in Warrington, and in an increasing number of other

places, offending books are *not* banned. They're just put in the back of the bus. They're taken off reading lists, but kept in the library. Often, moreover, they're kept in the library on restricted shelves, or are just plain hidden. Or they're taken out of lower-school curriculums and placed, maybe, on high school lists. Usually optional lists. Whatever the device, the books are made less accessible to kids. And so they're less often read. If they're read at all.

This is not the kind of stuff that makes for pungent newspaper or broadcast coverage. Actually, this sort of "compromise" is seldom covered at all. I was only the second reporter in two years to talk to school officials about the Incident in Warrington. The principal of Tamamend Junior High School was surprised to hear from me. "We're not having any racial riots, any racial problems here," he told me. "That takes the fun out of your story, I guess. And we're not banning anything either. I don't believe in going into the censorship business. Besides, then the civil liberties groups get after you."

"The only story here," another school official told me, "is that we worked out a compromise by which everybody wins."

Except the kids, black and white, who are being treated with such "sensitivity" and "kindness"—but not with respect. Respecting a child means you work with him so that he can keep discovering more and more of his potential. So that he can keep learning what his strengths are, including his strengths of character. What's going to happen to a kid when he gets into the world if he's going to let a word paralyze him so he can't think?

But the principal of Tamamend Junior High School told me *Huck* had to be taken out of his school because black kids' feelings were hurt. Again, where were the teachers—to connect those feelings to who Huck and Jim actually are?

And the principal of Mark Twain Intermediate School in Fairfax County, Virginia, went along with the banning of *Huckleberry Finn* (before he was overruled by the district superintendent) because "I just felt that a student of any race or nationality shouldn't be made to feel uncomfortable in a classroom."

And in school districts around the country, similar nice people have said similar nice things in justifying the removal of *Huckleberry Finn* and other books from required high school as well as junior high school reading lists. Some school folks, however, refuse to yield to this milky niceness. They figure kids aren't that fragile. And they figure that when educators *are* softly obeisant to those who want to limit what youngsters read, the result is yet another generation of adults who never learned in school how to think—and see—for themselves.

So it was in Davenport, Iowa, when an attack was made on *Huck Finn* which was required reading in an American literature high school course called Great American Authors. A black student and the parent of another black student wanted this "racist" novel taken off all required reading lists.

The demand was turned down. The student was told she could read another book if she wanted to, but, said the English faculty, "It's impossible to have a class called Great American Authors without including Mark Twain." And *Huck*.

Back in Warrington, Pennsylvania, a black girl in junior high school asked for *Huckleberry Finn* awhile after the incident. She'd heard somewhere it was a good book. Although still available in *her* lower school (for a few more months), it had not been chosen by her teacher. The black student read *Huckleberry Finn* and thought it was one hell of a book. She liked it a whole lot. Didn't find it racist at all. Quite the opposite.

If I were to name the town, you would have to look it up in an atlas. It's not a village—being big enough for a school population of sixteen thousand—but it's no metropolis. Hardly any news comes out of this town that's of interest to anyone but the folks who live there, and they'd like to keep it that way.

Especially the man in charge of coordinating the English program in the town's classrooms wasn't looking to be on the nightly news when I talked to him. A black parent had just complained to him about *Huckleberry Finn,* which is required reading in the ninth grade. I mean it's really required. No child leaves the ninth grade in this town without getting on the raft with Huck and Jim.

The black parent was disturbed that his child, that any child for that matter—but especially a black child—should have to read a book with the word "nigger" in it. All the way through it. At this point, the black parent was not demanding that *Huckleberry Finn* be removed from the curriculum and from the library. He was objecting to the book being *required* reading.

The discussions had been low-keyed and informal. No newspaper or wire service or broadcast station had any idea that this place might join Fairfax County, Virginia; Davenport, Iowa; Warrington, Pennsylvania; and Houston as yet another battleground over whether Mr. Twain's novel does injury to young readers, particularly young black readers.

The school official in this unnamed town agreed to let me hear him think out what he's going to do—he's not sure yet—provided I didn't name him or the town.

"You see," he said, "I've kept a file on the attacks on *Huckleberry Finn* around the country, and one thing that's clear to me is that as soon as the press gets into this, it gets a lot harder to keep the talks between the school and the parents low-keyed. Anyway, there is no story here. Yet. We're trying to figure things out. The parent doesn't want to come across as a censor. And I don't want to come across as being callous on this thing."

He paused, and then said slowly, "When a person is offended, a person is offended. You can't say to him, 'Well, you shouldn't have been offended, or it's ridiculous to be offended by this book.' But on the other hand, it's difficult for me to agree to allow any child to go through our school system without reading *Huckleberry Finn*. There's no other book I know of that is so important—in so many different ways—for kids to know. Especially ninth-grade kids. It seems to me I'd be falling down on my job if I didn't keep that book on the required list. On the other hand, I've got to be sensitive to other people's sensitivities. So I don't know what I'm going to do."

He was aware of the travails of *Huckleberry Finn* in Warrington, Pennsylvania, and the ultimate grand compromise there which took the book out of the junior high schools and removed it to the high school where it was to be only one of eight titles from which teachers can choose.

In Warrington, the protest began with one set of black parents. The wire services picked up the story, followed by some of the big papers in the area, notably the *Philadelphia Inquirer.*

Thereupon, other black parents came forward. They reported—and this impressed school officials—that their children had not only suffered emotional harm because they'd had to read

Huckleberry Finn, but their classwork in other subjects as well had been adversely affected. All because of Mr. Twain's creature.

I asked the language arts supervisor in the Warrington school system whether there had been any such reports of damage to black children during all the previous years in which *Huckleberry Finn* had been on the required reading list in the junior high schools.

No, there had been no such reports.

I asked if she and other school officials had investigated this alleged correlation between *Huck* and those black children's failing grades—a correlation that revealed itself only after the press reports on the single initial complaint against the novel.

Well, no, the school officials had not really looked into whether such a connection could actually be demonstrated.

My own theory, which I also can't prove, is that a kind of group loyalty was in operation among the black kids who claimed to have been injured by the book. The parents of one of their own had complained about *Huckleberry Finn,* and in a show of solidarity, other black children began protesting against the book. And to make their points all the more vivid, they also began showing symptoms that the presence of that book was so malign that they couldn't concentrate on their other studies either.

Every one of those black children may well have thoroughly believed all this to be true. The function of the school, however, is to try to find out if it is true. And it didn't even try.

But let us suppose it is true that *Huck* had paralyzed those black kids. All the more reason for them to get all the way into understanding *Huckleberry Finn.* Otherwise, what a terrible thing for a child to learn! That he is so fragile, so vulnerable, so without intellectual and emotional resources that a book can lay him low. And that is what the teachers and supervisors of the junior high schools in Warrington, Pennsylvania, had allowed the black children in their care to learn.

As for the conflict over *Huck* in the other small town in Pennsylvania, the coordinator of the English curriculum was telling me one morning that he is riven between his desire to avoid a racial conflict in the community and his desire to "keep the best literature we can in the classroom."

If he wanted a way out, I told him, Russell Baker, among others, had given him one. In *The New York Times,* Baker, an admirer of *Huckleberry Finn,* nonetheless claimed: "It's a dreadful disservice to Mark Twain for teachers to push *Huckleberry Finn* on seventh-, eighth-, and ninth-graders.... *Huckleberry Finn* can be partly enjoyed after the age of twenty-five, but for fullest benefit it probably shouldn't be read before age thirty-five, and even then only if the reader has had a broad experience of American society."

Dr. Kenneth Clark had snorted when I read him that Russell Baker passage on the phone.

But how did this schoolman in a small Pennsylvania town— worrying about a possible racial confrontation over this book— react to what Baker had said? He *could* tell the black parents that, on reflection, he had decided that this book was not right for any child in the secondary schools. And, for that matter, he could recommend that even on their own time, all teachers under thirty-five stay away from the novel.

No, the man decided not to take this escape route. "No, neither Russell Baker nor my concern about other people's concern over the use of the word 'nigger' is going to change my mind about what's right educationally. *Huckleberry Finn* is well placed, very well placed, in the ninth grade. And I'll tell you why.

"First, the story is told by an adolescent: and there are few *quality* novels where a youth is dealing with adults entirely from his perspective, in his language, through his experiences.

"Second, in terms of craftsmanship and flow, it's a simple novel. In the ninth grade, students are just learning the structure of the novel. It's really our first opportunity to teach the novel as a form, and there's nothing better to do that with than *Huckleberry Finn.* Especially the way it's tied in so nicely with the river.

"Also, it's a chronological novel. Not all novels are. For instance, when you jump into Charles Dickens at grade ten, you've got a different, more complicated structure to the novel than you have with *Huckleberry Finn.* So Twain's book is a great introduction to the form of the novel.

"Then," the schoolman continued, "it ties in very well with the pre–Civil War history that this school district, and most others, are studying at this grade. Twain has a lot to say about America during that period. He gives adolescent kids a great deal to learn and think about.

"Take the word 'nigger.' It's during the *adolescent* years that kids ought to be dealing with that word, its history, and the kind of people who used it then, and those who still use it. Good Lord, Twain spends three-quarters of his book trying to make clear what a damnable word 'nigger' is, because it shows the whites who used it didn't *see,* didn't begin to understand the people they were talking about."

I mentioned a letter I'd received recently from a librarian in Twain's home state, Missouri. She was focusing on books as a vital part of what she calls the initiation rites of children. Books, she insisted, are among the ways teenagers move into adulthood. "And," she continued, "to deny them the books that can most help them make that transition is inhumane."

"Well, sure," said the schoolman. "That's another reason I've insisted on requiring that all kids in this town read *Huckleberry Finn.* That book is *about* Huck's rites of passage. To put it more prosaically, a large part of it has to do with an adolescent's growth. But that book also has such a sweeping magnitude to it. It has so many things in it. It's about adolescence; it's about the race thing; it's about con men, the Duke and the Dauphin; it's about the murderous foolishness of pride, the Grangerfords. Oh, I could go on all morning."

The schoolman's voice became low. "It would be such a shame for a kid never to get to read this book."

I asked him how he felt about such "compromises" as the one that had been worked out in Warrington, Pennsylvania, to spare kids from Huck Finn in junior high and maybe allow them to read the book in high school. But even then, in the majority of such "compromises," *Huckleberry Finn* has carefully been removed from *required* reading lists in high schools.

"It's insidious," the schoolman in the small town said. "I mean, it's not outright censorship, so nobody has to defend himself against that charge. But this kind of 'compromise' does make it harder and harder for the kid and the book to come together. Oh, some self-starters will seek out *Huckleberry Finn* in the library or ask if they can choose it for independent study; but in those school districts that have compromised, *most* kids will never get to read the book.

"And you know what that's an extension of? The way we underestimate kids. This is a classic case of just that. We underestimate the capacity of black kids to understand why and how 'nigger' is used in *Huckleberry Finn.* And God knows we underestimate Mark Twain."

"Yeah, but so much of this book is Twain's satire," I said. "And John Wallace, the black administrator at Mark Twain Intermediate School in Fairfax County, said that it was asinine to think that most children understand satire."

The schoolman laughed. "What could be a more perfect underestimation of kids than that? Look at what kids read on their own. Sometimes I think they live on satire."

"Well, it seems to me you've made up your mind that Huck's going to stay here," I said. "In the ninth grade. And on the *required* reading list."

"I don't know," he sighed. "I know I'm right about the book, but the key thing is this—you have to be sensitive to someone else's sensitivities. I can talk about the book to the black parents, just the way I've been talking to you about it now. And I can assure them we teach it sensitively, and they'll say, 'It still hurts my child.' And I'll say the child can choose another book. But what book can replace *Huckleberry Finn?*"

The schoolman had another appointment. "I'd say," he bade me farewell, "that it's a toss-up right now as to what's going to happen. This is just one of those little battles fought in remote places. Only we'll know in this place how it turns out."

In time, and with accumulating pressure, the school system in that town did agree to a compromise—*Huckleberry Finn* could be one of three books ninth-graders could select for their English class. It was no longer *required* reading.

The national press did not carry the story from this "remote place."

The schoolman who had such high regard for *Huck* sighed when I spoke to him last. But he knew that I understood he would not continue to fight for *Huck,* even though "it would be such a shame for a kid never to get to read this book."

In Plano, Texas, in November 1990, David Perry, the only black member of the City Council, demanded that *Tom Sawyer* and *Huckleberry Finn* be taken off the school district's required-reading list. These Mark Twain novels, he charged, were "racist and degrading." On reading *Tom Sawyer*, he said, his twelve-year-old daughter had become upset.

At a series of meetings before the curriculum review committee and other bodies, many black residents of Plano supported Perry while English teachers and administrators insisted that the novel was anti-racist while it also skewered the hypocrisy and bigotry of whites.

For more than twenty years in Plano, all seventh-graders had read *Tom Sawyer*, and all eleventh-graders got to know Huck Finn and the runaway slave Jim. Blacks compose some 5 percent of the students in the district.

Mr. Perry and his supporters focused on the seemingly endless use of the word "nigger" in *Huckleberry Finn*. However, Dr. Jocelyn Chadwick-Joshua, thirty-five, an assistant professor of English at the University of North Texas, had a distinctly different point of view.

She is black and recalled that fifteen years ago, when she was teaching *Huckleberry Finn* to eleventh-graders in Irving, Texas, she was aghast that Twain had called black people "niggers" about three hundred times in the novel. But then she started to study Twain, his life and works, and became convinced that it was important for black youngsters to read and understand what's going on in *Huckleberry Finn*. The professor has since become a leading advocate for keeping the book on required-reading lists, having consulted for twenty school districts, spoken at conferences on the issue, and visited forty high school classes.

She does believe that before students actually get to the book, they have to know its history and the history of racism and slavery—including the punishments for runaway slaves and those who helped them.

Some years ago, I was talking about *Huckleberry Finn* at a library in Indiana during Banned Books Week. There were reporters there, and one stayed after everybody had left. She was in her mid-twenties and black. "Intellectually," she said, "I agree the novel should be taught, but I can't read it. When I was in high school in a small town in Nebraska, I was the only black in the class. We started on *Huckleberry Finn* without a word of context, of historical background, of who Mark Twain was. I dreaded that class. Every time 'nigger' came up, I flinched. You just can't throw the book at kids; you have to prepare them."

Actually the year before Councilman Perry's complaint, the school district hired Dr. Chadwick-Joshua in order to teach two hundred teachers during the summer how to deal sensitively with the novel.

David Perry did not believe teaching teachers would do any good. And he added that removing the book from the required reading list was not censorship. "I see it as an issue of racial hurt."

Eventually, the school board refused to take the Twain novels off the required reading lists, but did allow students to choose alternative titles. Few of the district's classes have more than one or two black students, but most of the youngsters, including the black students, did not select different books.

Some of the black youngsters said they went along with Twain because they didn't want to call attention to themselves by asking for another book.

Sixteen-year-old Treshel Washington started the book warily even though she had sworn not to. When she finished Chapter 9, she said to the *Dallas Morning News,* "I've been told that Mark Twain was an abolitionist, so I thought I'd see what it was all about."

And in Chapter 31, she will have seen—as Clay Reynolds, a professor at the University of North Texas wrote in the *Dallas Morning News*—"the tremendous power that rests in Huck's ultimate decision to forfeit his immortal soul rather than send Jim back to slavery [and how] Huck comes to understand that Jim is not merely a piece of property ... or subhuman baggage, but how this runaway slave has become both his friend and his surrogate father." (Huck had written a letter, turning in Jim to his owner, and he believed he would be doomed for eternity if he did not send it. But he couldn't. "All right, then," he said to himself, "I'll *go* to hell.")

Because of the controversy, the school district is adding programs on black history and other multicultural studies. *Huckleberry Finn,* it should be noted, is a multicultural course in itself. Ralph Ellison once wrote that when he was coming up, "I could imagine myself as Huck Finn."

While *Huck* was in the dock in Texas, I spent an afternoon with a public high school class—all the students were black—in Brooklyn.

They had read a novel of mine for young readers, *The Day They Came to Arrest the Book,* which is about attempts to ban *The Adventures of Huckleberry Finn* from a public school. There are, as I have noted, black parents who want to ban it because of its profuse use of the word "niggers." Fundamentalist Christians want to ban it because Huck doesn't go to church and uses profane language, and like most of the other people in the book, acts as if there were no God. And feminist students are eager to banish the book because, they say, all the women in it are portrayed as being dumb or flighty and subservient to men.

I asked the students what they thought of the fierce arguments about *Huck Finn* that run throughout my book. Did it belong on a public school reading list?

"Well," one young woman said, "I learned that what 'nigger' means depends on how it's used in the conversation."

Another student, after reading about Huckleberry Finn, bought a copy of the Mark Twain book, and now the others were curious to read it.

None thought the book should be banned. They laughed at the idea. "How are you going to learn anything that way?" several said.

In most of the schools I know about, students seldom find teachers or administrators who are unafraid of enabling students to think for themselves. An exception was in a classroom at the Ditmas Junior High School in Brooklyn. The teacher, Rose Reissman, was at least as lively as her eighth-grade students. They were white, black, Oriental, and otherwise reflected the dauntless pluralism of New York City.

It is Rose Reissman's abiding conviction that no one can grow up effectively independent without knowing how to think. And part of learning how to think is knowing how to make connections. Accordingly when, each year, she taught *Huckleberry Finn,* her students learned about the history of the period and of the places where the novel is set. They were also bombarded with contemporary accounts, sometimes as fresh as last week, of attempts to remove the book from public school systems around the country.

Her students having absorbed all this, she peppered them with questions. Why does the word "nigger" appear so often in the book? Does seeing that word again and again in the book do harm to black children? What is its effect on white kids? Should the First Amendment protect a writer who uses such words?

Being kids who are encouraged to think for themselves, the eighth-grade students argued and matched experiences with each other, with Miss Reissman, and with anyone visiting their classroom. In one discussion about *Huckleberry Finn*, a student who is black told me that when a white classmate had kissed her, just for fun, a few days before, she saw what she described as an awful look on another white student's face.

The young woman paused, waiting for me to ask her if she thought all those "niggers" in *Huckleberry Finn* had had anything to do with that awful look. I asked her, and she said she didn't know. But her mention of the incident during this conversation about the book indicated to me that she thought *Huckleberry Finn* could have been the cause of her hurt.

Did she think the book should be banned? No, she did not. At first, reading it had been painful for her, she said, but then she saw what Mark Twain was up to, and she could take it. What she did want to say was that people do get hurt sometimes by having the freedom to read. She just wanted that out in the open.

A year later, when another of Rose Reissman's classes had been digging into *Huckleberry Finn* in the course of a lesson plan about censorship, I was greeted outside the school one morning, just before the class began, by four male eighth-graders, all of them black. They were so eager to straighten me out that they were practically hopping up and down. What made them so angry, they said, was that there are people out there—they pointed in the general direction of Topeka—who think that black kids are so dumb they can't tell the difference between a racist book and a book that's against racism. Like *Huckleberry Finn*.

Year after year, Rose Reissman's students conferred and diverged on such engrossingly volatile subjects as whether handicapped infants have the right to live even if their parents want to let them die; how to deal with the daily danger to lives—their own lives—on the streets; and just what kids' constitutional rights are in the school building.

By the time they moved into high school, Miss Reissman's once and former eighth-graders had developed a decidedly personal interest in such matters as due process, equal protection of the laws, and the shrinking Fourth Amendment. They had also done intellectual battle over the meaning of cruel and unusual punishment, there being no unanimity among these kids about the death penalty. Or about anything else.

Rose Reissman was not exactly cherished by school administrators in her district. Some considered her irresponsible—the sort of person who incites children to understand and exercise their rights, particularly their First Amendment rights because all their other rights flow from that one. Talking like that to children could only lead to trouble in the school.

But since her workshops for other teachers, and occasional mentions of her in the press, seemed to reflect well on the district, she was warily allowed, for a time, to continue to teach unreconstructed Americanism. In time, however, she had to move on elsewhere in the city and, with remarkable resourcefulness, she continues to teach children and teachers how to be unafraid to think and to speak their minds, even to principals.

II

The Right Not to Read a Book with Whores in It

"The right of freedom of thought ... includes both the right to speak freely and the right to refrain from speaking at all."

In our system, state-operated schools may not be enclaves of totalitarianism. School officials do not possess absolute authority over their students. Students in school as well as out of school are "persons" under our Constitution.—U.S. SUPREME COURT, *TINKER V. DES MOINES INDEPENDENT SCHOOL DISTRICT* (1969)

Compulsory unification of opinion achieves only the unanimity of the graveyard.—U.S. SUPREME COURT, *WEST VIRGINIA STATE BOARD OF EDUCATION V. BARNETTE* (1942)

It was a grand victory for the right of students to read a book that some people in the town considered vulgar and downright filthy. You may remember the story. It was on network television and on many front pages around the country. Studs Terkel, the author of the beleaguered book, came himself to the high school auditorium—in Girard, Pennsylvania—and convinced all but a stiff-necked minority that his book ought to be in the schools because the people in it are so real, so wide-rangingly American. And I would have said, if anyone had asked me, that kids can learn more from that one book about what it's like out there—where they're going to spend the rest of their lives—than from any other single volume I know. Not just about the inside of many different kinds of jobs, but about why some people get a hell of a lot of satisfaction out of what they do for a living, and why many more do not.

The book was *Working* (Pantheon; Avon paperback). Over some three years, Studs had talked to farmers, hookers, garbage men, cops, dentists, housewives, jazz musicians, gravediggers, editors, and many more of us. One of the voices that stays in my head is that of a fireman—Tom Patrick, from Brooklyn. And it's also one of the passages that got the book in trouble in Girard, Pennsylvania.

"The fuckin' world's so fucked up. But the firemen, you actually see them produce. You see them put out a fire. You see them come out with babies in their hands. You see them give mouth-to-mouth when a guy's dying. You can't get around that shit. That's real. To me, that's what I want to be.

"I worked in a bank. You know, it's just paper. It's not real. Nine to five and it's shit. You're lookin' at numbers. But I can look back and say, 'I helped put out a fire. I helped save somebody.' It shows something I did on this earth."

When there was talk that this book, *Working*, should be thrown out of the school or at least out of class, Kay Nichols, a teacher at the high school who had recommended the book in the first place, talked to Studs on the phone about what was going on. That's when Studs decided to go there, to put himself on the line in Girard, alongside his book. At a student assembly in the high school, he got two standing ovations and, according to *The New York Times*, "deafening applause." He also did well with the adults at another session in the high school auditorium that evening.

Stud's visit was on February 2, 1982, and on March 22, the Girard School Board affirmed the rightful place of *Working* in the high school and refused, furthermore, to provide an alternative book for any student who objected to being forced to read *Working* against his or her moral or religious principles. (Or those of his or her parents.) There was a little zinger in the school board statement. It recognized, on the one hand, that some of the language in the book might be "legitimately offensive" to some parents and children.

But the school board also noted that "with all deference due the parents, their sensibilities are not the full measure of what is proper education."

Another result of Studs's having come to Girard was a letter to him from the junior class of the high school. Printed in the March 6, 1982, *Nation*, the letter said:

"We, the members of the Junior Class of Girard High School, would like to thank you for coming to Girard High School and presenting your viewpoints to us. We also would like to apologize for any insulting remarks made to you by either the students or the community as a whole.

"You have represented America to us, you have widened our horizons and you have given us the ability to see what America is truly about.

"Mr. Terkel, your trip to Girard was not in vain, you have won the respect and admiration of the entire school and this is a gift we can never repay.

"Again, many thanks for your interest in the youth of today."

In an editorial, the *Nation* said of this letter from the Girard High School junior class: "The students' response shows that the 'youth of today,' at least, have a sense of 'what America is truly about,' and it is eloquent testimony to the power of free speech in action at least when the speaker is Studs Terkel."

I remember getting a natural high, like the *Nation*, from the reports of Studs's trip to Girard. But there's another part of this story that has not been reported, except in the local county papers in that part of Pennsylvania. It has to do with what preceded Studs's visit and with what happened after he left. None of what follows in any way diminishes *Working* or Studs's characteristically forthright decision to come to Girard and speak for the kids' freedom to read.

But I am not so sure that the Girard School Board, the high school principal at the time, and the key faculty member in this story understand a fundamental First Amendment corollary of the right to read. And that is the right of a student to not be forced to read a book that goes against his conscience. The right to say no to authority, the right to nonviolently "sock" a school system.

I didn't know there was an unreported part of the Girard story until I read a book review in the March 1983 *Inquiry*. The book was Stephen Arons's *Compelling Belief: The Culture of American Schooling* (New Press/McGraw-Hill). Its reviewer in *Inquiry* was William Bentley Ball, a constitutional lawyer for whom I have great respect. He successfully argued the landmark *Wisconsin* v. *Yoder* case before the Supreme Court in 1972 (the right of the Amish, on the grounds of religious liberty, not to send their children to school past the eighth grade).

Ball's particular expertise is the illumination of First Amendment protection against any state interference with the free exercise of religion. This sometimes brings him very unpopular clients (for instance, Bob Jones University); but if a First Amendment lawyer does not have unpopular clients, he is like someone trying to play the saxophone without a reed.

In the review of the Arons book—titled "Separating School and State"—William Ball wrote:

"We have, of course, heard much about 'book burning,' but much less about 'book forcing.'" He then noted "incidents much as that which arose in Girard High School in Pennsylvania. There the school board voted to deny diplomas to two fundamentalist Christian boys who refused to read Studs Terkel's *Working*—with its chapter on a prostitute's 'working' and its frequent blasphemous language."

I looked at that last sentence again. In Girard, you refuse to read a book, and on that ground alone, all your previous years in the school system are wiped out? I called William Ball. I got the court papers in the suit (argued by Ball) by the two seniors, claiming they surely had a right to be graduated. And I talked to the boys' teacher, Kay Nichols (Karolyn Nichols in the court papers).

The case has to do with some of the constitutional law that has to do with the right to say "No!" It's a very important liberty, and it is seldom taught in the schools—for obvious reasons.

For instance, a 1977 Supreme Court decision, *Wooley* v. *Maynard*—prosecuted by David Souter, then New Hampshire attorney general. The case involved a Jehovah's Witness. (Members of that faith have contributed greatly through the decades toward expanding liberty of conscience through constitutional lawsuits.) A resident of New Hampshire, the Jehovah's Witness objected to the state requirement that whenever he drove his car, he had to use license plates with the state motto, "Live Free or Die."

The Jehovah's Witness considered it offensive, and against his conscience, for the state to make him advertise a secular eschatology to which he did not subscribe. So he taped over those words on his license plate, and the state—having nothing better to do—went after him.

"We begin with the proposition," said the Supreme Court in *Wooley* v. *Maynard,* "that the right of freedom of thought protected by the First Amendment against state action includes both the right to speak freely and the right to refrain from speaking at all." Thus did the High Court establish a First Amendment right to silence rather than having to surrender your conscience—at least in this context—to the state.

Later in the decision—and this is the section that characterizes an abiding principle of William Ball—the Court said: "Here ... we are faced with a state measure which forces an individual as part of his daily life ... to be an instrument for fostering public adherence to an ideological point of view he finds unacceptable.... *the First Amendment protects the right of individuals to hold a point of view different from the majority and to refuse to foster ... an idea they find morally reprehensible.*" (Emphasis added.)

So, who are those two fundamentalist Christian boys who refused—even on pain of not being allowed to graduate—to read Studs Terkel's *Working?* And who were these school professionals who refused to give the two students an alternative book, commanding instead that they do their assigned reading in *Working?* Or else. Keep in mind the lines above from the Supreme Court's *Tinker* decision: "In our system, state-operated schools may not be enclaves of totalitarianism."

The boys who insisted they had a right not to read *Working* as a matter of conscience were Robert Burns, Jr., and James Richardson. Both were enrolled in the twelfth-grade vocational English class at Girard High School. The parents of the two students are, according to the court papers, fundamentalist Christians who do not, however, "seek to supervise the work of the public school in which their children are enrolled." But the parents do "believe that they have a duty in conscience to assure that the education provided to their children in the public school does not violate traditional Christian moral values and beliefs."

When I send a book out into the world, the feeling is somewhat like waving good-bye to a child leaving home. Actually, it's worse. If a son or daughter gets into trouble, you can still help, but there's usually not much a writer can do for a book that's in a jam. But you try anyway. Sometimes you may help rout the censors by testifying for your book in court. Or you can maybe, just maybe, win the battle at the start by showing up as soon as you hear of a move to throw your book out of the library or the classroom. Then, as in *High Noon,* you go up against the thought police, no matter how many of them there are, and blow them away with the First Amendment.

That's what Studs Terkel did in Girard, Pennsylvania, when *Working,* the child of his typewriter and tape recorder, was in trouble. After Studs left, *Working* wasn't in trouble anymore. But two fundamentalist Christian boys were—for continuing to refuse to read Studs's book. Why? Because, the two seniors and their parents said, it offended their moral and religious beliefs.

Too damn bad, said the school administration. If these two persisted in not conforming to the curriculum, they'd better not make any graduation plans.

I remembered what Justice Robert Jackson had said in the 1943 Supreme Court decision vigorously supporting the right of the children of Jehovah's Witnesses in West Virginia *not* to salute the flag in public schools. "If there is any fixed star in our constitutional constellation, it is that no official, high or petty, can prescribe what shall be orthodox politics, nationalism, religion, or other matters of opinion or *force citizens to confess by word* or *act their faith therein.*" (Emphasis added.)

Kids have a First Amendment right to *be* different, to *believe* differently, in the public schools. And, Justice Robert Jackson added, "Freedom to differ is not limited to things that do not matter much. That would be a mere shadow of freedom. The test of its substance is the right to differ as to things that touch the heart of the existing order."

That's just what those two seniors at Girard High School in Pennsylvania claimed as their right—to differ as to things that touched the heart of their beliefs. Even though their teacher, their principal, and the school board said the two boys had no right to go against the existing order of the school system, especially its required reading lists.

During a conversation I had with their teacher, Kay Nichols— the paladin of every student's right to read Studs Terkel's *Working* (whether they want to or not)—she said something that struck me as peculiar. "Those two boys were not heroes!"

"I beg your pardon, I'm not sure I heard you right."

"They were not heroes. They were alienated from the rest of the class. They were scorned."

"Why?"

"Because of their actions," she said sharply, as if to a slow student.

A quite different perspective is that of First Amendment lawyer William Ball. He represented the boys when nothing—not Kay Nichols, not the principal, not the presence of Studs Terkel himself—had been able to make them bend and agree to read *Working*. Said Ball in the court papers:

"Plaintiffs not only hold their religious beliefs sincerely, they hold them with enough moral courage to withstand the conformist pressure of community powers, not to mention the national media." (He meant Studs Terkel's widely covered triumphant visit to Girard to defend his book.)

The two boys seem like heroes to me. It's what that heretic Henry David Thoreau used to say: "Let your life be a counter friction to stop the machine."

But why specifically did Robert Burns and James Richardson so stubbornly refuse to read *Working* on the grounds of religious conscience? The language, for one thing. Not only such appoggiaturas as "fuckin'" and "shit," but also the abundance of blasphemy, as the boys and their parents see it. There was more. William Ball emphasized in one of the court papers that Burns's and Richardson's moral and religious beliefs cause them to oppose the *"entire theme"* of *Working*.

In his introduction to the book, Studs described work as often doing violence "to the spirit as well as the body.... To survive the day is triumph enough for the walking wounded among the great many of us."

Well, these fundamentalist Christians believe, says William Ball, "that God has directed them to view work as a positive, joyful, and sacred duty which enables them to please God and come closer to Him. They believe that the Bible directs them to avoid foul and offensive language, immoral situations, and activities which might lead them into sin. As a result, they cannot, in good conscience, read from and therefore assent to a book which is shot through with foul language, blasphemies, and views of life and work which are deeply offensive to their Christian convictions."

In the complaint, filed in the U.S. District Court for the Western District of Pennsylvania, Ball pointed out: "The plaintiff parents do not seek to suppress the author's expression of these views but they vigorously object to the author's view of life, morality and work being imposed upon their children by the state."

> I had assumed that the welfare of the single human soul was the ultimate test of the vitality of the First Amendment.— WILLIAM O. DOUGLAS, *GILLETTE* V. *UNITED STATES* (1971)

> Every man—in the development of his own personality—has the right to form his own beliefs and opinions. Hence, suppression of belief, opinion and expression is an affront to the dignity of man, a negation of man's essential nature.— THOMAS EMERSON, *TOWARD A GENERAL THEORY OF THE FIRST AMENDMENT*

> [State-sponsored education] is a mere contrivance for moulding people to be exactly like one another; and as the mould in which it casts them is that which pleases the predominant power in the government, whether this be a monarch, a priesthood, an aristocracy, or the majority of the existing generation, in proportion as it is efficient and successful, it establishes a despotism over the mind.—JOHN STUART MILL, *ON LIBERTY*

Graduation was in sight for the vocational educational students in Kay Nichols's twelfth-grade English class at Girard High School. It was the second half of the term, and all the kids had to do was keep their eye on the ball until emancipation day. But Bob Burns and Jim Richardson continued to be annoyingly difficult, stubborn, downright unreasonable. It was as if the dybbuk of Bartleby the Scrivener had somehow entered both boys, for Burns and Richardson chorused, again and again, "I prefer not to." Although at first they tried to do the required reading assignment.

The two fundamentalist Christian boys did complete the first assignment in *Working*. On finishing that assignment, the boys yelled the Christian equivalent of *Trayf!* Not kosher! Unclean! Not only was the language profoundly offensive to them and their parents (like "motherfucker"), but many of the concepts of work in the initial assignment mocked, to say the least, what God had told them.

The day after reading that first assignment, Burns and Richardson told Kay Nichols they could not, in conscience, have anything more to do with that book. The teacher sent the boys to the office of Walter J. Blucas, principal of Girard High School. Blucas had the answer. Read on, he told the mulish boys. Just skip the language and concepts you find unacceptable.

"You see," Studs Terkel told me later, "they did give the kids an option. They didn't have to read the passages that offended them."

I reminded Studs that for Orthodox Jews, the *whole* pig is *trayf.* You can't pick and choose among its parts if you want to be on the right side of G_d. For these kids, *Working* was a seamless series of invitations to sin. Furthermore, how are you supposed to know when to skip the offensive parts? At the point you've been offended again, right? What kind of deal is that?

The professional staff at Girard High School, however, kept trying to force the book into those fundamentalist Christian heads. Kay Nichols told me that after Burns and Richardson first objected, "I assigned them only sections of the book that would not offend them. I assured them they would not be offended." She then added—in an aggrieved tone: "But they said *anything* between the covers of that book would be offensive."

Nichols had another argument. "If I present certain material to students and tell them, 'You have to believe this is correct,' then I am violating their rights of conscience. But in that class, I was not limiting or circumscribing their reaction to the material. They could disagree with any of it. So I was not violating the rights of those two students."

William Ball, the First Amendment lawyer for Burns and Richardson, points out in response that when a fundamentalist Christian kid in a public school is told he cannot choose an alternative book but *must* read the teacher's wholly offensive choice or he will fail—or, worse yet, not be graduated—then the state is forcing him to go against his moral and religious beliefs. The very forced act of reading, even if the student is allowed to disagree with the material, is a violation of his conscience.

"These boys at Girard," Ball says, "could have been told they don't have to believe that 'motherfucker' is a nice word, but that it's not offensive in a particular context. So, although the word greatly offends their beliefs, Burns and Richardson—had they yielded to the state in this matter—would have, in their own minds, assented to the use of that word because they would indeed have been using it in the act of reading it."

The wonder of this story, whether you agree with Ball or Nichols, is the energy, the sheer demonic energy, with which the educators of Girard, Pennsylvania, tried to cram this book into these nay-sayers. William Ball thinks there could have been a touch of "elitism," as he puts it, involved. "These kids," he says, "were in a vocational-technical track, and maybe the feeling was that to get the right stuff into this kind of kid you had to simply take their minds and stamp into them what ought to be there."

Maybe so. Maybe, not knowing the abundance of autodidacts in the working class, the authorities at Girard figured this might be the best time Burns and Richardson would be vulnerable to an idea, and wanted to fill them up to their meager capacity. However, I think most of the lust to make these kids conform came from the chronic passion of any agent of the state to keep things nice and regular. And that's why, in the public schools, as John Stuart Mill has said, much of the professional staff see their mission as turning out graduates "exactly like one another."

After principal Blucas and teacher Nichols refused to give the boys an alternative book, Burns and Richardson were removed from the classroom by Blucas (who marches through my imagination with the gait of Charles Laughton), and were isolated in the library whenever the class discussed *Working*. While in the library, those miserable sinners against the secular order were given no alternative work to do and indeed, according to William Ball's court papers, "were specifically directed not to move about or leave their seats."

Linda Burns, mother of Bob, then moved that *Working* be reconsidered for use in the high school. She asked, first, that it be withdrawn entirely from the school district. There she was wrong. No parent has the right to decide what the kids of other parents are going to be saved from. More logically and constitutionally, she asked that students who objected to the book for reasons of religious conscience be given something else to read.

On February 2, 1982, Studs Terkel himself came to Girard, and had the high school auditorium resounding with cheers. On March 22, the Girard School Board denied Linda Burns's request to reconsider *Working* as part of the curriculum in twelfth-grade vo-tech English.

Said the board: "The objecting students have not been required to read the chapters they feel to be offensive. The teacher has told the class that she will, in advance of each reading assignment, advise them that they may find sections of that particular assignment objectional [*sic*], and those ["objectional"] assignments are not mandatory."

Once again, I marvel at the concentrated zeal with which all these grown-ups were determined to force-feed these primitives. But why couldn't they have given the boys another book?

"To require," said the Girard School Board, "that the objecting students be provided with alternative books would be tantamount to delegating to any recusant segment the Board's right to select instructional materials. The Board has to make the ultimate determination."

We're talking about *one* book in *one-half* of *one* course, and the school board acts as if providing an alternative book would so shake the firmament that the high school would fall apart. And the board said nothing of the boys' right to free exercise of their religion by not being forced by the state, under these circumstances, to be apostates in school.

We are not talking, by the way, about some fundamentalist Christian students in a public school who object to being forced to take a course in biology that spends a good deal of time on evolution—and none on "creationism." That kind of requirement involves the very foundation of part of the curriculum—not just one book among others on a class reading list.

As William Ball concedes, "When you have a direct challenge to the curriculum itself, as in your biology example, it's a much more difficult situation to contest in the courts." And my prediction, as a clubhouse lawyer, is that the courts would decide for the school if the student, needing those biology credits to graduate, refused to take the course and was denied his degree. His recourse then would be to transfer to a religious high school.

The events in Girard fall far short of that kind of irreconcilable conflict between religious beliefs and secular education. Anyway, after the school board said the Christian kids had no choice but to read *Working*, principal Blucas told the boys that if they kept on shunning the book, they would not be allowed to graduate in June 1982.

William Ball went to Federal District Court, and a settlement was reached that obviated a trial. Bob Burns and Jim Richardson were indeed allowed to graduate, even though they did not open the pages of *Working* again.

But benevolent school personnel sped the boys into adulthood with a parting reminder of the magnanimity of true professionals, even when those professionals have suffered a defeat. Both Burns and Richardson were flunked for the second half of their English course with Kay Nichols. Why? They hadn't done their assignments in *Working*. After all, said acting schools superintendent Dr. Jan Calhoun, it is the district's right to choose the books to be taught; the teacher of this class organized it within the framework of approved curriculum guides; and the two students chose not to participate, even though they had full knowledge of the foregoing facts.

Or, as Bartleby's employer said to him, "Either you must do something, or something must be done to you."

William Ball, having won the final event, was still brooding, as I am, about Girard High's final kick in the rear to Bob Burns and Jim Richardson. Ball wrote a letter to the *Erie Times*. "It is grossly unfair to have given these boys a failing grade. Up to here they had maintained a 'C' average in the course. They stood ready, to the last, to perform an alternative reading assignment (and there is a whole world of wonderful readings from which such an assignment could have been made). To have flunked them appears to be an act of meanness."

Most acts of meanness in the public schools, however, do not rise to constitutional levels. And I suppose that for some teachers and administrators, this power to be mean—with near impunity—provides a psychic income of no small value. What a pleasure it must have been to stamp the two F's on the records of those Bible-spouting misfits!

III

The Thought Police—with the Very Best of Intentions

"We took a vote and we removed those words."

What follows was a precursor of the "political correctness" orthodoxy on college campuses—and beyond, in parts of the feminist and civil rights movements, as well as among conservative cadres.

Though the issues and priorities are obviously different in these various groups, the description that binds them together is that they are—as art critic Harold Rosenberg once said—"herds of independent minds."

In the June 25, 1979, letters section of the *Village Voice*, fourteen of its editors and writers grandly dissociated themselves from the Jules Feiffer strip in the same issue. Why? Because it "ends with the racial slur, 'nigger.'" Therefore, said these clanking wardens of appropriately sensitive language, "Whatever its intentions, the cartoon plays into, and not off, a reactionary sensibility. We find it not only offensive but far from funny and not in the least illuminating."

At least two of the signers clearly wanted the Feiffer strip killed entirely. As for the rest, my own guess is that a poll of the fourteen would have resulted in a majority also voting to censor the strip.

In the offending cartoon, a frustrated man (white) says: "Can't say 'fag' anymore. Can't say 'dyke' anymore. Can't say 'fruit' anymore. Can't say 'queer' anymore. I can only take so much tolerance. I'm going back to 'nigger.'"

Feiffer was obviously driving in the point that the one 1960s "movement" that generated all the others has benefited least and indeed is slipping back fast because of the pervasive racism that Feiffer skewers.

Yet fourteen *Voice* editors and writers, exercising their inalienable right to behave like schmucks in public, scornfully found this strip "not in the least illuminating." The only specific reason they gave is Feiffer's use of "nigger."

The word "nigger," said a senior editor who was trying to kill the strip, profoundly offends all blacks and other right-thinking people. Why, he asked me meaningfully, didn't Feiffer use "kike" in the final panel? Because it doesn't make the point. It doesn't shock the reader into recognition of how *he* may be thinking about blacks. Sure, anti-Semitism is lively enough throughout the land, but not nearly so powerful and destructive as racism.

The signers, in their towering obtuseness, had stripped Feiffer of his history. Almost from the very beginning of the *Voice*, Feiffer most vividly and consistently exemplified the spirit of the paper. From Presidents to readers, no one has been immune from his swift, leaping wit. Also among Feiffer's targets are the most cherished shibboleths of not only bigots but also liberals yearning to be accepted by blacks.

The battle over the strip is not over. Fundamentally, there remain two factions at the paper. Some of us believe that the reader can be—has to be—trusted to make up his or her own mind and so there ought to be many perspectives and no restrictions on ideas and language. But one member of the thought police, lobbying against the Feiffer strip, told me, in all befuddled sincerity, "We're not censoring ideas. We're just getting rid of language that can be written in a better, less offensive way."

The thought police honestly feel that the paper's mission

should be to adhere to the "correct" anti-establishment line in all things, including language.

I know the authoritarian mind well, having grown up in a neighborhood abounding with Communists and certain wholly inflexible Trotskyite sects. My first reporting was as an infiltrator into various fascist groups while I was still in my teens; and in the years since, I have had to deal with true believers among radicals, Zionists, PLO-types, educators, parents, blacks, Hispanics, the National Organization for Women, Operation Rescue, and homicide detectives.

Whatever his sanctified line, the true believer is wholly convinced he or she is acting in the very best interests of both the proximate and ultimate truth. And if he is on a newspaper, it is his responsibility to see to it that the readers are told what to think; that they are not distracted by ambivalences and ambiguities; and that no language be used that could possibly offend any group whose side the paper should be on.

A copy editor at the *Voice* was telling of how a piece came into that department bearing certain words she considered offensive to feminists. "We took a vote," she proudly continued, "and we removed those words." Presumably, the hapless author was not there, but even if he or she had been, the censors would have prevailed.

And an editor advised another editor, "You can't use that reporter on this piece. She doesn't have the right line."

At a meeting, a staff writer was vehemently censorious of another writer because the latter has an appalling tendency to present both sides of stories. (Why, sometimes he finds more than two sides.) The target of her reeducation campaign was further pilloried because, she charged, he seems even to identify with some of those people in his stories who do not have the right ideas.

And then there was the notorious (within the shop) incident of a story by a woman who lived on Christopher Street in Greenwich Village and was not much pleased with what was happening on that and adjacent streets. Her purpose, as she told me, was to write a kind of neighborhood story. Her neighborhood was now turning into a Tenderloin district.

The problem with the piece among certain sensitive staff members was that those transmogrifying the neighborhood, as the writer saw it, were homosexuals. She was not putting down all homosexuals, but rather the kinds of behavior—whether engaged in by gays or rhinoceroses—that made it unpleasant for her to live there. She was not advocating the removal of the new Tenderloiners, finally moving out herself, but was simply telling what had happened.

The writer, anticipating that this piece might stir up certain folks at the *Voice* as being homophobic, asked the then-editor not to make it available in the office until it was in better shape. The story did need some work, but far sloppier pieces have been printed in the *Voice*. Somehow, a copy of the article was sprung, disseminated around the office and to a gay publication outside, and a concerted campaign was instituted by the thought police at the paper to kill the article. The writer began to hear of vitriolic speeches, both at the *Voice* and in her neighborhood, denouncing her. And she heard of insistent pressures being placed on the editor and managing editor to suppress the piece. It never ran.

I do think that those among the signers of the anti-Feiffer letter who were editors performed a useful service. Any potential new writer for this paper, with its roots in Lenny Bruce and I. F. Stone, would now know whom to try to avoid as an editor. Unfortunately, those who succeeded in killing the article about Christopher Street did not identify themselves publicly. These censors left no fingerprints.

"The professor was denounced as sexist and racist; and then, by other names, most vilely abused."

The National Council of Teachers of English has battled attempted censorship in the schools for years.

NCTE pamphlets, like "The Student's Right to Read," served as welcome ammunition for teachers and librarians who choose to confront the thought police in their districts. That particular document proclaimed: "The right of any individual not just to read but to read whatever he wants is basic to a democratic society." There is, of course, an inexorable corollary to that resplendent dictum: the right of authors to use their own language in their books and articles—rather than have to adjust their choice of words to the ukases of some authorizing committee.

Yet the National Council of Teachers of English at one point became infected with the zeal to censor, and precisely on the point of writers' freedom to have their own, unbleached voices.

In 1975, the NCTE's Board of Directors approved a resolution condemning the use of "sexist language" on the ground that it "warps our perceptions, whether we are the writer or speaker, reader or listener." Simple denunciation being insufficient, there came to be a set of "Guidelines for Nonsexist Use of Language in NCTE Publications." The editors of the various journals of the Council—*Elementary English, College English, The English Journal, et al.*—were not commanded to adopt those guidelines; but most of them—good soldiers in the jihad for nonsexist language—did enforce them.

At NCTE headquarters, the source of copious publications, the nonsexist guidelines were totally, uniformly enforced, not only in reports, papers, articles, NCTE books and monographs but also in each piece of correspondence coming from that beacon of positive thinking.

In 1977, the Council accepted for publication a collection of papers that came from a conference on stylistics. In February 1978, a University of Illinois–Chicago Circle professor who had written one of the articles received a letter from NCTE's director of publications. This nonsexist commissar of right-thinking language informed the professor that in view of NCTE policy against the use of "man" in occupational terms, two of his words were being replaced. Policeman had been changed to police officer. And chairman had been purged to read chair.

The professor, a chronic individualist, objected that he should be allowed to use whatever terms he preferred.

He was rebelling against the kind of foolishness, no matter how noble the intent, that George Orwell was referring to in "Politics and the English Language":

"A man may take to drink because he feels himself to be a failure, and then fail all the more completely because he drinks. It is rather the same thing that is happening to the English language. It becomes ugly and inaccurate because our thoughts are foolish, but the slovenliness of our language makes it easier for us to have foolish thoughts."

The by-now controversial author wrote to Professor Harold Allen of the University of Minnesota. Allen had been a member of the NCTE since 1924 and was particularly active in the free-speech wars that organization fought outside its own councils. Allen, for instance, had been given the initial responsibility for creating "The Student's Right to Read" pamphlet.

On hearing the Chicago professor's complaint that he was being denied the freedom to write those two words, Allen pointed out to the NCTE's director of publications that the directive implementing the "Guidelines for Nonsexist Use of Language" did not say they *must* be used. It said they *should* be used. And for the director to insist on the removal of those words was rather embarrassingly inconsistent with the NCTE's general policy against censorship.

The director of publications was unpersuaded. Those demeaning words must be censored. The Chicago professor, stubbornly maintaining that his freedom of speech was more important to him than being included in this NCTE book, withdrew his article from the anthology, even though it was already in page proofs.

Herbert Allen, much disturbed to see a virus of censorship entering the NCTE's bloodstream, as it were, made a proposal at the annual NCTE convention during Thanksgiving weekend in 1978. It seemed a modest enough suggestion:

"That the policy opposing the use of sexist language in NCTE publications shall not be so construed as to prevent the use of such language by an author if an accompanying editorial comment indicates that its presence is the result of an author's express stipulation."

Had that resolution been adopted, the NCTE's own devotion to nonsexist language would remain pristine. And all the editors, copy editors, proofreaders, and secretaries at NCTE publications would also be free of any sexist blemish. The blame would lie fully on any maverick author who insisted on being so chauvinistic as to be perversely literal about the word "chair," for instance. And that, of course, is where the blame ought to be. That's why there are bylines. The reader will hold only the writer responsible for what appears in print.

Professor Allen submitted his resolution. Thereupon, Neil Postman reported in the spring 1979 issue of *ETC./A Review of General Semantics,* Allen was "denounced as sexist and racist; and then by other names, most vilely abused."

Why racist? Well, thought police are so used to thinking in herds that they do not see their "enemies" as three-dimensionally discrete but rather as being all alike. As that resonant anti-Semite of the 1930's airwaves, Father Charles E. Couglin, interchangeably used "Jew" to mean both Communists and international bankers, so the new wardens of language consider that a sexist must also be a racist and, if he is a heterosexual, a homophobe besides.

That is not all that happened to Professor Allen. "After a period of unseemly hooting," Postman continues, "a large group mobilized itself to sing 'We Shall Overcome' with that unique and somewhat unnatural fervor that is customary at those moments."

Consider this twisted legacy of the 1960s. What were they overcoming? "Sexism," right? But also, free speech.

At last, as Postman says, "in defamation, Allen's proposal was defeated."

The forces of blinding light in the NCTE savored their triumph. Linda Reed, writing for the NCTE's Women's Committee, proclaimed that "NCTE has an opportunity—and a responsibility— to be in the forefront of social change. The editorial policies and procedures of the NCTE Publications Department reflect that image of the organization.

"... We may not know the actual impact for many years, and we may frustrate a few authors along the way, but surely it is worth the wait, and the sacrifice."

In *ETC.,* Neil Postman elaborated on what was lost along the way:

"In defending both this debacle [the overcoming of Professor Allen] and the policy itself, one member of the triumphant forces told me that there is no difference between an editor's insisting on correct spelling and an editor's insistence on non-sexist usage. This I regard as complete and dangerous nonsense, worthy of a Commissar to whom political opinions, like spelling, are viewed as either correct or incorrect, and from which no deviation from the established truth may be permitted.

"Make no mistake about it: the labeling of someone's language as 'sexist' involves a political judgment and implies the desirability of a particular sociological doctrine. One may be in favor of that doctrine (as I believe I am), but it is quite another matter to force writers by edicts and censorship into accepting it.... Writers like to say things in their own way and for their own reasons, and it is always nasty business when editors tell them what level of consciousness their language must be at."

That a majority of delegates representing 100,000 members of the National Council of Teachers of *English* did not understand these basics is rather scary. In view of the homogenous nature of most American textbooks, which are developed by publisher-controlled committees to offend no one, the teacher is the only hope a child has that he or she can learn in an atmosphere free of rigid strictures as to inquiry and expression. But if teachers are to make political judgments about language usage—possibly giving negative grades to kids who won't see chairs as actual human beings—then students will learn, even more than ever, that right thinking comes from right-minded authority that can be questioned only on pain of being considered a deviant. A sexist, for instance.

"The fight against bad English," George Orwell warned, "is not frivolous and it is not the exclusive concern of professional writers."

"The thick black wings of the monstrous crow"

He was a Stalinist and I, having read *Darkness at Noon* when I was fifteen, was his political enemy. Otherwise, we were friends. An actor of rising renown, he moved inside Chekhov, O'Neill, Shaw with power and ease. He had just broken into movies when Joseph McCarthy—with the thick black wings of the monstrous crow in *Through the Looking Glass*—put the land in shadow.

My friend, blacklisted, took the part of a salesman in a haberdashery. The money was what you'd get for a walk-on, but he could have his shorts at a discount. One of his few pleasures was to taunt me about "this bourgeois Bill of Rights in *your* democracy. I am free to say what I think," he would mumble, "and they—all the creeps with their lists and their phone calls and their boycotts—are free to punish me for what I say. Let them argue with me. Let them have a fistfight with me, one at a time. But to take my livelihood away! You can freeze to death from such freedom."

So he won a lot of pyrrhic points in our debates. Later, when the blacklists crumbled, some of the banished came back from limbo to resume their careers. My friend did not. He tried, but he had mislaid his confidence and never found it again.

In the late 1970s, when an official of the Florida Citrus Commission intimated that Anita Bryant—then the national spokeswoman for the Florida orange—might be sacked because of her off-hours crusade against homosexuals, I thought of my Stalinist friend.

Around the country, in contempt of Anita Bryant's right of free expression, campaigns to boycott orange juice were organized. And not only by her targets. Some indignant heterosexuals also switched to tomato juice or, if they're particularly cosmopolitan, Calvados. Legions of letter-writers warned the Florida Citrus Commission to jettison its spokeswoman or suffer a blight more fearful than any in the annals of nature. Economic threats were also directed against the Miami tourist bureau and a Miami bank for which Anita Bryant had done television commercials. Bryant said indignantly, "I'm a victim of blacklisting."

Ira Glasser, then–executive director of the New York Civil Liberties Union, concurred: "Anita Bryant has taken certain public positions, and certain people who disagree with those positions are trying to punish her economically. This is exactly what happened during the McCarthy years. I see no difference between blacklisting people then through *Red Channels* and blacklisting Anita Bryant now."

There is, of course, a counterargument. Many of us have boycotted particular brands of California grapes and lettuce in support of Cesar Chavez's struggle to persuade California growers that serfdom is not an especially gracious way of life for their workers. And many of us boycotted the textile products of J. P. Stevens & Company, an employer dedicated to preserving the sort of early–Industrial Revolution approach to workers that enabled Karl Marx to make a name for himself.

So what's wrong with boycotting Anita Bryant? I asked Floyd Abrams, one of the republic's leading First Amendment lawyers. Abrams declared himself "very disturbed" at the mounting of any economic boycott aimed at any individual who has spoken out, however outrageously, on any issue.

"The boycotts of California growers and of J. P. Stevens," Abrams said, "are against *actions* by these employers in their business—when they resist workers' attempts to get a fair wage, for example, or violate their employees' collective bargaining rights. But Anita Bryant is being boycotted because she has engaged in *speech*, including political speech, that has nothing to do with her work advertising orange juice. If this kind of boycott against an individual happens often enough, there has to be a dangerously inhibiting effect on a lot of other people's speech."

No civil libertarian, including Floyd Abrams, would claim that boycotts directed against Bryant should be prohibited by law. After all, organized peaceful protests are also protected by the First Amendment. But when such protests aim at curbing speech through economic intimidation, the boycotters ought to be reminded that blacklisting is not a right-wing monopoly. Instead, it is a pernicious process available to any group eager to suppress ideas that enrage it.

In fact, not all gay organizations approved the blacklisting of Anita Bryant. When great pressure was being put on the Singer Sewing Machine Company to reject Bryant for television commercials, the National Gay Task Force noted: "We are not happy to see that kind of discrimination, even when the victims themselves are discriminators."

Although Bryant's contract with the Florida Citrus Commission was finally extended, the boycott continued. And when a boycott is on, the target, if he or she is a performer or writer or artist, may well lose other jobs without knowing that they've been lost. Employers don't like controversy. Bryant claimed, moreover, that talk-show appearances were being canceled because other performers would not sit alongside her. And in Bryant's line of work, when that kind of exposure dissolves, it's the *Red Channels* effect all over again.

Let us suppose, however, that Anita Bryant had been applying her off-hours to the fervent advancement of gay rights. In that event, the odds still being what they were at that time, a landslide of abuse would already have denuded her of employment as the lady of the oranges. And of all other gigs. Meanwhile, gays and their allies—including many who were trying to strip her of all gainful employment as a homophobe—would be clamoring for Bryant's right to speak freely. And they would be denouncing those trying to shut her up.

What do we learn from this confusion? That in defining free speech and those who are entitled to exercise it, most Americans agree with Humpty Dumpty:

"When *I* use a word, it means just what *I* choose it to mean—neither more nor less."

And that is why, every once in a while, the skies darken as the monstrous crow spreads its thick black wings to choke off an individual's dissent.

"We believe you have made a tragic mistake in this matter in creating a false 'free speech' issue, when the real issue is the practice of racial discrimination."

> *I don't think anybody in his right mind thinks I want them here.*
> *No, I don't want them here. But they have a right to play here.*
> —ERASTUS CORNING II, MAYOR OF ALBANY, NEW YORK

When word came to the *Village Voice* in September 1981 that Hugh Carey, commander-in-chief of the military and naval forces of the state of New York, had apparently made it impossible for South Africa's Springboks rugby team to play in a city-owned stadium in Albany by denying it state protection, a colleague of mine yelled, "Great!"

The genuine, noble-minded exaltation in that utterly wrong-headed cry echoed elsewhere in the land as the Springboks were banished from other cities, including New York City.

"A fabulous victory," said Richard Lapchick—an organizer for the nationwide coalition, SART (Stop the Apartheid Rugby Tour)—when Hugh Carey overruled the mayor of Albany and showed that he knew how to use a South African method to keep the public peace. "A moral victory," said a spokesman for Operation PUSH in Chicago as the Springboks were being forced to scurry around the Midwest looking for private places to play, because public stadiums had been denied them.

A moral victory for whom? And what is the moral?

This was Skokie all over again. Then, it was mainly Jews who were furiously insisting that Nazis had no First Amendment rights to demonstrate on that tour where many Jews, including Holocaust survivors, lived. ("Freedom of expression," said one opponent of the American Civil Liberties Union's defense of those rights, even for Nazis, "has no meaning when it defends those who would end those rights for others.")

In this case, blacks and many whites outraged by apartheid saw no First Amendment issue in closing public stadiums to a team then representing the most viciously racist government in the world. As Judge William Booth, president of the American Committee on Africa, wrote to Dorothy Samuels, then executive director of the New York Civil Liberties Union: "We believe you have made a tragic mistake in this matter in creating a false 'free speech' issue, when the real issue is the practice of racial discrimination."

Nonetheless, the New York Civil Liberties Union persistently and successfully supported the Springboks' First Amendment right to play—all the way through the federal courts.

The New York Civil Liberties Union knew that the consequences of yielding to the ban-the-Springboks pressures would be dangerous—to every controversial group on any side of any political battle. As the Albany *Times-Union* emphasized in a September 18 editorial, "We will live to regret it. That decision to prohibit the Springboks from playing will prove to be far more important and will have greater unfortunate consequences than any rugby game ever could have had." The paper also emphasized:

"... Public officials cannot be allowed to pick and choose which political demonstrations they will allow and which they will ban. This was the practice in America's South for many years, the practice that often made it impossible for black civil rights marchers to get a permit to parade. Now Mr. Carey has established this same precedent in New York...."

But how does a commercial rugby game become a First Amendment matter in the first place? It is true that the Supreme Court has extended First Amendment projections to movies and theatrical productions. The Court, though, had yet to rule directly on whether a sporting event can qualify as protected symbolic speech.

In this instance, however, it could not be more obvious that all the protests against the Springboks had nothing whatever to do with rugby but had everything to do with this being a South African team. So these were indeed political protests. Moreover, Lauren Anderson, associate director of the National Conference of Black Lawyers, accurately wrote New York mayor Edward Koch that South Africa "views its sports policies as very political. The Government of South Africa has made it very clear that they seek to use international sports competitions as a means of obtaining legitimacy for their racist and illegal policies." (She and the Conference wanted the match canceled.)

It was even revealed that a South African businessman with close—and in the past, secret—public relations ties to the government gave $25,000 to the Eastern Rugby Union (sponsors of the Springboks' trip) to help "legitimize" South African sports in this country. All in all, it was clear that the Springboks hadn't come here just to play rugby.

This made their presence all the more odious, but the First Amendment does not make an exception for the odious—whether they're from South Africa or the Ku Klux Klan. Or, as Federal District Judge Bernard Decker of Chicago said in the case of the Nazis and Skokie: "The ability of American society to tolerate the advocacy even of the hateful doctrines espoused by plaintiffs without abandoning its commitment to freedom of speech and assembly is perhaps the best protection we have against the establishment of any Nazi-type regime in this country."

Another part of the Constitution was at stake with regard to the rugby game—the Equal Protection Clause of the Fourteenth Amendment. In their *amicus* brief for the New York Civil Liberties Union in the Springboks case, Steven Shapiro and Arthur Eisenberg pointed out that "when a municipality regulates access to the streets, sidewalks, parks or public facilities, *it cannot grant or deny such access because of the political or religious values, the race, the color or the national origin of those who seek to use these facilities."* (Emphasis added.)

Commander-in-Chief Carey, therefore, was in further violation of the Constitution because "the decision to exclude the Springboks turned exclusively upon the team's country of origin, the political policies of that country, and the political values that have, therefore, been ascribed to those South African players."

But the governor and Mayor Koch had a "nonpolitical" rationale for banning the Springboks. They claimed they shut out the Springboks because the anti-apartheid demonstrations at the matches might well become violent, and also because the extra law-enforcement personnel required would be very costly. In terms of public safety and of being a drain on the taxpayers' money, the Springboks were too troublesome to be borne.

Actually, the organizers of both the New York and the Albany demonstrations made it clear that they were not advocating violence. But let us assume Carey and Koch felt they had sufficient reason to anticipate a riot to cancel the game. This brings us to what is called "the heckler's veto"—the power of the threat or apprehension of violence to cause public officials to suppress unpopular speech or assembly.

To begin with, as William O. Douglas said in *Terminiello* v. *Chicago* (1948): "A function of free speech under our system of government is to *invite dispute*. It may indeed best serve its purposes when it induces a condition of unrest ... or *even stirs people to anger.*" (Italics mine.) But when free speech does stir people to anger, what is the responsibility of government?

A classic answer was supplied by the Bill of Rights Committee of the American Bar Association in a successful 1939 *amicus* brief for the CIO, which Mayor Frank ("I Am the Law") Hague wanted to kick out of Jersey City:

"It is the duty of the officials to prevent or suppress the threatened disorder with a firm hand instead of timidly yielding to threats.... *Surely a speaker ought not to be suppressed because his opponents propose to use violence.* It is they who should suffer for their lawlessness, not he." (Emphasis added.)

Mayor Hague lost, and this has become settled constitutional law. As one of the courts said in the Skokie case: "Courts have consistently refused to ban speech on the possibility of unlawful conduct by those opposed to the speaker's philosophy."

In New York City and New York State, however, Carey and Koch came very close to legitimizing "the heckler's veto." An official who worked for Koch and insisted on anonymity told me after the Springboks were vetoed out of a September match in New York City: "It's scary. With these precedents, any sizable group of people who don't like the politics of a visiting team or a dance troupe or a theater company, can decide—by stirring fears of violence—what the rest of us can and can't see" (as happened in San Francisco in June, 1981, when then Mayor Dianne Feinstein canceled a Turkish Folkloric Ballet performance in the face of Armenian wrath and threats of attacking the performers).

As for the money argument, just what is the price of the First Amendment? At what number of cops or state troopers, at how many hours of overtime, does it become too costly to protect greatly unpopular speech? Would the same cost, however, be bearable if a different set of players were involved? To quote Dorothy Samuels, then head of the New York Civil Liberties Union: "If a black African team wanted to play and the Ku Klux Klan threatened to disrupt it, the governor would be the first to offer the protection of the state police. The only difference here is that the group [the Springboks] is an unpopular group."

In all of this, the one statement by a public official that got straight to the core of the First Amendment came from, of all people, the patriarch of one of the last of the old-time political machines—Erastus Corning II, mayor of Albany for forty years. While those "politically correct" statesmen Carey and Koch picked up political points behind the shield of public safety, Corning said:

"... Our Constitution guarantees an individual the right to publicly espouse an unpopular cause, and the same right to a number of individuals in peaceful assembly. For that reason, it is wrong to prohibit an individual or group from taking part in a public athlete event because of their beliefs or the policies of their government.

"There is a vast difference between a ban or prohibition and a boycott or peaceful demonstration.... Individuals are free to act as their conscience dictates—approve, watch or ignore the game, boycott it, or demonstrate and protest peacefully."

Then Hugh Carey took Corning's statement and, in effect, tore it up by refusing to permit the game to go ahead. But the federal courts put it and the First Amendment back together again.

Said Federal District Judge Howard Munson in Albany on September 21: "By enjoining the scheduled sporting event, the governor of New York seeks to destroy the very constitutional freedoms which have enabled the more than a century-long struggle to ensure racial equality in this country.

"Surely," the judge went on, "the American citizens must realize that the benefits of such a constitutional heritage must not be commanded by executive fiat and extended or withheld on the basis of changing popular demand."

Most Americans realize no such thing. Whether racists or antiracists, they passionately believe that certain kinds of speech are too vile, too harmful, to be permitted as are representatives of vile, harmful nations.

In the course of the Springboks journey through the court system, which ended at the Supreme Court of the United States, the New York Civil Liberties Union declared, in a memorandum of law:

"What began as an athletic contest has been elevated by events into an important test of constitutional principles. This case is not about apartheid. For purposes of this lawsuit, the South African Springboks could just as well be any other unpopular group. The question for this Court to resolve is what obligation the government has when a group's unpopularity raises the possibility of a violent reaction by those opposed to it. That problem is not unique to the present situation. It has arisen before, and will undoubtedly rise again, in many other contexts. In this case, defendants' response has been to cancel a game which has plainly disturbed a great many people. In our view, the Constitution commands that the government instead protect both the players and those who are opposed to the message they believe the game represents.

"In *Police Department* v. *Mosley* 408 U.S. 92 (1972) the Supreme Court held a Chicago ordinance unconstitutional where the ordinance prohibited all forms of peaceful picketing within 150 feet of a public school except for picketing arising out of a labor dispute.

The *Mosley* decision rested upon the observation that the Chicago ordinance selectively granted the right to picket based upon the content of the speech and the labor affiliation of the speakers. In this regard, the Court declared: 'Under the Equal Protection clause, not to mention the First Amendment itself, government may not grant the use of a forum to people whose views it finds acceptable, but deny use to those wishing to express less favored or more controversial views.'

"The decision to prohibit the Springboks Rugby Club from playing in a municipal park turns upon either of two judgments that have been made with respect to these South African players.

"Some ascribe to the players, themselves, the political values of a racist South African government. Under this view, the players are being denied access to Albany's municipal facilities because they are thought to espouse and represent the political values of that racist regime. In such an instance, the Springboks are plainly being denied access to public facilities because of the political values that they espouse or are thought to espouse. Such a denial thus constitutes discrimination on the basis of political beliefs in violation of the 'equal access' principles articulated above.

"Alternatively, others might concede that the Springbok players, themselves, do not necessarily support the South African government; but they insist that all white nationals of South Africa must, nevertheless, be barred because of the policies of the South African government. In such a circumstance, the Springbok players are being denied access not because of any affinity that they have to the South African government and not because of any values that they personally espouse but, simply, because of the politics of their country of origin.

"To ascribe to an individual the characteristics and values of their country of origin is precisely the sort of group stereotyping that the Fourteenth Amendment was meant to forbid. Accordingly, defendants' decision, in this regard, constitutes discrimination on the basis of national origin which similarly offends the 'equal access' principles as set forth above."

The Second Circuit Court of Appeals sustained the decision of the Federal District Court and, in a last-minute move to get the game canceled, representatives of the state of New York, in the name of

Hugh Carey, rushed to the Supreme Court of the United States.

This was the response:

Application denied.

Thurgood Marshall

9/22/81.

Three days later, in a lead editorial, the *Los Angeles Times* said: "...The issue was clear...rugby fans had a right to attend the games; and the protesters had a right to express their views in peaceful demonstrations against the matches...the duty of government officials was plain. They should have acted to protect the rights of all involved."

Not only Hugh Carey failed his obligation to the Constitution, the *Times* continued. "Mayor Edward Koch of New York opposed the appearance of the Springboks, and Mayor Tom Bradley of Los Angeles urged cancellation of the games.... Constitutional rights cannot be held hostage by threats of violence."

I should note that I started the process by which the Springboks were able to play. (The game, by the way, proceeded without incident.) There had been a brief notice in the paper one Saturday morning about the governor's decision to cancel the game. I called the associate director of the New York Civil Liberties Union at home (I was on the board of directors at the time), and the Springboks' introduction to American constitutional law was under way. My involvement on the "wrong side" was incomprehensible to a number of white liberals and black lawyers who were friends of mine.

"This is a nice liberal cause which costs nobody anything— except, of course, blacks being deprived of books in South Africa."

> Between the idea
> And the reality
> Between the motion
> And the act
> Falls the Shadow.
>
> —T. S. ELIOT, "THE HOLLOW MEN"

During the 1980s a majority of the student editorial board of the *Georgetown Law Journal* struck what they thought was an exemplary blow against apartheid. It had been discovered that one of the subscribers to the law review was the University of South Africa. That institution was summarily informed that its subscription was cancelled.

"Each firm or organization that does business with South Africa," said the majority of the editorial board, "whether it sells machine guns or law reviews, must evaluate doing business with a ...government that systematically disregards the most basic human rights.... [We had] to decide whether to continue a contractual relationship with a university that is an arm of a racist and repressive government.... We simply could not in good conscience continue that relationship."

There was a dissenter on that student editorial board. His name was John Kastelic and he decided to try to overturn that decision even though he risked being called a racist and worse. Kastelic organized a few other dissenters, and they issued a free-speech analysis of what had been done.

"South Africans," the counterattack began, "probably experience enough censorship without our help."

I heard about Kastelic's uphill battle, and I talked to him as well as to those students on the editorial board who vigorously supported canceling the subscription to the University of South Africa.

Then I called Randall Robinson, director of Trans-Africa. More than anyone in this country, Robinson had focused public attention on the indivisible evils of the South African government. He orchestrated an insistent series of demonstrations and arrests in front of South African consulates that started in Washington and spread throughout the country. At the same time, Robinson and his allies were instrumental in moving Congress into more action against apartheid than anyone would have thought possible five or six years before. Of course, by their own resistance to P. W. Botha, black South Africans helped enormously to concentrate Congress's mind; but someone of Robinson's strategic expertise was needed to help pull things together on this end.

I told Robinson about the removal of the University of South Africa from the subscription list of the *Georgetown Law Journal*.

"While I applaud students struggling to be principled," he said, "I have problems with the specific action they have taken. Our movement wants to end American investments there, but not the circulation of American ideas. *We need a free flow of ideas.*

"As a matter of fact," Robinson continued, "South Africa can only benefit from knowing what is thought about it by American law students and scholars." I also spoke to Eleanor Holmes Norton, former head of the Equal Employment Opportunity Commission and then a professor at the Georgetown University Law School. Norton had worked closely with Robinson on the anti-apartheid demonstrations and other actions against the South African government.

She was appalled at what the Georgetown students, with the best will in the world, had done. She, too, felt that what South Africans needed was *more* exposure to ideas, not less. That racist government, after all, was in the business of restricting the flow of information. Why help it?

The National Law Journal wrote a piece about the civil war at the *Georgetown Law Journal.* So did I. And there was also a lead editorial in the *Washington Post,* making essentially the same points that Randall Robinson and Eleanor Holmes Norton had made.

Another vote of the student editorial board took place: John Kastelic's free-speech view finally prevailed, and the University of South Africa was told that it would be getting future issues after all. As an important dividend of the battle, the board passed an amendment to the constitution of the *Georgetown Law Journal.* Henceforth, the journal would "not consider the political, ideological, or religious views of present or prospective subscribers in deciding whether to terminate, initiate, or review subscriptions."

I expect that the lesson learned by the law students in that debate was an important as anything they picked up in three years of classes at the Georgetown Law Center.

There is another banning of ideas to South Africans of all colors and classes that is far more vast and harmful than the *Georgetown Law Review*'s stab at censorship.

A number of the largest American book publishing houses—along with major distributors of books, and journals, as well as key distributors of research material on microfilm—stopped sending anything to South Africa years ago.

The principle involved has nothing to do with the companies' revulsion at apartheid. The principle is profits. At least seventy-five American cities had passed measures of some kind that were aimed at isolating South Africa and thereby increasing the pressure on the government there to end apartheid in all its dimensions. These municipal measures were aimed at American companies that do business with South Africa. If those companies wanted to sell their goods to these American cities, they had to agree to stop dealing with South Africa.

These selective purchasing agreements are not always absolute, but some cities make no exceptions for books and research materials. If you sell textbooks or children's books to South Africa, that's enough to exclude you, for instance, from doing business with Detroit, Pittsburgh, and Los Angeles.

A publishing house can make a lot of money selling textbooks to the school system of a big American city, as well as to public colleges and universities. Accordingly, among the book firms that have been helping keep ideas out of South Africa are Simon and Schuster and its subsidiaries, including Prentice-Hall; McGraw-Hill; and Macmillan-Scribners. One of the exceptions was Random House and its allied components because of the firm conviction of its then-head, Robert Bernstein, that a publisher should send all the books he can to a country that is not free.

Once a firm signs an agreement to keep books out of South Africa, it applies to all the corporation's publications—from textbooks to fiction to children's books. Included are books critical of apartheid.

Also involved in this brave blow against blacks as well as whites in South Africa has been Baker & Taylor, this country's largest distributor of books, magazines, journals, video software, and audio material. It may be the largest distributor of these carriers of ideas in the world.

The book publishers and Baker & Taylor can certainly be blamed for abandoning the most basic principle of publishing: there shall be no cooperation with suppression of thought. But a great deal of the culpability for this circle of censorship through the years lies with the unthinking members of American city councils and school boards who ardently believe they are helping the fight against apartheid in this Orwellian way.

As a small illustration of the money involved, Baker & Taylor is owned by the W. R. Grace Corporation. When the latter stopped all commerce with South Africa, that decision included Baker & Taylor. And just in time, as reported to the January 9, 1987, *Publishers Weekly:*

"Public libraries that passed anti-South Africa ordinances had threatened to seek another supplier if Baker & Taylor's parent company continued to do business with South Africa.... These included the Chicago public library system, which accounts for $1.8 million of business annually; the Los Angeles Public Library, $225,000; and the San Francisco Public Library, $350,000."

Also part of the boycott because of a decision by its parent company was University Microfilms limited, an indispensable source of research material.

Practically everyone who gets a Ph.D. in this country files his or her dissertation with University Microfilms. The firm also has reproduction rights to about 90 percent of the scholarly journals published here. No university anywhere in the world can afford to subscribe to every scholarly publication, so access to this research material on microfilm is essential. University Microfilms also has a division specializing in out-of-print books, scholarly and otherwise.

None of this material could be sold to South African scholars—whether they are for or against apartheid.

The parent conglomerate of University Microfilms is Bell & Howell. Among its many other holdings is the Merrill Publishing Company, a textbook firm, along with an extensive electronic network for transmitting various on-line research data. It also sells *The New York Times* on microfilm to libraries. But all these services, a Bell & Howell spokesman told me, were no longer available in South Africa.

Another mighty blow against apartheid.

Bell & Howell is proud of the information from medical and legal journals that it sends to such customers as teaching hospitals. The corporation's spokesman informed me that Bell & Howell used to send "the newest discoveries in medicine and in treatment on microfilm" to South African hospitals. "Otherwise," he said, "it would have been prohibitively expensive for them to keep up with all the books and journals, but this way they could have it all quickly and conveniently."

The patients in those hospitals are both black and white. But since the boycott, as their contribution to combating apartheid, the patients had to do without the latest news in medical treatment.

In the course of talking to book publishers about their participation in cutting off ideas and information to black as well as white South Africans, I ran into a candid publishing executive, Bernard Finnegan, then the chairman of Collier-Macmillan International Sales. He readily told me that his corporation no longer sells to South Africa.

"My own personal view," he said, "is that this is counterproductive, but there are school boards that insist on these selective purchasing contracts. And there are college professors who write us to say that if we sell to South Africa, they will never write another book for us.

"When we were selling there, by the way, the majority of our textbooks were used by black students." And unlike many of the textbooks produced in South Africa, the American volumes did not teach apartheid as a subtext for nearly every subject.

This ban, moreover, not only deprived blacks of textbooks. Children's libraries were also put in Coventry by American publishers. Again, libraries are used by black children as well as white children. A bookseller in Capetown asked Gloria Miklowitz, a visiting American writer of children's books: "What good does it do our children, black and white, to be denied books?"

"Well, you see," Bernard Finnegan of Macmillan told me, "this is a nice liberal cause which costs nobody anything—except, of course, those, including blacks, being deprived of books in South Africa."

Judith Krug, director of the Office for Intellectual Freedom of the American Library Association, has always refused to collaborate with censorship of any kind, and that fierce consistency sometimes makes her a target of the left as well as the right. Of this boycott, she said: "The very publishers who now won't let their authors' ideas get into South Africa are the very same people who file *amicus* briefs against book censorship in the United States."

A South African who has been working in this country for years as a strategist for an anti-apartheid organization told me: "When I was sitting inside South Africa, I was desperately trying to get books in. And the government, my enemy, was trying to keep them out. Many of us smuggled many books in many directions. Now I'm sitting here trying to keep books out of South Africa. I don't feel very comfortable about that."

The most surprising conversation I had on the self-censorship of publishers with regard to South Africa was with Andre Schiffrin. One of the most intelligent—and usually one of the more farseeing—publishers, Schiffrin was then in charge of Pantheon Books.

Yet in our conversation, Schiffrin kept defending those book publishers who have signed suppression agreements.

"Well," Schiffrin said, "you wouldn't want a textbook on police torture methods sent into South Africa, would you?"

I asked him how many books on police torture methods had been printed in America last year. Or in any year.

There was a pause. He couldn't think of any titles, but added that various technical books could help South Africa's police-state apparatus. Yes, they could, but a number of cities, which did not forbid sending all books to South Africa—expressly ruled out selling any books, technical or otherwise, to "the police, the military, the prison system, the Armaments Development and Production Corporation, the national intelligence services, the council for scientific and industrial research, the Atomic Energy Corporation," *et al.* Such specifics could be inserted in any selective purchasing contract.

Unlike Andre Schiffrin, John Ryden, the director of the Yale University Press, did not try to find justifications for the grubbiness of those American publishers who will no longer send *any* books— texts, children's books, trade books, medical books—to South Africa.

"When book publishers become censors for an abhorrent regime," Ryden told me, "it's wrong. It's always wrong. And through our books, we can give South Africans a chance to learn what they didn't learn in their own schools."

"Do you know," a source at the Association of American Publishers told me, "that the International Publishers Association issued a strong statement opposing this kind of self-censorship by American publishers?"

Datelined Geneva, the statement by the International Publishers Association said forthrightly:

"The suppression of the provision of books to or from countries with governments which practice unacceptable policies, of whatever persuasion, is more likely to confirm those policies than to ameliorate them.

"Further, such suppression would deny the essential support of ideas and information to those who oppose the policies, and to the population at large, in such countries. The availability of books is essential to the education and eventual freedom of those who are oppressed.

"Equally, availability in other countries of works by authors who live in countries with unacceptable regimes is essential to international knowledge of those countries. The existence in each country of authors who comment on their societies is basic to social change. They deserve and need an international audience....

"The International Publishers Association is ... fundamentally opposed ... to any restrictions on free international trade in books between all countries, of whatever persuasions or policies, or to any policies which seek to restrict the availability of books in any country or the availability in any country of books from any other country."

There are prominent American book publishers who could not sign such a statement. And the Association of American Publishers Freedom to Read Committee did not rebuke the book-banning publishers in their ranks because they were powerful members of the AAP, and the AAP is a trade association, not a free-expression association. That meant that the Freedom to Read Committee had to censor itself when any of the Association's members violated the freedom to read.

I told Eleanor Holmes Norton about the Orwellian notion that the way to freedom is banning books. She is black and was a fierce litigator against racism while with the American Civil Liberties Union, and since—including extensive protests against the racism of the government of South Africa.

"I can't believe it!" she said. "I can't believe what you're telling me. It is so disturbing to see such reflexive reactions on the part of those cities and public library systems that support the boycotting of books to South Africa. We can defend divestment, but to take away books and ideas means we're not taking advantage of the contradictions in the South African system. It means we're not trying to penetrate that system.

"Remember," Eleanor Holmes Norton said, "that James Baldwin, in the middle of Harlem, found his voice and power by going to the library. Are we so arrogant as not to believe that there are no white Afrikaaners who, by going to the library and reading American books, can break away from the dogma of their government?

"This is just not a hard issue," she continued. "There are hard issues on the best ways of ending apartheid, but this isn't one of them."

Over the years, I have been asked to speak before state library associations around the country, from Virginia to Wyoming. And I have come to know a fair number of other public and school librarians while covering stories about posses of "Concerned Citizens" trying to remove or keep books out of libraries.

What I invariably say to audiences of librarians is that they clearly are on the very front line of First Amendment wars. Journalists like me come into a town to cover a censorship story and after a few days, we leave. But the embattled librarians have to cope with the bristling hostility of the "Concerned Citizens" for months and years.

Their national organization, the American Library Association, has been consistently helpful to the troops in the field in providing firm, clear professional principles and support in times of siege. The principal instrument of that support is Judith Krug, director of the ALA's Office for Intellectual Freedom.

I've known Judy Krug a long time, and like certain jazz musicians I much admire, she is a continuing inspiration. She is tough, resilient, resourceful, and will not, under any circumstances, compromise when it comes to the letter and/or spirit of the First Amendment. She also has a ready wit, unlike many of the would-be suppressors of books—on the right and the left—with whom she battles.

In towns where Phyllis Schlafly's face might well have been

proudly imprinted on the placemats in the local restaurants, librarians, their backs against the wall, have reached for Judy Krug's phone number and thus armed, go on to smite the yahoos.

This is a story of a fight Judith Krug lost, and it happened, of all places, at the 1987 annual conference of the American Library Association in San Francisco.

The ALA would rise as one to defy a school board chairman who declares: "Censorship is the board's sworn obligation under the law and is not a negotiable item." I did not make that up. The chairman was Wayne Montgomery and the town is Wasco, California, where a censorship war was under way over whether students should be exposed to John Gardner's *Grendel*.

In the summer of 1987 what the ALA found abominable in a place like Wasco it did to itself in San Francisco. At issue was the policy set by a number of city councils and school boards around the country that forbade a city or any of its agencies from dealing with any American firms—including book publishers—that do business with South Africa.

There was another dimension to American book publishers and research firms keeping information out of South Africa. The censorship worked both ways. American libraries were also stripped of essential resources when a city's selective purchasing contract included books and other such materials. Firms that did not agree to stop sending books to South Africa were forbidden to sell their books, journals, and microfilm to *American* public schools and libraries.

What happens, then, to the First Amendment right of *Americans* to receive ideas and information? Well, some said this cost was worth paying as an act of sacrifice to help South African blacks. But of what help was it to South African blacks to deprive *them* of information, too?

Some librarians came to that ALA annual conference in San Francisco determined to do something about this two-way censorship of ideas that was helping no one except the South African government.

Two of the dissenting ALA members submitted the following resolution:

"Units of [American] government, in their legitimate desire to express solidarity with the anti-apartheid movements in the Republic of South Africa and in Namibia, have passed laws and ordinances prohibiting any unit of government to trade with any vendors having business dealings with these countries;

"Such laws and ordinances result in the inability of [American] libraries to purchase a diversity of materials [from blacklisted publishing firms] and

"The imbalance of collections is depriving citizens of their right to a full range of viewpoints and information, thereby creating an apartheid of the mind; and

"This also puts libraries in conflict with the American Library Association resolution, 'Abridgement of Human Rights in South Africa,' which urges American libraries '... to develop collections on South Africa that reflect the full diversity of viewpoints and experience in that country.'"

The resolution presented at the ALA conference in San Francisco continued:

"Be it resolved that the ALA and its members reaffirm that free access to information is pivotal in the individual's freedom of choice, and that access to materials, information, and ideas must not be abridged because of the social or political ideologies of the creators of such materials or the geographic origin of their source....

"*Be it further resolved that these restrictions violate the First Amendment to the U.S. Constitution,* and ... the imposition of penalties upon vendors exercising their First Amendment rights to disseminate information is to be challenged whenever and wherever it occurs...." (Emphasis added.)

How could members of the American Library Association oppose a resolution based on the First Amendment, which has been both sword and shield to librarians all over the country—especially since the beginning of Ronald Reagan's presidency, during which hordes of "Concerned Citizens" have descended on public and school libraries to purge the shelves of wicked books?

The ALA then had more than 42,000 members. Some 12,100 members and other registrants were at the annual conference in San Francisco. Of these, 500 to 600 were at the membership meeting at which the First Amendment resolution was proposed.

It didn't have a chance.

The resolution had been offered by Jean-Anne South of the Baltimore Public Library, and was seconded by Dorothy Broderick, a persistent defender of young people's First Amendment rights—and everybody else's, too.

At the membership meeting, speaking for the resolution, Dorothy Broderick emphasized that librarians ought to understand the need to oppose efforts "to restrict the right of U.S. citizens to a full range of ideas.... Good intentions do not justify depriving people of their constitutional rights to a full range of publications."

Had I been an ALA member, I would have completed the circle by pointing out that if there is not an exception for information in these purchasing contracts, book publishers who sign them are also depriving South Africans, very much including those without political rights, of ideas that could be of help in obtaining those political rights.

Among those speaking against the resolution was ALA member Herbert Biblo, who accused the resolution's sponsors of "going around the back door...to undermine the struggle for human rights in South Africa.... We're defending intellectual freedom while people are dying and starving and being abused."

Also opposed was E. J. Josey, a former president of the ALA and a professor at the University of Pittsburgh's graduate school of library and information science. Professor Josey, who must be an unforgettable model of clear thinking to his students, told the membership: "This is a racist document."

Said Judy Krug later: "How can anyone involved with libraries stand up and go on record and say, 'We are going to solve problems by withholding information'?"

The vote was open, with members standing. When the supporters of the resolution—including Judith Krug, director of the ALA's Office of Intellectual Freedom, stood—a number of the librarians turned around and hissed them. The resolution was roundly defeated.

Speaking at the Opening General Session of that ALA conference in San Francisco was Theodore Roszak, a history professor at California State University/Hayward and the author of, among other influential books, *The Cult of Information, The Folklore of Computers,* and *The True Art of Thinking.*

Roszak made the valuable point that in an age of glistening high-tech information machinery, librarians will nonetheless continue to be essential to all those people who can't afford to buy access to these gee-whiz information services. "It will be a long time," Roszak said, "before we have information services called Welfarex, Pauperserve, or Joblessnet."

Librarians, he continued, are also crucial "in a society that seems obsessed with the self-defeating prospect of mechanizing everything." As an antidote, "Librarians can offer what no machine can—a living mind, a human presence."

Something more is needed, however, than a living mind and a human presence. Most of the time, librarians also know how to *use* their minds, how to think. How to think independently. How to avoid being trapped by emotional whirlpools into denying their very reason for being librarians—complete access to all ideas.

The majority of the ALA members who battered down the free-flow-of-ideas resolution, while hissing its supporters, were, however, indulging in what W. H. Auden called "rehearsed responses." Like a low-grade computer.

Every fall, the American Library Association is one of the nationwide sponsors of "Banned Books Week." Throughout the country during that week, librarians display exhibits of books that have been banned in schools and libraries. They should include books banned from South Africa by American publishers—with the approval of the American Library Association.

David Henington, director of the Houston Public Library, strongly opposed apartheid. He also opposed limiting what people who use the library could read. There was a painful time when both those goals appeared to be in irreconcilable conflict. But Henington was not convinced that the fight against apartheid necessarily had to be at odds with the fight for everyone's freedom to read.

In July 1987, Kathryn Whitmire, the mayor of Houston, successfully proposed that the City Council pass an ordinance aimed at economically isolating South Africa and Namibia. Among its provisions were purchasing restrictions on American companies doing business with, or in, South Africa.

"Any company the library system dealt with," Henington told

me, "had to sign a notarized affidavit that it was not dealing with South Africa."

The effects of that selective purchasing contract on the public library soon became all too clear to Henington.

"The *Wall Street Journal*," he says, "refused to sign the affidavit because they have subscribers in South Africa, and they also have a correspondent there."

So it was no longer possible for users of the Houston public libraries to read the *Wall Street Journal* there. But that was only the beginning of what residents of Houston could no longer find in their public libraries.

"We became unable to buy services that are very basic to a public library," Henington notes. "For instance, the *Reader's Guide to Periodical Literature*. It's published by H. W. Wilson, and that company refused to sign the affidavit."

Among its other research resources, H. W. Wilson publishes comprehensive indexes of articles in the arts and sciences, as well as *Current Biography*.

"We no longer were able to buy from *Encyclopaedia Britannica*," Henington continued. "I don't mean only the encyclopedias but also their audiovisual materials. Not having them is a great hardship. They're fantastic, especially in the arts and sciences."

Another supplier refusing to sign the affidavit was a national black Methodist church organization. "We buy a directory from them every year," Henington explained, "but they violate the purchasing contract because they're 'in contact' with South Africa. That contact consists of providing food and clothing to people in need there."

Henington decided he had to do something. Like any public library director, he was a politician. He had to be. He had to lobby for and defend his budget. He had to secure allies in the city government and elsewhere who would help him protect the First Amendment when groups of "Concerned Citizens" would demand that certain books and periodicals be removed from the library shelves and, preferably, burned.

"I had to persuade people on the City Council," Henington told me, "that there should be certain exceptions for the library within that selective purchasing contract. The one thing I did not want to do was to dilute the very strong message the City Council was sending to South Africa. And I made that clear."

Henington then explained to the council members and other involved parties that the restrictions on the public libraries in Houston were impinging on their own constituents' freedom of access to ideas and information. Black constituents, Hispanic constituents, white constituents.

He also pointed out that the restrictions prevented the library from getting some of the books being published in South Africa. By black as well as white writers. Surely, he said, "we want to hear what black writers there are telling us."

Until the ban, moreover, the Houston Public Library had been subscribing to two newspapers published in South Africa. "They were windows into the country," Henington said during his lobbying. But the windows were now closed.

Henington kept working, quietly, to open other windows that had been closed. "I didn't go to the papers. This is a very emotional issue. I lobbied the members of the City Council individually. I told them how deeply opposed to apartheid we were at the library.

"Initially, they didn't understand what I was trying to do. Some said I was working to get approval of apartheid. But I told them that what I was trying to get was free access to information for people in Houston.

"It took me several months," Henington says, "but they came around—the members of our library board and the members of the City Council."

Houston is the fourth largest city in the country and its public library system encompasses the central library (three buildings), thirty-two branch libraries, and extension services. All are heavily used.

On October 21, 1987, the libraries in Houston no longer had to limit what their users could read.

The City Council passed an ordinance exempting from the selective purchasing contracts "publications, where the public official responsible for the procurement certifies in writing that such procurements are necessary to provide adequate levels of service to the public."

When the American Library Association met in San Francisco

on June 29, 1987, it was known that this resolution by the Houston City Council was about to be passed. That's one of the reasons the ALA membership was asked to pass its own resolution alerting Houston and all other American cities to the dangers of restricting information—at home or anywhere else in the world.

Like David Henington, the proposers of the ALA resolution in San Francisco were against apartheid, and they also believed that censorship in America could only help the South African regime.

That resolution at the ALA convention, calling for the availability of "a full range of ideas" in American libraries, failed badly. So David Henington did not get any support from what one would have thought were his natural allies—the nation's librarians. He was left to his own resources, and fortunately, he knew how to use them.

In the course of researching this mass banning of books by American publishers, I was told by some of the participants that I oughtn't to worry because South Africa was getting American books through third parties. That is, if an American book is published in England, it can be shipped to South Africa. There are other networks to South Africa by way of Europe. But not all American titles are published in England, to say the least, and not all American titles are distributed by alternative routes in other countries.

The fact is that many American books, periodicals, and much invaluable research on microfilm were *not* getting through. For instance, in the October 9, 1987, *Publishers Weekly*, Gloria Miklowitz wrote about the unavailability in South Africa of American children's books dealing with racial injustice. Then she added:

"Dean Dall of the University of Cape Town Medical School [told me] that they cannot keep up with the latest American medical books and journals ... because some American publishers ... are unwilling to ship to them.

"'Some 80 percent of our patients are black,' Dall said, 'and we serve doctors of all races, so we find it difficult to comprehend why the latest treatment should be denied patients in integrated hospital wards—in the name of fighting apartheid.'"

As for the limited number of American books that did get

through by means of third parties, this was hardly a secret maneuver. Nearly everyone in book publishing knew about it—as did those anti-apartheid organizations monitoring the selective purchasing contracts that have been set up by a considerable number of American municipalities and school boards. So that meant the school boards and council members could easily have been told about the ploy.

The subject came up in a conversation I had with Erwin Glickes, president and publisher of The Free Press, vice president of Macmillan, and then chairman of the Freedom to Read Committee of the Association of American Publishers. Macmillan had cut off all books to South Africa. (Yet the Freedom to Read Committee saw nothing peculiar about having as its chairman someone involved with banning books. But then again, there were other committee members in the same position.)

Glickes, a bright, thoughtful, engaging man, told me: "Books are still getting to South Africa through third parties, international distributors. But if you expose what's happening, the American cities and school boards with selective purchasing contracts will widen the affidavit that they make book companies sign. They'll insist that American firms not ship their books to a third party. So, if you write about this, those books won't get to South Africa."

Journalists get used to a lot of chutzpah, starting with our own. But this was stunning. Forget for a moment that a lot of American books and research materials were not getting through to South Africa at all. The point here was that Glickes and the other American publishers involved in the banning wanted this third-party operation to continue in order to assuage their own guilt at being censors.

In case some municipalities didn't know about the third-party route, Glickes wanted me to help him and his colleagues in the cover-up. That way, they remained in conformity with the selective purchasing contracts they had signed around the country while softly cheering on the alternative "underground railway" carrying books they themselves had burned.

The president of the Association of American Publishers is Nicholas Veliotes, an impressively urbane former ambassador to Jordan and Egypt. When I talked to him, he was unequivocal in his opposition to boycotting ideas, "most particularly when trying to influence a dictatorship. We can't change a closed society by keeping it closed."

Veliotes also gave me this astonishing statement: "No publishers I know of, no one in my association, is in favor of restricting books to South Africa."

That was utter nonsense. Simon and Schuster, Macmillan–Scribners–The Free Press, and McGraw-Hill are all members of his association. Each one had signed agreements to no longer send books to South Africa.

What had to be done—as Irving Louis Horowitz, the Hannah Arendt Professor of Sociology and Political Science at Rutgers, kept urging—was the education of school boards and city councils around the country. They had to be told that, indeed, you cannot change a closed society by keeping it closed. And you cannot strip Americans of their First Amendment right of access to ideas in public schools and libraries by insisting that firms that sell to these places must strip people in other countries of their right to read.

But who was to do this educating?

Meanwhile, the Association of American Publishers finally issued a pious declaration of opposition to the banning of books anywhere. It was modeled, in part, on an earlier statement by the International Publishers Association.

But the new AAP proclamation ignored the fact that some of its most prominent members were doing exactly what the AAP statement condemned—that hypocritical statement talked about publishers being "forced" to stop selling their books to South Africa. Forced by whom? Their own greed had made them censors.

At last, the American Publishers International Freedom to Publish Committee and the Fund for Free Expression decided to bring some light to the darkness created by the book publishers. They sent Robert Wedgeworth and Lisa Drew to South Africa to see what results, if any, the boycott has had. At the time, Wedgeworth was dean of the School of Library Services at Columbia University, and Drew is vice president and senior editor of William Morrow.

In November 1989, their report—"The Starvation of Young Black Minds: The Effect of Book Boycotts in South Africa"—was released. Wedgeworth and Drew had spoken to teachers, librarians, writers, publishers, bookstore owners, students, and others who have had direct experience with the boycott.

All of them—black and white—unanimously called for an end to the boycott. Of particular significance is the position of the African National Congress. In the American cities that require disengagement from South Africa, the strongest supporters of total isolation have often insisted that the ANC is entirely behind the boycott—including books. Actually, from the beginning, the ANC expressed doubts about banning ideas in a country whose government already specialized in doing just that. But now, the ANC has clearly stated that although it wants other boycotts to continue, it does not favor suppressing the "inflow of progressive cultural products and ideas." (Fortunately, the ANC has not described what "progressive" means, thereby avoiding, it is hoped, another form of censorship.)

One impact of the boycott has been, according to the report, that "black students are using out-of-date textbooks." Wedgeworth, who is black, notes that the overall poverty of educational resources available to black students "is the most devastating situation I've ever seen in my professional life." And he adds that "with the government spending five times more on education for whites than blacks, the book boycott weakens the meager alternative resources for blacks."

Soon after the report was released, a number of American librarians and educators called Robert Wedgeworth, who is black, an Uncle Tom. It's their way of helping those black kids in South Africa. The report he and Lisa Drew wrote had yet to have any significant impact.

"A woman cannot make an informed choice between two options when she cannot obtain information as to one of them."

Nearly five years into the tenure of Chief Justice William Rehnquist and ten months after the retirement of Justice

William J. Brennan Jr., the Supreme Court is no longer in transition. It has become the Court it will most likely be for the next generation.—LINDA GREENHOUSE, *THE NEW YORK TIMES*, MAY 26, 1991

Landmark decisions of the Supreme Court do not always call for the ringing of the Liberty Bell. Some can be terribly destructive of liberty. *Dred Scott* v. *Sanford* (1857) said that no blacks, free or slave, had any rights "which the white man was bound to respect." They were only property.

Plessy v. *Ferguson* (1896) held that it was constitutional for blacks to remain segregated. The Court thereby gave its imprimatur to the pernicious myth of "separate but equal."

Korematsu v. *the United States* (1944) ruled that it was constitutional to imprison Japanese-Americans in concentration camps solely on the basis of their ancestry.

Bowers v. *Hardwick* (1986) removed an entire class of people— gays—from the protection of the constitutional right to privacy. According to a majority of the Court, a homosexual can be criminally prosecuted for sodomy in his own bedroom, while heterosexuals committing sodomy do not have to fear the knock on the door.

On May 23, 1991, the Rehnquist Court delivered another landmark decision that will affect millions of Americans for a long time to come. *Rust* v. *Sullivan* has generally been written about as an abortion case. And that it is—and more. From now on, five million poor women—who can only get medical help from the nation's 3,900 federally financed family-planning clinics—would no longer be able to obtain complete medical advice and treatment from the physicians in those clinics.

The core of *Rust* v. *Sullivan* was the free-speech rights of these women and their doctors, nurses, social workers, and counselors. According to the federal regulations mandated toward the end of the Reagan administration and supported by Reagan's successor, no doctor or other health-care worker in these federally subsidized clinics can even mention the word "abortion." In the past, these family-planning clinics could not perform abortions under the law but they could advise women about abortions and refer those who asked to places where abortions are performed. No more. It had become like prohibiting any mention of Trotsky in Stalin's Russia.

And now, for the first time in American history, the Supreme Court said that the government can censor what a doctor must ethically say to a patient. Even if a doctor in one of these federally funded clinics believes a woman could, down the line, be in serious danger if she carried a fetus to term, he can't tell her she may need an abortion. Nobody in the clinic can tell her that.

Rust v. *Sullivan* has also set another precedent in terms of suppressing speech. In his dissent, Justice Harry Blackmun said:

"Until today the Court never has upheld a viewpoint-based suppression of speech simply because that suppression was a condition upon the acceptance of public funds. Whatever may be the government's power to condition the receipt of its largesse upon the relinquishment of constitutional rights, *it surely does not extend to a condition that suppresses the recipient's cherished freedom of speech based solely upon the content or viewpoint of that speech.*" (Emphasis added.)

The contrary argument of the Reagan and Bush administrations was succinctly expressed by Nabers Cabannis, a Health and Human Services official who watched over the family-planning clinics: "If you don't like our rules, you don't have to receive our funds."

The Rehnquist Court has now made this position into constitutional law. If you take any benefits from the government, you will have to, on demand, surrender your First Amendment rights.

So *Rust* v. *Sullivan* goes far beyond a physician's freedom of speech—and his or her patient's First Amendment right to receive that information.

On May 25, the *Washington Post*'s Supreme Court reporter, Ruth Marcus, quoted a crucial Rehnquist sentence in his majority decision:

"Within far broader limits than [the clinics] are willing to concede, when the government appropriates public funds to establish a program, it is entitled to define the limits of that program." And that includes setting limits to what those involved in the program are allowed to say. Or, for that matter, to write.

Rehnquist made only one exception to this kind of government gag order: colleges and universities.

The First Amendment, he said, limits the government's ability to "control speech" in an academic setting when it supplies any funds. That's because of the tradition of freedom of expression there. There is apparently no such tradition anywhere else in the nation.

It doesn't take long to recognize the scope of this now constitutional censorship of speech. Duke University law professor Walter Dellinger notes that *Rust v. Sullivan* "is especially alarming in light of the growing role of government as subsidizer, landlord, employer, and patron of the arts."

The government, therefore, can mandate politically correct speech in much more than the doctor-patient relationship. And there is no reason to believe that a Democratic administration will be able to resist the temptation to put speech conditions on certain federal grants. Imagine the role of Tipper Gore (the Phyllis Schlafly of pop and rock music)—if Al Gore were to be elected President—in scrutinizing NEA grants to music and the other arts.

And Ruth Marcus of the *Washington Post* asks: "In the President's proposed school choice program, for example, could the government support vouchers only for those schools that agree not to discuss abortion in their sex education classes?

"Following the [family planning] clinic regulations, teachers could be instructed to tell students who ask ... that the school 'does not consider abortion an appropriate method of family planning.'"

This was an astonishing attack by the Rehnquist Court on the First Amendment. We have been accustomed to its remorseless shrinking of the right of habeas corpus and such other contractions of the Bill of Rights as its admission of coerced confessions into evidence. But until now, there was some hope that the majority of the Court had a modicum of respect for the First Amendment.

This, however, is not a Supreme Court that believes in judicial restraint. It can be a sweepingly activist court. Consider more fully what it has now done to the doctor-patient relationship.

As Walter Dellinger wrote in the May 25, 1991, *New York Times:* "Thirty years ago Justice William O. Douglas noted that the 'right of the doctor to advise his patients according to his best lights seems so obviously within First Amendment rights as to need no extended discussion.'"

I cannot imagine any of the previous Supreme Courts—from the very beginning—tampering with the doctor-patient relationship.

When William Rehnquist was an Associate Justice, most observers doubted that he would ever have much long-lasting influence on the Court. He went his own way. Rehnquist was often on the short end of 8–1 or 7–2 decisions. Some of his clerks called him the Lone Ranger.

But Rehnquist began to have more influence when he became Chief Justice. There are hardly any more of those solitary dissents, and his views carry considerable weight with much of the rest of the court.

In his Lone Ranger days, some law professors and Supreme Court reporters charged Rehnquist with, on occasion, manipulating citations in his opinions to strengthen his argument by any means necessary.

Some of this disingenuousness remains. In *Rust* v. *Sullivan*, Rehnquist was aware that some people—doctors, for instance—were very concerned that preventing physicians from giving complete advice to the pregnant women in these clinics could greatly endanger the health of some of them.

Not to worry, Rehnquist said in his decision. First of all, he said, the regulations do not "significantly impinge upon the doctor-patient relationship" because patients who go to these clinics ought not to expect "comprehensive medical advice."

Like medical advice as to whether a continued pregnancy might shorten the life of a woman with heart disease.

Well, she could go elsewhere to find out about that.

But she has no money to go elsewhere. These are pregnant women without money.

Then Rehnquist had the chutzpah to go on to say that if an emergency should happen and an immediate abortion was indicated, the regulations "provide a specific exemption for emergency care" that requires the client's "immediate referral to an appropriate provider of emergency medical services."

He can't be that obtuse. A pregnant woman may have medical problems that can complicate pregnancy and so endanger her health over time that her physician may feel the need, well before there is an emergency, to tell her that an abortion may be advisable.

But Rehnquist and a majority of the Supreme Court say that

even so, her physician must remain silent—until there *is* an emergency.

As for David Souter, he made it very clear during oral arguments that he knew precisely what this case was about—and what was at stake. He kept pressing Kenneth Starr, the solicitor general, to admit that the government actually wanted to prevent a doctor from telling a patient what was in her best interest.

"You're telling me," Souter asked Starr, "that a physician can't perform his usual professional responsibility.... I think you're telling me that the secretary [of Health and Human Services] may preclude professional speech.... The time period to act may be very short. High blood pressure may result in a stroke within an hour. And a doctor can't give advice," Souter asked, not for family-planning purposes but for traditional medical purposes? Yet Souter voted with the majority.

One of the clinics affected is the Hub, a Planned Parenthood center in New York's South Bronx, where 99 percent of the patients are African-American or Hispanic. Its medical director is Dr. Irvine Rust, the named plaintiff in this Supreme Court suit. Rust's patients "don't have money," he points out. "They can't go to a private doctor. To not be allowed to give information [about abortion] is just an abomination."

The prohibition, Rust told the *Washington Post*, amounts to "giving the poor person, the black and Hispanic person, second-class care."

Worth remembering was a dissent below by Judge Amalya Kearse, in the Second Circuit.

A 1979 Jimmy Carter appointee, Kearse has become quite passionate about civil liberties, having written a stinging dissent against a majority opinion permitting the government to conduct a drug raid without a warrant.

In *Rust* v. *Sullivan*, Kearse had no patience with the opinion of the majority that the government regulations did not violate the First Amendment because they did not ban speech on the basis of its viewpoint.

Bluntly, Kearse noted:

"Plainly, the regulations facially discriminate on the basis of viewpoint, and control the content of the grantee's permitted speech."

As for the dangers to the women using the clinics, in arguing before the Supreme Court for Dr. Rust, Harvard law professor Laurence Tribe pointed out, according to *U.S. Law Week,* that "of the five million women served by federally funded clinics each year, nearly 60,000 have medical conditions such as cancer, diabetes, or heart disease—conditions in which a pregnancy might endanger their health or lives."

There is another fundamental argument against these government regulations. *Roe* v. *Wade,* while not in the best of health, is still the basis for women's constitutional right to an abortion. By what constitutional logic, then, can the government forbid speech about a constitutional right in a clinic receiving federal funds?

As Judge Kearse added in her Second Circuit dissent:

"The ... regulations plainly interfere with the pregnant woman's freedom to decide which course of action she prefers. In some cases, the information ban will delay the appropriate education of the patient to such an extent that she is denied any genuine choice. In some cases, the patient will never be fully informed for, as the Secretary of Health and Human Services [Louis Sullivan] has acknowledged, 'for many clients, family-planning programs are their only continuing source of health information.' [A woman] cannot make an informed choice between two options when she cannot obtain information as to one of them."

With evident relish, Kearse also pointed out that these changes in the Title X regulations were entirely due to old-time backroom political pressure in the course of which the First Amendment was sold down the river.

She quoted Sullivan, the unhappy middleman in implementing this raw act of government censorship:

"It is certainly true that one of the prime reasons for these regs is a stricter [separation] of abortion from Title X programs. That is a matter of policy. That is a matter of politics."

So compelling were these arguments against the gag rule that I was sorry, though not surprised, to see the pro-life groups so myopic as to be on the government's side. They have experienced fierce attempts to suppress their speech, from the RICO suits (see chapter IX) hurled against them by the National Organization for

Women to harsh limitations on their picketing by various courts and municipalities. (Punishment for blockading abortion clinics is quite different, because that action is illegal.)

Having their own First Amendment rights under siege so often, the pro-lifers should have realized that if the government wins this case, the diminishment of the First Amendment will eventually affect them, too. Another administration can condition government benefits that pro-lifers want—on their being willing to censor *themselves* to get funds.

Neither the pro-lifers nor NOW realizes that the First Amendment is indivisible.

Meanwhile, as Rachel Pine of the American Civil Liberties Union said in her brief to the Supreme Court: "Lured into Title X clinics by the apparent promise of reliable health care, indigent women leave the clinic not merely unenlightened, but affirmatively misled. The lives and health of women are thus directly jeopardized—not, in this instance, because of poverty but because of the mandatory misinformation the regulations require." Misinformation that is also mandated by the Supreme Court of the United States.

Several months before the decision came down, I talked about this case with a fifth-grade public school class in Brooklyn. The students laughed when I said that silencing doctors was before the United States Supreme Court.

"How could that be?" The kids were amazed. "How could anybody order a doctor to keep his mouth shut when he was treating a patient?"

I sure would have liked to see the Chief Justice explain himself in that classroom.

In March 1992, the White House, because of the opposition to the "gag rule," even within the Republican party, softened the regulations. Doctors in federally financed family planning clinics may give limited advice on abortion, even when a woman's life is not in danger. Nurses, counselors, and social workers—with whom patients are most often in contact—still may not speak about abortion unless asked, and then they must say they do not give information about abortion. But they, along with doctors, can refer the patient to a clinic whose primary function is not to provide abortions.

The change maintains government regulation of speech in these family planning clinics. The Rehnquist Court has not yet been overruled.

IV

The Education of Yale in the Glories of Free Speech

"If expression may be prevented, censored, or punished because of its content or because of the motives attributed to those who promote it, then it is no longer free. It will be subordinated to other values that we believe to be of lower priority in a university."

William Shockley, a Nobel laureate for his work in the invention of the junction transmitter, was much better known—and reviled by many—as a vigorous proselytizer for the view that blacks are genetically inferior. He advocated cash incentives for sterilization to all who do not pay income taxes—with a one-thousand-dollar bonus for each tax point below 100.

Shockley liked to lecture at colleges and universities about the inferiority of blacks, but he usually was drowned out by unremittingly hostile audiences. This happened to him again in 1973 when he spoke at Staten Island Community College in New York where a predominantly white group of students and faculty made it impossible for Shockley to be heard.

A black leader in New York—Roy Innis, head of the Congress of Racial Equality—was appalled at the actions of the largely radical whites who silenced Shockley. He described what happened as "the Schweitzer syndrome"—whites acting on behalf of blacks. Innis emphasized that blacks do not need whites to "protect" them against such hateful ideas as those expounded by Shockley. Blacks, Innis went on, do not intend to "hide like sniveling cowards behind the coattails of our Marxist friends."

The black students at Staten Island Community College also distanced themselves from the whites who were intent on denying Shockley freedom of speech. Before Shockley came to the campus, at a press conference at CORE national headquarters in Harlem, Orchid Johnson (president of the Black Student Union) and Leona Sanders (a member of the Black Student Union and also chairwoman of the community college's Student Senate) issued a statement emphasizing that the threats of violence against Shockley were coming from the largely white Progressive Labor Party (a radical Marxist group)—*not* from blacks.

They also said that while they supported Shockley's right to speak under the First Amendment, they and many other black students would boycott his appearance so that if there were any violence, or disruption, the responsibility for cutting off Shockley's First Amendment rights would be clearly that of the Progressive Labor Party.

"The Black Student Union," they said, "has taken an independent stand in defense of its own interest."

This tradition of black political independence in highly controversial contexts has a long history. During the 1930s, for example, there were a number of blacks who recognized that the Communist Party was trying to manipulate them for its own priorities. And in 1968, when students occupied Columbia University, black students separated themselves to secure their own interests.

The black animus toward the "Schweitzer syndrome," as Roy Innis called it, was based on the conviction that certain white radicals patronized blacks, believing they had to be told what to think.

Another dimension of the debate on Shockley and the limits of freedom of speech was illuminated at a conference shortly before Shockley's engagement at Staten Island Community College. Held at New York University, the Conference on Racism presaged the "politically correct" attitude toward speech on campuses nearly twenty years later.

For example, Dr. Garland Allen of Washington University addressed the Conference on Racism and was asked whether he believed that his theory of justified censorship would imperil the university as a forum for the free exchange of ideas.

Allen, according to the November 18, 1973, *New York Times,* said that he believed in academic freedom, but only in conjunction with the ideas of the local community. "It should be like what goes on in China," he said.

Some seven hundred professors and students from around the country attended that conference, having answered a call to the event in the form of an advertisement in the October 28 *New York Times.* The call also contained "A Resolution Against Racism," a manifesto that was signed by 1,400 professors throughout the country.

The resolution was further evidence that "politically correct" myopia is not limited to the 1980s and 1990s. Having said that "the doctrine of racial inferiority is ... unscientific as well as socially vicious," the resolution went on with a call to "our colleagues" to, among other things, "urge professional organizations and societies, academic departments, and editors of scholarly journals to condemn and refuse to disseminate racist research....

"... Nor, in the light of all the evidence, can the ideology of racism be legitimately called 'controversial' and open to debate."

Disagreeing with the authoritarianism of the majority of those at the Conference on Racism at New York University, a group of faculty members, students, and a secretary at Staten Island Community College issued this statement before Shockley's arrival:

"Shockley's conclusions concerning the relationship between intelligence and heredity are disturbing, but more profoundly, the social policy implications that might be drawn from them are dangerous and a threat to all people struggling to establish a truly equitable and democratic society in America.

"We must expose his fallacies, falsehoods, and inhuman policies. We must counteract his warped ideology with our moral beliefs. We must challenge his evidence with our evidence. If we fail to confront Shockley, we have failed ourselves and the chance to alter our society.

"We believe that any community that silences one person for what he thinks is not a safe community for any of us. The real danger of Shockley is *not* that he will persuade an audience to act but that some bureaucrat somewhere will encounter his ideas and assume that they must be correct because they have not been refuted. *Hence we cannot afford to be silent, nor can we afford to silence Shockley. The First Amendment is so essential that its protection must be given to all—even to William Shockley."* (Emphasis added.)

Shockley himself, after having been prevented from speaking at Staten Island Community College, said:

"The true failure exhibited here, I believe, is basically a lack of faith that reason can work and that man is a growing thing."

Roy Innis of CORE was heard from again:

"Black folks got to understand that we are on the firing line on this one.... In every generation there are a bunch of dudes like Shockley, going all the way back ... to those German anthropologists.

"Let me tell you this. People believe these guys in two ways— they believe them openly and consciously or they believe them quietly, subliminally, covertly. But they do believe them.... And let me tell you, I will [debate] these guys any day of the week and twice on Sunday.

"I believe that [when you debate], at least it's on the table. I can deal with it. I've got confidence in myself and my folks to deal with it. That's why I decided to take Shockley on up at Harvard. I wanted a very prestigious forum. I wanted to whip that dude publicly. I wanted to leave him as intellectually dead as a duck in a frozen pond.

"You know why? Because it's important, first of all, for black people. We got to show black people that there are black men some place who can stand up to any white man on any set of terms and defeat him in battle."

Roy Innis, as we shall see, was also eager to take on Shockley in debates at Yale, but the "Schweitzer syndrome" prevented him. By silencing Shockley, students at Yale simultaneously prevented a black man from decimating Shockley in debate.

In April 1974, William Shockley and William Rusher (then publisher of the *National Review*) were scheduled to debate on the Yale campus. The debate didn't take place.

As Donald Kagan, now dean of Yale College, reported in a 1975 address—"Freedom of Speech at Yale"—about a quarter of the audience that filled the hall "joined in concerted and prolonged disruption, forcing cancellation of the meeting."

This had happened to Shockley before, and not only at Staten Island Community College, but, wrote Kagan, "it was the first time in memory that an invited speaker had reached his lecture hall and been prevented from speaking at Yale." And the climate at Yale was such that no one with "unpopular views of a certain kind" could be confident he or she would be invited to speak or, if invited, would be allowed to speak.

"Not since the shameful days when Joe McCarthy rode roughshod over freedom of speech and other fundamental freedoms," Kagan continued, "has this situation existed. Indeed old hands tell me that it was not this bad at Yale even then. In those days, the attack on free speech was from the outside and, I am told, the better universities rallied their forces and resisted the attack on the most fundamental need of a university—the free exchange of ideas and opinions. Lately, however, the attack has come from inside and has been harder to resist...."

Kagan believed that the erosion of free speech at Yale began in the autumn of 1963 when the Political Union invited Governor George Wallace of Alabama to speak. Wallace was the most visible and hated symbol of southern resistance to full citizenship for blacks. And not long before he was to speak at Yale, four black schoolchildren had been killed in a black church in Birmingham.

Before Wallace was due on campus, the then-provost, Kingman Brewster (who was later to become president of Yale), declared publicly that he had asked the Executive Board of the Political Union "to consider the damage which Governor Wallace's appearance would do to the confidence of the New Haven community in Yale and the feelings of the New Haven Negro population."

The Yale Political thereupon censored itself and George Wallace, and withdrew the invitation. Kingman Brewster thanked the

Union, praising its refusal to let Wallace speak and thereby acting "in the interests of law and order as well as town-gown relations."

There was dissent, however, in the Yale community. In an editorial, the *Yale Daily News* emphasized:

"We think the issue is one of the right to speak: all voices have the right in an academic community and in a democracy such as ours.... As we believe the Reverend William Coffin [then Yale's chaplain] has the right to demonstrate in the South, so we believe Governor Wallace should not be denied the right to come and to be confronted by the Yale and New Haven communities, both white and Negro....

"The more we consider Yale's treatment of the invitation to Governor Wallace, the more painful it all becomes. This kind of action simply does not belong in this great academic community. The pressures of [the] time must not dull our allegiance to such a basic duty of a free university."

Among the dissenters on the faculty was John Perry Miller, dean of the graduate school, who was critical of the political pressure on Kingman Brewster from the mayor of New Haven, who had said that Wallace was "officially unwelcome."

Said Dean Miller: "It is highly regrettable that [the mayor] should be so insensitive to the nature of a university that he places the Political Union and Yale officials in a position where they apparently felt compelled to violate the principles to which a free university is committed."

And C. Vann Woodward, a nationally renowned Yale history professor, said:

"The university is in danger of sacrificing principle to expedience. If the South can afford the risk of violence in the struggle for the principle of Negro rights, New Haven, can, too, for the principle of freedom of speech."

The *Yale Daily News* reported that "feeling among faculty members and students" concerning the cancellation of the invitation to Wallace "appears almost overwhelmingly negative."

Moreover, the Reverend Edwin Edmonds, black pastor of the Dixwell Avenue Congregational Church, forcefully pointed out that if an individual's right to speak could not be protected at Yale in New Haven, "it would be the same thing that Wallace is guilty of in Alabama."

The *Boston Herald* called Yale's action "a disservice to the course of civil rights and liberties."

But there were those who contended that having Wallace on campus would have been in bad taste, and the beneficial effects of keeping him away would be more important than upholding the principle of free speech.

A student group, the Committee for the Protection of the Rights of Not Very Nice People, did not agree with that way of "balancing" freedom of expression and collected 250 signatures opposing the reversal of the invitation to Wallace.

The *Yale Daily News* came out with another editorial:

"One of the world's great academic communities has gone out of its way to stifle a voice which at least a group of its students wanted to hear." The editorial also quoted the words of an abolitionist printer decades before:

"We are more especially called upon to maintain the principles of free discussion in case of unpopular sentiments or persons—as in no other case will any effort to maintain them be needed."

Donald Kagan reported that "two groups of law students issued another invitation to Wallace, reaffirming 'the right of students to hear speakers of their own choosing without restraint or interference from those who would like to limit the right of free expression to those whose views coincide with theirs.'"

Provost Kingman Brewster answered that his "position and the university's position on free speech was uncompromising." Except for this time, when, Brewster implied, the threat of violence must be avoided.

When a new student invitation to speak was delivered to George Wallace, he declined, although he did appear at other Ivy League campuses.

In 1970, there was a Black Panther trial in New Haven, and the Yale administration, reacting to the fear of violence attendant on the many Black Panthers and their supporters in town for the trial, reacted in just the opposite way it had to the specter of the coming of George Wallace. The Yale administration opened the campus to the Panthers and their followers.

The situation, Donald Kagan wrote, "was immeasurably more dangerous than it had been in 1963. The possibility of violence seemed great. It is also true that the New Haven community was much more alarmed by the invasion than it had been by the prospect of Wallace's speech, and it seemed much more insulted and offended by the rhetoric of the Panthers and their friends than the New Haven black community had been by the prospect of a speech by Wallace.

"The Panther newspaper was all over New Haven urging people to kill policemen. This was certainly a situation that threatened law and order and town-gown relations—the reasons given for discouraging Wallace's appearance."

The Panthers took full advantage of Yale's invitation to make themselves home on campus. Dwight Hall was turned into the headquarters of the Panthers Defense Committee, and in a meeting elsewhere on campus, a Panther said:

"Basically what we are going to do is create conditions in which white folks are either going to have to kill pigs or defend themselves against Black folks.... We're going to turn Yale into a police state.... You have to create peace by destroying the people who don't want peace."

How did official Yale react?

"The administration," Donald Kagan said, "did not try to prevent any of these speeches. No statements even of personal opinion came either from the president or the corporation regretting the invitations to the speakers or deploring the provocation or the insulting nature of the speeches.... [Kingman Brewster and the Yale administration] still gave priority to safety over ideas or principles, but this time expediency dictated support rather than the suppression of free speech. They calculated that there was greater danger in trying to prevent the speeches—whose contents I believe they did not like—than in allowing them."

In April 1972, the Yale Political Union invited General William Westmoreland, United States Army Chief of Staff and the commander particularly identified with the war in Vietnam. Westmoreland never got to the Law School auditorium, which had already been occupied by anti-war groups who pushed their way in, screaming "Ho, Ho, Ho Chi Minh!" They occupied not only the seats but the stage as well. Westmoreland, on being informed of the guerrilla raid while having dinner at Mory's, declined to even try to speak.

Kingman Brewster, who by then had become president of Yale, sounded quite unlike the Kingman Brewster who had deplored the invitation to George Wallace:

"I am ... disappointed that there are apparently a significant number of people in the Yale and New Haven communities— whose feelings about the Southeast Asian wars and General West- moreland's role in them—overcame their concern for freedom of speech. This is wholly reprehensible in a free society, especially so in a free academic community. Precisely because of this conviction, it was the determination of the university to risk whatever con- frontation might have occurred in order to vindicate the Political Union's right to listen to speakers of their choice without interrup- tion."

Brewster's rhetoric aside, Donald Kagan summarized the dis- mal reality at this stage in Yale's troubled history of free speech: "For the first time in memory, violence and disruption had pre- vented a public speech at Yale. The university, moreover, though forewarned, had done little to protect the speaker's right before- hand and nothing to deter future repetitions of the affair by pun- ishing the evil-doers. Perhaps more troubling was the fact that, compared to 1963 [the furor over Governor Wallace], there was lit- tle public outcry at Yale."

Then—in January 1974—came William Shockley. Roy Innis of CORE had suggested to the Yale Political Union that he be invited to debate Shockley. Among opponents of the idea was Molly Backup of the Progressive Labor Party. She warned that Shockley would not be allowed to speak in any form. As for the principle of freedom of speech, it is, she said, "a nice abstract idea used to enable people like Shockley to spread racism." And the Reverend Robert Jones of the New Haven Black Coalition ominously promised a demonstration that would be "as peaceful as possible and as violent as necessary."

The Yale administration made no statement, one way or the other.

The debate was scheduled—even though Shockley-Innis encounters had been suppressed at Harvard and other colleges. The Political Union, announcing the forthcoming debate at Yale, noted that it felt a particular responsibility to host the debate "because such discussion has been denied elsewhere. The Union recognizes free speech and unimpeded academic freedom as fundamental democratic principles."

But the board of the Yale Political Union—in the face of threats of violence—canceled the invitation three weeks later by a vote of 200–190.

Another student group, Lux et Veritas, invited Shockley to come ahead but instead of Roy Innis, he would be debating a biologist. At this point, Kingman Brewster and the Yale Corporation intervened. Said Brewster, accusing Lux et Veritas of trying to provoke conflict and playing games with free speech:

"The occasion does not warrant departure from Yale's principles of free speech. However, the use of free speech as a game, the lack of sensitivity to others, the lack of consideration for the community, and the lack of responsible concern for the university as an institution seem to me reprehensible....

"From my point of view, the best way to avoid playing into the hands of the sponsors, the best way to avoid amplifying Dr. Shockley's views, the best way to show one's scorn and distaste for this provocation is to leave the speakers to an audience of their sponsors...."

Donald Kagan was furious: "...There can be no doubt that such strong and unusual language from such august sources must serve as a deterrent, not only to the group which is its target, but also to any other group wishing to make a similar invitation. The very introduction of the question of motive has the most dangerous implications. To begin with, the motives of the people inviting a speaker plainly have nothing to do with the legitimacy and desirability of the invitations or with the university's responsibility to protect his right to speak. Even in the unlikely event that the inviters publicly proclaimed that their motive was to provoke their opponents and test the university's claim to a proper regard for free speech, that would not reduce the university's responsibility one iota. To introduce the question [of motivation] in the context of freedom of speech, therefore, is an irrelevant distraction that can only serve to deter and intimidate."

In any case, Lux et Veritas finally decided they didn't want to be in the center of controversy, and so one more invitation was withdrawn. Another momentarily brave group, the Calliopean Society, came forward, but it, too, passed on the torch after two weeks because of "insufficient funds and the absence of logistical support in the face of extraordinary ... threats emanating from members of the Yale community...."

The president of the Calliopean Society told the *New Haven Register* that she had been directly harassed and believed the threats that had been made against her were "more than rhetoric."

As the debate about the debate went on, John Blassingame, professor of history, spoke to both the administration and to students: "I hope the Yale community will permit him to speak. Freedom of speech is not divisible. Denied to Shockley today, it can be denied to the president of the Black Student Union tomorrow."

Meanwhile, with Shockley still shut out of Yale, the history department of the suburban Amity Regional Senior High School indicated it was going to ask the local board of education to invite William Shockley to speak there. The idea had come from a teacher, Robert Burns, who had discussed the invitation with his classes.

A majority of the high school students, though hostile to Shockley's ideas, were in favor of the invitation in order "to demonstrate that this is a free society and any view, no matter how unpopular, has the right to be aired."

And Burns, their teacher, said: "It is very difficult to teach that this is a nation where you have the freedom to speak when the institution of higher learning down the street will not allow both sides of the question to be aired."

However, the Amity School Board said that it surely cherished the idea of free speech—but not this time. It was mindful of "the types of pressures brought upon Yale." Added one member: "If Yale's afraid of it, then it may be too much for Amity." The debate, therefore, was, after all, not held at the high school either.

At Yale, divisions among student and faculty concerning invitations to Shockley grew deeper. Elwyn Lee, chairman of the Black Law Students and a member of the Third World Coalition to Disinvite Shockley, wrote in an open letter to the Yale community:

"Yale is a private institution. Therefore, all the talk about free speech is misguided." (The First Amendment does not apply to private institutions.) And he expressed his hope and those of his colleagues that President Kingman Brewster would "exercise his power to stop the debate."

A group of Chicano students declared that "inasmuch as Yale considers itself a national university, it has an obligation to all minority students not to allow the connotation of legitimacy to the topic of genetic inferiority."

Another letter to the *Yale Daily News* began:

"We, Catholic, Protestant and Jewish chaplains at Yale, regret the necessity for great debate about a non-event.... We feel it necessary to share our anger that minority students have been pushed into a no-win situation where they must painfully defend themselves against a guest who defames them and another who exploits their distress."

The letter indicated that the Shockley-Innis debate should be canceled, but if that blessed resolution failed, then "the entire Yale campus should ignore it."

The question of sensitivity—which was to be a pervasive polemical concern in the campus debates about offensive speech in the 1990s—was also underlined in a letter to the Yale newspaper by Carlos Lumiet, a student:

"I am somewhat dismayed by the apparent lack of sensitivity to others betrayed by some of the more ardent advocates of the Shockley-Innis debate that I have encountered.

"These individuals have seemed disturbingly prepared to sacrifice the feelings and dignity of a substantial number of their fellow students on the altars of freedom of speech and academic freedom.

"Too bad they're not a little less concerned with abstract principles and a little more concerned with other people."

And at a meeting of all the black student groups at Yale, a statement was issued saying: "We hereby serve notice that we vehemently oppose the Shockley-Innis debate and will exert all necessary efforts to prevent its occurrence.... We admonish all right-thinking people who still believe that all men are created equal with certain inalienable rights to do likewise...."

On the other hand, Gregory Harris, a student, noted: "Even if Shockley is a crackpot, which I think he is, and Innis a demagogic publicity hound, which I think he is, the scheduled debate is still an excellent opportunity for Yale to vindicate itself by showing that it will allow heretics to speak, and will punish those who interfere with that freedom, no matter what interest group the disrupters represent."

Of particular interest was a letter printed in the *Yale Daily News* from Bob Greenlee, a reporter for the *New Haven Register* (the letter was originally addressed to Yale President Kingman Brewster):

"... As one who is outside of the Yale community, but a member of the working press, I am concerned about the black law students' demand that the debate not be held.

"As men and women who may soon enter the legal profession, I would ask them how they would have reacted in the period of the 1960s when a host of militant blacks were going around the country espousing their viewpoints on every subject under the sun, including the problems of a 'racist society and its oppression of blacks'—if any of these people had been refused a chance to state their views?

"For me, a black, it is especially painful to see the black law students fear a debate between two men, neither of whom is the acknowledged authority on the subject of genetics, espousing their idiotic views...."

"The best possible attack against Shockley's views, which the law students feel are repugnant, is for the students to compile adequate research on Shockley, detailing how he arrived at his views, his background, etc., and to pass out this information to those attending the debate.

"For the sake of argument, I wonder what the reaction of law students would be if the Yale Political Union invited Minister Louis Farrakhan, national spokesman for the Nation of Islam, to speak and a group of white Yale law students petitioned to have that invitation rescinded?

"In the final analysis, it must be noted that when the decision to deny freedom of speech and the espousal of unpopular views is granted, then the freedoms of all of us are in jeopardy!

"And finally, I hope that the Yale Political Union doesn't buckle under to pressure to prevent the debate from taking place.

After all, what with all of the other problems facing the New Haven community and the nation, this just might be the comic relief that we need."

An editorial, "Double-Standard Ban at Yale," in the *New Haven Register,* began:

"Some Yale students, in petitioning for an appearance at the university by Russian novelist Alexander Solzhenitsyn, state that the author's 'quest for truth will reaffirm Yale's tradition of free expression.' It seems to us that Yale can do much more for that tradition by its own example....

"Excuses can always be found for stifling expression. The Kremlin bureaucrats trotted out all the standard jargon in their vain bid to silence Solzhenitsyn. Academia has its own jargon when it chooses to employ a double-standard guideline for freedom of expression. Suddenly, free speech on the campus might offend the sensibilities of the community. There is the danger of provocation, the questioning of motives. There is objection on the ground that the speakers are not experts on the subject.

"But 'only yesterday,' Yale tolerated speaking engagements by a procession of inexpert individuals (the Black Panthers) who expounded radical views on social science that offended large elements of the community. And many used obscene language that hardly inspired respect for academia.

"Why the sudden solicitude, the sudden careful application of standards to qualify for a platform at Yale? We can only conclude that the extension of freedom of expression on campus shifts with the sands of time and with viewpoints. Opinion, it seems, can be stampeded onto and off the Yale campus."

In the *Yale Daily News,* there was a brief letter from C. Vann Woodward, Sterling Professor of History:

"Harvard recently disgraced itself and the academic community by stopping a Shockley-Innis debate. In doing so, Harvard students obligingly provided these two crude publicity seekers with precisely what they sought. I hope Yale students will prove more sophisticated and less imitative...."

Professor Vann Woodward was to be disappointed. The Shockley-Innis debate never took place at Yale because no other group was willing to sponsor it.

However, yet another group, Young Americans for Freedom, did come forward with an invitation to Shockley, and this time the other debater would be William Rusher.

Again, there were threats of disruption. One group warned: "We, as concerned members of the Yale community, intend to stop the Shockley-Rusher debate on Monday night. We will use nonviolent but effective means. Shockley has been kept out of Harvard, drowned out at Dartmouth and heckled out of Staten Island Community College. We feel that Shockley should not be allowed to speak at Yale."

By contrast with the strong support of free speech by Yale students in the debate over the invitation to George Wallace in 1963, the voices to suppress speech had become louder in 1974.

As for the debate, neither Rusher nor Shockley was allowed to speak. All that could be heard, wrote Donald Kagan, were "derisive applause and shouted obscenities."

One of the paeans to censorship, as reported in the *Yale Daily News,* was this chant: "Hitler rose, Hitler fell, racist Shockley go to hell!"

At the end of his 1975 article chronicling the free-speech wars at Yale, Donald Kagan wrote gloomily of the decline in faculty and student passion for freedom of expression:

"That is dangerous and worrying, but it should not be completely surprising. The truth is that hardly anyone really believes in free speech. We all believe in it for ourselves, for those who agree with us, and some of us, even for those who don't disagree too much. But we are generally not eager to defend the rights of those whose views trouble us, or frighten us, or threaten us.

"That is natural, and the founding fathers, in their wisdom, knew it. They knew that a free government required freedom of speech and that the majority could not be trusted to protect the freedoms of unpopular individuals or groups. That is why they insisted on the Bill of Rights, and especially on the First Amendment. Freedom of speech cannot survive unless it is rigorously protected by law, defended by the established institutions of society and their officers, and devotedly cherished by the citizens who understand its importance."

And how many such Americans are there—on or off any campus?

Universities, Kagan continued, must—as places of independent inquiry—adhere "to the broadest possible definition of free speech. They cannot find truth without listening to error, heresy and sometimes even blasphemy....

"Freedom of speech is vital, but it is not free; it has a high price. It compels us to go against our natures, to hear unpleasant and even hateful things, to tolerate unpleasant and even hateful people. It requires us to take stern measures against our own, and even ourselves.

"Here at Yale we have not been willing to pay the price. The fault is general: in our administration because they have failed to lead the defense of freedom; in our faculty because we have not protested that failure and demanded a more vigorous defense; and in our students because they have too easily been led astray. Unless these failures are swiftly repaired and the path we have taken in the last decade sharply reversed, the future for freedom of speech at Yale is bleak."

So wrote Professor Donald Kagan, a member of the history department at Yale, in 1975. What he did not know then was that a report would be issued in that very year that was about to set a standard of freedom of expression for Yale and for the rest of the nation. The committee responsible for the report was chaired by C. Vann Woodward, a renowned professor of history at Yale.

From the Woodward Report to the Fellows of the Yale Corporation:

"The following report is the result of the findings and deliberations of a committee ... charged with examining the condition of free expression, peaceful dissent, mutual respect and tolerance at Yale.... The president appointed a committee of thirteen—consisting of five faculty members, two members of the administration, three graduate students, two undergraduates, and one member of the Yale alumni....

"From the beginning of its investigations the committee has been aware that Yale's problems are shared by sister institutions at home and abroad. Correspondence with some of them has reinforced the impression that a movement which in its inception in California a decade ago proudly invoked the name of Free Speech has in latter days showed signs of repudiating its original commitment. While this investigation is confined to the experience at Yale, it has been the hope of the committee that its statement might inspire in other universities a rededication to the principles asserted in this report. 'If there is any principle of the Constitution that more imperatively calls for attachment than any other it is the principle of free thought—not free thought for those who agree with us but freedom for the thought that we hate' (Oliver Wendell Holmes, Jr., *U.S.* v. *Schwimmer,* 1928).

"The history of intellectual growth and discovery clearly demonstrates the need for unfettered freedom, the right to think the unthinkable, discuss the unmentionable, and challenge the unchallengeable. To curtail free expression strikes twice at intellectual freedom, for whoever deprives another of the right to state unpopular views necessarily also deprives others of the right to listen to those views.

"We take a chance, as the First Amendment takes a chance, when we commit ourselves to the idea that the results of free expression are to the general benefit in the long run, however unpleasant they may appear at the time. The validity of such a belief cannot be demonstrated conclusively. It is a belief of recent historical development, even within universities, one embodied in American constitutional doctrine but not widely shared outside the academic world, and denied in theory and in practice by much of the world most of the time....

"If a university is a place for knowledge, it is also a special kind of small society. Yet it is not primarily a fellowship, a club, a circle of friends, a replica of the civil society outside it. Without sacrificing its central purpose, it cannot make its primary and dominant value the fostering of friendship, solidarity, harmony, civility, or mutual respect. To be sure, these are important values; other institutions may properly assign them the highest, and not merely a subordinate priority; and a good university will seek and may in some significant measure attain these ends. But it will never let these values, important as they are, override its central purpose. We value freedom of expression precisely because it provides a forum for the new, the provocative, the disturbing, and the unorthodox. Free speech is a barrier to the tyranny of authoritarian or even majority opinion as to the rightness or wrongness of particular doctrines or thoughts....

"Above all, every member of the university has an obligation to permit free expression in the university. No member has a right to prevent such expression. Every official of the university, moreover, has a special obligation to foster free expression and to ensure that it is not obstructed....

"Shock, hurt, and anger are not consequences to be weighed lightly. No member of the community with a decent respect for others should use, or encourage others to use, slurs and epithets intended to discredit another's race, ethnic group, religion, or sex. [Yet] it may sometimes be necessary in a university for civility and mutual respect to be superseded by the need to guarantee free expression.

"We have considered the opposing argument that behavior which violates these social and ethical considerations should be made subject to formal sanctions, and the argument that such behavior entitles others to prevent speech they might regard as offensive. Our conviction that the central purpose of the university is to foster the free access of knowledge compels us to reject both of these arguments.

"They assert a right to prevent free expression. They rest upon the assumption that speech can be suppressed by anyone who deems it false or offensive. They deny what Justice Holmes termed 'freedom for the thought that we hate.' They make the majority, or any willful minority, the arbiters of truth for all. If expression may be prevented, censored or punished, because of its content or because of the motives attributed to those who promote it, then it is no longer free. It will be subordinated to other values that we believe to be of lower priority in a university.

"The conclusions we draw, then, are these: even when some members of the university community fail to meet their social and ethical responsibilities, the paramount obligation of the university is to protect their right to free expression. This obligation can and should be enforced by appropriate formal sanctions.

"If the university's overriding commitment to free expression is to be sustained, secondary social and ethical responsibilities must be left to the informal processes of suasion, example, and argument."

The Woodward Report then chronicled the turbulent history

of free speech—and its enemies—at Yale since the 1960s, and continued:

"This committee's account has revealed instances of faltering, uncertainty, and failure in the defense of principle on the part of various elements in the university community. Within the community has appeared from time to time a willingness to compromise standards, to give priority to peace and order and amicable relations over the principle of free speech when it threatens these other values....

"A significant number of students and some faculty members appear to believe that when speakers are offensive to majority opinion, especially on such issues as war and race, it is permissible and even desirable to disrupt them....

"The banning or obstruction of lawful speech can never be justified on such grounds as that the speech or the speaker is deemed irresponsible, offensive, unscholarly, or untrue....

"Disruption of a speech is a very serious offense against the entire University and may appropriately result in suspension or expulsion."

The Yale Corporation accepted the Woodward Report, and in its brief statement alluded—without naming any of those culpable—to past lapses of courage on behalf of free speech by certain Yale officials:

"[The Corporation] would not ... expect the president [of Yale] or any other officer to seek to dissuade any group from inviting a speaker except in the most unusual circumstances...."

Highly critical of the Woodward Report was Black Law Students Union chairman Michael Darnell, who said that "morality and moral perspectives are more important than the inviolability of free speech on campus."

C. Vann Woodward answered by saying that his committee had rejected the argument that "equality and freedom for the oppressed must come first. We know that we have not achieved equality. But in the meantime, we want free speech. It is not a luxury for intellectuals, but a vital, indispensable need for a free university." (He might have added that it is also a vital, indispensable need for achieving equality.)

Woodward and his report were also attacked by the Reverend William Sloane Coffin, Jr., the Yale chaplain who was much admired around the country by members of the civil rights and peace movements. Saying that freedom of speech ought not to be considered an end in itself but rather a means leading to the fulfillment of human potential and equality, Coffin faulted the Woodward Report for being more concerned with protecting freedom of expression than with promoting ethical responsibility:

"Equality is *the* moral imperative of our day, and so the Third World presents *the* moral problem of our day." Coffin went on to praise the work of the Third World Coalition at Yale, which had opposed William Shockley's appearance on campus.

History and classics professor Donald Kagan—who was later to become dean of Yale College—noted that while the faculty had endorsed the principles of the Woodward Report and while there had been much favorable press reaction to it around the country, "those of us who cherish freedom of speech have little cause for rejoicing. Private conversations, faculty debates, and the columns of the *Yale Daily News* reveal that a vocal portion of the community remains lukewarm toward, confused about, or even hostile to the defense of free speech on this campus."

In less than ten years, the case of Wayne Dick's fiercely controversial right to free speech would support Kagan's assessment of the continuing divisions within the Yale community on this matter. Dick, a student, greatly offended Yale's gay and lesbian community by making and distributing parody posters about gays and lesbians.

"If my sentence is not overturned, please advise me as to other views that I am also not allowed to criticize."

For twelve days in April 1986, the fifth annual Gay and Lesbian Awareness Days (GLAD) were the focus of attention on the Yale campus. Sponsored by the Gay and Lesbian Co-op in order to make the Yale community more knowledgeably aware of its gay and lesbian members, GLAD included lectures, an arts festival, discussions, a rally, and a dance.

Among the speakers were Larry Kramer, author of *The Normal Heart*, and Pat Califia, a columnist for *The Advocate*. Califia skillfully exposed the dangers to free expression in the heavy-breathing work of then–Attorney General Edwin Meese's Commission on Pornography.

On the Monday morning after the Gay and Lesbian Awareness Days ended, posters appeared on campus—at the Freshman Commons, the Law School, in Old Campus mailboxes, and other places. According to the April 16 *Yale Daily News*, "the author and distributor" of the "pink flyers" was unknown.

The flyer was a parody of the GLAD announcements. Distinguished neither by its wit nor its taste, it was nonetheless pure speech. Nothing in the text was legally obscene, and by any standard of state or federal law, nothing in the text defamed any particular person.

The headline was:

BAD Week '86

Bestiality Awareness Days

There followed a mythical schedule for BAD week. Among the events: "'PAN: the Goat, the God, the Lover,' a lecture by Prof. Baaswell"; "Bishop Bleatmore (grad. Dartmouth '69) speaking on THE IMPACT OF HOMO ERECTUS ON THE ORIGIN OF NEW SPECIES, Blight Hall"; "Lambda Lambda Lambda—Yale's own Animal House!! announces their first BARNYARD RUSH—Y'all come!!! all night at the Rockinghorse Club"; "Goat Lovers of Colour present a talk on PLAYING WITH KIDS Feta-compli, Blight Hall"; "Ms. Seal speaking on *Rover vs. Wade:* '13 Years of Bitches Choice: Repudiating The Silent Yelp,' Law School Auditorium."

As you might expect, a lot of people were offended, and not only members of Yale's gay and lesbian communities. A *Yale Daily News* story quoted Dean of Student Affairs Lloyd Suttle as thundering that the flyer had not been approved by the Dean's Office and should "absolutely" be taken down. (Apparently, at Yale, as in Britain centuries ago, printed expression must first be licensed by the Crown before it can be disseminated.)

The hunt was on for the anonymous satirist. One sleuth, canvassing the copying shops, found an employee who identified a regular customer as the man who had come in and had the flyer copied.

A word about faceless pamphleteers. In the public world outside the Yale campus, anonymous speech is protected by the First Amendment. The Framers of the Constitution were well aware that some of the British libertarian writers who had greatly influenced them did not use their right names for fear of being clapped into a cell.

Indeed, one of the most far-reaching civil liberties cases in England, a case that helped shape our own Fourth Amendment, began with the Crown's pursuit of an unsigned pamphlet attacking the government. The author was revealed to be John Wilkes, and the police, acting on a general warrant, confiscated all his personal papers. In *Wilkes* v. *Wood* the Chief Justice of England ruled that use of nonspecific warrants was "totally subversive of the liberty of the subject."

Nor, for that matter, were the Wobblies, in our own history, accustomed to signing their names to their posters and flyers. And as a youth, while involved in labor disputes with vengeful employers, I did not sign my name to various union pamphlets that harshly illuminated the bosses' cruel and usual behavior.

Ah, but these are illustrations of what is generally called political speech. By contrast, some would say, the anonymous flyer at Yale wasn't much different from what you'd find above a urinal. Yet, nasty as many at Yale found it, the text of the flyer was discussing a matter of public interest. And even if it had not clearly been political speech, as it was, once you start quarantining "good" speech from "bad" speech and punishing the latter, you are then giving the authorities the power to censor not only that "bad" speech but many other kinds.

In any case, the author of BAD week '86 was no longer anonymous. He turned out to be Wayne Dick, a sophomore from Florida. His father works for a road construction company, and his mother is a secretary. When she was young, his mother went to a Christian college in Indiana for a year, but couldn't afford to stay on. So Wayne Dick had become the first member of his family with a shot at getting a college degree. He then intended to go to law school.

Somewhere along the line, before coming to Yale, Wayne Dick acquired the notion that everyone in this country has a right to free speech. And he figured that this most basic of all freedoms would be particularly honored on the campus of so prestigious a university as Yale. Surely there, even if it is a private place, the spirit of the First Amendment would be nurtured.

But that was before Wayne Dick went on trial at Yale for unspeakable speech.

On May 2, Wayne Dick received a letter from Patricia Pierce, associate dean of Yale College, and secretary of the Yale College Executive Committee. The letter began by putting him on notice that Caroline Jackson, director of the Afro-American Cultural Center and a member of the Yale College Dean's Office Racial and Ethnic Harassment Board—joined by Yale senior Patrick Santana—had "submitted to the Executive Committee a complaint alleging harassment in the form of a BAD week '86 poster."

"If this allegation is substantiated," Wayne Dick was told by Associate Dean Pierce, "you may be guilty of a violation of the regulation against 'Physical restriction, assault, coercion, or intimidation of any member of the community (Chapter I, Section B, p. 6–7). [This encompasses] any act of harassment, intimidation, coercion or assault, or any other act of violence against any member of the community, including sexual, racial or ethnic harassment.'"

As Dick read on, the morning grew darker. In the same letter, Pierce informed the accused that she and the other two members of the Executive Committee Coordinating Group had decided that the complaint had merit and should be submitted to the full Executive Committee. The defendant was instructed: "It would be to your advantage to prepare a written statement concerning this matter."

Because his target had been the gay and lesbian community, Wayne Dick was now regarded by many as a campus pariah. His insufferable views could not remain unpunished.

The Executive Committee that was to decide his fate was composed of faculty and student members who conducted their proceedings in secret, issued no written opinions, or even a count of the final vote. (One never knew if there were dissents.) The accused student was permitted a faculty adviser, but that adviser was barred from taking a direct role in the trial—thereby being unable, for example, to cross-examine witnesses.

All decisions of this Court of the Star Chamber were final, although an appeal was possible if substantial new evidence were found. But the appeal was not heard by an independent body. The same Executive Committee that found the defendant guilty decided whether the new evidence was credible and, therefore, if the case should be reexamined. This was the procedure, mind you, not at some rural Baptist college but at that Camelot of the Northeast, Yale University.

In accordance with the procedures of the Executive Committee, the defendant wrote a letter to it prior to his appearance at its chambers.

In his letter to the Executive Committee, Wayne Dick said that he could hardly be charged with harassment in the face of the Yale Report on Free Expression, also known as the Woodward Report. As I noted earlier, this report is part of the college's undergraduate regulations and is therefore binding on students, faculty, and presumably even the dread Executive Committee of Yale College.

As Wayne Dick did at his actual hearing before the Executive Committee, I will quote from the Report of the Committee on Free Expression at Yale as it appears in the Yale University Undergraduate Regulations:

"... If a university is a place for knowledge, it is also a special kind of small society. Yet it is not primarily a fellowship, a club, a circle of friends, a replica of the civil society outside it. Without sacrificing its central purpose [to discover and disseminate knowledge], *it cannot make its primary and dominant value the fostering of friendship, solidarity, harmony, civility or mutual respect.... It may sometimes be necessary in a university for civility and mutual respect to be superseded by the need to guarantee free expression....*" (Emphasis added.)

"Even when some members of the university community fail to meet their social and ethical responsibilities, the paramount obligation of the university is to protect that right to free expression."

Wayne Dick told me that at one point he asked Patricia Pierce, associate dean of Yale College and secretary to the Yale College Executive Committee, how he could be brought up on charges at all when the text of his flyer seemed to be fully protected by the Woodward Report. Pierce told him, he says, that the Woodward Report does not protect "worthless speech"—and that's what his flyer was.

Dick ended his pretrial letter to the Executive Committee by saying: "I have always held dear the values lauded by the Woodward commission: friendship, harmony, civility, and mutual respect. I did not mean to violate the norms of civility in the poster, and they are not necessarily inconsistent with satire. I hope that I have not offended any member of the university community; and if I have, I apologize.

"But the Woodward Report is clear. Even if my poster had caused shock, hurt, or outrage, it is still protected. It may be properly subject to personal or moral criticism on that basis—although I do not believe my poster would merit such criticism—but it is not properly subject to university punishment.

"The Woodward Report says further that expression must not be prevented, censored, or punished because of its contents or motives.... If the Executive Committee finds me guilty of harassment, its members will be guilty of punishing free speech and will be in flagrant violation of the freedom of expression policy in the Undergraduate Regulations. The Executive Committee will have taken a giant step backwards and will have placed Yale on the road to becoming a forum where only the politically correct have a right to be heard, and those holding 'unenlightened' views will be silenced.

"Only by ruling that the exercise of free speech is not harassment and finding that I am innocent will the Executive Committee have justly interpreted its own rules and reaffirmed Yale's commitment to free expression."

The May 12 trial of Wayne Dick lasted two and a half hours. It was the defendant's impression, he told me later, that some members of the Executive Committee were of the belief that summary hanging might be the most appropriate way of terminating the case.

On May 13, Patricia Pierce delivered the verdict:

"The Yale College Executive Committee determined that Mr. Wayne Dick ... '88 was guilty of a violation of the Undergraduate Regulations. The Committee judged that the 'BAD week' poster produced by Mr. Dick constituted an act of harassment and intimidation toward the gay and lesbian community and towards individuals named in the poster."

The sentence: two years' probation.

According to Yale's Undergraduate Regulations, probation means "the student is in official jeopardy. The commission of a serious offense while on probation will normally result in suspension or expulsion."

What is a "serious offense"? There is no further definition.

The sentence of probation might well have affected Wayne Dick well beyond his undergraduate years—as in his planned application to law schools.

Furthermore, this part of Dick's record would also be included, a number of Yale administrators told me, in any other recommendations written for him. In Elizabethan times, publishers of bad thoughts—like dissenter John Stubbs in 1579—lost their right hand, and that was the end of it. At Yale, a black cloud would stay over your head.

John Stubbs, who had criticized the proposed marriage between Queen Elizabeth and the Duke of Anjou, looked at his severed hand, and with his left one, raised his hat, and cried, "God save the Queen!" He had learned his lesson.

Wayne Dick kept his hat on his head. On May 16, he wrote a letter to A. Bartlett Giamatti, then president of Yale:

"I am writing to you in the hope that you will help me. I have just been sentenced to two years' probation by the Executive Committee. My crime was a satirical poster ... which criticized GLAD week....

"I have been told that my poster is not protected by [Yale's] freedom of expression regulations because it is worthless and offensive. I have seen many posters that I thought were worthless and offensive, but I respect others' right to express their views. This respect for others' rights is something I have acquired at Yale.

"I was born and raised in a small town in Florida where the old southern political philosophy and prejudices were commonly accepted. By and large, I accepted these views without really considering them. When I came to Yale as a freshman, I found that my views were held by a small minority and I soon had to justify them for the first time.

"In defending my beliefs through conversation with various

people, I realized that some of my views were ill-considered. For those I have kept, I now, at least, have a philosophical basis for them. Of course, I can hardly claim to be all-wise after having just completed my sophomore year; but because of the free interchange of ideas, I have grown.

"I most often express my views on the defensive since I still find myself in a conservative minority. To avoid heated arguments and to avoid hard feelings, I have often kept silent, even when I had strong moral objections to a point of view that was being stated. Recently, though, I decided to criticize an event which was, until recently, considered morally repugnant. My main reason for deciding to state my opinion more publicly was that only one opinion on this issue was being heard. I saw no real criticism of this issue.

"I am of the opinion that homosexuality is not an absolute good. I saw it as being accepted as such by the majority of the campus. This year, since no one was seriously questioning GLAD week being a good thing, I decided to put out a poster.... With the poster I criticized the current acceptance of homosexuality as moral by comparing it to bestiality, which is, for now at least, considered a moral perversion.

"After being brought up on charges and found guilty of harassing the gay and lesbian community, I realized that criticism of the public acceptance of homosexuality as moral is prohibited by Yale University despite the Woodward Report.

"I ask that my sentence be overturned if the free-expression regulation is in force or that my sentence be reduced because of my ignorance of the special status of debate on homosexuality.

"*If my sentence is not overturned, please advise me as to other views that I am also not allowed to criticize, so that I won't unknowingly violate my probation and the standards of Yale University.*" (Emphasis added.)

A. Bartlett Giamatti made his scholarly reputation with a book, *The Earthly Paradise and the Renaissance Epic.* As David Remnick said of that book in the *Washington Post*, Giamatti, in exploring the garden in literature, from Eden on, was concerned with the "realms of equilibrium and truth."

On May 30, Giamatti answered Wayne Dick's letter:

"I have read your letter with care, and want first to assure you that your right to free expression of your opinions, on any issue, will be protected by the University in the future as it has been in the past."

That assurance must have made Wayne Dick burst into song. The Dear Occupant letter continued:

"It is the function of the Yale College Executive Committee to determine when the regulations concerning intimidation and harassment have been breached, as well as to protect the right of any member of the community to free expression.

"As you know, there is no appeal from a decision of the Yale College Executive Committee excepting to the Committee itself. I have consulted with Dean Patricia D. Pierce, Secretary of the Committee, and am satisfied that the Committee Procedures have been carefully followed in your case."

Just before taking over as president of the National League, A. Bartlett Giamatti delivered his last formal remarks as president of Yale University. It was at a baccalaureate ceremony, and Giamatti urged the new graduates to watch out for the "tyranny of group self-righteousness.

"There are many," he said, "who lust for the simple answers of doctrine or decree. They are on the left and right. They are not confined to a single part of the society. They are terrorists of the mind."

The departing president went on to excoriate all systems that bar the free exchange of ideas. He did not, however, mention Yale, despite the case of Wayne Dick.

Giamatti's successor as president of Yale was Benno Schmidt, formerly dean of the Columbia University Law School and a specialist on the First Amendment.

I wrote to the new president about Wayne Dick's case and received an answer on June 18:

"... I am not yet in office at Yale, and of course this entire matter predates any accession to responsibility on my part. I will consider this matter after I become president."

In the meantime, in looking into the postconviction history of this case, I talked to Sidney Altman, then dean of Yale College.

Dean Altman explained the procedures by which students are charged and tried before the Executive Committee. I told him I could not understand how Wayne Dick could have been found guilty of writing and distributing a poster, even if it was offensive to many on campus, in the face of the Woodward Report.

Well, said the dean of Yale College, it's a matter of interpretation as to whether the Woodward Report protects Wayne Dick. (A matter of interpretation or a matter of reading comprehension?) Dean Altman also told me that the sentence of two years' probation would indeed be part of Dick's record to be forwarded to law schools or medical schools or just about anywhere else his record had to be sent.

At one point, I told Dean Altman that the whole procedure—from the secret trial, to the defendant's "adviser" being forbidden to cross-examine witnesses, to the final decision without any reasons given for how the decision was reached—struck me as crudely one-sided.

Dean Altman answered, "It's a system that works for us."

I reminded him that Henry VIII used to say the very same thing as his wives' heads rolled off their shoulders.

When our conversation was almost done, the dean paused, and told me, "You realize I can't give you my *private* feelings on this matter. I'll just have to leave it at that."

I was getting discouraged as I made the telephone rounds of the Yale administration. I had yet to find anybody who saw anything wrong—or would say so—about how this radiant university had punished a student for having and expressing bad thoughts.

A friend of mine, Sid Zion, an alumnus of Yale Law School, suggested I call Guido Calabresi, dean of the school. The first surprise was that I had no trouble getting through to him. I started to tell him about the case, but after I'd said about ten words, Dean Calabresi broke in:

"Outrageous! I know the case. Outrageous! That student's treatment by the Executive Committee was absolutely dreadful!

"It would have been perfectly appropriate for the faculty and the administrators to say that the flyer was disgraceful and disgusting and that he should be ashamed of himself. But what he did was not in any way punishable, let alone this extraordinarily severe punishment.

"I have been a supporter of gay rights," the Dean said, "from the beginning, whether here at the law school or at the college or anywhere else. I am against discrimination of any kind. But with regard to speech, this is the university that said William Shockley had a right to speak here, and what he was peddling was more offensive than that poster.

"What the Executive Committee did," Calabresi went on, "was an ideological kind of thing. Put what they did to Wayne Dick alongside the very mild treatment the very same committee gave to the people, one of whom was my son, who were arrested during protests and counterprotests connected with pressuring the university to divest itself of investments in South Africa." (The arrests of the pro-divestment students were for blocking the entrances to a university building, which violates a Yale regulation against "interference with university functions," including the seizing or occupying of any university building "or part thereof.")

Calabresi noted: "I have no doubt what side I'm on with regard to gay rights," and he also made clear he has no doubt what side he's on with regard to free speech. The two are not contradictory.

Soon after I talked with Dean Calabresi, I was checking some facts on the phone with Wayne Dick. In passing, he mentioned that someone from Reed Irvine's Accuracy in Academia had contacted him, but Dick said he had told the caller that he was not interested in having AIA involved in his case. Although he considers himself conservative in some areas, Dick does not take kindly to students being used to grade their professors on their "liberalism" and then report back to AIA. "Students should do their own questioning," Dick said. "That's what education is about."

One afternoon, it suddenly—and belatedly—occurred to me to ask C. Vann Woodward what he thought of how the Executive Committee of Yale College had handled Wayne Dick's case.

I called Professor Woodward, and he said he would like to see the facts of the case. I sent them, and a few days later he called me.

"You're right," he began. "The Woodward Report was misused and abused by the Executive Committee in Wayne Dick's case. The report was intended to protect people in the use of their freedom of speech—not to punish them for that use. The Woodward Report does not guarantee that the speech has to be acceptable or pleasant or even correct. It simply guarantees the right to all to exercise their speech. Mr. Dick, it seems to me, was doing just that.

"It may not have been wise for him to say what he did on that poster," C. Vann Woodward continued, "but that isn't the question. I agree with Guido Calabresi, dean of the Law School, that the Executive Committee's action was a violation of Mr. Dick's freedom of speech. The Executive Committee was wrong."

Professor Vann Woodward paused. "After all, it's the unpopular speakers that need protection."

C. Vann Woodward became Wayne Dick's adviser and advocate. Free speech, he told the *Yale Daily News,* had not been protected by the original Executive Committee decision punishing the student.

Wayne Dick himself, speaking to *The New York Times,* cited a section of the original Woodward Report: "Even when some members of the university community fail to meet their social and ethical responsibilities, the paramount obligation of the university is to protect their right to free expression."

As for the new president of Yale, Benno Schmidt, he appeared to agree with the Woodward Report. In his inaugural address, Schmidt had said, "There is no speech so horrendous in content that it does not in principle serve our purposes."

In a meeting with Wayne Dick, Schmidt suggested strongly that he ask the Executive Committee for a new hearing. The student was reluctant, telling the president that the procedures by which the committee operated had not changed. There was still scant due process, and although he had asked that at least the proceedings be made public, that request had been denied. Schmidt, quite forcefully, advised the young man to nonetheless try for a new hearing.

When Dick told me about the conversation, I said it seemed to me that Schmidt was sending a message to him, that Schmidt knew what the new verdict would be. In any case, Dick had already decided to take the president's suggestion.

"Free expression," law school dean Guido Calabresi said before the second hearing, "is more important than civility in a university."

In an October 2, 1986, press release, Yale College dean Sidney Altman announced that the Executive Committee had voted "to reverse its decision of last semester to discipline Mr. Wayne Dick."

He added that the new decision was "in no way altered by the extraordinary publicity [that] surrounded this case." That "publicity" had come from the original reports on the case by this writer in the *Village Voice* and the *Washington Post*. It may have been that national attention to the case did not lead to the reversal of his punishment, but I expect that the presence of C. Vann Woodward on his side—and Benno Schmidt's strong views on free expression—were not lost on the Executive Committee.

President Schmidt noted officially that "Yale has exemplified in this decision one of the great assets of a community devoted to free expression, and that is the capacity to change its mind."

Wayne Dick was characteristically far from humble at his vindication. Said the twenty-year-old: "Not guilty was what I wanted to hear. But I'm not satisfied at all with the committee. Its rules are conducive to tyranny." However, he added, "there's now a clear precedent for upholding the Woodward Report at Yale."

Not everyone rejoiced. Said Tom Keane, coordinator of the Gay Student Center, "It's hard to imagine the same sort of thing happening if someone had done a parody of Hillel [the campus center for Jewish students]." And Millard Owens, a co-moderator of the Black Student Alliance at Yale, emphasized: "What we have is a statement to the minority community that the Executive Committee doesn't take seriously the rights of those who tend to be the victims of harassment." Keane added that the verdict "will just embolden some people" to attack gays.

Carrie Costello, a founder of the Ad Hoc Committee Against Defamation, said that the acquittal "will be mistaken by some people as a judgment against civility. That's too bad."

C. Vann Woodward's view was that "certainly I don't agree with [Dick's] ideas, but they all come under the protection of free speech."

On the "CBS Evening News" three days before the verdict, Yale professor Alvin Novick had a decidedly different perspective: "You can't use terms like nigger or kike, and you can't accuse gay and lesbian people of being like bestial people. Those are very heavy-duty pejorative views that are uncivilized."

In a lead editorial two days after the verdict, the *Washington Post* said:

"... The poster in question was in terrible taste. It probably offended many members of the university community. And the satire was rightly characterized by columnist Nat Hentoff in this paper as 'hardly equal to Jonathan Swift's.' But the First Amendment wasn't drafted to protect bland comments, inoffensive criticism or popular ideas. It was adopted specifically to ensure that controversial speech is not squelched and, in particular, to protect the free discussion of ideas.

"In order to do this, Americans put up with a lot of offensive material—everything from pornography to the ravings of the American Nazi Party. If it were otherwise, someone would have to be put in charge of deciding what speech is acceptable for citizens to hear, and that would be the beginning of the end of American liberty....

"Tolerance, respect for human differences and civility are the hallmarks of an educated person. Every university seeks to foster these qualities in its students. But these qualities cannot be taught by punishing a student for saying or writing what he pleases, even if he is wrongheaded and offensive to authority figures or organized groups of peers."

The ideas and principles in that editorial were to prove deeply offensive to many students, faculty members, and administrators in American colleges and universities in the years that followed.

"If fear, ignorance and bigotry exist on our campuses, it is far better that they be exposed and answered, than that they be bottled up...."

In the fall of 1989, Yale president Benno Schmidt spoke to the entering class. It was among a series of warnings that, I expect, will resonate for many years to come. "There is disturbing evidence abroad in the land that we need to reflect on the obvious. We need to renew our commitment to freedom at Yale with unmistakable determination....

"For many of you, your first year at Yale will be your first experience living in a community rigorously committed to freedom of thought. You may find the experience unsettling. I hope you will find it exhilarating....

"Because ideas live, because imagination is the key to wisdom, John Stuart Mill was surely right to contend that if we give in to the urge to suppress that which we are sure is error—even very offensive and dangerous error—we lose a benefit as great as truth itself, namely, 'the clearer perception and livelier impression of truth, produced by its collision with error.' ... Much expression that is free may deserve our contempt. We may well be moved to exercise our own freedom to counter it. But we cannot censor or suppress speech in a university, no matter how obnoxious its content, without violating the principle that is our justification for existence. All of us at Yale must strive for the courage to face ideas that we may regard as fraught with evil.

"Freedom of thought, like the most valuable lessons of life, is not easy to embrace. It is, indeed, the effort of a lifetime. It requires a willingness to take the long view, the courage to confront the unthinkable without losing one's composure, and a willingness to trust that reason and the good, if free to play their part, can overcome evil and insanity.

"This is a flabby and uncertain time for freedom in the United States ... Accordingly, I wish to express the view ... that the suggestion [by President George Bush] that we as a nation ought to amend the First Amendment to the Constitution to deal with the ephemeral obnoxiousness of a few hotheads who burn the flag in protest against something-or-other ought to be regarded as outlandish by everyone committed to freedom and the rule of principle in its defense....

"On some other campuses in this country, values of civility and community have been offered by some as paramount values of the university, even to the point of superseding freedom of expression. Such a view is wrong in principle, and if extended, disastrous to freedom of thought. I hope there will be no mistake about Yale's paramount commitment to freedom...."

Under Benno Schmidt, Yale became the leading university in the country in the defense of free speech. Schmidt, along with Donald Kagan and others, continued the spirit of the Woodward Report.

In March 1991, Schmidt, speaking at the 92nd Street Y in New York, said:

"The most serious problems of freedom of expression in our society today exist on our campuses. On many ... including some of the finest universities ... freedom of thought is in danger from well-intentioned but misguided efforts to give values of community and harmony a higher place in the university than freedom. The assumption seems to be that the purpose of education is to induce correct opinion rather than to search for wisdom and to liberate the mind. The issue of freedom in our universities is not only of critical importance to the quality and integrity of higher education. *Attitudes on campus often presage tendencies in the larger society. If that is so with respect to freedom of expression, the erosion of principle we have seen throughout our society in recent years may be only the beginning.* (Emphasis added.)

"Most free-expression controversies in our society engage strong institutions and powerful interests with a stake in freedom. In most, the press can be counted on to focus public attention on the cause of freedom. In most, there is a strong tradition of judicial intervention to protect First Amendment interests. The issue of freedom in universities is different. Here the institutions which ought to be fiercely devoted to freedom—the universities themselves—are distracted and confused....

"If freedom of thought is to be protected in universities, it is the universities themselves that must summon up the clarity of purpose to defend the principles of liberty on which the academic mission must rest. Perhaps the most important lesson universities can teach their students is to think and search for truth in freedom. For most students, this lesson is not easy. *They come to universities with little or no understanding of the theory and practice of freedom of thought.* (Emphasis added.)

"The problem of freedom of expression on our campuses lies at the intersection of two extremely disturbing tendencies. One is a general anxiety in our society that is eroding our commitment to enduring principles in our national life, an unsteadiness that especially threatens freedom of expression, the freedom that is the indispensable condition, as Benjamin Cardozo reminded us, of all our liberties. What the near-miss of amending the First Amendment to deal with flag burning, the political agitation over indecency in the arts, and the steady march toward an official-secrets-act regime of national-security secrecy all have in common is a pervasive doubt about the capacity of our society to live and flourish in conditions of freedom.

"The second tendency is the uncertainty and confusion that currently prevails in colleges and universities about the fundamental principles and values on which the enterprise of higher education rests, or ought to rest. The question of freedom of expression on campus is only one example of a drift that has many other manifestations, such as the exposure of the curriculum to the crudest pressures of the volatile politics of the campus, the willingness of many universities to do practically anything anybody will pay for, and the flabbiness of the traditions of liberal education in the face of the most shortsighted utilitarianism....

"Moreover, universities have become saturated with politics, often of a fiercely partisan kind. Universities have indeed become the anvil on which young people, and often old as well, beat out their resentments at the incompleteness of life. The economic and political insecurities of universities, from within and without, have produced a style of academic leadership that tends to be highly risk-averse, queasy about defending academic values, and inclined to negotiate and propitiate about almost anything.

"Thus, on many campuses around the country, perhaps most, there is little resistance to growing pressure to suppress and to punish, rather than to answer, speech that offends notions of civility and community. These campuses are heedless of the oldest lesson in the history of freedom of expression, which is that offensive, erroneous, and obnoxious speech is the price of freedom. Offensive speech cannot be suppressed under open-ended standards without letting loose an engine of censorship that cannot be controlled. Vague and unpredictable possibilities of punishment for expression on campus not only fly in the face of the lessons of freedom, but are in addition antithetical to the idea of the university....

"If fear, ignorance, and bigotry exist on our campuses, it is far better that they be exposed and answered, than that they be bottled up....

"To stifle expression because it is obnoxious, erroneous, embarrassing, not instrumental to some political or ideological end is—quite apart from the invasion of the rights of others—a disastrous reflection on the idea of the university. It is to elevate fear over the capacity for a liberated and humane mind.

"Then there is the problem of disruption of unpopular or controversial speakers....

"The first victims of such suppression are the students and faculty who do not have their own convictions tempered by exposure to other points of view, even if ultimately unpersuasive. But the more serious loss is suffered by the university, because these acts of suppression tend to contribute to a pall of conformity on many campuses. And yet, most universities ... do not ... respond as if their academic integrity is threatened by these disruptions. Even in an open society, history demonstrates that freedom of speech needs firm protection to flourish. Free speech and unorthodox thinking are for most people easily intimidated, and especially so in the close confines of the university.

"I believe that a university should virtually never bow to threats of disruption or even violence against an unpopular speaker. A university should not encourage or connive in a withdrawal of an invitation to an unpopular speaker. The principle that freedom must be protected, as best the university can, is no less in the case of an unpopular speaker threatened by lawless disruption that it would be if some misguided group threatened to burn offensive books in the university's library....

"The second and more vexing question of freedom of expression in universities today concerns not the lawless disruption of freedom within the university, but the actual use of university authority to suppress freedom....

"Its impact will be felt not only by those whose speech is punished; the greater problem is the vastly greater number of speakers who will steer clear of possible punishment by steering clear of controversial or unpopular views. The chilling effects of vague powers to punish offensive speech are likely to be far more damaging to freedom of expression than the actual applications of such rules...."

The New York Times took the position approvingly that ... a private university is not bound by the First Amendment, and so need not treat free expression as a paramount value and should therefore "balance" the needs of freedom and the needs of civility on campus. This is profoundly wrong.

"A university, by reason of its special character, ought to be more devoted to freedom than the larger civil society, which has other goals that compete with the search for truth. This search is the paramount end of the university, its very reason for existence. Moreover, universities have a special capacity to answer obnoxious speech. The communal character of the university, the fact that it is replete with opportunities for expression, the capacity of students, the faculty, deans and presidents to answer forcefully and promptly, all present manifold opportunities to counter offensive expression.

"Moreover, decades of First Amendment adjudication have shown that vague balancing formulas of the sort the *Times* is ready to approve for universities are, even in the hands of disciplined judges, a disaster for freedom. What can we expect of such formulations in the hands of students and faculty, however well-meaning?...

"It does not follow that because the university is committed to nondiscrimination, it should suppress any speech that can plausibly be thought to be racist. What is racial prejudice, after all, but a particularly vicious form of ignorance and fear? It is precisely the function of free expression to dispel ignorance and fear with the light of truth. A university ought to be the last place where people are inhibited by fear of punishment from expressing ignorance or even hate, so long as others are left free to answer.

"I have often heard the argument... that uninhibited freedom of speech was somehow more appropriate in the days when our universities were more homogeneous, while current conditions of far greater racial, religious, and cultural diversity call for controls in the interest of harmony and community. That so many people of goodwill would make such an argument shows how far we have drifted from our confidence in and commitment to freedom. I can only imagine what James Madison or Holmes would have thought of this complete inversion of the theory of free expression. It is precisely societies that are diverse, pluralistic, and contentious that most urgently need freedom of speech and freedom of religion....

"Freedom is not self-defining and it is never finally won."

"This demand for unanimity of outlook is antithetical to the spirit of feminism and has no place in a community dedicated to the free expression of ideas."

In 1985, I was excommunicated from the body of the Jewish people by a trio of circuit-riding rabbis. They held the dread ceremony in a motel in Tewksbury, Massachusetts. Blowing on a ram's horn, snuffing out a candle (presumably symbolic of my life as a Jew), the three rabbis cast my soul into perpetual goyishe darkness.

As their text of damnation, they used the language of the 1757 excommunication in Brode, Poland, of a band of Jewish heretics called the Satanic Sabbation Frankists.

My own utterly unforgivable act of satanic heresy had been to protest the 1982 Israeli invasion of Lebanon.

A good many other Jews that year, and since, have declared me beyond the pale for being less than wholly and undeviatingly supportive of Israel.

I tell them—as I wrote the rabbis who were casting thunderbolts from their motel room—that I do not recognize their authority to decide who is an authentic Jew and who is not. One of the earliest truisms I heard as a boy, in my Jewish neighborhood, was that where there are two Jews, there will sooner or later be three synagogues. There is no one Central Committee to pass on anyone's legitimacy as a Jew.

Years before my failed excommunication, I was talking with Charles Mingus, the formidable black bassist and bandleader, at the bar of the Five Spot in New York. The subject was the blues, and I was telling Mingus about Jewish blues, the largely improvised singing of the cantors in the synagogues. I was telling him of the "cry"—the *krechts*—in their voices that is similar to that of black blues singers.

Mingus was curious, but before we could explore comparative soul music any further, a tall black nationalist standing near us broke in. He was angry at Mingus. Not because of our conversation. He apparently had been angry at Mingus for some time.

"You've got no business to say you play black music," the nationalist said to Mingus. "You're too light to have real black roots."

Mingus raised his fist, but thought better of that way of communication. Instead, he leaped onto the bandstand, picked up his bass, and played a blues that was so black the room disappeared deep into the past that is always beneath the appearance of the present. The black nationalist also disappeared.

There are always individuals and committees who have anointed themselves purifiers of a political party, a race, a religion. Their power exists only if it is recognized.

This is the story of one such band of true believers—and of a group of "heretics" who would not be denied their legitimacy as feminists.

In March 1987, the Yale Women's Center approved a statement of purpose.

"The Yale Women's Center is a place for all women—of every race, ethnicity, age, ability, class, sexual orientation, religion—to gather together and to explore the richness and diversity of women's lives.... We work toward a world without discrimination, in which all women create, act, and achieve freely—in the classroom, on the playing field, in the work force, in the political arena, in social relations, and in our personal lives; *and we invite everyone in our communities to join us in the challenge of creating such a world.*" (Emphasis added.)

The Yale Women's Center pledged "to break down the barriers between women.... One of the visions for the Center will be to encompass a wider spectrum of women and women's experiences."

The women of the Center were acting entirely within the letter and the spirit of Yale University's stated Policy on Freedom of Expression. I quote from the August 1987 formulation of that policy in a pamphlet signed by Sheila W. Wellington, secretary of the university:

"Nothing is more conducive to the advancement of knowledge and the search for truth to individual growth and fulfillment, and to basic human liberties than a community, rare in human history, where all shades of opinion can be voiced and all avenues of thought and research pursued...."

Yale's Policy on Freedom of Expression quoted the 1975 Woodward Report:

"The history of intellectual growth and discovery clearly

demonstrates the need for unfettered freedom, the right to think the unthinkable, discuss the unmentionable, and challenge the unchallengeable."

Accordingly, the 1987 statement emphasized that Yale is committed "to the free and full expression of differing views. The conditions for maintaining free speech at Yale, as elsewhere, are to protect the expression of all views and to maintain a community with the *requisite ... access to facilities* and evenhandedness toward all opinions." (Emphasis added.)

This indeed sounds like the very model of a university. But as the Irish poet James Stephens used to say, there are always lumps in the pudding.

At Yale, there was a group called Yale Students for Life. It had no ties with any national or local right-to-life organizations. Its concern was with developing "a consistent ethic of life." In that respect, Yale Students for Life resembled, but was not part of, Feminists for Life of America. That organization—then in its fifteenth year—is based in Kansas City, Missouri, and has members throughout the country. They call themselves pro-life feminists. In the 1985 book *Pro-Life Feminism,* Gail Grenier Sweet explains what that means:

"[Pro-life feminists] realize that abortion is just one facet in a kaleidoscope of social ills, which harden our hearts and destroy our planet—ills including infanticide, euthanasia, capital punishment, war, and pollution. These [pro-life feminists] are like the earliest feminists who understood that civil rights meant recognizing the dignity of every human being, *especially* the defenseless."

Yale Students for Life opposed infanticide, euthanasia, capital punishment, and nuclear war. As for abortion, many of its members did not approve legislating against abortion. They wanted to change minds, not laws. They wanted to engage in dialogue. And that's just what the Yale Women's Center was all about, or so it seemed.

Having read the Women's Center's Statement of Purpose, and being aware of Yale University's Policy on Freedom of Expression, Yale Students for Life went to the Yale Women's Center and asked to become part of this place that said it wanted to "break down the barriers between women."

Well, said the students in charge of the Yale Women's Center—

which is funded by the university—they didn't exactly mean *all* women.

But, Students for Life reminded the Yale Women's Center, its invitation did say *all* women.

Hold on, said the Women's Center. We have to look at our guidelines again.

Hastily, a more specific set of guidelines was drawn up to determine which women's groups were entitled to share the Women's Center. These were the new guidelines: "A commitment to full rights for women under the law, a commitment to freedom of sexual orientation and expression, and a commitment to reproductive freedom."

That took care of Yale Students for Life's nerve in considering themselves "part of the diversity of women's lives." Admission to the Yale Women's Center was hereby restricted to only those women who were pro-abortion.

Katie Oberlies, a graduate of Yale College, a third-year law student at Yale, and active in Students for Life, told me her reaction to the new guidelines: "I would have no objection if they named it the Yale Center for Reproductive Freedom, but it *is* called the Yale Women's Center."

She was one of the signers of a letter by Students for Life in the *Yale Daily News*.

"… We are disturbed by the efforts of some at the Women's Center to restrict the definition of 'feminist' to those who hold a certain narrow set of political and moral beliefs and who have a limited vision of what is in the best interests of women.…

"This demand for unanimity of outlook is antithetical to the spirit of feminism and has no place in a community dedicated to the free expression of ideas.

"The Women's Center has room for women with diverse views on such vital feminist issues as pornography, surrogate motherhood, prostitution, and legislative protection for pregnant women in the workplace. We believe there should be room for us at the Women's Center as well."

Answering in the *Yale Daily News*, Linda Anderson, senior administrative assistant in Yale's Women's Studies Department, wrote:

"Women's Centers have been established during the second wave of feminism for the liberation of women. And liberation means, among other things, that we must have control over our bodies in every way possible, including whether we will bear children or not. This is a basic right according to feminist thinking."

Let's look at that last sentence again. It was impossible, according to Linda Anderson and those who ran the Yale Women's Center, to be a feminist without also being in favor of abortion. They thereby remove all legitimacy from Feminists for Life of America and from such other pro-life feminists as Juli Loesch, Mary Meehan, Liz McCalister, *et al.* Snuffing out candles, they excommunicate heretics.

So a woman who considered herself a feminist but failed the pro-abortion test was banished from a place called the Yale Women's Center. As I was banished from certain centers of Jewish dialogue because I publicly criticized Israel. As Charles Mingus was told he was not black enough to play the blues. The place for free expression, as for the homeless, is in somebody else's neighborhood.

As the debate intensified on campus, a student, Matthew Rendall, wrote a letter to the *Yale Daily News:*

"... As long as Yale funds only one Women's Center, it has no right to pick and choose which 'feminists' use it. For Yale to pick up the tab (however much or little) for one group of activists but not for their opposition would be ... grossly unfair."

Matthew Rendall presented a scenario:

"Imagine, for a moment, that avowed conservatives run the Yale Women's Center. Since 1980 the Center has fought abortion [and] comparable worth ... while urging that Old Campus be renamed 'Phyllis Schlafly Memorial Quadrangle.' All with $400 per semester of university funding.

"Now a 'pro-choice' group is challenging the conservatives' hegemony. Arguing that 'pro-life groups *do not* have a monopoly on women's issues,' the group demands to meet at the Center. The Center's coordinating committee tells them to go to hell. Would the campus stand for this? Of course not."

Joining the debate was Alice O'Brien, staffing coordinator of the Women's Center. To her, the issue could not have been more clear. Yale Students for Life, she said, had no place in the Women's Center because "they are an educational group concerned with life. That's not exclusively a woman's concern."

Katie Oberlies believes that a consistent ethic of life is of great concern to many women. It is not a concern that is exclusive to women, but it is so compelling, to say the least, that it connects what many women think about, and want to do something about.

"As a pro-life feminist," Oberlies says, "I see abortion inextricably linked to other life issues such as infanticide, euthanasia, capital punishment, nuclear war, and poverty. Just as women were central in the movement to bring about a nuclear freeze, women must be central in the quest to develop a consistent ethic of life."

Members of the Yale Women's Center Coordinating Committee told me that they permitted individuals in Yale Students for Life to come into the Center. But to give space to a pro-life *group* would subvert the principles of the Center.

I can imagine the indomitable Dorothy Day—who fought wars of liberation against the FBI, the national security apparatus, and local sheriffs while also upbraiding princes of her Church for their indifference to the powerless—watching this power play at Yale. And wondering why these young women at this privileged place were so determined to keep other women at the back of the bus. Day did not believe that liberation meant discrimination.

But what about this offer to let the members of the scorned Yale Students for Life into the Center if they come alone, checking their affiliation at the door? That might be fair if the Center allowed no other women's groups to meet there or to have the Center's imprimatur. But there were a number of women's organizations officially part of the Center. Among them: Women's Action Coalition (a pro-choice group) and Yalesbians.

Yale Students for Life, refusing to be segregated, circulated a petition on the Yale campus:

"We, the undersigned, support the effort of Yale Students for Life to become participants in the Yale Women's Center.

"The Yale Women's Center must be open to all women at Yale, regardless of their political, religious or moral beliefs. We urge the Coordinating Committee of the Women's Center to rethink their current position on the right of Yale Students for Life to be a part of the Women's Center.

"We also urge the Yale College Dean's Office to issue guidelines prohibiting inappropriate discrimination by organizations such as the Women's Center, which use Yale facilities and receive Yale funding.

"We, on all sides of the abortion question, believe that the Yale community is made richer and stronger by the diversity of its members. We must not allow some among us to suppress that diversity."

The Yale campus is hardly a cheering section for pro-lifers, but, to the surprise of Yale Students for Life, over three hundred students signed the petition. Many of the signers made clear that they were pro-abortion, but were offended by the banning of these women from a Yale facility because of their views.

At last, a pride of Yale deans assembled to study this matter. Among them were Sidney Altman (then-dean of Yale College) and Patricia Pierce (associate dean and dean of academic life). Both had been much involved in the celebrated case of Wayne Dick. With regard to the segregated and unequal rules of the Women's Center, the deans, particularly Altman, appeared to be more concerned with the protections due dissent than they had been in the Wayne Dick controversy.

On October 23, the *Yale Daily News* carried a story by staff reporter Jack Wills:

"The Yale College dean's office has told the Women's Center that Yale Students for Life must be included among its penumbral organizations.

"According to Cory Morganau, coordinator for publicity and outreach for the Women's Center, the Center had resisted admitting the group in the past because 'the anti-abortion sentiments they seemed to be promoting would have been at cross-purposes with our support of pro-choice.'"

In his story, Jack Wills quoted Dean Sidney Altman: "[The Women's Center] is a facility we provide simply for women to discuss problems and issues as such. As a facility provided by the dean's office, it should be open to all women and all women's groups."

Reacting with relief and pleasure to the decision, Kelly Askew, president of Yale Students for Life, noted: "Until now we have been second-class citizens."

Meanwhile, on October 26, the *Yale Daily News* got to the actual core of the dispute:

"The Yale College deans are at it again, making autocratic decisions without consulting students, a lot of folks were thinking this weekend.

"This time, however, the decision is the right one.

"Last week the administration told the Women's Center that it had to include Yale Students for Life, a student organization that is opposed to abortion. Members of the Women's Center had long resisted such a move.

"The anger of members of the Women's Center is understandable. The Center has long been a political organization with definite objectives—and members deeply committed to those ideas. Their passionate pursuit of these ideas, of the right of women to 'create, act, and achieve freely' is admirable, and laudable.

"Their unwillingness to recognize the validity of ideas different from their own—by not letting pro-life organizations into the Center—is not.

"The Women's Center advertises itself as 'a place for all women … to gather together and to explore the richness and diversity of people's lives' in its statement of purpose. Where is the diversity in attracting only those who agree with your position?

"Moreover, whether the Center has always had a distinct political orientation or not, and whether Yale's administration has 'tacitly approved' that stance by giving the Center space and money for several years, the fact remains that the organization's name is the Women's Center, and that it is university—not privately—funded. Any student at Yale concerned about women's issues, whatever their opinion on those issues, should be allowed the use of the Center.

"Nevertheless, by forcing the Center to admit Yale Students for Life, the administration has taken a stand that it must back with action. If the Center is to be a place, as Dean Altman asserts, 'open to all women,' it must have the space and funding to accommodate them. Three rooms … and $400 a term do not begin to meet these needs."

The argument went on. Linda Anderson of the Women's Studies Department wrote in a letter to the *Yale Daily News:* "Are we to see decisions in the future that allow the KKK to meet at the Afro-American Cultural Center or a neo-Nazi group to meet at the Yale Hillel?"

In answer, Steven Pelkin wrote in the same paper:

"Unlike the KKK's attitude toward blacks or the Nazi's attitude toward Jews, Yale students for Life are not constitutionally antithetical to the existence of women.... The saddest aspect of this dispute is that the Women's Center resistance comes off as liberalism gone astray into radical conservatism. When this happens, the use of all liberalism is cheapened."

The dispute also reflected the lust of certain groups—left, right, or beyond category—to delegitimize all dissent. Dissenters are not seen as individuals, and hardly as human. The members of Yale Students for Life are against capital punishment and euthanasia, as well as abortion. Yet they are compared to the Ku Klux Klan and a bunch of neo-Nazis.

As Elizabeth McCalister—the thunderous pro-life feminist, long active in civil rights and anti-war work—once wrote from prison after damaging some nuclear missiles: "We must widen the frame." Especially, one would think, at a university.

In time, Dean Sidney Altman stated firmly that Students for Life had to be given access to the Yale Women's Center. Altman's successor, Donald Kagan, told me that the access turned out to be short-lived because the membership of Students for Life became largely male.

V

The Pall of Orthodoxy on the Nation's Campuses

Doing in Democracy

> "Free speech to us is just a joke anyways. We don't own any
> major newspapers or radio stations."

There was much celebrating among the peace forces some years ago over the acquittal of Abbie Hoffman, Amy Carter, and thirteen others for blocking a CIA recruiter from appearing at the campus of the University of Massachusetts at Amherst. Forgotten during all the toasts were twelve students at the university who wanted to hear the recruiter on campus.

Their First Amendment right, at a public university, to receive information had found few champions. Even the Civil Liberties Union of Massachusetts was silent, as well as the national office of the ACLU.

I have no doubt the CIA has committed criminal acts. Nor do I object to civil disobedience, having been much influenced by the radical pacifist A. J. Muste, and having engaged in that tactic myself.

146

But shutting off debate is exactly contrary to what A. J. Muste was all about. Such tactics were used at the University of Colorado in Boulder, where stink bombs were thrown into the ventilation systems to gag CIA recruiters and students who had come to hear them. One of the latter noted angrily that the protesters were making decisions for him and he had not given them that power.

The headline in Boston's *The Phoenix,* a sizable countercultural weekly, saluted the Hoffman-Carter triumph as "Doing Democracy." Seen in an egalitarian light, however, prohibiting people from hearing what they came to hear was actually an elitist authoritarianism. The protesters see themselves as more knowledgeable and more humane than the clods lining up for the CIA interviews. And so the clods have to be protected from themselves.

The situation was somewhat different, when, as at Brown University a couple of years before, the administration acceded to a CIA demand that exchanges between its recruiters and critical students be almost nonexistent.

At Brown, it was the university that failed its responsibility of keeping the campus a place of free inquiry. Even under these conditions, however, those who wanted to hear the recruiters had a right to; and the protesters had a right to inform them, in any nonviolent way they could, of what they were not being told. But the protesters had no right to prevent the CIA recruiters from coming to the Brown campus.

There is another argument some of the righteous use to suppress speech. Abbie Hoffman used it in his closing statement to the jury in Massachusetts; and, as quoted in *The Chronicle of Higher Education,* it had also been stated by University of Colorado philosophy professor Ann Ferguson. She says:

"There is a distinction between the rights of free speech and the rights to recruitment on campus.... just as [the university] has no obligation to have vending machines on campus, it has no obligation for organizations to recruit on campus, especially when [they are] breaking the law or violating human rights."

Vending machines don't speak, and recruitment is speech. It is speech when either a public interest or a corporate law firm comes on campus to scout possible recruits. It is speech when the Peace Corps or the Marine Corps comes calling.

Partially echoing Professor Ferguson, Abbie Hoffman told the jury that organizations, "private or public," that break the laws of the Commonwealth of Massachusetts have lost their recruiting privileges on campus.

That took care of the admirable, as I see them, nonviolent direct-action groups that go into missile bases and smash components of nuclear weapons systems. And if an organization of blacks in Roxbury, part of Boston, commits civil disobedience by sitting in at City Hall, none of its members will be able to pass the gates of the University of Massachusetts, according to the rules of Chancellor Hoffman.

At that university, on that occasion, there would have been a free exchange between the protesters and the CIA recruiter. The rules allowed for a real debate. And under those conditions, the students could have demolished him with the facts. But the recruiter never did get on campus because, as one of the students proclaimed, "We are past dialogue."

That is not "doing democracy." That is doing in democracy. A prominent civil liberties lawyer in Massachusetts had sounded fanfares about the "victory" at the University of Massachusetts. I asked him what he thought about the denial of First Amendment rights to those who had wanted to talk to the CIA recruiter. There was a long pause. "I never thought about them," he said.

And, in the last conversation I had with Abbie Hoffman, he genuinely had no idea why I could not share in his victory over the CIA.

"Yes, Virginia, there are racist assholes. And you know what? The Constitution protects them, too."

In June 1991, on the Public Broadcasting System, I was a member of a Fred Friendly seminar on "Safe Speech, Free Speech and the University." We were discussing the rising tide of college speech codes—punishing students for a wide, vague spectrum of "offensive" speech. The session was held at Stanford University, which had enacted a typically slippery code that can ensnare students who have no idea they are breaking it.

There were two Stanford students—and one recently graduated Stanford alumnus—on the panel. Two were black; the other
was Asian-American. All were bright, articulate, and firmly in favor
of punishing speech for the greater good of civility on campus.

During the preceding two years, I had visited over twenty colleges and universities around the country—from Penn State and
Columbia University to the University of Utah and the University of
Tennessee. With some exceptions, I found that minority students—
and women of all colors—do indeed believe that the First Amendment (and its spirit in private institutions) must bend when hate
speech is at issue.

When I tell them that James Madison, the architect of the First
Amendment, intended it to be of most value in times of bitter cri-
sis, they point out, with various degrees of civility, that Madison, a
dead white male, lived in a time of slavery. So he and the First
Amendment are abstractions.

Many white students, faculty members, and administrators are
also convinced that speech must be limited if racism, sexism, and
homophobia are to be extirpated in and out of the classroom. And
that includes the punishment—and if necessary—the banishment
of professors infected with any or all of those viruses.

Indeed—again, with some exceptions—most of the white liberal students who consider themselves activists look at you with genuine puzzlement when you tell them how Oliver Wendell Holmes
described the test of free speech:

"If there is any principle of the Constitution that more imperatively calls for attachment than any other, it is the principle of free
thought—not free thought for those who agree with us but freedom of thought that we hate."

Another abstraction.

These new Jacobins are powered by a genuine faith that they
are working for an undeniable good—creating and sustaining true
equality on campus by eradicating speech that makes minorities,
women, and gays feel unwanted. Convinced that they are occupying the moral high ground, they see their opponents as raising the
issue of free speech as a cover for their own racism, sexism, or disgraceful indifference to these issues.

And they are joined by the undeniably influential editorial

writers of *The New York Times* who—on May 12, 1991—described as "sloganeering" any attempts to criticize "political correctness" on campus. "The real danger," said the *Times,* "is the rising tide of hate."

The *Times* approves of campus speech codes—as if it is essential to curb speech in order to curb bigotry. Educators presumably have no other way to educate students out of what they have learned at home or among poisoned peers.

Underlying this conflict between the relatively few free-speech students and administrators, on the one hand, and the censors-for-the-common-good on the other is a deeper debate: advocates of civil rights verses advocates of civil liberties. It has hardly been mentioned in the abundance of reports on the civil wars on the campuses.

Among the law professors on the Fred Friendly panel were Thomas Grey of Stanford, who is white, and Randall Kennedy of Harvard, who is black. Grey essentially wrote the Stanford speech code, and Kennedy—usually a proponent of free speech and thought—is nonetheless in favor of college codes.

Both Grey and Kennedy served as clerks to J. Skelly Wright on the District of Columbia Court of Appeals. Wright was a courageous, indomitable defender and implementer of civil rights. Both Grey and Kennedy also served as clerks to Thurgood Marshall on the Supreme Court. Marshall, while a consistent advocate of free speech, has been most influential as a paladin of civil rights.

Throughout the country, both on campus and off, there is an intense conflict between civil rights and civil liberties students, administrators, and law professors. In the American Civil Liberties Union—whose national board finally declared its opposition to college speech codes—the legal director, John Powell, who is black, still maintains that a balance has to be struck in these matters between the First and the Fourteenth Amendments. The latter guarantees everyone equal protection under the laws. Powell and the civil rights legions maintain that this means students have to be protected from demeaning and denigrating speech if they are to be—and feel—equal on campus.

This split between civil rights and civil liberties forces has been dramatically evident during debates about college speech codes on various boards of affiliates of the ACLU. Black board members, with exceptions, have called for support of the speech codes. The more fundamental issue—which will be debated for many years to come—is whether the First Amendment goes too far.

A conclusion from this division among people of good intentions is that when the First Amendment is put up against such desirable goals as the control of bigotry, it fades—for many people—in importance.

Furthermore, civil liberties have to do, most of the time, with protections of the *individual* from the government. Civil rights, on the other hand, are usually regarded, and litigated, as *group* rights that the government must implement for individuals. And that, too, is a basic conflict in the battle over curbing speech on and off campus. (With regard to pornography, for another example, these feminists who want to outlaw it base their attack on group rights claiming that pornography debases and degrades women and therefore puts them in a subordinate position in society.)

So, too, with race. On the "MacNeil/Lehrer NewsHour" (June 18, 1991), Professor Molafi Asante, chairman of the African-American Studies Department at Temple University, said:

"You have certainly the individual's right to say whatever he or she pleases to say. I mean, that is fundamental to the Constitution itself. You have the other point to this, of course, which is the collective interest.... What is the collective interest? What is best for the community? What is best for the society? And certainly I think the whole question of insensitivity is basic to this issue. And if an individual is insensitive to his or her peers or colleagues, then I think that certainly the university should be concerned about this."

His approach—more carefully wrought than most—exemplifies the ritual of balancing free speech into the back of the bus. Yet, though free speech is "fundamental to the Constitution itself," when the chips are down, the university must put "sensitivity" first.

By rather lonely contrast, there is the view—and practice—of Yale President Benno Schmidt. The great majority of college presidents have either put a speech code in place as a quick, cheap way of pretending they're doing something about bigotry on campus, or they hunker down and try to avoid the subject. Benno Schmidt continually, consistently, confronts the question of free speech versus the university-as-a-community, a community with its concerns of civility and sensitivity.

On Fred Friendly's Public Broadcasting System program, Schmidt said:

"I take a completely different view of what a university is ... I don't think the university is first or foremost a community. It's not a place, first and foremost, that is about the inculcation of thought [and] habits of mind that I might agree are correct and constructive.

"The university has a fundamental mission which is to search for the truth. And a university is a place where people have to have the right to speak the unspeakable and think the unthinkable and challenge the unchallengeable.

"Now, it's not a place of violence. It's not a place for threats.... There's no place for violence, or threats of it, in a regime of freedom. But beyond that, I think that these [speech] codes make a terrible mistake.... Students think that they are codes about building communities that are based on correct thoughts, and that's antithetical, I think, to the idea of a university."

The group-rights codes have actually succeeded in helping to divide the university into a number of splintered "communities." And contrary to some of what's been written, they have not succeeded—on any campus I know of—in squashing or even intimidating conservative students. (A number of professors who march to their own drums, however, have been bedeviled into dropping courses because of the heat—including classroom disruptions by the ultra-orthodox.)

Conservative students are enjoying their role as champions of free speech, taking great sardonic pleasure in depicting the righteous left as neo-McCarthyites. On many campuses, conservatives—usually with the help of funds from highly conservative foundations—are publishing alternative papers. They tend to be quite lively and witty (humor being in exceedingly short supply among the Jacobins). And these papers take much muckraking pleasure in exposing the surrenders, small and large, of university administrators to the demands of the ultra-orthodox.

Those most stifled by the pall of orthodoxy on campus are students who are liberals but of an independent mind—and moderates. On campus after campus, from Brown to Stanford, I have talked to students who say there are some views they hold—or questions they want to ask—that they no longer bring up in class or in most places outside of class. It's not worth the hassle—or being placed in Coventry. Questions, for example, about affirmative action. How far should it go? Should the progeny of the black middle class get preference? And questions about abortion. Should the father have any say at all in what happens to the fetus?

One brave student at New York University Law School, Barry Endick, actually signed his name a few years ago to a complaint about this bristling orthodoxy in a letter in the law school student publication, *The Commentator.* He told of the atmosphere in the law school created by "a host of watchdog committees and a generally hostile classroom reception regarding any student right of center." This "can be arguably viewed as symptomatic of a prevailing spirit of academic and social intolerance of ... any idea which is not 'politically correct.' ... We ought to examine why students, so anxious to wield the Fourteenth Amendment, give short shrift to the First. Yes, Virginia, there are racist assholes. And you know what? The Constitution protects them, too."

On the other side of the nation, Louis Freedberg, who covers higher education for the *San Francisco Chronicle,* began an article, "A Campus Fear of Speaking Freely" (October 30, 1991):

"The student looked nervously over her shoulder, 'Please don't use my name. There are things you wouldn't want to talk about around certain people.'

"The interview did not take place in the pre-Gorbachev Soviet Union but in Sproul Plaza at the University of California at Berkeley, site of the Free Speech Movement, where students fought for the right of free expression twenty-seven years ago.

"The student's fears reflect widespread apprehension on several Bay Area campuses that certain topics—mainly centering on race relations, feminist issues, and gay rights—are off-limits for open discussion in social situations and even in the classroom.

"Their fears appear not to be a figment of politically conservative imaginations. In an era when issues such as multiculturalism and ethnic diversity have gained ascendancy, even liberal educators concede there is a lack of completely open discussion on many college campuses....

"The students who express these fears are mostly white, but not exclusively so, and tend to be conservative. But some who regard themselves as 'moderates' or 'liberals' also say they feel constrained."

The reporter quotes Devon Courteau, a student who describes himself as a "moderate Republican":

"A lot of times I don't want to speak up in class. Otherwise, I'd have 40 percent of the class on me saying I'm a counterrevolutionary racist fascist. I'm normal. I don't want everyone to hate me for my views."

A twenty-six-year-old graduate student at Stanford University, Alexander Van Dyck, says he is a liberal but on the issue of date rape on campus, among other subjects, he censors himself: "If I were to say something about the rights of the accused, lots of people would see it as an affront."

Deanna Cunningham, a black reporter on the staff of the student newspaper at San Francisco State, noted that there are students who will not let her use their names in the paper: "People are afraid, period. No matter if they have conservative or liberal views.

"In many interviews," the reporter went on, "students talked about being afraid to talk about concerns or ideas that could not remotely be regarded as blatantly racist or sexist. Rather, they are afraid to say anything about a controversial topic that they feel could be misconstrued."

Contributing to this atmosphere of fear of being condemned or ostracized by fellow students are such vivid lessons in the swift application of orthodoxy as Berkeley senior David Allen recalled for the *San Francisco Chronicle*:

In an economics class, black students walked out of the room because a foreign student kept using the term "black" instead of African-American. The black students and the professor had objected, but the foreign student persisted, and so the exodus took place.

Said David Allen: "If you're a white male and you say something, you're wrong. I'd just as soon write my paper and hand it in and not say anything."

A student at San Francisco State, who would not give his name to the *Chronicle*, talked about "an unwritten suspension of free speech," but will not challenge it. "I want to blend in with the community. And nothing I could say would do any good anyhow. It doesn't make sense to go against the grain. It's not that [speech] is controlled by the police, but it's controlled by... our peers."

The story continues: "At Stanford, Kaydee Culbertson, a junior born on an Indian reservation, says students are so careful about saying the wrong thing about native Americans that she has no idea what they are really thinking.

"'*When it reaches the point where sensitivity stifles communication, it has gone too far,*' said Culbertson, who is co-chair of Stanford's Native American Student Association." (Emphasis added.)

And there are law schools with speech codes. The most egregious is that of the New York State University of Law at Buffalo. It begins with an obligatory obeisance to freedom of speech and thought—which it then takes away:

"Every intellectual community worthy of the name thrives on sharp and heated controversy—on the free and full expression of opposing ideas and values; on impassioned arguments for, and equally passionate arguments, against. Given the particular professional skills required for the practice of law, law schools—including this one—especially prize and encourage such unencumbered give-and-take, the more lively and uninhibited the better."

However, "because the common law and two centuries of constitutional tradition have long given American lawyers a special role in assuring fairness and securing equal treatment to all people, our intellectual community also shares values that *go beyond a mere standardized commitment to open and unrestrained debate.* We support the particular values shaped by the special traditions and responsibilities of the legal community to which all of us—students and faculty alike—belong." (Emphasis added.)

Any and all expressions of "bigotry, prejudice and discrimination are abhorrent to these traditions; they not only detract from the person uttering them, but reflect poorly upon the profession as a whole."

Therefore, "by entering law school, each student's absolute

right to liberty of speech must also become tempered in its exercise, by the responsibility to promote equality and justice."

So, with astonishingly imprecise, vague, and overbroad language, the law school faculty goes on to say that it will crack down on any and all remarks directed at another's race, sex, religion, national origin, age, or sexual preference as well as "racist, sexist, homophobic and anti-lesbian, ageist and ethnically derogatory statements." As if that weren't broad enough, also beyond the pale at the University of Buffalo Law School are "other remarks based on prejudice and *group* stereotype." (Emphasis added.)

The sins of bad speech, moreover, will pursue the student after graduation: "Where such acts indicate that a student may lack sufficient moral character to be admitted to the practice of law, the school can and will make appropriate communication to the character and fitness committees of any bar to which such a student applies—including, where appropriate, *its conclusion that the student should not be admitted to practice law.*" (Emphasis added.)

I first learned of this vengeful view of law students' free-speech rights in Buffalo from two students at the law school. Both were members of the conservative Federalist Society. On inquiry, I found that indeed the only students against the policy were also members of the Federalist Society. On the left, the law school chapter of the National Lawyers Guild was all for the restrictive code; and later, the National Lawyers Guild came out for speech codes on all campuses.

Only one professor at the law school criticized the punishment of law students' speech.

Around the country, most law professors—even the First Amendment specialists—have been silent about the speech codes, as well as other strictures on speech in the name of equality. Similarly, many other professors, including liberals, have shied away from any direct confrontations with the ultra-orthodox, even when other professors have been relentlessly attacked because of their heresies.

There is fear among professors on some campuses, fear of being put on a list of undesirables. And in these colleges and universities, administrators do not protect those professors accused of being "racist," "sexist," and so forth.

In March 1991, a reporter for the *Chicago Sun-Times*, Basil Talbott, told of the ordeal of Al Gini, forty-seven, an associate professor at Loyola University in Chicago. He had won three teacher-of-the-year awards.

During a class on business ethics on January 22, 1990, Gini was talking about unethical behavior, and how it can lead to sanctions, including being fired. It has become improper, he said, to call a black person a Negro now. Worse yet, he said—pointing to a student, Sandra Westmoreland—"if I called this student a nigger student and really meant it, it would be grounds for termination."

Gini was trying, he explained later, "to make people realize how wrong it was to use words like that."

After class, Sandra Westmoreland went up to the professor and said she had been offended by his use of the word "nigger." Gini said he had not intended to offend her, but since he had, he apologized.

Three months later, writes Basil Talbott, Sandra Westmoreland "called a press conference to complain that Gini had singled her out as a 'nigger.' She demanded Gini's dismissal. Charges were lodged with the United States Education Department."

Gini was then subjected to investigations conducted by four Loyola University offices and the Office of Civil Rights of the Education Department. Eight months later, the federal investigators ruled that Sandra Westmoreland had not been discriminated against by reason of race. Still, the pressure was on Loyola to get rid of this "racist." The administration did not fire him. He was tenured. But the university, feeling it should do *something*, set up a speech code.

After months of living under suspicion of being a racist, Gini told me that teaching will never be the same for him. "If it were possible, I think I would quit teaching." After twenty-four years as an educator, "I don't feel free in the classroom anymore. And many junior faculty members say, 'If this can happen to him, we're all vulnerable.'"

Sandra Westmoreland still feels very offended. "I felt dehumanized. It came out of the blue in a strong, dominating voice. I don't know his initial intent. I just know how I felt."

Clearly, she had felt vulnerable. The word "nigger" knocked

out of her mind the context in which it was being used. But Al Gini also suffered much pain and anxiety that were entirely unnecessary.

When Westmoreland made her complaint, it should have been easy—through the other students in the room that day—to determine what the professor had actually said. And that should have been the end of it.

"A lot of professors," Al Gini said to me, "are taping their classes" so that they can defend themselves. And not only at Loyola. Also, says Gini, some professors are dropping controversial cases. Also, not only at Loyola.

Harvard law professor Alan Dershowitz—among the boldest and bravest of First Amendment defenders—writes:

"I feel this problem quite personally, since I happen to agree, as a matter of substance, with most 'politically correct' positions. But I am appalled at the intolerance of many who share my substantive views. And I worry about the impact of politically correct intolerance on the generation of leaders we are currently educating."

Leaders will indeed emerge from the ranks of these college and university graduates. Among them will be the lawyers, judges, educators, legislators, and Supreme Court Justices of the future. And the mind-set with which some leave the campus in these years is: some censorship is okay—provided that the motivations are okay.

In the course of a two-year debate on whether Stanford should have a speech code punishing language that might wound minorities, women, and gays, a letter appeared in the *Stanford Daily*. Signed by the African-American Law Students Association, the Asian-American Law Student Association and the Jewish Law Students Association, the letter called for harsh punishment for offensive speech. It reflected the letter and the spirit of a 1989 declaration by Canetta Ivy, black, and a leader of student government at Stanford during the period of the grand debate. Her major was African-American studies, and she intended to go to law school.

"We don't put as many restrictions on freedom of speech," she said, "as we should."

Reading this letter by the rare ecumenical body of law students (so pressing was the situation that even Jews were allowed in), I thought of twenty, thirty years from now. From so bright a cadre of graduates from so prestigious a law school would indeed come some of the leaders of the future.

The debate at Stanford ended when the president, Donald Kennedy, following the prevailing winds, surrendered his previous position that "suppression of free expression inevitably results in assaults on the life of the mind." Stanford adopted a speech code.

The leader of the opposition at Stanford was law professor Gerald Gunther, arguably the nation's leading authority on constitutional law. But Gunther did not have much support among other faculty members, conservative or liberal.

Gunther pointed out during the campus debate that he received his elementary school education in a very small town in Nazi Germany. There his teacher, classmates, and other townspeople would address him as "Judensau" (Jew pig). That, he recalls, was one of the milder ways in which they used to make his day.

Professor Gunther, knowing what constant harassment by vilification feels like, learned, he says, in Nazi Germany and in his life here that it's necessary to denounce "the bigots' hateful ideas with all my power yet at the same time challenge ... any community's attempt to suppress hateful ideas by force of law."

The way to deal with bad speech, Gunther emphasized, is "with more speech, with better speech, with repudiation and contempt."

Before the speech code was voted in at Stanford, Professor Gunther predicted that the university "will be on record as adopting an anti-speech regulation—a hideous precedent for a university that boasts of the winds of freedom and claims to be bound [through a private institution] by the principles of the First Amendment."

The effect of this "hideous precedent" at Stanford and many other colleges with speech codes is the intimidation of a considerable number of students so long as these codes exist.

Jeff Shesol, a graduate of Brown who then became a Rhodes Scholar at Oxford, became nationally known while at Brown because of his comic strip, "Thatch," which, not too kindly, parodied "politically correct" students. At a forum on free speech at Brown before he left, Shesol said he wished he could tell the new students at Brown to have no fear of speaking freely. But he couldn't tell them that, he said, advising the new students to stay clear of talking critically about affirmative action or abortion, among other things, in public.

At that forum, Shesol told me, he said that those members of the left who regard dissenters from their views as racist and sexist should realize that they are discrediting their goals.

"They're honorable goals," said Shesol, "and I agree with them. I'm against racism and sexism. But these people's tactics are obscuring the goals. And they've resulted in Brown no longer being an open-minded place."

At that point, there were hisses from the audience.

A vigorous dissent from political orthodoxy on campus was made by a black Harvard Law School student during a debate on whether the law school should start punishing speech. A white student got up and said that the codes are necessary because without them black students would be driven away from colleges and thereby deprived of the equal opportunity to get an education.

The black student rose and said that the white student had a hell of a nerve to assume that he—in the face of racist speech—would pack up his books and go home. He'd been all too familiar with that kind of speech all his life, and he had never felt the need to run away from it. He'd handled it before, and he could again.

The black student then looked at his white colleague and said that it was condescending to say that blacks have to be "protected" from racist speech. "It is more racist and insulting," he emphasized, "to say that to me than to call me a nigger."

But that would appear to be a minority view among black students. Most are convinced they do need to be protected from wounding language. On the other hand, a good many black student organizations on campus do not feel that Jews have to be protected from wounding language.

There is a strong strain of anti-Semitism among some—not all, by any means—black students. They invite such speakers as Louis Farrakhan, the former Stokely Carmichael (now Kwame Toure), and such lesser but still burning bushes as Steve Cokely, the Chicago "activist" who has declared that Jewish doctors inject the AIDS virus into black babies. That distinguished leader was invited to speak at the University of Michigan.

And the black student organization at Columbia University brought to the campus Dr. Khallid Abdul Muhammad. He began his address by saying: "My leader, my teacher, my guide is the honorable Louis Farrakhan. I thought that should be said at Columbia *Jew*niversity."

Many Jewish students have not censored themselves in reacting to this form of political correctness among some blacks. A Columbia student, Rachel Stoll, wrote a letter to the *Columbia Spectator:* "I have an idea. As a white Jewish American, I'll just stand in the middle of a circle comprising... Khallid Abdul Muhammad and assorted members of the Black Students Organization and let them all hurl large stones at me. From recent events and statements made on this campus, I gather this will be a good cheap method of making these people feel good."

At UCLA, a black student magazine printed an article indicating there is considerable truth to the *Protocols of the Elders of Zion,* a venerable anti-Semitic tract. For months, the black faculty, when asked their reactions, preferred not to comment. One of them did say that the black students already considered the black faculty to be insufficiently militant, and the professors didn't want to make the gap any wider. Like white liberal faculty members on other campuses, they want to be liked—or at least not too disliked.

Along with quiet white liberal faculty members, most black professors have not opposed the speech codes. Many believe, along with many of their white counterparts, that minority students have to be insulated from barbed language. They do not believe that an essential part of an education is to learn to demystify language, to strip it of its ability to demonize and stigmatize, and that the way to deal with bigoted language is to answer it with more and better language of your own.

Consider University of California president David Gardner. He imposed a speech code on all the campuses in his university system. Students are to be punished—and this is characteristic of the other codes around the country—if they use "fighting words," derogatory references to race, sex, sexual orientation or disability.

The term "fighting words" comes from a 1942 Supreme Court decision, *Chaplinsky* v. *New Hampshire,* which ruled that "fighting words" are not protected by the First Amendment. That decision, however, has largely been in disuse at the High Court for many years. But it is thriving on college campuses.

In the University of California code, a word becomes a "fighting" word if it is directly addressed to "any ordinary person." (Presumably, extraordinary people need no protection.) These are the kinds of words that are "inherently likely to provoke a violent reaction, *whether or not they actually do*." (Emphasis added.)

Moreover, he or she who fires a fighting word at any ordinary person can be reprimanded or dismissed from the university because the perpetrator should "reasonably know" that what he or she has said will interfere with the "victim's ability to pursue effectively his or her education or otherwise participate fully in university programs and activities."

Said Gary Murikami, chairman of the Gay and Lesbian Association at the University of California, Berkeley: "What does it mean?"

A principle had been set at these and many other campuses that free speech is merely situational, merely relative to each administration's fears of the time. As times change, as college presidents and other administrators change, as the hegemony of the right replaces that of the left, so will the extent of free speech.

This was a point of danger finally recognized by the national board of the American Civil Liberties Union when, after months of dissension among some of the affiliates—and on the national board itself—a vote was taken in October 1990.

The first speaker in that climactic session—and I think she had a lot to do with making the final vote against speech codes unanimous—was Gwen Thomas.

A black college administrator from Colorado, she is a fiercely persistent exposer of racial discrimination.

She started by saying, "I have always felt as a minority person that we have to protect the rights of all because if we infringe on the rights of any person, we'll be next.

"As for providing a nonintimidating educational environment, our young people have to learn to grow up on college campuses. We have to teach them how to deal with adversarial situations. They have to learn how to survive offensive speech they find wounding and hurtful."

* * *

A particularly illuminating civil war concerning free-speech rights on campus was fought for much of 1990 within the board of the Civil Liberties Union of Massachusetts (CLUM). It helps illuminate many other civil rights versus civil liberties battles around the country—conflicts that will increase and deepen in the decades again because there is a fundamental conflict between the two movements on the issue of whether "hate speech," hurtful speech, offensive speech should be protected under the First Amendment.

One of the combatants was the Reverend Grayson Ellis-Hagler, pastor of the Church of the United Community in Roxbury and a forceful citywide civil rights activist. He described the opposing camps as the First Amendment Absolutists versus the Frontierists. Hagler is a firm member of the second group.

The Frontierists, he said, are those who understand that this is a class as well as a constitutional issue. There are those—blacks, for instance—who have had different experiences than the "purist" civil libertarians. And the board members in his own camp, Hagler added, include people who identify with those experiences. Not only black members of the board, but also white lawyers from community and legal services organizations, and gays and lesbians.

Those, moreover, whose direct experience has included vicious verbal harassment, Hagler said, certainly know that "we need to send a clear message that some forms of speech cannot be permitted." And not only on college campuses. Hagler was opposed to the ACLU defending, in 1977, the Nazis who wanted to demonstrate in Skokie, with its large Jewish population—including Holocaust survivors.

Among those on the other side is Natasha Lisman, a Boston attorney. During one of the debates she was told, "You don't know what being black is like." Calmly, she answered, "You don't know what being a Jew in Poland was like." Lisman lived in the Ukraine and Poland as a child, and fleeing the Nazis, came to America. She, it should be noted, thought the ACLU had no choice but to defend the Nazis in Skokie even though it was "a very painful" decision.

"The First Amendment," she says, "is the source of all our rights. So, yes, so far as it's possible, I am an absolutist."

On the staff of CLUM is Nancy Murray, who is in charge of one of the more far-reaching efforts in the country to involve teachers and students in making the Bill of Rights much more than ceremonial words on paper. Yet, to my surprise, she was not aligned with the First Amendment Absolutists. "The situation on college campuses," she told me, "is such a cause of concern that we have to try something. There are too many crazy people saying all kinds of things."

I reminded her that John Adams and the Federalists felt that way when they instituted the Alien and Sedition Acts only seven years after the First Amendment and the rest of the Bill of Rights had been ratified.

Nancy Murray closed the conversation by saying, "We need to find out what the blacks think." Which blacks? A number of blacks on the CLUM board are in agreement with Hagler, but there is also Byron Rushing, a forthright member of the Massachusetts House of Representatives. "Bigotry thrives underground," Rushing told me. Rather than curb speech on campus, he added, "we need to train people in how to deal with free speech." Without hesitation, he calls himself "a First Amendment Absolutist," having learned the crucial importance of free speech, he points out, during his work in the civil rights movement in the 1950s and since. And Rushing notes how effective Martin Luther King, Jr., and Malcolm X were by vigorously exercising their freedom of speech.

I asked Natasha Lisman why she thinks there has been such a division within the ACLU—not only in Boston—on whether free speech is too costly when it comes to minorities and women being verbally harassed on college campuses. While the Michigan and Wisconsin affiliates supported the free-speech position—and have brought lawsuits against colleges with speech codes—the Northern California affiliate has actually promulgated its own college code that does not so much "balance" the First Amendment as twist it badly out of shape.

"I think," Natasha Lisman said, "there has been an influx into the ACLU of what are essentially representatives of other interest groups. They arrive with the agenda of those groups and look on the ACLU as a vehicle for promoting that agenda.

"What they do outside the ACLU is admirable, as are the

groups they belong to. But the ACLU has its own agenda, and a basic part of it is protecting everyone's First Amendment rights.

"From 1972 on, I have seen a gradual politicization of the ACLU—a blurring of distinctions between civil liberties and other good causes."

For example, she said, a proposal was made at an ACLU Biennial meeting that the organization give the rights of the poor special priority. Who among the decent folk of the nation—and especially of the ACLU—would not vote for that? But should that policy—phrased in so broad and vague a way—be an ACLU policy?

Is every right of the poor a *civil liberty?* The poor are entitled to many civil rights *from* the government. They are also entitled to *civil liberties.* New York federal district judge Leonard Sand was correct—though overruled by higher courts—in deciding that the First Amendment includes, as a civil liberty, the right to beg in the subways. It's not only a form of speech, it's a form of political speech. The beggars are calling attention to a certain inequality of incomes in the society.

But if the ACLU is going to take on all the *rights* as well as the *liberties* of the poor, it will be a muddle of an organization.

When that proposal—that the ACLU should give the rights of the poor special priority—was made at the biennial meeting, Natasha Lisman rose and offered a counterproposal:

"The ACLU should make a special priority of those civil liberties that have a special impact on the poor."

Her counterproposal narrowly passed.

In many ways, the ACLU can—and has been—of use to the poor without diluting its particular reason for being. Lawsuits, for example, barring welfare agents' invasions of clients' privacy through surprise visits have been litigated by the ACLU. And a continuing battlefield—the provision of due-process hearings before governmental benefits can be cut off—has long been an ACLU priority.

"The ACLU," Natasha Lisman emphasizes, "is such a unique organization. It does not represent any particular interest groups." It exists to protect individual liberties from the government—from those of high school journalists resisting a principal's censorship of their articles to a person on death row who has been denied adequate counsel below.

"Because the ACLU represents a set of principles rather than interest groups," says Lisman, "it is foolish and irresponsible to undermine the organization by diminishing its uniqueness."

The battle to attenuate that uniqueness is continuing in affiliates around the country, particularly in—but not limited to—California. The Civil Liberties Union of Massachusetts ultimately decided—by a very narrow margin—to oppose campus speech codes. But as the composition of the board changes and as other issues arise—for instance, the conflict between certain sexual harassment laws and the First Amendment as interpreted by the courts—there is no guarantee that the principle of free speech will continue to prevail in that affiliate of the ACLU. Or in others.

Free expression in the workplace, as on many college campuses, can be limited if it creates a "hostile working environment." That has come to mean *Playboy* pinups on locker doors or dormitory doors, as well as language that offends some women, though not all. Where is the line to be drawn between harassment and protected speech? Two federal circuit courts have decided that the line is to be determined by the perspective of "a reasonable woman"— not, as in the past, by the perspective of "a reasonable person."

Thus the First Amendment has been balkanized by gender. As previously in obscenity cases, the First Amendment has been balkanized by making local community standards determine the outcome of obscenity trials. Thus there is no longer a national standard for the First Amendment when it comes to obscenity. With regard to sexual harassment charges, only one gender—female— determines the outcome in an increasing number of jurisdictions.

And, as Wayne State University law professor Kingsley Brown points out, "You've got employers censoring workers' speech out of fear of being held liable by the government. It is still government censorship, even if the mechanism is a civil action by private parties."

Clearly, *physical* sexual harassment is not protected. Nor is verbal harassment when it is a threat, including threats of loss of a job or reduced status if the women does not yield to sexual demands. But when the speech encompasses pinups on the wall that offend some women or when jokes are told that offend some women— should there be punishment? There often has been.

Robyn Blumner, executive director of the Florida affiliate of the American Civil Liberties Union, is clear about this kind of speech in the workplace.

"Even sexists," says Blumner, "have free speech rights."

Federal and state workplace rules concerning sexual harassment have been incorporated in many college speech codes—particularly sanctions for the creation of a "hostile atmosphere" for students. These codes began in response to crude racial and sexist scrawls and epithets. But indeed, the language being punished increasingly extends to any words that create a "hostile atmosphere" or any language that "involves an express or implied threat to an individual's academic efforts." Whatever that may mean.

There is also the damaging effect of these "protective" regulations on the very people who are insisting they be safeguarded. Malcolm X used to talk about the need to learn how language works, how to dissect it, how to use it as both a shield and sword. Above all, he felt, blacks should not be fearful of language. They should not let language intimidate them but rather fight back— when words are used against them—with more powerful words of their own.

If you read Malcolm X's collected speeches and listen to his recordings, it's clear he was an extraordinarily resilient, resourceful, probing master of language. How did he get that way? Not by being protected, as he grew up from wounding language.

I've debated black students about these speech codes. They are highly articulate and quick with polemical counterpoint. And I've asked them why on earth they are running away from language when they could turn a campus into a continuing forum on racism—by using the vicious racist language directed at them to illuminate and counter what's going on at that college.

Moreover, by turning to censorship instead of challenge, these students can well cut off speech they themselves want to hear.

On ABC-TV's "Nightline" several years ago, debating Barbara Ransby (a Ph.D student in political science at the University of Michigan and a founder of the United Coalition Against Racism there), I asked her response to this quite possible scenario. A group of black students invite Minister Louis Farrakhan to lecture in a political science class at a college. He comes and says, "I want to explain what I said about Judaism being a gutter religion. I meant it, but I want to give you the context in which I said it."

There are Jewish students in the class, and they claim that—according to the university's code, which includes outside speakers—Farrakhan has created a hostile atmosphere for them.

In my view, I said, Farrakhan ought to be able to speak anywhere he chooses, and certainly on a college campus. So long as the students have the right to question him and argue with him, they'll have something to gain from the experience. But under some of the speech codes at more and more colleges, Farrakhan—having created a "hostile atmosphere"—would quite likely not be permitted on campus again.

Is that what the black students pressing for speech codes want? To have black speakers they invite on campus rejected because of what they say and how they say it? Do women students want radical feminist Andrea Dworkin barred because of possible charges that she creates a "hostile environment" for nearly all men?

Also overlooked by students especially concerned with artistic expression is that a "hostile atmosphere" can be created by a painting or a piece of sculpture because obviously, "expression" can be graphic as well as verbal. When the University of Wisconsin's speech code was being debated before the state's Board of Regents, E. David Cronon, dean of the university's Madison College of Letters and Sciences, testified that the code would indeed chill students' rights to artistic expression.

Furthermore—and this is a poignant dimension of the rush to virtuous censorship—it won't do a bit of good. Let us suppose these codes were in place on every campus in the country. Would racism go away? Racism would go underground, in the dark, where it's most comfortable.

The language on campus could become as pure as country water, but racist *attitudes* would still fester. The only way to begin to deal with racism is to bring it out in the open—not pretend it has been scared away.

According to the Stanford speech code, "Speech or other expression constitutes harassment by personal vilification if it:

"a) is intended to insult or stigmatize an individual or small number of individuals on the basis of their sex, race, color, handicap, religion, sexual orientation, or national and ethnic origin; and

"b) is addressed directly to the individual or individuals whom it insults or stigmatizes; and

"c) makes use of insulting or 'fighting' words or nonverbal symbols."

But how is it determined that someone *intended* to insult? Intended to "stigmatize"? Which "nonverbal symbols" can get you suspended or expelled?

And what is a "fighting word"? To whom?

Fighting words, according to the Stanford speech code, are words that by their "very utterance inflict injury or tend to incite to an immediate breach of the peace."

That hardly helps prevent you from getting into trouble unless you know, in advance, what particular set of words will ignite each particular student. The least Stanford can do is interview every student and then provide all students with a list of the specific words that will cause each of the other students to explode.

And, by the way, when does a word "tend" to incite? What measuring rod is used?

Stanford prides itself on being one of the elite universities, and yet the majority of its faculty and students have yet to learn so basic a historical truth as this—stated by Eleanor Holmes Norton, former chairwoman of the federal Equal Employment Opportunity Commission:

"It is technically impossible to write an anti-speech code that cannot be twisted against speech nobody means to bar. It has been tried and tried and tried."

Steven Rohde, a constitutional lawyer, who was co-chairman of the Los Angeles Bar Association Bill of Rights Bicentennial Committee, points out:

"A university campus, whether public or private, must be a place for robust, wide-open, and free discussion. Students bring to college all their prejudices, their fears, their doubts, their misconceptions. If they spend four years cooped up under repressive regulations, they might well dutifully obey the rules, offend no one, and leave with all their prejudices, fears, doubts, and misconceptions firmly intact.

"Punishing bigoted speech only treats the symptoms, not the disease. It often creates martyrs and drives them underground, where they attract new, impressionable followers on the pretext that they themselves [the bigots] are an 'oppressed minority,' whose 'truths' are so powerful they are banned by the Establishment."

Stanford has also gone beyond the continuous chill of speech codes to institute a policy that some people should have more free speech than others.

One of the leading supporters of the speech police is law professor Robert Rabin, who was chairman of the Student Conduct Legislative Council. During the debate in the Faculty Senate on whether the Stanford speech code should pass, Professor Michael Bratman offered Rabin a hypothetical:

In an angry exchange with a white student, a black student calls him a "honky son-of-a-bitch." I assume, said Bratman, that language would be prohibited under the speech code.

"No," said Professor Rabin. As reported in a document of the Student Conduct Legislative Council, Rabin went on to explain that the proposed Stanford speech policy takes the position that the white majority, as a whole, should not be protected from hateful speech as much as groups that have suffered discrimination.

Accordingly, "calling a white a 'honky,'" said Professor Rabin, "is not the same as calling a black a 'nigger.'"

The Stanford Sliding Scale of Free Speech.

Under this notion that some people deserve more free speech than others, punishment of bad speech is measured by which *groups* have been more discriminated against over time. Members of those groups get extra free speech.

One assumes, then, that a student charged with anti-Semitism will get a heavier punishment than someone who has insulted a WASP because Jews, Lord knows, have been discriminated against more often and certainly longer than any other religious group.

As for ethnicity, what about Native Americans? In view of the length of their brutal mistreatment here, shouldn't they be allotted more free speech than any other ethnic group? What about Italian Americans? They claim, with justification, that they have historically been the targets of deep-rooted discrimination. Will a Stanford student suffer greater punishment for insulting an Italian Catholic student by contrast with making a Presbyterian feel bad?

A visiting professor at the Stanford Law School at the time was Mari J. Matsuda, who has become one of the more renowned advocates nationally of a sliding scale of free speech. According to *The New York Times* (June 29, 1990), she says—as paraphrased by the *Times*—that "freedom of speech should belong mainly to the powerless rather than those in power. In her view, the powerless are all members of 'outsider' groups, like blacks and women, no matter how affluent and influential the individual."

In some circles, this is a version of "communitarianism." (The values and priorities of the community—or a group—should prevail over an "undue" emphasis on individual rights and values.) Individual free-expression rights, therefore, can and should be subordinated to the group equality rights of minorities, women, gays and lesbians, *et al.*

Individuals *within* those groups are expected not to engage in deviationism (i.e., individualism). If they do, the time may come when—as in the French Revolution or Arthur Koestler's *Darkness at Noon*—they may find themselves weightless.

I have confronted group-think in many settings, including the offices of the *Village Voice,* but the most striking occasion was on a visit to Michigan State University in November 1990. I was to lecture on the widening spectrum of attacks on free expression—from speech codes on college campuses to arrests of rap groups to Jesse Helms's profound interest in federal funding of the arts.

There were about four hundred in the audience, forty of whom were ardent members of a group called As One. They were black, they were disciples of Minister Louis Farrakhan, and they were as disciplined as the forces of the late Rabbi Meier Kahane.

In the previous February, Minister Louis Farrakhan had spoken at Michigan State. Among his other customary tributes to Jews, he had charged that Jews control the music business and exploit black artists:

"You suck the blood out of the black community and you feel we have no right, now, to say something about it?"

Farrakhan had also indicted Jews for controlling movies and

the curriculum of the public schools, thereby creating stereotypes of blacks that psychologically damaged them.

Not surprisingly, the Hillel Jewish Center on campus protested. The center did not contest Farrakhan's right to speak at Michigan State but insisted that "Jews on campus also have a right to call attention to anti-Semitism when it manifests itself at the university." Hillel was also still engaged, at the time I came, in a campaign to get the president of Michigan State to say publicly that Farrakhan had, in parts of his talk, been anti-Semitic.

As One, meanwhile, had been resolutely defending Farrakhan and attacking Hillel. In a letter to the director of Hillel, As One said: "There is a new Black Man and Black Woman on the scene, and we will not bow down to you or anyone else out of fear or ignorance.... Farrakhan is our Hero, our Black uncompromising, unvanquished champion.... *We will not turn our back on him.*" (Emphasis added.)

That night, As One had seated themselves in two solid blocs, one directly in front of me, the other to the right. As the evening went on, I noticed that each of the blocs had a conductor who signaled various group punctuations to my talk—vivid disbelief; shouting indignation; scorn at such misinformation about Farrakhan, the etymology of anti-Semitism, everything.

For a while, however, As One was relatively quiet, though very watchful. They vocally approved my observation that bigotry is based on ignorance, as is illustrated by the fact that most white college students know little or nothing about the Holocaust of the Middle Passage, during which untold numbers of Africans died before they could become slaves in America. They were packed so tightly together that some killed those next to them so they could breathe. And I added that there is widespread ignorance among students of such vital figures of black liberation in the 1960s as Robert Moses, the Reverend Fred Shuttlesworth, and Fannie Lou Hamer.

I even heard a few cheers from As One at this point. Those were the last of the evening. They became surly and silent when I started talking about Malcolm X, whose killing, after all, had been celebrated by Farrakhan, for Malcolm X had turned on the Nation of Islam and the Honorable Elijah Muhammad.

I told of my friendship with Malcolm during his last years and of the card he had sent me—and a good many others—on his way back from Mecca. The card said that while he still believed that blacks must organize themselves separately for political and economic power, he could now see that some whites could be allies.

Looking at As One, I spoke of the time that Malcolm, not long before his death, was lecturing at a college and during the question period, a black student rose and delivered a blistering philippic against Jews. Every Jew in creation, past and present.

Before the student finished his steaming statement, Malcolm—walking past the moderator, who had been fielding the questions—strode to the microphone and told the student that he was speaking out of sheer bigotry, the same hurtful and harmful ignorance that is so often aimed at blacks. That sort of thing, Malcolm said, doesn't help anybody.

Members of As One shook their heads, not in approval. They were even less taken with a passage from one of Malcolm's last speeches—in February 1965:

"We don't judge a man because of the color of his skin. We don't judge you because you're white, we don't judge you because you're black. We judge you because of what you do and what you practice.... So we're not against people because they're white. We're against people who practice racism."

There was some applause from the general audience, but not from As One. Everything they did, including silence, was in unison.

I then went into a discussion—with specific references to sections of his resounding speeches—of Minister Farrkahan's anti-Semitism. For the rest of the night, as the college paper, *The State News,* reported the next morning, "Hentoff was in the center of the ring of fire."

The conductors of the two blocs of As One began to get busy when I quoted from a 1990 interview with Farrakhan in the *Washington Post* in which he said a Jewish film producer had told him that a small group of men meet regularly in an apartment on Park Avenue, or in Hollywood, to "study trends" around the world. And if they don't like what's happening, "we produce [the trends we want] through our writers and people that have the same mind, and [we] move the people according to the way we feel the trends should be."

Who was "we"? "Well," said Farrakhan, "when [the film producer] said, 'We,' and he was Jewish, I do not know whether he meant a small group of Jews or a small group of like-minded people."

Either way, Farrakhan made clear he believed this conspiracy out of James Bond does indeed exist, and he has believed it for the past twenty years. He cited no evidence except for this alleged conversation with the Jew who, rubbing his hands, could have come right out of the *Protocols of the Elders of Zion*.

I looked at his devoted followers in the audience and suggested that if they tried some independent thinking, they might come to the conclusion that theirs is an eerie leader indeed.

What I did not say, and should have, is that looking at the individual students in As One, it seemed to me that many, maybe all, had as yet unknown capacities, as individuals, for liberating their intelligence so they could free themselves from the bondage of this group-think.

By this time, they were shouting, loud enough to try to drown me out. It worked once, but the moderator, with indignant allies from the rest of the audience, restored just about enough order so I could be heard.

I called Farrakhan a classic anti-Semite—someone who not only hates Jews but believes, or says he or she believes, that Jews create baleful conspiracies that ensnare millions of innocent people.

Now they were yelling, and I was not surprised. Farrakhan's Nation of Islam is unusually sensitive to what they consider to be the proper usage of "anti-Semite." So was Malcolm X when he was a commander in the army of Elijah Muhammad. He and I were on a television panel once and somebody charged Elijah Muhammad with being anti-Semitic. Malcolm smiled condescendingly: "The honorable Elijah Muhammad is by belief a Muslim, and many Semites practice that religion, so how can he be an anti-Semite?"

After ten minutes of variations on the clamorous theme "Look in your dictionary!" I made a concession to As One, but they did not appear to take kindly to it. "I will grant your point," I told them, "and instead I'll say that Minister Farrakhan is anti-Jewish."

And so the rest of the evening went—with the rhythms of a heavy sea. As I watched the members of As One, being true to their name as they responded to every signal of their conductors, I remembered seeing the tumultuous followers of Ariel Sharon. They would make him King of Israel. Who knew what each of them was before *they* became as one?

Looking at *this* As One, I wondered if any of them could be the next Malcolm X. After all, he used to be one of them.

At one point, the conductors gave the signal to walk out, and they all did, going as far as the stairs leading to the exits. But somehow, they couldn't go all the way. They lingered, listening to the dialogue between me and the rest of the audience. And they went back to their seats. A somewhat hopeful sign, I thought.

As if to indicate that their seeming lack of resolve actually meant they had decided to stay in order to demolish the speaker, they became louder and angrier than ever.

One of their members, tall and straight, rose to address me accusingly. With his white shirt and bow tie, he looked like a member of the Fruit of Islam, Farrakhan's palace guard.

"I am not anti-Semitic. I am not anti-Jewish," he declared. "I am a soldier of Allah! And you have to pay the price when the day comes!"

Rousing cheers from everyone in As One.

I asked him what the price will be.

"When the truth comes"—he pointed at me—"you will be eaten—if you do not submit to the voice of the truth as spoken by the voice of Louis Farrakhan!"

"*Sieg heil!*" an unruly member of the opposition in the audience shouted.

(Not long before, students at Trinity College in Hartford had told me that in a speech, before my coming there, a lieutenant of Farrakhan in that region had called me "the anti-Christ." But he gave no job description. And I wondered what a Muslim was doing invoking the specter of the anti-Christ.)

At Michigan State, I told As One of my designation as the Anti-Christ. They neither affirmed nor denied.

There were Jewish students in the audience. I knew they were Jewish because they said so. Some demanded of any supporters of Farrakhan that they renounce their leader's anti-Semitism. (They got nowhere.) And there were Jewish students who agreed with As One that racism was the fundamental issue at Michigan State, as everywhere else. They knew they could not sit with As One, although they'd have liked to, but they wanted As One to know they were with them in spirit.

Toward the end of the evening, a young woman, white, stood up, denounced me for typical white obtuseness, and praised As One. They did not object. Another young woman, white, stood up and said, loud and clear, from the back of the auditorium:

"The people that are ignorant are the people that are bigots. The people that are ignorant can only see and think in generalizations. They only see blacks as a so-called minority."

As One was nodding in concurrence.

The young woman continued: "I am a Jew. Nobody knows that by looking at me so I hear worse things than blacks do—because the bigots don't know they're talking about me. I hear all the time that Jews should be driven out of every country.

"I'M PISSED OFF! I'm a Jew and I'm a good—a DAMN GOOD—person! I don't care what anybody is. If you're a good person, you'll be my friend."

There was big applause. The biggest of the night. None from As One. But they didn't condemn her.

The conversation resumed, heated and full of generalizations. As One joined in again.

When it was all over, a soft-spoken black man—who I later found out was the faculty adviser to As One—came up on stage and said to me, "I want to thank you for the way you handled the evening. I want you to know it was nothing personal." He paused. "It was only business."

It took me a while to figure out what he meant. As One is in the business of being loyal to and protecting Minister Farrakhan. I was some white Jew who was attacking Farrakhan. An itinerant speaker, identity unknown and immaterial. Since they didn't know me, there *was* nothing personal about that evening so far as As One was concerned.

And that was too bad. For me and for them, too. I can still see, from time to time, those staring, angry faces, like marionettes. And those faces, on campuses around the country, are not only black.

* * *

Some college administrators consider it their responsibility to erect walls between "vulnerable" students and those who would hurt them with speech, including symbols.

For instance, James T. Laney, president of Emory University, wrote proudly in *The New York Times* of the philosophy of official suppression of speech on that campus:

"I would suggest that when a fraternity sells T-shirts that portray women in demeaning sexual positions, at least one of the historic exceptions [to free speech] applies."

Women students, then, are incapable of creating their own T-shirts portraying men in demeaning sexual positions? Women students are incapable of using their own ways of expression to teach those fraternity dolts something they never learned at home or at school?

Laney and the other college presidents who have decided that it is vital to suppress speech in order to nurture learning and civility on campus are saying to the bigots: We can't cope with your disgusting speech. Your words are too powerful for us administrators and faculty. We don't know how to educate against it. So, in this place of higher learning and free inquiry, we're going to shut you up. We are too weak in resources, skills, creativity and courage to do anything else.

As for the students who demand censorship of speech, Nadine Strossen, president of the American Civil Liberties Union, makes this point:

"There is an ultimate irony in the 'politically correct' movement. To think that granting the oppressive, as they say, power structure the additional power [of punishing 'offensive' speech] will improve the lot of the oppressed strikes me as politically naïve." And that power, as Benno Schmidt says, becomes open-ended.

In 1952, a majority of the Supreme Court upheld—in *Beauharnais* v. *Illinois*—a conviction for group defamation, for offensive speech against blacks. Beauharnais, who headed a white supremacist group, had published a leaflet calling blacks, all blacks, rapists and robbers. The 5–4 decision has not been overruled in succeeding years, but is no longer an active element in the Court's reasoning.

William O. Douglas dissented in *Beauharnais*, saying: "Today a white man stands convicted for protesting in unseemly language against our decisions invalidating restrictive covenants [forbidding the sale of homes to blacks]. Tomorrow [under the precedent set by the Court today], a Negro will be hauled before a court for denouncing lynch law in heated terms."

In another dissent in the same case, Justice Hugo Black said:

"If there be minority groups who hail this holding as their victory, they might consider the relevancy of this ancient remark: 'Another such victory and I am undone.'"

The "rules and prohibitions" enacted by two universities to punish offensive speech have been struck down on First Amendment grounds by federal district courts.

First to be declared unconstitutional was the University of Michigan's. These were some of the reasons:

In a class on entrepreneurship, as part of a public-speaking exercise, the professor told each student to compose a limerick and read it aloud. One student made fun, in his limerick, of the alleged homosexuality of a well-known athlete.

Another student in the class who did not think it was funny filed a complaint against him for violating the university's "Policy on Discrimination and Discriminatory Harassment." The policy—a response to racist and anti-Semitic remarks on the campus radio station—provided punishments for "any behavior, verbal or physical, that stigmatizes an individual on the basis of race, ethnicity, religion, national origin, sex, sexual orientation, creed, ancestry, age, marital status, handicap, or Vietnam-era veteran status."

The student who wrote and read the offending limerick quickly apologized. But more was required. He had to attend a gay rap session and write a heartfelt apology in the *Michigan Daily*, the student newspaper.

He signed his statement of penance: "Learned My Lesson." As a federal judge noted later, although the University of Michigan is a public university, "No discussion of the possibility that the limerick was protected speech (under the First Amendment) appears in the file or in the administrator's notes."

Also at the University of Michigan, a file was opened on a black student. He was attending an orientation session of a preclinical dentistry class. By widespread reputation the class was regarded as the toughest course a second-year dentistry student could take.

At the orientation session, intended to answer any apprehensions felt by prospective students, the black student said that he heard minorities were not fairly treated in the course and accordingly had a very difficult time. He had heard this from, among others, his roommate, who was black.

Later, a minority professor who taught that particular course heard what the student had said. The professor filed a complaint against him under the university's speech code. What the student had said, the professor charged, was unfair and would damage her chances for tenure.

The black student's "rehabilitation" began with counseling sessions in which he was stripped of his illusion that the university is a place of free speech and free inquiry. He then had to write a three-page letter of apology to the professor in charge of the course. Although all he had done was ask a question based on what former black dentistry students had told him, the young man confessed, in his letter of apology, that he should have verified the allegation before giving voice to it.

But to verify what he had heard, he had to ask about it at the school, and that is exactly what he was doing at the orientation session, held precisely for that purpose—to answer fears and concerns of students thinking of taking the course.

It should be noted that a primary purpose of the University of Michigan's speech code—as it is at a number of colleges and universities—was to make black and other minority students feel more at home on campus.

In September 1989, the University of Michigan's restrictions of speech were declared unconstitutional by Federal District Judge Avern Cohn. The American Civil Liberties Union had brought the suit, and its volunteer attorney was Wayne State University law professor Robert Sedler. The latter is not only an ardent civil libertarian but also has one of the most distinguished records in the country as a litigator against segregation and other forms of racism.

Judge Cohn let stand the university's prohibition of physical acts of harassment. It was the prohibition of speech that he found violative of the First Amendment because, he said, the speech section of the code was too vague and overly broad. At the end of his decision, Judge Cohn quoted Thomas Cooley, a former justice of the Michigan Supreme Court and professor at the University of Michigan Law School.

In a treatise on constitutional law, Cooley had noted that even if speech "exceeds all the proper boundaries of moderation, the consolation must be that the evil likely to spring [from the deeply offensive words] will probably be less, and its correction by public sentiment more speedy, than if the terrors of the law were brought to bear to prevent the discussion."

In October 1991, another lawsuit by the ACLU against a college speech code—the University of Wisconsin's—was successful. (Neither the University of Michigan nor the University of Wisconsin appealed.)

The Wisconsin rule prohibited speech intended to create a hostile learning environment. Such speech was described as language that demeaned other students' race, sex, religion, color, creed, disability, sexual orientation, or ancestry.

Federal District Judge Robert Warren made a number of illuminating points in his decision. For instance:

"[The University of Wisconsin] Board [of Regents] states that the proscribed speech lacks social utility because it (1) is not intended to inform or convince the listener; (2) is not likely to form any part of a dialogue or exchange of views; (3) does not provide opportunity for reply; (4) constitutes a kind of verbal assault on the person to whom it is directed and (5) is likely to incite [violent] reaction...."

Disagreeing, the court said: "Most students punished under the rule are likely to have employed comments, epithets or other expressive behavior to inform their listeners of their racist or discriminatory views [and to attempt] to convince their listeners of their positions."

As for the charges that the prohibited speech is not likely to be part of a dialogue and so does not provide opportunity to reply, the court said that those criteria come from the tradition that speech should be part of a "marketplace of ideas." Generally, said the court, that's true, as is its corollary that speech is free so that the truth [through dialogue] will eventually be known. (Accordingly, racial epithets are hardly conclusive to dialogue.)

However, Judge Warren emphasized, "the Constitution does not make the [eventual] dominance of truth a necessary condition of freedom of speech. To say that it does would be to confuse an outcome of free speech with a necessary condition for the application of the [First] amendment."

With regard to the rationale that says speech codes are necessary to prevent verbal assaults on students, Warren said that the Supreme Court has already ruled that such speech is protected under the First Amendment.

That is, speech such as "snakes," "slimy scum," "atheist Communistic Zionist Jews"—all of these words were used by Arthur Terminiello in a Chicago speech. Speaking for a majority of the Supreme Court, Justice William O. Douglas ruled in *Terminiello* v. *Chicago* (1949) that "a function of free speech under our system of government is to invite dispute. It may indeed best serve its high purpose when it induces a condition of unrest, creates dissatisfaction with conditions as they are, or even stirs people to anger. Speech... may have profound unsettling effects as it presses for acceptance of an idea."

As for the fifth argument for speech codes presented by the University of Wisconsin, Judge Warren dealt with the claim that the speech prohibited by the university has no First Amendment value because of its tendency to incite violent reaction.

"The Supreme Court," said Warren, "has clearly defined the category of speech which is unprotected due to its tendency to incite violent reaction. This category of speech is limited to speech which by its very utterance tends to incite an immediate breach of the peace." In sum, "fighting words." But the University of Wisconsin's rule was so broad, said the judge, that it also encompassed speech that did not incite violent reaction and therefore is protected by the First Amendment.

But what about a claim by the university made by its chancellor, Donna Shalala, many minority students, black state legislators, members of the Board of Regents, and a good many members of the faculty? Judge Warren addressed that claim directly:

"The Board [of Regents] first asserted compelling interest in increasing minority representation to add to the diversity of the University of Wisconsin System campuses. Increasing diversity is 'clearly a constitutionally permissible goal for an institution of higher education.' However, the UW rule does as much to hurt diversity on Wisconsin campuses as it does to help it. By establishing content-based restrictions on speech, the rule limits the diversity of ideas among students and thereby prevents the 'robust exchange of ideas' which intellectually diverse campuses provide."

Summing up, Judge Warren said: "There exist many situations where, in the short run, it appears advantageous to limit speech to solve pressing social problems such as discriminatory harassment. However, the suppression of speech, even where the speech's content appears to have little value and great costs, amounts to governmental thought control."

Thought control can come from other sources than the government or the administration of a university, public or private. In October 1991, conservative students at the University of Wisconsin in Milwaukee tried to hold a "pro-American" rally that would include a debate on the university's cultural diversity policy that requires every student to take a three-credit course in minority studies.

As reported by the *Milwaukee Journal*, one of the speakers at the rally—a radio talk-show personality, Mark Belling—was prevented from speaking. "The protesters," said the *Journal*, "many from minority student groups, mobilized partially in response" to the advertised debate on the mandated course in minority studies. Some of them threw coins, hard candy, and otherwise silenced Belling.

Particularly illuminating was the reaction to the prior restraint on the speaker by the assistant chancellor for student affairs, William Mayrl. The *Milwaukee Journal* reported: "Campus administrators cautioned against reading too much into what they see as spontaneous violence at a rally.... Mayrl saw the protest as 'an old-fashioned disruption of a speaker' rather than a plan to silence debate over minority studies."

After all, said the university's Chancellor, John Schroeder, Mark Belling's use of "stereotypes and insults" on his radio show made that sort of reaction inevitable.

The chancellor of a major university thereby legitimized the "heckler's veto." If what a speaker says inflames an audience, the speaker should expect to be silenced. Under First Amendment case law, however, it is the responsibility of the authorities—in this case, Chancellor Schroeder—to protect the speaker and enable him or her to keep on speaking.

Not all the students at the conservatives' rally came to commit violence. But few saw anything wrong in the silencing of the man from the radio show. The *Milwaukee Journal* interviewed Svovata Edari, president of the Black Student Union. "Minority students," Edari said, "don't need to hear views such as Belling's spoken again.

"Free speech to us is just a joke anyways," Edari said. "We don't own any major newspapers or radio stations. How can you have free speech when you can't be heard?"

By continuing to speak. As Malcolm X and Frederick Douglass and William Du Bois and Martin Luther King had. They were heard. Obviously, there is an enormous imbalance in institutional resources, but no change in the laws would have been accomplished without free speech and assembly—including speech by those who did not own any major newspapers or television stations.

In 1966, for instance, the case of 187 black high school and college students came before the Supreme Court (*Edwards v. South Carolina*). While on a march against racial segregation in Columbia, South Carolina, they were arrested and convicted of the crime of breach of the peace. The Court reversed the convictions on the ground that their rights to free speech, free assembly, and the freedom to petition for redress of grievances had been violated.

Writing for an 8–1 majority, Justice Potter Stewart noted that when the students had been told to disperse or be arrested, they did not disperse but instead "sang patriotic and religious songs.... There was no violence or threat of violence on their part....

"They were convicted upon evidence which showed no more than that the opinions which they were peaceably expressing were sufficiently opposed to the views of the majority of the community to attract a crowd and necessitate police protection."

The state, Justice Stewart emphasized, is not permitted "to make criminal the peaceful expression of unpopular views.... As in the *Terminiello* case, the courts of South Carolina have defined a criminal offense so as to permit conviction of the petitioners if their speech 'stirred people to anger, invited public dispute, or brought about a condition of unrest.' A conviction resting on any of these grounds may not stand."

By bringing this case, the black high school and college students helped strengthen precedents that have brought about more demonstrations, more speech, in protest against discrimination and other forms of injustice.

But Svovata Edari, president of the Black Student Union at the University of Wisconsin/Milwaukee, sees free speech as a "joke" so far as "minority students" are concerned. They don't own major newspapers or radio stations, so what's the sense of exercising their free-speech rights? And since free speech is a joke for minorities, then it's only fair to suppress the speech of those with whom they disagree, like the conservative talk-show host.

It's like William Roper—in Robert Bolt's *A Man for All Seasons*—saying to Sir Thomas More in astonishment: "So.... you'd give the Devil benefit of law!"

"Yes, what would you do? Cut a great road through the law to get after the Devil?"

"I'd cut down every law in England to do that."

"Oh? And when the last law was down, and the Devil turned round on you—where would you hide, Roper, the laws all being flat? This country's planted thick with laws from coast to coast—man's laws, not God's—and if you cut them down—and you're just the man to do it—d'you really think you could stand upright in the winds that would blow then? Yes, I'd give the Devil benefit of law, for my own safety's sake."

Those of all colors who would beat down the devils of racism, sexism, homophobia, *et al.* by suppressing speech will, of course, find that, inescapably, they will have no protection when the winds blow.

Back at Stanford, in the student newspaper, there was a letter from a senior, Dan Blumenthal, who is majoring in computer science and Japanese. Writing about a black fraternity, he said:

"A flier for this weekend's Omega Psi Phi Jamm '91 party

depicted a black man holding in one hand a sword and in the other the severed head of a white man.

"If this had been reversed, it is obvious what would have happened. It would have been universally condemned, it would have made the front page of *The Daily* and the fraternity would no doubt have been placed on probation. But here (I am only guessing) it is seen as a very PC expression of rage at white oppressors.

"The fact is, however, that racism is racism. Showing a white man killed by a black is hardly constructive.

"Incidentally, although I find this flier racist and offensive, I believe in the fraternity's right to publish it. I simply find it sad that so many people who should be working to fight racism are so busy propagating it."

In the October 28 issue of *The Stanford Review*, an independent conservative newspaper, Michael Newman noted: "The university has striven to protect the legitimate rights of minorities to be free from harassment, but in doing so it has granted them harassment privileges which the majority does not enjoy. How else can one explain the university's lack of response to the Omega flier? The same officials who went ballistic after [a] Beethoven [poster] received an afro have no problem with this violent expression of hate... These guys should lose their house, even if they don't have one."

Those responsible for the flier with the severed head of a white man could not be charged under Tom Grey's interpretation of the Fundamental Standard. The flier was not directly addressed to an individual or a small number of individuals. A few months later, another incident occurred which received much greater attention and created a greater anger on campus, but it too was not punishable under the speech code.

A law school student was accused of screaming homophonic epithets at a Resident Fellow at Otero Hall. The comments included: "Faggot! Hope you die of AIDS!" and "Can't wait 'til you die, faggot!" The issue initially became clouded when the Resident Fellow told the *Stanford Daily* that he thought the comments "were about me, but they were not spoken to me." They had been aimed at his cottage. Furthermore, he said, he is not homosexual. The Dean of Students, Michael Jackson, said while university officials wanted to prosecute the vilifier, it couldn't be done because the epithets were not hurled face-to-face. Tom Grey disagreed. The architect of the code said, "Yelling at the door knowing that the person is there" is just a like a face-to-face encounter. It's harassment, said Grey, "as long as the words were *intended* to be communicated to a particular person."

This confusion did little to support the contention of Stanford's Judicial Affairs Officer, Sally Cole—before the code had been adopted—that "if people know what the rules are, then they needn't be concerned about inadvertent violations."

There was yet another problem about dealing with the incident at Otero Hall. The alleged target of the homophobic slurs was not a student. He was a Resident Fellow. Therefore, said Grey, the speech code did not apply because "under the harassment aspect of the standard, only students are protected."

The Dean of Students, Michael Jackson, was not particularly concerned about whether the perpetrator could be formally prosecuted. "People need as much latitude as possible in their speech," he told the *Stanford Daily*. "I am exercising my speech to say that I object to the way in which [the student] spoke out." And, he added, the community ought to be informed. "If 25,000 to 30,000 people know that you said something like that, you're probably being punished."

Meanwhile, Judicial Affairs Officer Sally Cole was troubled about the narrowness of the Tom Grey speech code especially because it applies only to students. The Otero incident, she said, might call for rewriting and broadening the code. But Cole also thought it useful to encourage public discussion of what had happened. A public forum, she said, "may be more effective than a confidential process that nobody ever hears about." It was her hope that "people view it as a positive example of an appropriate way to respond to conduct that cannot be legislated by a judicial process." University officials agreed, and that is how the Otero incident first became widely public.

The result as recorded in a front-page headline in the *Stanford Daily* was that the law student's "Comments on 'faggots' [was] derided across University." Third-year law student Christy Haubegger said, "Everyone is taking care not to make him a First Amendment martyr. But we do want people to know we find the comments really offensive. He has held himself out as an example of the Law School, and we want to diassociate ourselves from that."

More than 400 law school students, faculty, deans and staff signed a petition that appeared as a half-page advertisement in the *Stanford Daily*. "An Open Letter to the Stanford Community" said: "We members of the staff, faculty and student body of Stanford Law School were saddened, angered and embarrassed to learn of the expressions of hatred that were inflicted on this campus on January 19. We have been reminded that ignorance can survive education and escape formal repercussions. But as members of this community, we condemn bigotry in any of its forms."

Paul Brest, dean of the law school, said that the advertisement "seemed just the appropriate way for the institution to respond— not with official sanctions nor with vituperations, but just by putting itself on record."

Second-year law student Suzanne Woods said, "I think there's a remarkable consensus that he has the right to make the comments—no one has denied that. But we are exercising our free speech rights to tell him that we—as a community—don't share his views."

Meanwhile, a move had already been underway on campus to do away with the Tom Grey speech code. The impetus initially came from the federal district judge in Wisconsin declaring that university's code unconstitutional. John Overdeck, one of the four presidents of the student body—the Associated Students of Stanford University—co-authored a bill to that effect.

"I think it's dawning on people again," Overdeck told the *Stanford Daily*, "to what extent [the Grey interpretation] is a severe limitation on free speech. I don't feel confident enough in the University to place in their hands the ability to restrict constitutional rights."

Tom Grey answered by saying that whatever happened in Wisconsin did not apply to Stanford because the University of Wisconsin is public, Stanford is private, and therefore the First Amendment has no official standing at Stanford. Professor Gerald Gunther, not surprisingly, disagreed. He reminded the community that the university had always been proud of its commitment to the First

Amendment, even though it was not legally obliged to pay it any attention. Therefore, said Gunther, the Wisconsin decision "deserves careful study." Douglas Bone, a graduate student senator in the Associated Students, added: "I don't think that Stanford should take away rights that are available to other students elsewhere."

The student senate passed the bill opposing the "fighting words" restrictions on speech but the measure's future is uncertain because it cannot take effect unless it also is approved by the Stanford Conduct Legislative Council (six professors, five students and the Dean of Students) that affirmed the original Tom Grey restrictions on speech. Whether the Grey interpretation is overturned or not, the incident at Otero Hall appears to indicate that many on campus prefer an open discussion of hurtful speech than its suppression by sanctions. In a November 1991 editorial, the *Stanford Daily* emphasized: "Hate speech is abhorrent—but freedom of expression must be maintained in a university."

"We have ex-slaves in this class who should know about— and celebrate—the Thirteenth Amendment."

Of all the stories I've covered concerning the ascent of the relentlessly orthodox on or off college campuses, one of the most dismaying has been the initiation into modern times of Murray Dolfman, legal studies senior lecturer at the Wharton School, University of Pennsylvania.

These events began in February 1985, but to this day, President Sheldon Hackney of the University of Pennsylvania says—through a spokesman—that Dolfman was treated fairly in view of his remarks in class which, the university points out, grievously offended black students.

At the time of the incident, Dolfman had been a part-time lecturer in the Legal Studies Department for twenty-two years. He is a practicing lawyer in Philadelphia but, as he has told me, he likes to teach. And he teaches so well that even the university committee that found him guilty of "offensive speech" noted that no previous complaint had ever been made against Dolfman. It also noted that he was an "extremely popular teacher" with "outstanding course evaluations," and that students competed vigorously to get into his classes.

So what did Dolfman do to create a campus-wide demonstration against him—led by black professors and students—in which one distinguished black academic charged that Dolfman had turned his classroom "into a cesspool"?

What had Dolfman done to lead the university's Committee on Academic Freedom and Responsibility (strangely named in this case) to condemn him for behavior that should not take place at the University of Pennsylvania?

Murray Dolfman teaches the way Charles Kingsley (portrayed by John Houseman) taught in the television series "Paper Chase." He makes demands of his students. He challenges them. He will single out a student—of whatever color or creed—and drill him in a point of law or a section of the Constitution. If you come unprepared to Dolfman's class, you are in peril.

On the fateful day that was to make Murray Dolfman a pariah on the University of Pennsylvania campus, he was lecturing about personal service contracts. Dolfman was making the point that no one can be forced to work against his or her will—even if a contract has been signed. A court may prevent you from working for someone else so long as the contract you signed is in effect, but, said Dolfman, there can "be nothing that smacks of involuntary servitude."

Okay, said the professor, where does this concept come from in American law? Silence. Finally, a student screwed up his courage and said, "The Constitution?"

"Where in the Constitution?"

Silence.

Dolfman finally told them where it came from—the Thirteenth Amendment. "What does that Amendment say?" he asked.

No one knew.

Dolfman often tells his students, "We will lose our freedoms if we don't know what they are." He tried to bring in a personal note. As a Jew, he said, and as an ex-slave, he and other Jews begin Passover every year by celebrating the release of Jews from bondage under Pharoah.

"We have ex-slaves in this class," Dolfman said, "who should know about—and celebrate—the Thirteenth Amendment."

Dolfman later told me, "I used that approach because I wanted them to think about that Amendment and know its history. You're better equipped to fight racism if you know all about those post–Civil War amendments and civil rights laws."

He started asking black students in the class if they could tell him what's in the Thirteenth Amendment. None could.

The Thirteenth Amendment, he said, provides that "neither slavery nor involuntary servitude... shall exist within the United States."

He asked a black student to stand and read the Amendment and to repeat it.

Four black students later complained to higher authorities that they had been hurt and humiliated by the way Dolfman had taught them the Thirteenth Amendment. They resented being called "ex-slaves." Furthermore, they said, why should they be grateful for an Amendment which gave them rights that should never have been denied them—and that gave them little else?

They had made none of these points in Dolfman's class.

Three of them later went to see Dolfman. He said he certainly had not meant to offend them and apologized if he had. He added that he should have said "descendants of slaves" rather than "ex-slaves." The students did not accept his apology.

Charges were filed, and university committees conducted a probe. One thing they came up with was that Dolfman had always taught this way. He had always zeroed in on students, not only blacks, to force them to think. But the university had to set an example—all the more since there were rising black-Jewish tensions on campus on other matters. A sacrifice was needed, and who better than Dolfman? He was part-time, without a contract, and without a union.

Dolfman's class was disrupted on February 13. Seven days later, there was a rally at which Houston Baker, Albert M. Greenfield Professor of Human Relations and director of the Center for the Study of Black Literature and Culture, declared:

"We have people here who are unqualified to teach dogs, let alone students, and they should be instantly fired."

Four days later, a vigil and rally took place in front of the home of the president of the university. According to the *Daily Pennsylvanian,* Professor Baker thundered: "We are in the forefront because some asshole decided that his classroom is going to be turned into a cesspool.... This administration is bull shit." To spell Professor Baker and other speakers, recordings of speeches by Martin Luther King and Malcolm X were played. And Ralph Smith, associate professor in the law school, declared, "Dolfman must go!" Both professors are black.

The Black Student League called Dolfman "a racist," adding "we will not be satisfied until we are convinced that actions such as those undertaken by Senior Lecturer Murray Dolfman will NEVER, NEVER take place again at this university."

University president Sheldon Hackney did not defend academic freedom, free inquiry, common sense, or Murray Dolfman. And Dolfman said to President Hackney: "If a part-time professor can be punished on this kind of charge, a tenured professor can eventually be booted out, then a dean, and then a president."

Having no epaulets that could be stripped from him, Dolfman had to make a public apology to the entire university. It was, he told me, a forced apology. He also had to attend "a sensitivity and racial awareness" session, sort of like a Vietnamese reeducation camp. But that wasn't punishment enough. He was exiled from the campus for a year. A good many of the faculty, black and white, was sorely disappointed. They thought he should be fired.

June Axinn, professor of social work and former Faculty Senate chairman, observed that the punishment was fair. "They found that Mr. Dolfman made racist remarks and was insensitive, and I hope an educational institution would find a way to educate him."

It is worth noting that, so far as I can find out, none of the law school professors, including those specializing in civil liberties, defended Dolfman. Nor did the liberals elsewhere on the faculty. If they had, they might have been called racists!

Nor, I might add, did the American Civil Liberties Union of Pennsylvania get involved. But other ACLU affiliates are likely to have defended Dolfman's free-speech rights.

I have left out one of the charges leveled against Dolfman. It was held against him that he had told a black student to change his pronunciation from "de" to "the." He also corrected the speech of white students, and had routinely instructed students to omit the repetitive "you know" from their ways of speech, and to get their hands out of their pockets when they talk. But it was the changing of "de" to "the" in the black student that offended the University's Academic Freedom and Responsibility Committee.

When Dolfman was finally permitted to teach again, he took his students—as he had previous classes—to hear oral arguments in Pennsylvania's Supreme Court. On that day, the diction of one of the lawyers was so bad—full of "deses" and "doses"—that the students found it difficult to concentrate on his argument.

When they were outside the courtroom, Murray Dolfman told the class, "Now you see why I stress the need to speak well."

The lawyer in the courtroom who had been using all those "deses" and "doses" was white.

Later, when Louis Farrakhan was invited by black groups to speak at the University of Pennsylvania, the student newspaper urged that the invitation be withdrawn. President Sheldon Hackney demurred: "Open expression is the fundamental principle of a university," he said.

VI

Speech Wars Among Women

"No one can make you feel inferior without your consent."

At Arizona State University, Nichet Smith—a junior majoring in justice studies—was going with three friends to visit a student in the Cholla Apartments on campus.

The four women, all of them black, stopped suddenly in front of the door of one of the rooms. On it was a flyer:

WORK APPLICATION

(Simplified form for Minority Applicants).

The next line said: BLACK APPLICANTS—It is not necessary to attach a photo since you all look alike.

Among the questions on the form were:

NUMBER OF CHILDREN CLAIMED FOR WELFARE

NUMBER OF LEGITIMATE CHILDREN (if any)

LIST APPROXIMATE ESTIMATE OF INCOME AND INDICATE SOURCE—THEFT:—WELFARE:—UNEMPLOYMENT

MARITAL STATUS:—COMMON LAW:—SHACKED UP:—OTHER

"It hurt real big-time," Nichet Smith said. "I wonder how many people actually feel that way."

Along with hurt, there was rage. The four black women went to the resident adviser at Cholla and said they intended to confront

193

the students who had put that poster on their door. And that is just what they did.

The women, it should be emphasized, did not turn to the administration to "protect" them. They did not demand that Arizona State's anti-harassment speech code be invoked. (The code is as afraid of free speech as all of its many equivalents around the country.)

The four black women, powered by their own anger, knocked at the door of the apartment and found one of its inhabitants, who assured them he'd had nothing to do with putting up that flyer. And yes, he understood why they were so furious and yes, yes, he would take it down right away.

It didn't end there. The four women spread the word and were the main force in organizing and leading an open meeting the next evening at the Cholla Apartments. About fifty students, half of whom were white, showed up. One of the whites on hand, Tami Trawhells, said: "It's offensive for me as a white person because it looks like all white people feel that way."

Also present was Charles Calleros, a laid-back, shrewd assistant dean of the law school and a professor there. Some of the students wondered why the hell the administration—rather than letting the four women do it—had not ordered the poster taken down.

Arizona State, however, is a public university. And so the First Amendment applies. Calleros carefully explained to the students that the First Amendment protects even the most offensive speech. Furthermore, the rules of the Cholla Apartments make it clear that students living there can post whatever they like on their doors. There was no constitutional way, therefore, for officials of Arizona State to rip that flyer from the door.

The four black women, however, are not agents of the state, and so they got it done.

Professor Calleros pointed out—as the women had already demonstrated—that the First Amendment did not prevent anyone offended by the poster from telling the offending students and anyone else how they felt about it.

The four women delivered that message very clearly. And repeatedly. And black students organized a rally and a press conference, along with an evening program at Cholla on African-American history. Rather than rhetoric, the evening was focused on a compelling Public Broadcasting program about the black lawyers, headed by Charles Houston of Howard University Law School, who fought to end segregated schools during the twenty years preceding *Brown* v. *Board of Education.*

There were also a march and rally and a session organized by student members of the NAACP at which race relations at Arizona State were forcefully discussed before a hundred or so students. A strong thread through all these discussions was the need for more multicultural education at Arizona State. Not propaganda in the guise of education, but the real stuff.

As for the black women, one of their themes, as described by Charles Calleros, was:

"They expressed pride in being identified not just as persons but as black women; yet they demanded that others recognize that each of them is unique rather than a collection of stereotypical physical and emotional characteristics."

An obbligato to these dialogues on campus—sparked by the Work Application poster—was a stream, sometimes a torrent, of letters in the college paper, the *State Press.*

One of the letters ("names withheld upon request") read:

"We would like to extend our sincerest and deepest apologies to anyone and everyone who was offended by the tasteless flyer that was displayed on our front door.... and was mentioned on the front page of the *State Press....*

"We did not realize the hurt that would come of this flyer. We now know that we caused great distress among many different people and we would again like to apologize to whomever was offended."

When I was at Stanford a couple of months later, I told the Arizona State story to a number of black and Latino students, many of whom believe that speech codes—including severe punishments for offensive speech—are necessary to protect them from racists and sexists on campus.

I told them what the four black women at Arizona State had done about the flyer on the door and what happened afterward. At the meeting on campus, the four women had emphasized that at first—when the pain of seeing that flyer hit them—they felt like victims. But after confronting the perpetrators of the flyer and then creating much of the momentum for what followed at the university, they no longer felt like victims. They now felt empowered.

Speech codes, on the other hand, weaken those they ostensibly protect by not enabling them to protect themselves.

Charles Calleros made another useful point. Because they were not punished, those who were responsible for the flyer were not—he emphasized—turned into "First Amendment martyrs." Had they been made into martyrs for free speech, much attention would have been diverted from the racism on campus and how to deal with it.

As for the students who had put that flyer on their door, Charles Calleros tells me that some time later, the director of the residence hall came into their room and saw two of them watching a program on Martin Luther King with great interest.

Some of the most lasting education takes place outside the classroom. As, for further instance, what happened during a student rally where a student of color recalled what Eleanor Roosevelt once said:

"No one can make you feel inferior without your consent."

Those four black women not only refused to consent but made those who tried to make them feel inferior recognize where the sense of inferiority properly belonged.

In April, Arizona State's chapter of the NAACP presented its annual Image Awards to those students "who exhibit positivity where negativity once prevailed."

One of the recipients of the award had helped bring Malcolm X's daughter to campus. Other winners included the four black women who had refused to be victims of racism.

But still, the University Student Code—which was *not* invoked by the self-empowered four black women—remains in effect. It includes speech as a form of harassment, and the term "harassment" is so broad and vague that the code is in contempt of the First Amendment. Professor Calleros is trying to "improve" the code but does not understand that the only way to protect free speech—as Justice William Brennan told me in an interview after his retirement—is to abolish *all* speech codes. Not "improve." Abolish.

In a letter to the president of the university—published in

April in the *Devil's Advocate,* the law school student newspaper—
Mark Morita took a scornful look at the code, which reads:

"It shall be a violation of university policy for any faculty member, staff member, administrator or student to act on the basis of another's status, with the purpose or effect of creating an intimidating, hostile, or offensive working, residential, or educational environment. Status means race, sex, color, national origin, religion, age, sexual orientation, handicap, or Vietnam-era status."

The way to deal with this impenetrable fog, says Morita, is "get rid of it." And he cited the "chilling effect" of the Correctness Code:

"Last semester, during Ethnic Food Day, I jokingly suggested forming a White Men's Law Student Association, so we could serve baloney on white bread with mayonnaise! My companions, with genuine fear in their eyes, hushed me up. 'Don't even make jokes,' they whispered. 'If someone hears you, you could get into big trouble.'"

Also in the *Devil's Advocate,* there was a letter by Arizona State law professor Fernando R. Teson about the dangers of speech codes to free expression:

"... Every week I hear colleagues in different parts of the country tell me that they prefer to conduct their classes in a bland and noncontroversial manner because they just don't want the headache of having to defend themselves against... zealots."

Professors also need to be empowered themselves.

"A duel between symbols I hate"

> If all of mankind, minus one, were of one opinion, and only
> one person were of the contrary opinion, mankind would
> be no more justified in silencing that one person, than he, if
> he had the power, would be justified in silencing mankind.
> —JOHN STUART MILL

Seeing Robert Bork on C-Span, I heard him say that freedom of speech means written or oral speech. It doesn't mean symbols. If the Framers had wanted to include symbolic speech, they would have said so.

Bork is not alone in this view. His is no longer the mainstream interpretation of free speech, but some constitutional scholars and even judges still put symbols in the back of the First Amendment bus. The Supreme Court barely protected symbolic speech in the flag-burning cases, but Justices Brennan and Marshall have left the Court, and so there is no telling how it will rule in the future on whether symbolic speech is protected by the First Amendment.

Meanwhile, symbolic speech remains deeply important to many people. In his enduring book, *Freedom Spent* (Little, Brown; paperback), Richard Harris wrote:

"For many people, symbols provide the only means of expressing their deeper feelings, and the visible manifestation of the invisible—an engagement ring, a flag, a beard...a crucifix, a pair of blue jeans—often expresses more in an instant for and about them than their words or acts ever could....

"[T]he innate power of symbols that can arouse the most passionate feelings of reverence, hope, and love in one person can arouse equally passionate feelings of scorn, fear, and hatred in another."

This is the story of just such a clash—the most bitter, complex, personal clash of symbols in a good many years.

In February 1991, Brigit Kerrigan, twenty-one, a pre-law senior at Harvard who is devoted to southern history, hung a Confederate flag from her fourth-floor window at Kirkland House.

Why? Out of regional pride, she said, but she also enjoyed sticking it to what she described as "Harvard's Northeast liberal establishment." Whether she thought of how black students would react is unknown.

Kerrigan was, however, clearly aware of certain terms very much in use at college campuses.

"If they talk about diversity," she told Carol Stocker of the *Boston Globe*, "they're gonna get it. If they talk about tolerance, they better be ready to have it."

While some students supported her right—as symbolic speech—to fly the flag of the Confederacy, there was a great deal of outraged, prolonged, and vehement opposition.

Protest marches took place; furious letters appeared in the various student publications; forums were held; and there was both local and national media attention.

Some of Kerrigan's hardest times were at Kirkland Hall, where she lived. Her fellow students had a fiery session with her, and even the faculty house masters wrote a letter to each member of "the Kirkland House community" that further inflamed the posse going after Kerrigan—determined to force her to pull the damn flag down.

Instead of agreeing with John Stuart Mill, James Madison, Thomas Jefferson, and Dr. Kenneth Clark that freedom of speech is indivisible, they treated Brigit Kerrigan as if she had a most disgusting infectious disease.

Reported in the *Boston Globe,* the letter from these Harvard faculty members said: "We empathize with those for whom public display of the Confederate flag is a source of pain.... [S]ince Bridget [*sic*] is unwilling to join this community spirit by removing her flag, we shall try to concentrate our attention on the positive qualities and personalities among us, set aside our sadness over this situation, and move forward with confidence that the action of one individual need not undermine all that is admirable about this House."

Obviously, the faculty in residence at Kirkland House consider freedom of expression to be "admirable" only so long as it is their own and only so long as it does not embarrass them. So much for Benjamin Cardozo's radical notion that freedom of speech "is the indispensable condition of nearly every other form of freedom."

Kerrigan, because of her notoriety, was the subject—or rather, target—of a full-page profile in the *Harvard Crimson.* The indefatigable reporter, as the *Boston Globe* noted, "dug up the fact that she was the driver in a car accident that killed her best friend when she was in the twelfth grade."

"It broke my heart," Kerrigan told *Globe* reporter Carol Stocker. The disclosure, she said, was irrelevant to the free-speech battle, but so painful that she thought for a while of taking down the Confederate flag. But she didn't because to do so would be "caving in to terrorists."

Meanwhile, Jacinda Townsend, a nineteen-year-old Harvard junior from Kentucky, was infuriated by the Confederate flag. She is black, has a photograph of Malcolm X on the wall, and has a lot of courage.

"Even though I know there's no one waiting for me with a

rope," she told Carol Stocker, "the sight of that flag is very frightening to me. It's a violent flag." It is a symbol of genocide to her, Jacinda Townsend emphasizes. "I don't see it so much as a part of free speech, but as a threat of violence."

Jacinda Townsend decided to get that flag down. First, she spray-painted a Nazi swastika on a white bed sheet, and hung it out of her window. With the swastika blowing in the wind, she thought, the administration would be so outraged it would order her to take the sheet down, but it would also order the terribly offensive Confederate flag to be removed.

When students left angry messages about the swastika on her answering machine, she would leave a return message telling the callers to get in touch with the dean and ask him to *make* her take down the swastika.

The administration did not oblige. The then-president of Harvard, Derek Bok, declared that the display of both highly offensive symbols was "insensitive and unwise," but added that Harvard's commitment to free speech prevented the banning of either form of expression "simply because [they offend] the feelings of many members of the community."

Jacinda Townsend's swastika finally did get hauled down. Jewish students were very, very offended. Townsend hadn't anticipated that reaction because "I had never met a Jewish person before I came to Harvard. I just thought of the swastika as a symbol offensive to me and to everyone." But not of particular offense to Jews.

The Black Student Union had been having discussions with Harvard/Radcliffe Hillel, and finally some members of the BSU went to Jacinda Townsend and asked her to take down the swastika lest it exacerbate black-Jewish relations on campus.

She didn't want that disintegration to happen. "It would be a real pity if that broke out," she said, "since that wasn't the intent." She was annoyed, however, with the Black Student Union because it had hurt her by denouncing her unfurling of the banner with the swastika. "They didn't have to endorse it," she said in the *Boston Globe*, "but they shouldn't have condemned it because we were all working for the same end goal." In any case, she took the swastika down.

Brigit Kerrigan's Confederate flag, however, kept flying until graduation week was over.

Both Brigit Kerrigan and Jacinda Townsend intend to practice law. (Kerrigan entered the University of Virginia Law School that fall.) Kerrigan is not likely to practice the kind of law Jacinda Townsend wants to engage in. Kerrigan was a founder of a conservative publication at Harvard that wrote satirically of homelessness, feminism, and affirmative action.

Townsend is going to be a lawyer back in what she calls "the New South." As the *Boston Globe* describes her vision, "she wants it to be a place where it is easier to be black, where the flags that are flown are ones 'we can all get behind.' And where symbols of hate are not tolerated, even at the expense of free speech."

With regard to hate speech, including symbols, Jacinda Townsend agrees with many college students I have talked to in recent years on campuses all over the country. They think hate speech of any kind should be punished. Often, the subject of the homegrown Nazis who wanted to march in Skokie, Illinois, in the 1970s comes up. (There were many Jews in Skokie, 7,000 of whom were survivors of the Holocaust.)

Says Jacinda Townsend: "I don't think the Nazis should have been allowed to march in Skokie." In that respect, she joins a majority of Americans of all backgrounds, ages, and classes. They would also agree with her about the Confederate flag at Harvard.

At one point in the duel of the hate symbols, Brigit Kerrigan appeared on "CBS News" and said: "If it takes a Confederate flag to stand for freedom, that's the way it's going to have to be."

And when speech—and the symbols of speech—appear to be opposed to free expression, they must be protected. For as long as such messages are openly seen and heard, they can be defeated.

VII

Law Schools That Require Loyalty Oaths

"The legal problem was an affront to our law school's values and thus there was no need for further debate."

In law schools, a particularly challenging way of learning what it's going to be like outside, in the arena, is participation in moot courts. Students brief cases and participate in oral arguments before judges who are lawyers, actual judges in the community, and, once in a while, justices of the United States Supreme Court.

You may have seen student moot court competitions on C-Span being judged by, among other visitors from the High Court, Antonin Scalia and Anthony Kennedy. Scalia's sardonic machine-gun questions are just about as daunting as those with which he assaults lawyers before the Supreme Court. A law student who can hold Scalia to a draw has little to fear from judges he or she will have to deal with in the decades ahead.

New York University Law School—one of the nation's best— has a prestigious moot court program. There are schoolwide competitions and national tourneys in which NYU students compete.

In 1990, however, a fierce debate took place at NYU Law School—among students and faculty—as to whether the choice of a legal problem for the fall's moot court cases was too "offensive" to be argued at all.

The debate at NYU reminded me of the ACLU's Jewish attorney David Goldberger, who defended the American Nazis who wanted to demonstrate in Skokie, Illinois. He found their ideas profoundly "offensive," but he believed those ideas should not be suppressed. He took a sometimes terrifying amount of heat from people who considered themselves liberals and civil libertarians. As I found out one day, Goldberger eventually disguised his voice on the phone until he knew who was calling. But he never backed down. (David Goldberger is now a law professor at Ohio State University.)

The war at NYU focused on the Orison S. Marden Competition, which is schoolwide and open to all second- and third-year students. It is administered by the student-run Moot Court Board.

The hypothetical case that enraged a number of students is *Mike Brody* v. *Carol Brody.* Mike Brody has come to court for a divorce and for sole legal and physical custody of their only child, five-year-old Cindy. There is no evidence that the mother—with whom the child lives except on weekends when she's with her father—is not a loving parent. But the father wants the child out of the mother's house because Carol is a lesbian and is living with a lesbian.

The decision of the Family Court judge in Honolulu is that sole custody of Cindy be awarded to her mother in the "best interests of the child."

The judge continued: "The petitioner [Mike Brody] urges that residing with a homosexual parent who lives in an open relationship with his or her lover cannot be in a child's best interests. We reject this argument. The evidence in this case shows that Cindy is a well-adjusted, happy child. Cindy has lived with her mother for the past year and a half, and has expressed a desire to remain in the care of her mother. Moreover, petitioner has failed to show any negative impact on Cindy from living with respondent."

A justice of the Supreme Court of Hawaii has given Mike Brody leave to appeal the decision. And that's where the NYU students begin their work. Some will brief and argue the case for the father, and others will advocate the case for the mother.

Nina Ruskin, a law student, wrote a letter to all those assigned to argue the petitioner's case in the Marden Competition. She was assigned to that side, too:

"... I have talked to some of you on the phone and it seems the consensus is that our side of the issue [the father's side] is an offensive one to argue and is also very weak when compared with the argument on the other side.

"It is very important to me to compete in moot court and I am unwilling to withdraw. However, I do have a proposal to make. If the majority of us threaten to refuse to argue the side of the petitioner, the Moot Court Board will be forced to offer us another problem (since it is impossible to have an argument when only one side is represented)."

She went on to note that the father's side of the argument is not only "offensive" but is "fueled by hatred." Furthermore, "it consists of biased beliefs and attitudes and thus it is impossible to write a meaningful brief on this side of the issue."

That's not all. Adding to the unfairness of having to represent someone who doesn't believe a lesbian makes a good parent is another problem. Because the mother's arguments "are so much stronger than ours, we are severely disadvantaged in the competition."

But the core of Nina Ruskin's objection would seem to be that "writing arguments on the side of the petitioner is *hurtful* to a group of people and thus *hurtful* to all of us."

The goal of a college education—both in undergraduate and graduate schools—has become, for many, the avoidance at all costs of hurt feelings and of hurting other students' feelings. If, as in college speech codes, certain words must be forbidden, it's better to do that than educate people out of their bigotry. And, among some students at NYU Law School, the new orthodoxy became that certain issues should not be briefed and argued if discussion of them might wound members of the law school community.

Meanwhile, Kris Franklin, co-facilitator of the Lesbian and Gay Law Students, was quoted in the law school student newspaper *The Commentator* as saying of the issue presented in the moot court competition:

"We thought [the case] presented a question that we didn't feel was debatable. If they substituted race or gender for sexual preference, the question wouldn't be asked."

At first it seemed as if the School of Law Moot Court Board would not surrender to those who believed that law students must be protected from issues that so offend them that they don't want to even debate those issues.

Charles Bidwell, moot court chairman, said he regarded the legal problem in the case "an opportunity for valid academic inquiry" into gay and lesbian custody rights. And the Marden Competition editor, John Magri, wrote in a memorandum to moot court competitors: "In searching for topics, we are often confronted with issues which have received widespread public attention and are the focus of mixed sentiments.

"Although the discussion of such topics may sometimes fuel tensions, they nevertheless represent real-life issues which are the subject of debate in other forums."

Other forums where presumably the law students are not as fragile as some of those at NYU Law School.

But then the Moot Court Board caved in. In a letter to participants in the competition, the board announced that the child-custody case had been kicked out of Marden Competition—the first time this had ever happened at the law school. A majority of the board concluded that the case and the issue were not "appropriate." This was "partly brought to our attention by Marden participants."

The rationale of "appropriateness" sounds like a high school principal censoring a student newspaper.

Why was it not appropriate? The board explained:

"For some members of the Moot Court Board, the issue of whether awarding custody to a homosexual parent is presumptively contrary to a child's best interests *was not an open question in a law school community that has a policy of condemning anti-gay biases, both in the law and society.*

"For these members, *the [legal] problem was an affront to our law school's values and thus there was no need for further debate.* (Emphasis added.)

"They argued that debate concerning the suitability of custody by an African-American parent would be inappropriate and that the Marden problem [of custody by a lesbian] was similarly inappropriate."

A minority on the moot board believed that the custody case should not be banished "because it raised an unsettled question of law, and fostered productive debate."

Clearly, those people were among the more insensitive members of the law school community.

Following the decision to censor by a majority of the Moot Court Board, other members of the student body and the faculty—who were stunned at this reversal of the fundamental values of any self-respecting law school—began to be heard from.

In *The Commentator,* Andrew John Carboy, a student, wrote: "... By buckling to criticism, the Moot Court Board is engaging in censorship.... If Marden participants objected to the original problem because they thought current case law placed them at a hopeless disadvantage, they should reconsider why they are planning on becoming attorneys. It is inconceivable for a practicing lawyer to reject or abandon clients simply because he or she believes the state of the law makes their cases weak."

In place of the inappropriate and insensitive child-custody case, the Moot Court Board distributed a substitute case that was utterly without controversy. The issue was homeowner tort liability. Or, as law student Barbara Busharis put it, "We were so unwilling to make a politically incorrect argument—or, maybe, afraid of being perceived as agreeing with it—that we fled to the safety of arguing whether or not homeowners have to trim their trees."

NYU Law School, like many institutions of higher learning around the country, had become infected with the obsessive need by some students and faculty to have thought police on campus.

At one point, however, NYU law professor Anthony Amsterdam wrote a letter to the Moot Court Board. Amsterdam is a long-term opponent of the death penalty and has engaged in a number of key cases in that specialty. He has expertise in a number of other areas of the law and is respected for both his brilliance and his integrity.

His letter to the Moot Court Board—also printed in the student newspaper, *The Commentator*—should be given to every entering law school student in the country and, for that matter, should be read and discussed in various undergraduate courses:

"... Members of your Board apparently believe that the idea that 'awarding custody to a homosexual parent is presumptively contrary to a child's best interests' is a wrong idea. I agree that it is a wrong idea. But the only acceptable or enduring way to demonstrate that it is a wrong idea is by putting it to the test of debate, not by putting it beyond the pale of debate.

"Your memo says that the 'Marden [moot court] program is designed to improve advocacy skills.' A critical advocacy skill is to be able to formulate an argument that you do not believe in—particularly one which leads to conclusions you abhor, and in which you identify with people you detest—so that you can contest against it most effectively."

(A variation of that self-discipline is needed in a good many newsrooms. Reporters and editors ought to try to understand where people—with causes they personally detest—are coming from. Not so that they can contest them—that ought not to be the job of a reporter—but so that they can more accurately explain them to their readers.)

Amsterdam continued about the need to formulate arguments that you yourself don't believe in:

"This is not an abstract platitude. A number of years ago I was involved in a Kentucky case in which a divorced mother was denied custody of her child because she was white. She had married a black man after her divorce, and the judge believed that the [white] child's best interests would not be served by putting them under the pressure of life in an interracial household.

"One of the finest and most dedicated civil rights lawyers in the United States led the mother's defense team [on appeal]. This lawyer didn't do it by declaring that the judge's reasoning and the opposition's arguments were unthinkable. The lawyer did it by thinking through every conceivable argument that could be advanced in support of the judge or the opposition and formulating those arguments as strongly as they could be formulated, so as to be able to rebut them before any court in the land.

"That is what advocacy is all about. The Marden [moot court] program cannot responsibly or credibly profess to be designed to improve advocacy skills when you run it in a way that advertises that you don't know the first thing about advocacy.

"Your memo," Amsterdam continued, "attributes to some members of the Board the view that 'the nature of the petitioner's [the father's] argument would hinder those assigned to argue that side in presenting a strong case.' This is a wholly unjustified public slur on your fellow students. It accuses them of inability to exercise a level of self-control indispensable to any lawyer. I do not believe that NYU students are the intellectual and moral weaklings you assert they are, but if I took your word for it, I would regard that as a serious condemnation of the student body.

"Your action in discontinuing use of the child custody case," Amsterdam emphasized, "disserves the very interests that you seem to think you are promoting.

"a. How can we ever rid our society of anti-gay biases unless we formulate the strongest arguments we can possibly make against those biases? And how can we do that if we don't also formulate the strongest arguments that could be made to support the biases?

"b. Courageous spokespersons, at high personal cost, have finally begun to bring homosexuality and the issues surrounding it out of the closet. Now you want to put it back in. Can't you see the message you are sending?

"c. More basically, once you begin to exclude ideas from the discourse of a community on the ground that they are wrong or offensive, you start in motion a process that inevitably ends up justifying suppression of the unpopular ideas of unpopular minorities. It is fanciful to think that bigots cannot beat you at the game you have begun. They always have and they always will.

"I recognize that if you reconsider your decision about using the child custody case, this vacillation will make you look... bad... but keep in mind two things.

"First, you couldn't possibly look worse than you do now. There's no way at all to defend your present position. Your memo [explaining why the Moot Court Board withdrew the child-custody case] invites outrage and ridicule.

"Second, if, as I suggest, your position is seriously flawed on the merits—if it's not just flawed as a matter of some close judgment call in weighing competing considerations but is fundamentally off-base when examined from any and every angle—that's even worse than being indefensible. It is, quite simply, *wrong*. Please give yourself a chance to come out right in the end by having the guts to reconsider whether you got it wrong (and how badly) on the first take...."

Meanwhile, the members of the Moot Court Board had been reexamining their original position among themselves, and a majority of the board decided they had indeed been wrong. (I expect, however, that the Amsterdam letter had some impact.)

Anyway, the board issued a statement saying it was going to bring back the dread child-custody case. But it was also going to keep, as an option, the homeowners' tree-trimming case, which it had originally substituted for the question of whether a child should grow up in a lesbian home.

The board made a bad mistake in presenting the "safe" optional case. A precedent has been set that if a case is too "offensive," too "hurtful" to those who have to take a side they don't like, then they should be able to choose another case.

Indeed, the Moot Court Board, in its announcement that it had erred the first time by banishing the child-custody case, also said this:

"Conscientious objection to a problem is entirely justifiable, and in the future the Board may exercise its discretion not to select a problem that many students will feel compelled not to argue, but we want to avoid setting a precedent that dual problems are necessary whenever arguments on one side of an issue are offensive."

In other words, future Moot Court Boards are advised to play it safe and avoid offending students by not choosing controversial cases. Splendid training for future lawyers.

Toward the end of the partial reversal by the Moot Court Board of its surrender to "politically correct" students, there is a decided echo from the Anthony Amsterdam letter:

"We also believe that the examination of the child-custody issue will be fundamentally beneficial to students who intend to remain vigilant on behalf of gay rights and other progressive causes. The moot court forum provides a great opportunity for participants to expose weaknesses in... arguments [against gay rights] and to prepare themselves to confront similar arguments outside the law school."

* * *

... we should not give bigoted arguments credence and power by forcing students to propound such regressive views; as many of us are personally and painfully aware, those views are espoused all too often by all too many people.... We urge the Moot Court Board to use their unique position to encourage challenging debate that will foster education, not bigotry.

—NYU law students Julie Goldscheid, Barry Gilman, Tim Clark, and Boris Thomas, protesting the assignment of a moot court case on whether a lesbian mother should be deprived of custody of her child.

Effective advocacy in the real world does not consist of pronouncing moral anathemas on your opponents' positions. It requires painstaking analysis and persuasive refutation—and that requires a sophisticated understanding of the arguments on the other side.

—NYU law professor Burt Neuborne

What has happened at New York University Law School indicates that institution may be in more trouble—in terms of retaining its reason for being—than its faculty and students realize. But it is not alone in this regard, among other law schools, colleges, and universities.

The arguments among students and faculty over the assigned moot court case reflect the increasing politicization of the school.

Some non-gay and non-lesbian students maintained that to take the father's side of the case was deeply offensive, hurtful to themselves and to others. Although there were gay and lesbian students who felt they would learn something by taking a side that personally repels them, others said the question presented by the case was not debatable.

Not many of the faculty spoke out publicly. Yet I would think that a professor—in his or her direct teaching role—has an obligation to state publicly where he or she stands on an issue like the attempted censoring of a moot court case on the ground that the subject was too repellent for discussion. That's part of teaching, too.

Some of the other professors did make their views known in

The Commentator. They weren't hiding, and what they have to say adds to the debate, although much of it is profoundly wrong-headed. These professors are attuned to what are politically correct views among students and faculty who want to be part of doing the right thing. And they all know exactly what the right thing is.

In an issue of *The Commentator,* professors Claudia Angelos, Peggy Davis, Sylvia Law, and Nancy Morawetz began their contribution to this dialogue—in their letter, "Dilemmas of Conscience"—by denying that the initial decision of the Moot Court Board to expel the child-custody case was "censorship."

The board, said the four professors, was simply acting on its "responsibility to insure that it is providing a pedagogically valuable experience for Moot Court participants." But what of the gravely offended students who pressured the board by threatening to organize so much opposition to the case that there wouldn't be enough students to make for a debate? This isn't attempted censorship?

Also, when the Moot Court Board announced that it was deep-sixing the child-custody case, it pointed out that the decision was based in large part on the convictions of some of its members that "the issue of whether awarding custody to a homosexual parent is presumptively contrary to a child's best interests was not an open question in a law school that has a policy of condemning anti-gay biases, both in the law and in society.... the [moot court] problem was an affront to our law school's values and thus there was no need for further debate."

You can turn that upside down and translate it into Sanskrit and back, and it still comes out pure censorship.

As for providing "a pedagogically valuable experience," the four professors who would protect students from unpleasant thinking are apparently unmoved by Professor Anthony Amsterdam's point:

"How can we ever rid our society of anti-gay biases unless we formulate the strongest arguments we can possibly make against those biases? And how can we do that if we don't also formulate the strongest arguments that could be made to support the biases?"

Similarly, if you are arguing in the courts against censorship, you will be a lot more effective if, by stretching yourself, you have worked out beforehand the strongest possible arguments of the censors.

In Idaho, I have spent time with some born-again Christians who were working hard to get some books out of the local public school system. I didn't convert them, and they didn't convert me, but I now can present their arguments about as well as they can, and that's been a great help in understanding their strategies and goals with which I profoundly disagree.

The four NYU Law School professors who wanted to protect the censors in the student body emphasize that students should not be required "to espouse views that they find deeply morally abhorrent." The Moot Court Board, the professors say, should "seek out alternatives that allow students to benefit from Moot Court without paying that price of conscience."

There are divisions about conscience among lawyers who are in practice. I know some who, in conscience, feel compelled to take clients whom they abhor personally, ideologically, and for the crimes they've committed. I don't mean lawyers who will take any client if the money's right. I mean lawyers who believe that everyone is entitled to the "best defense" he or she can find. And these lawyers think they're pretty damn good. So there is also the challenge: am I good enough to get this sleaze bag off?

Then there are lawyers who draw a line. They will not, for example, work for a chiseling defense contractor or defend a big-league drug dealer. But what is a Legal Aid lawyer supposed to do? Whether he or she can provide the "best defense"—and some can—they are the last defense for those without resources. The four feel-good professors at NYU might bring up that dilemma of conscience in their classes.

In any case, these questions of conscience are different for lawyers in practice than for law students. Out there, what you do or don't do affects people's lives. If you are clever enough to get a murderer off, for instance, and you know he actually did it, you may brood about whether you should have taken the case in the first place, and your conscience may be quickened in this regard the next time around.

But in law school, you're learning how to analyze, how to argue, and you cannot do any harm to anybody—yet—because you are not representing anybody real. Except yourself. And when these four professors want to exempt law students from "paying [the] price of conscience," the result is to exempt law students from growing, to exempt them from facing the abhorrent and learning how to deal with it *without* surrendering their principles.

Why not become an advocate for the most repugnant position you can imagine? And why not do it in public, in a moot court setting? See if the sky falls. Or instead, will the experience make you a far better defender of ideas in which you believe than if you had chosen the cocoon these four professors would design for you?

The four professors also say in their letter to the Moot Court Board in *The Commentator:*

"We hope and trust that sensitive exploration and debate on controversial issues will flourish at the Law School in a wide variety of contexts. But we do not believe that the Moot Court Board is compelled by any first principles to impose dilemmas of conscience on unwilling advocates...."

If the future of the moot court at NYU Law School—or any law school—involves more issues that will prove too "controversial" for "unwilling advocates" who must be politically correct in all they do, there will eventually be fewer and fewer controversial cases assigned. And the result will be a mush court. As well as a decline in the law school's standing in the country.

And more fundamentally, if more law professors do not join the law students supporting free inquiry, Anthony Amsterdam's prophecy will come true:

"More basically, once you begin to exclude ideas from the discourse of a community on the ground that they are wrong or offensive, you start in motion a process that inevitably ends up justifying suppression of the unpopular ideas of unpopular minorities. It is fanciful to think that bigots cannot beat you at the game you have begun. They always have and they always will."

Commenting on the civil war at NYU Law School, Arthur Leonard, a professor at another school (New York Law School), pointed out:

"For too long, lesbian and gay legal issues have been virtually invisible in the nation's law schools. Those of us who advocate lesbian and gay rights should be celebrating when a student-run moot court board decides to use a problem dealing with anti-gay bias, because the students on both sides will have to research the issues (issues frequently not addressed in their classes) and form their own conclusions based on that research. It is impossible to deal with an issue in the intense experience of moot court without some students having to argue a position with which they strongly disagree; but that's part of the educational process.

"I am the founder and first president of the Bar Association of American Law Schools' Section on Gay and Lesbian Legal Issues. I also have been named cochair of the Special Committee on Lesbians and Gay Men in the Legal Profession of the Association of the Bar of the City of New York. I get calls from all over the country from students asking for suggestions for gay and lesbian issues for moot court topics. I hope this trend continues. Furthermore, even if the 'politically correct' at NYU contend that the issue of custody rights of lesbian mothers should be 'beyond debate,' the fact is that many state supreme courts disagree with them, and students who want to practice in this area have to be well-armed to deal with the courts' biases."

And a lawyer from Peaks Island, Maine, John S. Whitman, told me of his reactions on hearing about the law students who objected to having anything to do with an "insensitive" moot court subject:

"As a lawyer who spends a substantial amount of time and energy representing indigent criminal defendants, I could feel the bile rising in my throat in thinking about those law students whose delicate sensibilities were offended by the moot court argument they were called on to make....

"If Nina Ruskin *et al.* are unwilling to take a politically correct position in a civil custody case, I wonder how they're going to defend alleged murderers, arsonists, child molesters or, for that matter, any other person whose case is seen as repugnant.

"For the sake of the legal profession, I hope these students choose another career."

In the *Los Angeles Daily Journal,* a legal newspaper, Arthur Gilbert, a justice on the Second District Court of Appeals in Ventura, California, wrote:

"... There are indications that the very people who once championed an unpopular cause want to make sure one subscribes to the 'politically correct' point of view.... Pressure is being placed on students and faculty in some colleges, for example, to express the correct views or suffer the consequences....

"[At NYU Law School] the students thought denying the lesbian couple custody just because of their sexual preference was offensive. Of course it is. That's why we need lawyers. They are there to protect all points of view, however offensive. The Bill of Rights was enacted just so that politically incorrect points of view could be expressed.

"If lawyers become intimidated by enforcers of correct thought, then we are in big trouble. The students who refused to participate in the moot court competition because the cause for which they had to argue was not a just one, unwittingly sabotaged the very principles they profess to support.

"It's okay to feel strongly about your position. But when your certainty of the correctness of your position demands that the opposition be silenced, you have already undermined your own position. You have become like your enemy.

"If lawyers forget this, we will ultimately have a society where ideas are crimes. *Fahrenheit 451, Brave New World* and *1984* will have been written in vain.

"The people who fought for minority rights, whether they be gays, blacks, Jews, women, or atheists, should be particularly sensitive to preserving the right of others to be heard, no matter how odious their point of view.

"It was hard for Jews in Skokie, Illinois, to countenance Nazis marching in their neighborhood. Nothing could be more understandable, but it was even more understandable that Jewish lawyers defended the rights of the Nazis to march. If the Nazis didn't have that right, neither would the Jews, or any other group."

After the battle over the moot court's sensitivity was over, I received several letters from law students and clerks to state court judges around the country telling me of cases moving through the courts that almost exactly paralleled that of the hypothetical which caused a civil war at New York University Law School.

And there was a letter from New York Law School professor Arthur Leonard. He told of a case in which "the trial judge appears to have denied a woman custody of her child due to her sexual orientation. This story reinforces my contention that the NYU moot court problem is an example of what students may confront in the real world.... This case is not an isolated phenomenon (as witness any of several Missouri appellate decisions over the past five years, or a notorious 1985 decision by the Virginia Supreme Court)."

The priority given to students' sensitivities at New York University Law School—and others, including the District of Columbia Law School, as we shall see—is an effective training ground for those lawyers who may, in the future, have to obey rules by state bar associations that also stress the need to maintain the correct attitudes and language required of members of the profession in good standing.

As an augury, there was a proposal by the State Bar of California in 1991 and 1992 that would have required the 128,000 lawyers in the state to watch what they say much more carefully.

Drafted by the State Bar's Committee on Women and the Law, the proposed rule says:

"An attorney shall refrain from manifesting—by words or conduct—bias or prejudice based on race, sex, religion, national origin, disability, age, sexual orientation, or socio-economic status—against parties, witnesses, counsel, or others.

"This Rule does not preclude legitimate advocacy when race, sex, religion, national origin, disability, age, sexual orientation or socio-economic or other similar factors are issues in the proceedings."

Punishments for violations of the rule could range from public reprimand to disbarment.

As Philip Hager reported in the *Los Angeles Times,* members of the bar—who, after all, are advocates, not dispassionate judges—have expressed concern that "a lawyer could even be punished for criticizing a church on its abortion policy or telling an ethnic joke to a colleague."

Ramona Ripston, executive director of the American Civil Liberties Union of Southern California, said: "The rule doesn't say *where* it can be broken. In a lawyer's office? On the street? It is very vague and so it is unconstitutional." (The First Amendment applies because the state bar is the official California state agency that supervises the legal profession.)

Another attorney, Stephen Rhode of Los Angeles, notes: "One major problem in attempting to regulate speech is that it is impossible to settle on a universal consensus of what words manifest 'bias or prejudice.' Would attorneys risk punishment for calling members of the Unification Church 'cultists'? Or for calling followers of Louis Farrakhan 'racists'? Or Zionists 'imperialists'? Palestinians 'terrorists'? Could a black lawyer be disciplined for calling another black lawyer an 'Uncle Tom' or for calling a white lawyer 'Mr. Charlie'?"

Adds another Los Angeles attorney, Michael Klein: "Are lawyers permitted to speak only if they are 'politically correct'?"

Leading to the current proposal were two studies by the Committee on Women and Law and the State Judicial Council that firmly documented a pattern of sexual bias in California's legal system. The Judicial Council's probe, as reported in the *Los Angeles Times,* found that "women attorneys were often propositioned by male lawyers and subjected to offensive jokes and sexual innuendoes."

Sheila James Kuehl, managing director of the Southern California Women's Law Center, has reminded the State Bar not only of the presence of gender bias but also of prejudice based on "race, national origin, language, sexual orientation, and physical ability."

She told me that the language of the rule ought to be clarified, but the need for it is compelling. In making the argument for speech control, she sounds very much like college administrators and certain law professors who justify campus speech codes. Says Kuehl:

"Nor is it sufficient to say that all attorneys have the privilege of castigating each other. To hurl an epithet based on race or gender at a person of a disadvantaged class, does not, in reality, allow an equivalent from a person of a disadvantaged class. It is as though both men and women, or Anglos or people of color, were issued guns, but only the white men got the bullets.... All insults may be equal, but in American society, some insults are more equal than others."

Where, then, did Malcolm X get his verbal bullets? And Dr. Kenneth Clark, and Eleanor Holmes Norton, and the non-Anglo law professors—Richard Delgado and Mari Matsuda—who are vigorously leading the fight to impose speech codes on college campuses?

Although they sometimes claim otherwise, Delgado and Matsuda have plenty of bullets.

Sheila Kuehl and the other advocates of censoring lawyers are engaged in the politics of victimization—not the politics of empowerment, which comes with knowing how to deal with all kinds of speech, without ducking.

"Civil liberties," said the dean of the law school, "are not the focus here."

I got a call one afternoon in April 1991 from a staffer at the student-run *Georgetown Law Weekly* in Washington. All hell was breaking loose. The paper had published an article, "Admissions Apartheid," by a senior, Timothy Maguire, which charged that "in every area and at every level of post-secondary education, the achievements of black applicants to [this] law school [and those accepted] are far inferior of those of whites." In college, they'd had lower grade-point averages, he wrote, and their Law School Admissions Test scores were considerably lower than those of whites applying to the law school.

Maguire said he had based this inflammatory analysis on a "random sample" of school records. Having worked for three months as a file clerk in the admissions office of the law school, Maguire was suspected of having mined confidential data.

Of two thousand students at Georgetown Law Center, 11 percent are black; and most of them—along with a good many white law students—were furious. At Maguire. And at the student paper that had printed this article.

The staffer who called me said that pressure was building to force Claudia Callaway, editor-in-chief of the *Georgetown Law Weekly*, to resign. And maybe much of the rest of the staff, too. (Callaway, a strong advocate of affirmative action, had been getting a lot of heat for printing even stronger African-American viewpoints. Now, some black students were charging her with conspiring with Tim Maguire to break confidentiality.)

My advice—and I doubt if Callaway needed it, in view of what she wound up doing—was to tell the student body what a newspaper is supposed to do: print the news, whether it hurts people or not. And Maguire's article—along with the reaction to it—was certainly news.

In an editorial in the April 16 edition of the *Georgetown Law Weekly*, Claudia Callaway wrote:

"In striving to represent the views of all students, the Editor in Chief should never inflict her views on another author's writing....

"The principles of the First Amendment and academic freedom do not cease to operate when the speech at issue is controversial or even painful....

"The emotion and passion raised by the article should be directed not at punishing the *Law Weekly* for publishing the article, but at changing the minds of those who agree with Maguire.

"Instead, the law center community is engaged in a classic confrontation between the right to an open forum for all ideas, however unpopular or ill-conceived, and the forces, on both left and right, who seek to limit speech only to those ideas that pass some *a priori* standard of political or moral certainty....

"The community must resist calls for restraints on the *Law Weekly*.... The staff of the *Law Weekly*, regardless of our personal and/or individual views, and regardless of any threats or reprisals, remains committed to the principles of the First Amendment and the free expression of opinion."

The *Law Weekly* survived, and formal charges against Callaway for breaking confidentiality were dropped, but the verbal assaults on Timothy Maguire continued. "The central issue," Gillian Caldwell—white, and a second-year student—told the *Washington Post*, "is racism. I think the article is assaultive. People were injured. I think that kind of speech is outrageous."

Talbert Weeks, president of the Black Law Students Association, said that Maguire's article was aimed at reducing Georgetown's "commitment to legal education for African Americans."

And the Black Law Students Association demanded that the law school withhold Maguire's degree. The association also filed a formal complaint against Maguire for violating the confidentiality of school records, and that set in motion the Law Center's disciplinary procedure. Maguire was in the dock, and he would have to face a faculty prosecutor.

Meanwhile, tensions in the school kept building. Saundra Torry reported in the *Washington Post* that "the school's faculty is so liberal, some said, and the student body so vocally left-wing, that it is difficult to take any stand that differs from the expected....

"Gina Elzy, a black second-year student, believes [however, that] many students subscribe to Maguire's views, 'but never had the courage to come out and say it.' Some, she said, subtly question the credentials of black students, particularly if they didn't attend an Ivy League school.

"But several white students said anyone who questions affirmative action is labeled a racist."

On the other hand, "I think a lot of blacks feel threatened," said Charlene Bryant, who is black. "My roommate... says she is tired of justifying her presence at every academic institution she attended."

On May 21, Saundra Torry wrote what seemed to be the final story on the matter of Timothy Maguire. He would be allowed to graduate with both his degree and a letter of reprimand.

Caroline Smith, a member of the Black Law Students Association, expressed displeasure that the school's administration "would okay somebody's racial harassment of a group of students." (Claudia Callaway, by the way, had been accused of being more pernicious than Maguire, because she gave him a forum.)

What further angered Maguire's critics was that, according to the settlement of his case, the formal reprimand would not be part of his official transcript.

The Center for Individual Rights, a conservative law office, was involved in Maguire's defense but was not—as we shall see—his actual representative in negotiations with the Georgetown Law Center.

The Center for Individual Rights said it was "elated" with the settlement, and that added to the dismay of Maguire's opponents.

Maguire did admit, in the settlement, that he violated his responsibility not to disclose information he had obtained while working at the admissions office. But the dean of the law school, Judith Areen, had her own admission to make. Confidential data about test scores and grade points had been circulated to the faculty in previous years—before Maguire did it. "It is a mitigating factor," she said, "that confidentiality had been compromised in the past." Maguire's skillful lawyers had found that out.

Maguire, in interviews, did some mitigating himself, apologizing for "offensive and inappropriate" language in his article. But Maguire stood by his conclusions.

Dean Areen, finally acknowledging the spirit of the First Amendment, said that Maguire was reprimanded solely for "violation of the trust placed in him as an employee of the Law Center, not for publishing controversial views in the student newspaper."

But the case wasn't over for the two volunteer lawyers who had come forward to represent Tim Maguire.

There are two lawyers in Washington—Bob Catz and Tom Mack—who could well serve as role models for law students curious about a career making the Fourteenth Amendment—"equal protection under the laws"—actually work for people who couldn't get past the receptionist at a big law firm.

Some lawyers' group ought to send Catz and Mack on a tour of law schools, where they could tell about their cases, the satisfactions in winning against huge odds, and what they learn in losing.

They could also bring a very important message to law students everywhere: the Bill of Rights is for *everyone*, even the politically incorrect. And then Catz and Mack could tell what happened to them at their own law school when they defended the free-speech rights of someone in the city who was detested by many of their colleagues and students.

First, some background. For five years, Bob Catz practiced law full-time with the Migrant Legal Action Program and the Legal Aid Society of Omaha, Nebraska. While teaching at various law schools, he has also continued to practice public law in the federal courts of appeals and the Supreme Court.

Catz was part of the defense team in the congressional impeachment proceedings against a black federal district judge, Alcee Hastings. And he was responsible for the deinstitutionalization of patients at the Forest Haven Facility for the Mentally Ill in Laurel, Maryland.

Tom Mack was general counsel to the Community Services Administration and regional director of the Office of Legal Services of the Office of Economic Opportunity. He has worked with the Chicago Legal Aid Bureau and the San Francisco Neighborhood Legal Assistance Foundation.

In 1990, Tom Mack went way against the odds when he represented ten inmates at Lorton, a prison housing many Washington, D.C., lawbreakers. It is not a country club prison. His clients claimed they had been severely assaulted by guards. It's the kind of case that is exceedingly difficult to win—the guards' testimony against that of the prisoners. Tom Mack won a $175,000 judgment for the prisoners.

Mack and Catz are law professors at the District of Columbia School of Law. It's a rather unique school, one that—in its aims—would, I think, delight Justice William Brennan. Established in 1987 as the successor to the highly socially conscious Antioch School of Law, the D.C. School of Law is the only publicly funded law school in the District of Columbia. Its mission is to encourage more members of minority groups to take up the law; it also welcomes the enrollment of women, the poor, and older students.

Through its clinical programs, the school represents—with its students—many of those minorities and the poor in the District of Columbia who need legal help.

In a letter to prospective applicants, the D.C. School of Law emphasizes that its "fundamental philosophy" is "that legal education and lawyers must be sensitive and responsible to the public interest.... By bringing the best minds to our social, political, and economic problems, we creatively and meaningfully fashion those solutions which serve the greatest good.

"We at DCSL believe that public service is the best and highest use of educated minds. This spirit of dedication is infused throughout the DCSL experience.... We offer an exciting and unique approach to the study and practice of law. Those who accept the challenge find that study at DCSL carries its own rewards...."

A perfect match. Tom Mack and Bob Catz—highly skilled in various dimensions of public-interest law—becoming part of a school that exists to teach and practice public-interest law.

The two law professors did well there, but then they made a grave mistake. They took on an unpopular client. Not the "correct" kind of unpopular client. If they'd done that, they would have been applauded by their colleagues and students. The heresy they committed was to take on a client who had criticized—in a newspaper at another law school—affirmative action.

It was Tim Maguire, who had written that article, "Admissions Apartheid," in the student-edited *Georgetown Law Weekly.* The piece—and the resultant ferocious reaction—had been reported in newspapers around the country.

Maguire was now on trial at the law center for having used confidential files for his article. A member of the faculty was appointed his prosecutor, and Maguire needed a lawyer. It was a serious proceeding. Maguire was in official danger of losing his law degree, among other possible punishments.

The defendant did have representation—lawyers from the Center for Individual Rights, but they were not that experienced in the rules of evidence in academic disciplinary proceedings. So the Center tried to get various lawyers around the city to take the case of this notorious young man. There were no takers. (When Claudia Callaway, editor of the Georgetown paper, asked a professor there to help *her* get a lawyer when she was up on charges, he refused because "it wouldn't be politically good for me.")

At this point, Tom Mack and Bob Catz themselves became notorious. They took the case, and that got them into a lot of trouble at their own D.C. School of Law, where many law students were just as angry at Tim Maguire as were the students at the Georgetown Law Center.

What followed revealed a curious flaw in the leadership—and among some of the faculty—of the D.C. School of Law. They had neglected to compellingly teach their students a fundamental constitutional liberty—the right to free expression, however obnoxious and hurtful. And the right of lawyers to defend, on free-speech principles, clients with whose views they thoroughly disagree.

During one stormy meeting at the D.C. School of Law, Bob Catz and Tom Mack were told by some of the students to drop Tim Maguire as a client. The two professors were accused by both black and white students of violating the school's mission to bring more racial and ethnic minorities into the practice of law as well as to champion social justice.

Reporting on that meeting, which lasted over two hours, Saundra Torry of the *Washington Post* wrote that "Mack and Catz defended their position, arguing that Georgetown was prosecuting Maguire because he expressed unpopular views and that many D.C. lawyers had shunned Maguire's case for that very reason.

"Mack argued that despite his disagreement with Maguire's article, it was crucial to defend Maguire's right to express his opinion.

"'There is great danger to us—not to the Maguires of this world—when you don't defend the right to express views that are unpopular.'"

Did that argument take? Maybe some students understood this rather vital point, but many did not. And there were faculty members who did not. Meanwhile, in an open letter to everyone in the law school, a student charged the two professors with the appalling crime of "making a politically incorrect statement."

Still trying, Tom Mack told the students and faculty: "The First Amendment and the rule of law" include "everything, not just... what is politically correct."

Bob Catz made another point, somewhat more subtle but just as fundamental. Reported Saundra Torry: "Catz added that Georgetown [by prosecuting Maguire] 'is hurting the cause of racial justice' by stifling debate on affirmative action—and punishing dissent. 'In the long run,' he told the students, 'it will come to haunt you.'"

Duke Ellington and I would talk of various things, but not of the First Amendment. That would have been redundant. He was the very embodiment of freedom of expression, and he utterly believed in everybody else's rights to play and compose freely. He hated constricting labels, although he would have preferred "Negro music" to jazz, if there had to be a label on music. Ellington suggested that to Fletcher Henderson in the 1920s, but Henderson could not be convinced.

Ellington grew up in the segregated city of Washington, D.C. Among class divisions in the black community, his family was not far from the top tier, but that meant nothing to the whites downtown. To them all blacks were beyond the pale. Whether you were a maid or a black physician, you couldn't eat in a restaurant in downtown Washington.

In public, Ellington, who had traveled far from home, never appeared vulnerable. Regally self-assured, he was more elegant than any President (including Franklin Delano Roosevelt). Sometimes—from his great height as the legend he knew he was—Ellington liked to tease. As when, one night, he tapped me on the shoulder from behind and said, "You don't know who I am, but I know who you are."

In private, he could be angry and hurt. For instance, he never got a Pulitzer Prize for music. In 1965, however, the three-man music jury had given him a token award, a special prize "for the vitality and originality of his total production." But the overall Pulitzer board took even that away from him, overruling the music jury.

In public, Duke, smiling, waved away the insult. "Fate is being kind to me," he said. "Fate doesn't want me to be too famous too young." He was sixty-six. A couple of nights later, he said to me, "You see, European-based music is still the only respectable kind in this country." He spoke with cool anger.

What hurt and angered him more than this traditional form of segregation by white arbiters of culture was the charge by some young black civil rights activists in the 1960s that Ellington was insensitive to their struggle. To the struggle of black people.

"People who think that of me," Duke said with some sadness, "have not been listening to our music. For a long time, social protest and pride in black culture and history have been the most significant themes in what we've done. In that music we have been talking for a long time about what it is to be black in this country."

Among so many such works, still resounding, are "Black Beauty," "Black, Brown and Beige," "Harlem Suite," "Harlem Air Shaft," "Portrait of Bert Williams," and "Black and Tan Fantasy."

Ellington and the sometimes dissonant dimensions of black pride came to mind as I was exploring the events at the District of Columbia School of Law as a result of two of its white law professors—Robert Catz and Tom Mack—defending Tim Maguire.

First of all, it was a free-speech issue. Maguire should not be deprived of his law degree for expressing his beliefs.

Furthermore, the professors pointed out, if Georgetown succeeded in punishing Maguire—while refusing to discuss its admissions policies openly—that would harm the rights of minorities throughout the country. What is Georgetown hiding? What are other schools with affirmative action hiding?

Nonetheless, Mack and Catz were being attacked at their own law school for taking on the defense of this "racist" student at Georgetown. "This was the first time" in his public-interest work, Catz said, that "I've had to worry about attacks from people around me." At an open meeting at the D.C. Law School before a largely hostile audience, Mack emphasized, as reported in *Legal Times:*

"Georgetown's reaction to this is all wrong. Ordinarily what you do with dissent is you answer dissent, you don't punish it."

Furthermore, Tim Maguire, like him or not, was a whistleblower, and it's important, the two professors tried to point out, to protect whistle-blowers. It's the principle that's vital.

What if a student at another school had discovered—through access to the admissions records—that the law school had been discriminating against *blacks?* The very D.C. Law School students who were attacking Mack and Catz for their "disloyalty" would have very much wanted Mack and Catz to defend *that* student.

But many of the black students remained angry. One scornfully told the two professors that this First Amendment that they so prized "drove my family out of Alabama" because the Ku Klux Klan had had the First Amendment right to speak and demonstrate. But had the First Amendment not been available to black protesters in the South, the marches and demonstrations that led to the Civil Rights Act might well have been crushed.

A black professor walked out of the open meeting, and one black student spoke for many when she said to Mack and Catz: "I don't question either of your right to go out and defend this man, but when you stand in front of a classroom of 50 percent black and minority students, I think that maybe you have to be sensitive about how that is going to impact that group of people. A professor at a place like DCLS has to be different."

There was an emphatic round of applause.

I spoke to the dean of the D.C. Law School, William L. Robinson.

A graduate of Columbia Law School, Robinson has one of the most distinguished records in civil rights law in the country. A former director of the National Lawyers' Committee for Civil Rights Under Law, he was associate general counsel for the Equal Employment Opportunity Commission and first assistant counsel for the NAACP Legal Defense and Education Fund. In both positions, he was involved in key civil rights legislation.

At the American Bar Association, Robinson has been chairman of the influential Section on Individual Rights and Responsibilities and is now a member of the ABA Standing Committee on Lawyers' Public Service Responsibility.

Robinson speaks with an easeful authority that reminds me somewhat of Ellington. We spoke at first about jazz. Robinson had read some of my writing on the music. I enjoyed the conversation because Robinson is very knowledgeable about jazz, very much including Ellington, and I seldom get much of a chance to talk about the music these days. Most of the people I interview on Bill of Rights matters think Bird is a general description of ornithology.

Finally, Dean Robinson and I talked about the two professors at his school who had been put on the defensive—because of their choice of client—by students and faculty.

Mack and Catz, the dean said, are on "a kind of probation with some segments of the student body and with some faculty. Their relations with those people, I'd say, are damaged. It is not a formal probation, but I think it may take their doing some outstanding public-service legal work before they may, grudgingly, get back their standing here."

I was stunned. What had Catz and Mack done that they should be on "probation" and have to redeem themselves when they had long since achieved a record in public-interest law that not many law professors in the country could equal? And the case for which they were being so severely criticized involved a fundamental liberty—free expression.

Well, Dean Robinson told me, "civil liberties, while being within the pale, are not the focus here. Faculty members must keep in mind the hurt their actions will do to the community of the law school."

Here again, as in far too many institutions of higher learning, students are being taught to see themselves as fragile victims. That is not the way to learn empowerment.

Dean Robinson did tell me that he would protect the professors' right to have taken on Tim Maguire as a client, but it was clear that he wished they hadn't.

Ellington came back into my mind. Here was this law school in his city, committed to bringing more blacks, women, the poor, and older and nontraditional students into the law. Duke would probably have wanted to do a concert for it. But here was this same school oblivious to how vital it is for lawyers to defend free expression, even of views they hate. Yet, without the best defense of free expression, everyone's right to speak and write and paint and create music is endangered, because freedom is indivisible.

In reporting on the open meeting at the D.C. Law School when Mack and Catz were being accused of being politically incorrect and insensitive to the school's mission, *Legal Times* noted: "Those accusing the two men of insensitivity toward blacks tended to be blacks and other minorities, while most emphasizing Maguire's right to free speech—and the professors' right to represent him—tended to be whites."

This is one division that ought not to exist between blacks and whites—especially not in a law school.

Tom Mack and Bob Catz are still at the D.C. Law School, teaching the Bill of Rights—all of it with more of the free spirit of Duke Ellington than the dean and many of the faculty and students possess.

"Outside law schools, the Constitution stays alive."

In 1991, during the Bicentennial Year of the Bill of Rights, it was too bad that public television hadn't been shooting a documentary of what was happening in Amherst, Massachusetts. This is a place where the Constitution never sleeps because there are so many loud arguments over what it means.

The previous fall, for instance, Amherst's Citizens Review Commission proposed a new bylaw that would forbid the public use of "fighting words" that "by their very utterance inflict injury" on the person or group addressed and that "tend to incite an immediate breach of the peace."

But the bylaw did not specify what particular offensive words would be punished. In an editorial, the *Daily Hampshire Gazette* reminded the townsfolk of what many colleges and universities around the country have forgotten: "The First Amendment protects even offensive speech."

And an attorney, Alan Rubin, testified before the commission that the proposed bylaw "makes me fighting mad." (Presumably, if the bylaw had been in effect, the commissioners might thereby have been found guilty of committing "fighting words.")

William Newman, an American Civil Liberties Union lawyer, warned that this proposed cure for racism, sexism and other verbal assaults "was not a cure but in fact a disease." But William Norris, representing the NAACP, asked: "Why should 'fag' be protected? What treasured First Amendment right are you expressing when you use that word?"

The proposed bylaw was laid aside—unhappily by some—to be tumultuously debated at a later time.

Amherst was also divided over the Amherst Pelham Regional High Schools' no-nonsense policy concerning sexual harassment. Among the official definitions of sexual harassment were staring or leering with sexual overtones and "spreading sexual gossip."

Gus Sayer, superintendent of schools, told John Leo of *U.S. News & World Report* that a single stare—not a pattern of stares—could be enough to have a kid found guilty of sexual harassment.

Leo asked: "What if a student told a friend, 'I think Marcie and Allen have something going'?" The superintendent answered that this passage of gossip would qualify as sexual harassment.

The *Daily Hampshire Gazette* wondered at what point "a look of affection becomes a harassing leer." School administrators familiar with the ways of the world will know.

The sexual harassment code still exists, but the superintendent of schools—who presumably reads the newspapers—now explains that it is an educational tool, not part of the disciplinary code. (At first, punishment ranged from a mandated apology to expulsion.)

Amherst was also involved in a spirited church-state war. For twenty years, there had been a Christmas tree in the children's room of the Jones Library, a public institution. As Christmas neared last year, the board of trustees, by a 5–1 vote, ruled that there would no longer be a tree there. In an ecumenical gesture, the trustees also evicted a menorah that had been in the library in honor of Hanukhah.

Fred Contrada reported in the *Springfield Union News* that Nonny Burack, a library trustee who is particularly identified with the ban, has since received a goodly number of phone calls advising her to go back where she came from. Some of the callers add: "Don't you know this is a free country, and we were nice enough to let you in?" Burack is a further annoyance to such callers when they learn she was born in the United States.

Other critics of her insistence that a Christmas tree does not belong in a public library point out that the U.S. Supreme Court ruled in 1989 that a Christmas tree is a secular symbol.

Burack's response—in the noneuphemistic, assertive spirit of Amherst—is:

"I've heard ad nauseam the argument that it's a pagan symbol. A Christmas tree is a Christmas tree. That's what it's called. It's an adjunct to a religious holiday."

It's encouraging to find a place where not only are there these continuing debates but they take place at town meetings, in drugstores, in bars—without a single political consultant or TV anchor "framing" the issues. Just as the Framers of the Constitution hoped they would.

VIII

Sweet Land of Liberty

"The government cannot mandate by fiat a feeling of unity in its citizens."

The very purpose of a Bill of Rights was to withdraw certain subjects from the vicissitudes of political controversy, to place them beyond the reach of majorities, and to establish them as legal principles to be applied by the courts.

One's right to life, liberty, and property, to free speech, a free press, freedom of worship and assembly, and other fundamental rights may not be submitted to vote; they depend on the outcome of no elections.—SUPREME COURT JUSTICE ROBERT JACKSON, SPEAKING FOR THE MAJORITY OF THE COURT IN THE FLAG-SALUTE CASE, *WEST VIRGINIA STATE BOARD OF EDUCATION V. BARNETTE,* 1943

This may seem very hard for you to even believe, but my opponent vetoed a bill that required the teachers in Massachusetts schools to lead the kids in the Pledge of Allegiance.—GEORGE BUSH ON THE CAMPAIGN TRAIL, *THE NEW YORK TIMES,* AUGUST 24, 1988

And in a CBS-New York Times poll... 70 percent of those surveyed said they disagreed with Dukakis on the pledge issue, saying that teachers should be required to lead classes

231

in the Pledge of Allegiance. Half said they felt that way even
if that policy was found to be unconstitutional.—*NEWSDAY*,
SEPTEMBER 14, 1988

Judge Learned Hand warned:
"Liberty lies in the hearts of men and women; when it dies
there, no constitution, no law, no court can save it."

In a *Wall Street Journal* column on September 15, 1988, Hod-
ding Carter III put it another way:

"... the average high school senior mumbling his way through
the National Anthem at every football game doesn't have a clue as
to what is contained in the Bill of Rights, let alone the whole Constitution, and couldn't explain why such knowledge is important if
asked."

Not only is the average high school senior ignorant of "such
knowledge," but so, alas, are most of his teachers, his parents, his
relatives, and probably most of the staff of the local newspaper.
Journalists know that the First Amendment says something about
freedom of the press, but what else do many of them know about
the Constitution or even about the rest of the First Amendment?

The attempts by President Bush and the Congress of the
United States to remove Old Glory from the First Amendment was
a historic occasion—recalling other historic occasions concerning
laws and court decisions that tried to insulate the flag from the
clear commands of the Constitution.

At eighty-three, William Brennan was the Supreme Court's most
vigorous, passionate defender of free expression. Indeed, he had
written more landmark First Amendment decisions than anyone
since the Court started sitting in 1790. (It should be noted, though,
that the Supreme Court did not begin to take a more substantive
view of the First Amendment until the mid-1920s, when the Court
finally ruled that the amendment applies to the individual states as
well as the federal government.)

Brennan's majority opinion in the flag-burning case, *Texas* v.
Johnson, 1989 was not, however, a landmark. As he noted in the text,
and in a conversation with me, the ruling that the First Amendment protects flag-burning as a form of expressive conduct flows

logically from a series of earlier Court decisions. As *The New York Times* accurately noted in a lead editorial, "Justice William Brennan's majority opinion was in the eloquent tradition of Justices Holmes, Brandeis, and Jackson."

It was Robert Jackson who wrote one of the most luminous definitions of Americanism in the history of the nation when he declared—in *West Virginia State Board of Education* v. *Barnette* (1943)—that the children of Jehovah's Witnesses could not be expelled from school for refusing to pledge allegiance to the flag:

"If there is any fixed star in our constitutional constellation, it is that no official, high or petty, can prescribe what shall be orthodox in politics, nationalism, religion, or other matters of opinion or force citizens to confess by word or act their faith therein." (This was written at the height of American involvement in World War II.)

Brennan quoted that line in *Texas* v. *Johnson*. He also referred to an incisive constitutional point made by the Texas Court of Criminal Appeals, which had earlier ruled that to punish Johnson for burning the American flag would be to attack the First Amendment. Building on the 1943 Jackson decision, the Texas court said:

"The government cannot mandate by fiat a feeling of unity in its citizens. Therefore, that very same government cannot carve out a symbol of unity and prescribe a set of approved messages to be associated with that symbol *when it cannot mandate the status or feeling the symbol purports to represent.*" (Emphasis added.)

So Brennan was saying nothing new. As Geoffrey Stone, dean of the University of Chicago law school put it, "The only astonishing thing is that the opinion [by the Supreme Court] was not unanimous."

If Brennan's decision in the flag-burning case had come down on the same day as the *Webster* abortion ruling, far less attention would have been paid to it. Even George Bush—*at first*—did not cry that the sky was falling. He didn't like the decision, he said, but "I understand the legal basis for that decision, and I respect the Supreme Court. And as President of the United States I will see that the law of the land is fully supported."

Soon after, however, Lee Atwater got the President boogying to tapes of the Dukakis Chain Saw Massacre of 1988. After that session, the President called insistently for a constitutional amendment to rescind what five appallingly unpatriotic members of the Supreme Court—led by that "activist" Brennan—had done to the Grand Old Flag.

And how did the Democrats respond? Did they remind the President of his initial statement: "I respect the Supreme Court..."? In fear and panic, the Democrats scurried away from any possible guilt by association with that Court. House Speaker Thomas Foley lashed at the Brennan decision as "deeply offensive."

Senate Majority Leader George Mitchell, a former federal judge, said—in fear of Lee Atwater—"I do not believe that Americans have to see the flag that symbolizes their freedom to speak devalued and cheapened in the cause of preserving that freedom."

Read that one again. It has all the coherence of a man suddenly seeing a python in his bed. And it was the same distinguished Democratic majority leader who helped shepherd a resolution through the Senate that expressed "profound disappointment" at the Supreme Court's having defiled the First Amendment by putting "such reprehensible conduct" under its protection.

Mario M. Cuomo also took care to disassociate himself from Brennan. Said the governor of New York: "I don't think you should be able to burn the flag." Cuomo prides himself on his deep knowledge of the Constitution.

Then there was a Senate resolution severely reprimanding the Supreme Court. The vote in its favor was 97–3. In dissent—in the tradition of Holmes, Brandeis, Jackson, and Brennan—were Ted Kennedy, Howard Metzenbaum, and Gordon Humphrey. The latter is so conservative a Republican that his recorded ACLU rating at the time was 14 out of 100. Yet on this flag matter, Humphrey told the stampeding majority of his colleagues that they were engaged in "an exercise in silliness.... and a bit of hypocrisy."

Ted Kennedy did more than vote against the resolution. He also released a statement on June 22:

"... if the First Amendment stands for anything, it means that the government cannot punish someone for criticizing our society—even if that criticism is as nasty and obnoxious as the conduct at issue in the *Johnson* case.

"The genius of the constitutional democracy symbolized by our American flag is evident in our system of an independent federal judiciary, sworn to uphold our Constitution's bulwark against the swollen tides of public outrage....

"This body ought not to go on record criticizing the Supreme Court for discharging the solemn duty to vindicate the freedoms protected by the Constitution and symbolized by our hallowed flag."

On that day, Kennedy and Howard Metzenbaum stood alone among Senate Democrats as protectors of the Constitution.

What about the House's reaction to the Great Flag Scare? A resolution was also brought before that body. It began: "Resolved, that the House of Representatives hereby expresses its profound concern over the Supreme Court decision in *Texas* v. *Johnson.*"

During the previous term of the Court, had the House expressed its "profound concern" over the Court's approval of the execution of sixteen- and seventeen-year-olds? Did the House trumpet its "profound concern" when the Court decided that indigent prisoners on Death Row do not have a constitutional right to a lawyer for a second round of state court appeals—even though many of those appeals have turned out to be successful?

Only in the flag case did the members of the House rend their garments and cry vengeance against the Court. Surely there were dissenters? Just five. The only one from New York was Ted Weiss of Manhattan. And there were four dissenting black congressmen: George Crockett of Detroit, William Clay of St. Louis, Gus Savage of Chicago, and Ronald Dellums of Oakland, California.

Of the dissenters in both chambers, Ted Weiss had the most cogent analysis of the developing panic: "We have nothing to fear from the flag-burners, but we have a great deal to fear from those who have lost faith in the Constitution."

As if to illustrate Weiss's point, a Democrat, Douglas Applegate of Ohio, proposed that Supreme Court Justices be subject to a reconfirmation vote by the Senate after six years of service.

Congressional veterans remembered what happened when the federal flag-desecration statute—which was on the books until struck down by the Supreme Court in *Texas* v. *Johnson,* along with the state flag statutes—came up for a vote in 1967. "Fifteen of us," Congressman Don Edwards told me, "voted against it. Just fifteen.

One of us, John Dowd of upstate New York, was defeated because of it. The rest of us lost a lot of votes. I lost twenty thousand."

There is no indication—either in the text of the Constitution or in our cases interpreting it—that a separate judicial category exists for the American flag alone.... We decline... therefore to create for the flag an exception to the joust of principles protected by the First Amendment.
   —Justice William Brennan, majority opinion, *Texas* v. *Gregory Lee Johnson,* June 21, 1989

   "Shoot, if you must, this old gray head,
   But spare your country's flag," she said.
   —*Barbara Frietchie,* by John Greenleaf Whittier, quoted by Chief Justice William Rehnquist in his dissent in *Texas* v. *Gregory Lee Johnson*

Soon after the Supreme Court ruled, 5–4, that burning an American flag is a protected form of expression, I was traveling in the Southwest.

Before I left, I'd been reading about, and seeing on television, the days and nights of rage in Congress over the callous disregard shown by Justice William Brennan for the American people's awe and love of Old Glory.

The members of Congress kept saying that they were reflecting the shock and indignation of the folks back home. So on the road, I picked up local papers, regional papers, and tuned in the local television and radio news. There was almost nothing on the Texas flag-burning case; but every day, there was a lot of space—news reports, local columnists, syndicated columnists, editorials—on the *Webster* abortion case.

Meanwhile the Republican apparatchiks in Washington predicted that if the Democrats did not join the President's demand for a constitutional amendment to sanctify the flag, they would be burned off the rolls of Congress by an inflamed electorate.

The amendment: "The Congress and the States shall have the power to prohibit the physical desecration of the flag of the United States."

The press, print and television, reported all this as if there really was a roaring mob out there in the country, bearing fire-brands, pitchforks, and hemp. And most of the Democrats believed the press, and they cowered in fear and panic.

Said House Speaker Thomas Foley: "There is no justification for the burning and disrespect to the American flag—no cause, no issue, no circumstance justifies that."

I called Justice Brennan. As the author of the notorious opinion, had he been deluged with letters demanding he go back where he came from—which was Newark?

Some Justices don't like to read uncivil letters, but Brennan made a point of reading them all. He wanted to know what people think, even if the letters were unspeakably nasty. So I knew he'd have seen whatever came to his chambers on the flag case.

He had gotten about two dozen letters, he told me. By contrast, Brennan had been steadily getting a flood of letters about the abortion case.

Then I asked Toni House, who runs the Supreme Court's public information office, about the extent of mail the Court as a whole had been receiving on *Texas* v. *Johnson*. "I'd count it by the dozens," she said, "maybe by the hundreds, but nothing compared to the abortion mail."

If large numbers of the populace were all that fired up about cutting the First Amendment down to size, you might expect many more letters to the Supreme Court than a few hundred. The veterans' organizations alone—the American Legion, for instance—would have been able to orchestrate much more mail than that.

I called Don Edwards, a congressman from California who heads the House Subcommittee on Civil and Constitutional Rights. The subcommittee had been holding hearings both on the flag amendment and on a statute proposed by the Democrats as an alternative to a constitutional amendment. Edwards has two offices in his district, and between those two and his office in Washington, there had not been much mail. Far less, he added, than the torrent that came in when Congress was considering a pay raise for itself.

Other members of Congress told me that while they had not heard a lot from their constituents on this allegedly inflammatory matter, some of their colleagues had heard rumblings. But those intimations of thunder seemed to have faded.

And the *Washington Post* reported that "from conservative Oklahoma, Democratic Senator David L. Boren had gotten no more than 500 letters and calls on the flag issue, a fraction of the 10,000 communications he received on the congressional pay raise issue earlier this year...."

In the Lone Star State, when the Texas Court of Criminal Appeals ruled in April 1988 that the First Amendment is strong enough to protect Gregory Lee Johnson's burning of the flag, there was very little reaction among the brigades of patriots there. Indeed, after the Supreme Court had affirmed the Texas court's decision, although there had been a few protests in Texas, there had been no sustained declarations of outrage.

On the floor of the Senate, Senator Bob Kerrey of Nebraska—a Congressional Medal of Honor winner who lost part of a leg in Vietnam—told of the night he was wounded. "With the smell of my own burning flesh in my head," he had been happy he was going back to "the home of the free and the brave [which] does not need our government to protect us from those who burn a flag."

Bob Kerrey, far from being in trouble at home, reported that the folks in Nebraska, although they had at first felt a constitutional amendment was the way to go, now agreed with him that it would be a dangerous route. And on the Senate floor he added: "On the face of the evidence at hand, it seems to me that there is no need for us to do anything."

Kerrey also attacked the President for failing to lead the nation in protecting the Bill of Rights from mutilation by constitutional amendment—and instead joining the mutilators.

Meanwhile, a Washington attorney, Ivan Warner—who had been imprisoned by the North Vietnamese from 1967 to 1973—wrote about the flag furor in the *Washington Post:*

"In March of 1973, when we were released from a prisoner of war camp in North Vietnam, we were flown to Clark Air Force base in the Philippines. As I stepped out of the aircraft I looked up and saw the flag. I caught my breath, then, as tears filled my eyes, I saluted it. I never loved my country more than at that moment. Although I have received the Silver Star Medal and two Purple Hearts, they were nothing compared with the gratitude I felt then for having been allowed to serve the cause of freedom.

"Because the mere sight of the flag meant so much to me when I saw it for the first time after five and a half years, it hurts me to see other Americans willfully desecrate it. But I have been in a Communist prison where I looked into the pit of hell. I cannot compromise on freedom. It hurts to see the flag burned, but I part company with those who want to punish the flag burners. Let me explain myself.

"Early in the imprisonment, the Communists told us that we did not have to stay there. If we would only admit we were wrong, if we would only apologize, we could be released early. If we did not, we would be punished. A handful accepted, most did not. In our minds, early release under those conditions would amount to a betrayal, of our comrades, of our country and of our flag.

"Because we would not say the words they wanted us to say, they made our lives wretched. Most of us were tortured and some of my comrades died. I was tortured for most of the summer of 1969. I developed beriberi from malnutrition. I had long bouts of dysentery. I was infested with intestinal parasites. I spent thirteen months in solitary confinement. Was our cause worth all of this? Yes, it was worth all this and more.

"I remember one interrogation where I was shown a photograph of some Americans protesting the war by burning a flag. 'There,' the officer said. 'People in your country protest against your cause. That proves that you are wrong.'

"'No,' I said. 'That proves that I am right. In my country we are not afraid of freedom, even if it means that people disagree with us.' The officer was on his feet in an instant, his face purple with rage. He smashed his fist onto the table and screamed at me to shut up. While he was ranting I was astonished to see pain, compounded by fear, in his eyes. I have never forgotten that look, nor have I forgotten the satisfaction I felt at using his tool, the picture of the burning flag, against him.

"We don't need to amend the Constitution in order to punish those who burn our flag. They burn the flag because they hate America and they are afraid of freedom. What better way to hurt them than with the subversive idea of freedom? Spread freedom.... Don't be afraid of freedom."

* * *

You've got to remember your past, or you're not going to have your country anymore.

—Joseph Stinson, twenty-five, a Bush voter, explaining why teachers should be required to lead students in the Pledge of Allegiance, St. Charles, Missouri, *New York Times*, September 17, 1988.

The creator of the Pledge of Allegiance was Francis Bellamy, a writer at *Youth's Companion* magazine. He crafted the Pledge in 1892 in celebration of the four-hundredth anniversary of Columbus's discovery of this place. Bellamy was vice president of the Society of Christian Socialists, and wanted to nationalize most of the means of production in this very nation.

As David Whitman has noted in the *Washington Post*, the first state to insist that all students recite the Pledge every single day was New York. Whitman adds that the vote in Albany "came one day after the United States declared war on Spain and was the start of a long pattern in which state legislatures would typically pass mandatory pledge salutes to…forcefully inculcate patriotism."

The Massachusetts legislature decided the Pledge was not dependable enough to verify the patriotism of young scholars, and teachers were ordered to include a special loyalty oath after the Pledge. Elsewhere, especially ardent advocates of the Pledge during the 1920s were members of the then-powerful Ku Klux Klan.

All of this is a prelude to the Pledge of Allegiance's curved and bloody path to the Supreme Court. In Minersville, Pennsylvania, a mining town mired in the Depression, the school board decided on November 6, 1935, to "demand that all teachers and pupils…. be required to salute the flag of our country as a part of daily exercises. That refusal to salute the flag shall be regarded as an act of insubordination and shall be dealt with accordingly."

Before the edict, the kids in Minersville had already been compelled by school authorities to treat the flag as a sacred object every morning. So why the formal ruling? Three kids had been respectfully and stubbornly refusing to have anything to do with the ceremony. They were Lillian and William Gobitis (ages twelve and ten) and Edmund Wasiewski (whose age is not on the record). On the day the formal school board rule came down, all three were expelled.

All three were Jehovah's Witnesses, and they had been taught by their parents that the Bible commands all believers to "flee from idolatry" (1 Corinthians 10:14). And in Exodus, the Bible had made clear: "Thou shalt not make unto thee any graven image.... Thou shalt not bow down thyself to them, nor serve them."

The flag, to Jehovah's Witnesses, was and is such an "image," for the government it represents is of the world—and not of Jehovah.

In his valuable book, *Prophets with Honor* (1974), Alan Barth describes the trial of these heretics. The lawyer for the kids brought in an expert witness—Frederick William Franz, a member of the editorial department of the Jehovah's Witnesses' Watchtower Bible and Tract Society. The lawyer asked him:

"Now, Mr. Franz, what would be the penalty, if any, to a Christian, or one of Jehovah's Witnesses, who disobeys such commandments [as the need to flee from idolatry]?"

"Eternal annihilation, destruction."

The superintendent of schools testified that these were "very good children," but if the precedent were set that kids could back out of their patriotic obligations, even for reasons of conscience, the public welfare and safety would be endangered.

The federal judge conducting the trial, Albert B. Maris, was lucky that this wasn't going on during the time of Joe McCarthy. The judge actually said in open court that the flag-salute requirement "although undoubtedly adopted from patriotic motives, appears to have become in this case a means for the persecution of children for conscience's sake."

The kids won. Down there. Then the case went up to the Third Circuit Court of Appeals, which unanimously agreed with Judge Maris. At that point, the Minersville school board decided to go all the way. After all, there had been three previous compulsory flag-salute cases before the highest court in the land, and each time the flag had come out waving. Why should this case be different?

On the other hand, from the Jehovah's Witnesses' point of view, there was reason to believe that this time the Supreme Court might rule that an individual's conscience should be protected by the First Amendment, even when it shuns the Stars and Stripes. Look at who was on the Court by then: William O. Douglas, Hugo Black, Frank Murphy (also a devoted civil libertarian), and Felix

Frankfurter, the distinguished and widely influential former Harvard law professor and defender of Sacco and Vanzetti. Also on the Court was Harlan Fisk Stone, a believer in the preferential place of the First Amendment and former dean of the Columbia University Law School. And the Chief Justice was the magisterial Charles Evans Hughes, a powerful defender of the First Amendment.

Surely the Gobitis children and their schoolmate had more than a fighting chance.

The decision came down on June 3, 1940. Eight to one *against* the Jehovah's Witnesses children.

Before the decision was announced, there had been an intense effort by Felix Frankfurter, who wrote the majority opinion, to make the decision unanimous. The holdout was Harlan Fisk Stone. Frankfurter sent Stone a five-page letter. He emphasized that judges, including those on the Supreme Court, should not be legislators. A democratically elected body had passed that flag-salute edict. Furthermore, he said, the Pledge of Allegiance helps "to evoke that unifying sentiment [in the nation] without which there can ultimately be no liberties, civil or religious."

Stone wrote back that he was "truly sorry not to go along with you."

On the day of the decision, Harlan Fisk Stone—in a rare move for him—read his dissent from the bench. In the course of the dissent, he said: "History teaches us that there have been but few infringements of personal liberty by the state which have not been justified, as they are here, in the name of righteousness and the public good.... The Constitution may well elicit expressions of loyalty to it and to the government which it created, but it does not *command* such expressions.... The constitutional expression of freedom of speech and religion [cannot be overridden]." (Emphasis added.)

Once news of the decision spread, patriots throughout the country engaged in strenuous measures to purge Jehovah's Witnesses of their foul disloyalty. In one instance, Archibald Cox writes in *The Court and the Constitution* (Houghton Mifflin, 1987), a stubbornly errant Jehovah's Witness was castrated to teach him the vengeance of the spurned flag.

There is a contemporary account by the Jehovah's Witnesses of what happened to many of their members after the Supreme Court affirmed that the Pledge of Allegiance was an essential act of national security:

"In Kennebunkport, Maine, Kingdom Hall was burned. At Rockville, Maryland... police joined a mob attack on a Bible meeting. At Litchfield, Illinois, a crowd of a thousand townsfolk milled around sixty canvassing Witnesses, burning their tracts, overturning their cars.

"At Connersville, Indiana, the Witnesses' attorney was beaten and driven out of town. At Jackson, Mississippi, a veterans' organization banished the Witnesses and their trailer houses from the city. Similar incidents occurred in Texas, California, Arkansas, and Wyoming. The Department of Justice traced this wave of violence directly to the Court's decision in the first Flag Salute case. [There was mob violence against the witnesses in forty-four of the forty-eight states.]

"Jehovah's Witnesses have been... kidnapped, driven out of towns, counties, and states, tarred and feathered, forced to drink castor oil, tied together and chased like dumb beasts through the streets, castrated and maimed, taunted and insulted by demonized crowds, jailed by the hundreds without charges, and held incommunicado and denied the privilege of conferring with relatives, friends, or lawyers.

"Many other hundreds have been jailed and held in so-called 'protective custody'; some have been shot in the nighttime; some threatened with hanging and beaten into unconsciousness.... Many have had their clothes torn from them, their Bibles and other literature seized and publicly burned; their automobiles, trailers, homes and assembly places wrecked and fired...."

Witnesses were charged with sedition, and some were put on trial for that heavy crime. Some were held as "Nazis." And "in Indiana, two harmless women have been convicted of 'riotous conspiracy' because of possessing literature which the American Legion terms as being 'against the government' and have been sentenced to ten years in the penitentiary....

"In almost every case where there has been mob violence [including during trials], the public officials have stood idly by and refused to give protection, and in scores of instances the officers of the law have participated in the mobs and sometimes actually led the mobs."

There have been many aggrieved dissents in the annals of the United States Supreme Court, but none has begun on so personal, so autobiographical, a note as Felix Frankfurter's in the next flag-salute case before the Supreme Court.

In 1940, Frankfurter had grandly won a sweeping Supreme Court victory for his belief that it was entirely constitutional to expel from school children of Jehovah's Witnesses because they would not salute the flag. Now, only three years later, he was on the losing end of a 6–3 decision which stated unequivocally that no one—including Jehovah's Witnesses kids—could be forced by the state to say what he or she does not believe.

The children of three Witnesses in West Virginia had been expelled from school for refusing to salute the flag. The 1942 mandatory rule by the State Board of Education included abundant quotes from Felix Frankfurter's majority decision in the 1940 flag-salute case.

In his dissent, Frankfurter reminded his colleagues of his Jewish roots:

"One who belongs to the most vilified and persecuted minority in history is not likely to be insensible to the freedoms guaranteed by our Constitution. Were my purely personal attitude relevant, I should wholeheartedly associate myself with the general libertarian views in the Court's [majority] opinion....

"But as judges we are neither Jew nor Gentile, neither Catholic nor agnostic. We owe equal attachment to the Constitution and are equally bound by our judicial obligations, whether we derive our citizenship from the earliest or the latest immigrants to our shores."

Frankfurter was saying that if he had been a member of the legislature that had passed the flag-salute law in this case (*West Virginia State Board of Education* v. *Barnette*), he would have voted for exceptions to the statute that would have allowed kids to refuse, for religious reasons, to salute. But as a judge—indeed, as a Justice of the Court of last resort—he had to exercise judicial restraint. He had to suppress his personal views and affirm the state legislature's right to enact a law promoting good citizenship.

Frankfurter added: "Never before these Jehovah's Witness cases... has this Court overruled [one of its decisions] so as to restrict the powers of democratic government."

But the Supreme Court had begun, in a few cases, to overrule lower court rulings that had subordinated an individual's First Amendment rights to anti-free-speech decisions by democratically elected legislatures. (See Harry Kalven's *A Worthy Tradition: Freedom of Speech in America,* Harper & Row, 1988.)

But Frankfurter was right. This case far transcended flag salutes and the Jehovah's Witnesses kids. It was one of the important initial turning points toward special protection by the Court of our most fundamental individual rights and liberties.

As Archibald Cox emphasizes in *The Court and the Constitution,* when the 1943 Court turned itself upside down in these Jehovah's Witnesses cases, the way was further cleared for the Court's commitment to "a strict review of legislation [undercutting] the First Amendment" and its "preferred position."

Six years before, in a powerful statement of this "preferred position" (*De Jonge* v. *Oregon*), Charles Evans Hughes had written:

"The greater the importance of safeguarding the community from incitements to the overthrow of our institutions by force and violence, the more imperative is the need to preserve inviolate the constitutional rights of free speech, free press, and free assembly in order to maintain the opportunity for free political discussion.... Therein lies the security of the Republic, the very foundation of constitutional government."

In the second of the major flag-salute cases, the rights and liberties of the individual—as opposed to the weakening of those rights by a majoritarian legislature—were further strengthened.

In his majority opinion in *West Virginia State Board of Education* v. *Barnette,* Justice Robert Jackson said, in language as clear as country water: "The sole conflict [here] is between authority and the rights of the individual." And, he went on, the conflict goes beyond children of Jehovah's Witnesses: "While religion supplies appellees' motive for enduring the discomforts of making the issue in this case, many citizens who do not share these religious views hold such a compulsory rite to infringe constitutional liberty of the individual."

Then, in a passage that has often been quoted, Jackson became the first Justice, to my knowledge, to lay the foundation for subsequent court decisions supporting students' First Amendment rights in schools:

"The Fourteenth Amendment, as applied to the States, protects the citizen against the State itself and all of its creatures—Boards of Education not excepted. These have, of course, important, delicate, and highly discretionary functions, *but none that they may not perform within the limits of the Bill of Rights.*

"That they are educating the young for citizenship is reason for scrupulous protection of constitutional freedoms of the individual, if we are not to strangle the free mind at its source and teach youth to discount important principles of our government as mere platitudes." (Emphasis added.)

Jackson made the point that a lot of these school boards are in small towns where the press is less vigilant in reporting suspensions of the Constitution in schools, and thereby these local boards "may feel less sense of responsibility to the Constitution.

"There are village tyrants," thundered Jackson, "as well as village Hampdens, but none who acts under color of law is beyond the reach of the Constitution."

(John Hampden was a resister in the reign of Charles I, and so became a popular paladin of the rights of the individual against the tyranny of the Crown.)

The most vital part of Jackson's opinion came in answer to what Felix Frankfurter had maintained in the previous Jehovah's Witnesses case, *Minersville School District* v. *Gobitis*. In triumphing then, Frankfurter claimed that courts have no particular competence in deciding these matters. If people object to what the legislature has passed with regard to flag salutes, let them argue it out in "the forum of public opinion" rather than transfer the battle to the courtroom. That way, all the "effective means of inducing political changes are left free."

That argument convinced seven other Justices in 1940. In 1943, Robert Jackson blew it apart:

"The very purpose of a Bill of Rights was to withdraw certain subjects from the vicissitudes of political controversy, to place them beyond the reach of majorities and officials and to establish them as legal principles to be applied by the courts. One's right to life, liberty, and property, to free speech, a free press, freedom of worship and assembly, and other fundamental rights may not be submitted to vote; they depend on the outcome of no election."

And that is the least understood—though the most basic—element of American government.

As for George Bush, Justice Jackson had people like him in mind: "Compulsory unification of opinion achieves only the unanimity of the graveyard. It seems trite but necessary to say that the First Amendment to our Constitution was designed to avoid these ends by avoiding these beginnings.

"There is no mysticism in the American concept of the state or of the nature or origin of its authority. We set up government by consent of the governed, *and the Bill of Rights denies those in power any legal opportunity to coerce that consent.*" (Emphasis added.)

"... These principles grew in soil which also produced a philosophy that the individual was the center of society....

"... Those who begin coercive elimination of dissent soon find themselves exterminating dissenters.... Freedom to differ is not limited to things that do not matter much. That would be a mere shadow of freedom. The test of its substance is the right to differ as to things that touch the heart of the existing order."

George Bush failed to secure an amendment to the First Amendment of the Constitution that would guard the flag against any and all who would desecrate it.

The Democratic leadership in Congress, however, succeeded—for a time—in proving their "patriotism" by passing the Flag Protection Act, which held that anyone who "knowingly mutilates, defaces, physically defiles, burns, maintains on the floor or ground, or tramps upon" the United States flag is subject to a maximum prison term of one year and a $100,000 fine.

It was a disingenuous statute, purporting to remove any political content when punishing people for desecrating the flag. The law would go into effect if anyone harmed the fabric of the flag, regardless of the motivation and political views of the desecrators.

That same Democratic leadership had roundly criticized the President for jingoistically pressing for a constitutional amendment on behalf of the flag. And when the Democrats succeeded in blocking that raid on the First Amendment, the *Washington Post* editorialized that "people seem to understand now... that free speech is to be protected more than fabric, and that the right to protest is to be valued even above the material object that symbolizes the nation. The Senate, in refusing to change the Bill of Rights, has preserved something far more important than the flag."

But then the Senate and the House concocted the Flag Protection Act, which would have indeed protected the fabric of the flag more than free speech.

When protesters burned the flag nonetheless, Federal District judges in Seattle and the District of Columbia struck down this slippery new law on the ground that flag-burning is indeed an exercise of symbolic speech and so must be protected by the First Amendment.

Flag-burning was again before the Supreme Court and again Justice William Brennan, writing for a majority of five Justices, struck down the statute. The new law violates the First Amendment, he said, by "criminally prescribing expressive conduct because of its likely communicative impact."

But the government had claimed that a majority of the nation opposed flag-burning. Said Brennan: "Any suggestion that the government's interest in suppressing speech becomes more weighty as popular opposition to that speech grows is foreign to the First Amendment."

From the beginning, there were variously illuminating comments during the Great Flag War. Representative Jim Inhofe, a Republican from Oklahoma, declared: "There comes a time when freedom of speech is not in the best interest of this country, and we've reached that point [with regard to the Supreme Court's decision in the Texas flag-burning case]."

And in a letter to the *Dallas Morning News,* Dale M. Greer wrote:

"It doesn't make sense to think that we should imprison others for the sake of a flag which is supposed to represent liberty.

"On the one hand, if the flag is just a fancy piece of cloth, we've got no business telling people what they can or can't do with it, so long as they bought it or made it themselves, because then it's just a piece of property. On the other hand, if the flag is a symbol of freedom and of our democracy, then it represents ideas just as words represent ideas, and in that case we've got no more business telling people what they can or can't do with the flag than we do telling them how to think.

"The governments of some other nations try to tell their people how to think. The governments of Iran or China would almost certainly hang someone for burning their flags. Do we really want to emulate countries such as these?"

Attempts to place the flag outside the First Amendment were recalled by historian C. Vann Woodward in a July 18, 1991, *New York Review of Books* article dissecting the "politically correct" assaults on freedom of speech and thought at American colleges and universities.

"In a commencement address at the University of Michigan on May 4," Professor Woodward wrote, "President Bush spoke out for freedom—freedom 'to think and speak one's mind,' perhaps 'the most fundamental and deeply revered of all our liberties,' yet one now under assault 'on some college campuses.'" So said George Bush.

But the same President who spoke for freedom in 1991 had—Professor Woodward reminded us—"two years earlier... proposed an amendment to the Bill of Rights against flag-burning."

The President had no comment on an Italian citizen, studying at Seton Hall University, who was forced to withdraw from that college and from this country in 1991 because he declined to wear an American flag on his basketball uniform. Marco Lokar is against all wars, and so did not join his teammates in wearing the flag patch to support allied troops in the Gulf War. He also refused to wear an Italian flag.

As *The New York Times* noted in an editorial, Lokar was harassed on the basketball court and his family was "relentlessly threatened by telephone. Fearful of his own safety and that of his wife and the unborn child she carries, he quit Seton Hall and announced he was taking his wife back to Trieste"—and away from this sweet land of liberty.

"God, I understand how they feel, but when will they think?"

During the fall of 1977, she had been speaking at synagogues about the First Amendment—more specifically, about the First Amendment rights of American Nazis to demonstrate in Skokie, Illinois. (There were some fifty of them who wanted to wear their Storm-Trooper uniforms, and display the swastika and such signs as "Free Speech for White People.")

Her credentials: She had barely escaped the Holocaust herself, had grown up in Israel, and had long been active in American Jewish organizations. She was also on the board of directors of the New York Civil Liberties Union.

"I have been shouted down, cursed, vilified," she said to me of her synagogue journeys. "They tell me that Nazis have no rights, and I try to tell them the First Amendment has to be for everyone—or it will be for no one. They will not hear this. God, I understand how they feel, but when will they *think* again?"

Most Jews felt very strongly about Skokie, especially the 45,000 who lived there—3,000 of whom were Holocaust survivors. The total population was 70,000.

I, too, had been speaking in support of the American Civil Liberties Union's defense of the free-expression rights of those Nazis, and had experiences similar to those of the woman who had lived in Israel. One afternoon, a distinguished-looking white-haired lawyer in a New Jersey audience had earlier been talking with brilliant precision about various government invasions of First Amendment rights in a dreadful new federal criminal code that was then in the House of Representatives. But when Skokie came up, the lawyer started shouting that allowing Nazis to demonstrate in Skokie would lead to Jews being shoved into American ovens. I, also a Jew, desperately wanted him to know that keeping the First Amendment intact was the best defense against waking up one morning and hearing on a loudspeaker that all Jews must assemble in Times Square—or its equivalent in other cities—within an hour. I wanted him to understand that I have had that fantasy since I was a boy in rampantly anti-Semitic Boston, and that I do not entirely believe it to be, necessarily, forever a fantasy. But he would not listen and came very close to trying to punch me out.

So many liberals and self-defined libertarians were so infuriated by the ACLU's action in the Skokie case that 15 to 20 percent of ACLU's national membership of 250,000 resigned or did not renew as a direct result of Skokie. No other single controversy in ACLU history damaged the organization so badly. And in Illinois, where the state ACLU had been doing the legal work for the Nazis, some 30 percent of that affiliate's eight thousand members at the time left in raging disgust—leading to serious cutbacks in staff and programs.

No other group supported the ACLU. And the greatly respected former attorney general of the United States, Edward Levi, ducked out of a commitment to sign a public statement urging ACLU members not to desert it. Constitutional scholar Philip Kurland—like Levi on the University of Chicago faculty—disagreed with court decisions won by the ACLU affirming the free speech rights of the Nazis. And George Will said majority rule should have prevailed in Skokie. The furor over Skokie, therefore, was instructive—a blistering reminder of the selective belief in the First Amendment that characterizes many Americans.

The extent of the defections from its ranks came as a surprise, however, to officials and staff lawyers of the ACLU. They had expected to be badly bruised by the disclosure during the previous summer that from 1953 to 1959 certain officers of the ACLU had been secretly cooperating with the FBI's search for "Communists and subversives" within the organizations.

"I was sure we'd get a lot of resignations," a member of the ACLU staff told me, "from people who thought we had no credibility anymore—even though the present leadership could no more cooperate with the FBI than they could support prayers in the schools. Yet no resignations came because of the FBI revelations. But when Skokie erupted and we proved how much credibility we do have in terms of the First Amendment, that's when the earth really moved."

In the spring of 1977, the Chicago-based National Socialist Party of America (a coven of standardly noisome Nazis) decided to focus their demonstrations on suburban areas with sizable Jewish populations. Skokie very much suited their provocative purpose.

The Nazis intended to march in Skokie on May 1 and July 4, but the village obtained a state circuit court injunction preventing the demonstrations. Enter the American Civil Liberties Union, on the side of the Nazis, followed by a series of court skirmishes leading to a July 1977 decision by the Illinois Appellate Court that the Nazis could demonstrate or march in Skokie but were absolutely forbidden to display or wear the swastika.

"The swastika," declared the court, "is a personal affront to every member of the Jewish faith, in remembering the nearly consummated genocide of their people committed within memory by those who used the swastika as their symbol." And that symbol, the court added, is not protected by the First Amendment because it could very well provoke violent reaction among certain Jews of Skokie, particularly those who had barely lived through the Holocaust.

The ACLU filed an appeal on First Amendment grounds, arguing that the swastika is as fully protected symbolic speech as were the black armbands, in the *Tinker* case, worn by the school children in Des Moines protesting the Vietnam War. (See chapter XIII for more on *Tinker.*) To allow the state to decide which "symbols" are lawful, and which are not, is to weaken the First Amendment dangerously. After all, given that power, who can tell what the state will decide the next time controversial symbolic speech is tested?

Those supporting the village of Skokie countered by claiming that this particular form of expression was deliberately calculated to ignite violence, and surely would—as the Illinois Appellate Court had said. Indeed, Skokie officials had testified that they would probably not be able to control the town's fiercely anti-Nazi citizens if the homegrown fascists were to appear.

In answer, the ACLU pointed out that it is unconstitutional to ban speech on the basis of a "heckler's veto." If Skokie was so sure that certain hostile groups would be hard to control, the ACLU pointed out, why didn't the village seek an injunction against *them* to prohibit *their* unlawful actions? If extra police power were needed, it must be used to protect speech, even the speech of Nazis.

Also, keeping the First Amendment principle the same but changing the cast, what about historic "provocative" demonstrations? Recalling the Selma, Alabama, march led by Martin Luther King, the *Nation* noted that the Selma demonstration "would never have taken place if the authorities had been allowed to ban it on the ground that it would provoke the rage of white opponents of civil rights for black citizens and therefore endanger the peace."

This argument had no impact on the growing number of ACLU members who continued to send in their furious letters of resignation. Often they attached their membership cards—on the back of which, by the way, the First Amendment was printed. It was grotesque, many of them said, to equate the Nazis with Martin Luther King. As a letter to the *Nation* put it, "Martin Luther King's marches furthered human freedom and dignity, and aimed at spreading nonviolence, while the Nazis want to degrade and destroy freedom and dignity, and spread violence."

But nowhere in the First Amendment does it say that freedom of speech is limited only to ideas and symbols that further freedom, dignity, and nonviolence.

Those who opposed the right of the Nazis to march often offered a further argument against the ACLU's position: The Nazis, they said, aim at gathering the numerical strength to tear down the very institutions and principles that the ACLU presents as a shield for the Nazis. True, this particular Chicago cadre is small, but so was another seemingly ludicrous Nazi band in Germany. The more the Nazis are allowed to gain strength here, the more the freedoms of the rest of the citizenry—particularly those of Jews and blacks at first—will be in peril.

This viewpoint is a variation on the theory that the Constitution is not a suicide pact. Should a rational society permit unfettered freedom of speech to those who exist to destroy it? If it does, is this indeed a rational society?

Justice Oliver Wendell Holmes answered that question forcefully and lucidly in a 1925 dissent (*Gitlow* v. *New York*). Benjamin Gitlow and colleagues had been convicted of distributing literature proposing "revolutionary mass action" to replace the present government of the United States. The Supreme Court affirmed the conviction. Joined by Justice Brandeis, Holmes took another view:

"It is said that the manifesto [by Gitlow] was more than a theory, that it was an incitement. *Every idea is an incitement.* It offers itself for belief and if believed is acted on unless some other belief outweighs it or some failure of energy stifles the movement at its birth.

"The only difference between the expression of an opinion and an incitement in the narrower sense is the speaker's enthusiasm for the result.... Eloquence may set fire to reason. But whatever may be said of the redundant [Gitlow] discourse before us, it had no chance of starting a present conflagration. *If in the long run the beliefs expressed in proletarian dictatorship are destined to be accepted by the dominant forces of the community, the only meaning of free speech is that they should be given their chance and have their way.*" (Emphasis added.)

Holmes's logic is inescapable. If speech is to be free, there is always the risk that those who would destroy free speech may be sufficiently eloquent to use that constitutional freedom to end it. But if speech is to be limited to prevent that possibility, then the enemies of free expression have already won a significant victory— even as they are silenced. And once the concept of curbing speech is established, those enemies, each time the state suppresses speech, will have moved closer to their goal of destroying free speech.

And so it happened in Skokie. On May 3, 1977, in order to bar the Nazis, the village passed a set of ordinances imposing criminal penalties on certain forms of speech and assembly. Without mentioning the Nazis by name, the ordinances first required that no parade or assembly involving more than fifty persons could be held unless there was at least thirty days' notice for a demonstration permit—and unless a $350,000 insurance policy was obtained by the demonstrators. The latter, covering public liability and property damage, cost anywhere from $100 to $900, depending on the risk. An underwriter willing to insure also had to be found, and that was not always a real possibility—especially if the group was decidedly unpopular.

Also prohibited, under any circumstances, was any demonstration that would "incite violence, hatred, abuse, or hostility toward a person or group of persons by reason or reference to racial, ethnic, national, or religious affiliation." So much for Oliver Wendell Holmes's most basic principle of the Constitution—free thought must include free thought for those whose ideas we hate.

The lengthy notice for a permit, moreover, would prevent ad hoc demonstrations—sometimes the most valuable kind, since free speech often has to be timely to be effective. In addition, the insurance provision turned the First Amendment into a document that discriminates against the lower economic classes. Suppose you don't have $100 or $900?

Obviously the ordinances, as a whole, would smother free expression. And so Skokie, in vehement reaction to the Nazis' assertion of *their* right to free speech, had managed to greatly delimit *anyone's* right to free speech in that village.

Skokie, to be sure, had generally been described as a "liberal" community. But those liberals had now constructed a law that—as the New York Civil Liberties Union's then-executive director, Ira Glasser, said—"is the same kind of law that was used in Birmingham, Alabama, and throughout the South to stop civil rights demonstrators. It is the same kind of law that was used against the Wobblies in the earlier part of the century, and by Mayor Hague in New Jersey to stop labor organizers. And it is the same kind of law that was used repeatedly only a few years before to stop anti-war demonstrations."

These Skokie ordinances—trampling the letter and spirit of the First Amendment—also became part of the litigation in which the ACLU remained stubbornly involved, despite its quite stunning loss of membership.

At the end of January 1978, one of the court battles over the Nazis and Skokie reached the highest tribunal in the state, the Illinois Supreme Court. Overruling the Appellate Court, the justices, by a 6–1 vote, declared that the Nazis had a constitutional right to display swastikas in Skokie. Upholding the ACLU, the court explained: "The display of these swastikas—as offensive to the principles of a free nation as the memories it recalls may be—is symbolic political speech intended to convey to the public the beliefs of those who display it." Furthermore, the court said that anticipation of a hostile audience cannot justify prior restraint of speech.

The Illinois Supreme Court dismissed another suit as well. Brought by an organization called Survivors of the Holocaust, the suit argued that psychological and emotional wounds caused by imprisonment in Nazi death camps would impel the survivors in Skokie to try to stop the Nazi demonstration, quite possibly by violent means. (One of the complainants noted in an affidavit that he had watched his mother being buried alive by the German Nazis.) Here again, the threat of violence, however understandable the motivation, cannot be a reason, in law, to shut off speech.

Or, as New York State Judge Charles Breitel said seventeen years earlier in another case that got the ACLU into trouble—the defense of Nazi George Lincoln Rockwell's right to speak in a New York City park—"The unpopularity of views, their shocking quality, their obnoxiousness, and even their alarming impact is not enough [to prohibit speech]. Otherwise, the preacher of any strange doctrine could be stopped; the anti-racist himself could be suppressed if he undertakes to speak in 'restricted' areas; and one who asks that the public schools be open indiscriminately to all ethnic groups could be lawfully suppressed, if only he chose to speak where persuasion is most needed."

The United States Supreme Court refused to review the decision of the Illinois Supreme Court. (Justices Harry Blackmun and Byron White dissented. They wanted to hear arguments on the limits to freedom of speech.) For the battered ACLU, the run of resignations eventually stopped. In time, the ACLU grew again, eventually reaching a higher membership than it had before. But if another Skokie were to test the membership, many are likely to again fail the test because not all members of the ACLU are primarily civil libertarians.

Skokie turned out to be a double lesson in liberty. The case itself vividly illustrated the First Amendment importance of symbolic speech and the indivisibility of all free speech. Simultaneously, the reaction to the ACLU's position by so many who considered themselves liberals and even libertarians emphasized—as no other case in many years—how fragile throughout the land is support for the still revolutionary notion that the state has no business squashing anybody's ideas or symbols. *Anybody's.*

The ACLU has won more renowned victories than its Skokie success. But the ACLU has seldom won a more vital internal battle than its decision to stay with the First Amendment rights of Nazis even if the great majority of the membership were to fall away.

"Hell," a young Jewish ACLU lawyer on the case told me, "if worst came to worst and we had folded, these bastards and their fucking swastikas would still need representation. I'd have taken the case on my own."

Aryeh Neier, national executive director of the ACLU at the time, said: "As a Jew, and a refugee from Nazi Germany, I have strong personal reasons for finding Nazis repugnant. Freedom of speech protects my right to denounce Nazis with all the vehemence I think proper. Despite my hatred of their vicious doctrine, I realize that it is in my interests to defend their right to preach it."

But the National Lawyers Guild, a group of lawyers on the left, which has done valuable civil rights work and has defended the civil liberties of people with whom it agrees, accused the ACLU of "poisonous evenhandedness" in the Skokie cases.

And during a grim period of the ACLU, when members were resigning in angry hordes, David Goldberger, legal director of the ACLU and attorney for Frank Collin, the head of the National Socialist Party (the Nazis), wrote to many of Chicago's criminal defense lawyers for their support in order to offset fierce public criticism of the ACLU—and those membership losses. Goldberger thought that defense lawyers, above everyone else, would understand the bar's ethical responsibility to represent unpopular clients, and therefore would rise in spirited defense of the ACLU, not to mention the First Amendment.

"The response to the letter," said Goldberger, "was silence." Nor had he been able to find any volunteer attorneys.

During the long march through the courts, Goldberger, the lead lawyer on the case, suffered much verbal abuse and after a while, as I discovered, disguised his voice on the phone until he knew who was calling. He did receive a letter of support from a woman:

"I was one of the youth of Jehovah's Witnesses during World War II—stoned, spat upon, jailed without due process, urinated upon and reviled because my religion forbade me to salute the flag or buy war stamps in school. I resigned my ministry in 1951 but eleven years was long enough to learn the value of the First Amendment to a person espousing an unpopular viewpoint."

"This is the hour of danger for the First Amendment."

On December 4, 1991, there came before the United States Supreme Court for oral arguments a case that could have restricted freedom of speech more than any other case in many years.

R.A.V. v. *St. Paul, Minnesota* started with a cross-burning at 2:30 in the morning in the front yard of the first black family in a working-class neighborhood in St. Paul, Minnesota. Asleep were Russell and Laura Jones and their five children (ages three to ten). It was a family of Jehovah's Witnesses.

One of the cross burners was Robert Viktora, seventeen at the time of the crime. He is the R.A.V. in the title of the case.

His attorney, Edward Cleary, had recently obtained an acquittal for a black man charged with murder. Earlier, Cleary and his partner had defended a black gang member accused of shooting a young white girl. Cleary received a lot of verbal abuse from whites for taking on that client, and he has been reviled by some blacks and white liberals for having taken a court-ordered appointment in the case of the cross-burner.

Cleary told me and many others that the cross-burning was "repugnant and reprehensible" and that there was no question in his mind that Viktora should be punished. But Viktora was not charged under such laws already on the books as arson, trespass or destruction of property.

He was charged with assault with intent to cause fear of immediate bodily harm or death. But he has not come to trial yet on that count because the prosecutor, Tom Foley, was out for a bigger prize—the first successful prosecution under a St. Paul "hate speech" ordinance which would have been copied by towns and cities and colleges throughout the United States if the Supreme Court agreed with Foley.

That ordinance, *not* Robert Viktora, was being tried before the Supreme Court.

This is St. Paul City Ordinance section 292.02: Disorderly Conduct:

"Whoever places on public or private property a symbol, object, appellation, characterization or graffiti, including, but not limited to, a burning cross or Nazi swastika, which one knows or has reasonable grounds to know arouses anger, alarm or resentment in others on the basis of race, color, creed, religion or gender commits disorderly conduct and shall be guilty of a misdemeanor."

It is because of this ordinance that Ed Cleary took the case of *R.A.V.* v. *St. Paul* to the Supreme Court. When he rose before the Justices in December, Cleary, who is not a man given to hyberbole, told them: "This is the hour of danger for the First Amendment."

Harvard Law School Professor Lawrence Tribe pointed out in *The New York Times* that this case came before the Court at a time when the First Amendment is under siege throughout the country, and not only from the political and religious Right:

"... people in so many contexts—hate speech on campus, feminists against pornography, political correctness—are making the argument that you can suppress certain kinds of speech just because it does so much harm...

"The First Amendment is almost always tested with speech that is profoundly divisive or painful. But if you start making exceptions, and suppressing speech that is hurtful, these exceptions will swallow free speech, and the only speech that will be left protected will be abstracted, emotionally lightweight speech that doesn't pack any wallop."

Remember, the issue before the Supreme Court was whether the cross-burning that night in the yard of the black family should be punished. Of course, it should. The issue is whether it should be punished under so broad and vague and far-reaching a statute as the St. Paul ordinance.

In the best brief submitted to the Supreme Court on this case—written by Bruce Ennis for the Association of American Publishers and the Freedom to Read Foundation—Ennis makes the crucial point:

"... although in this case the ordinance is being applied to a 'message of racial supremacy' and was.... directed to a minority group, the ordinance covers far more than hate speech directed at minority groups. *There is no limitation on the subject matter of the speech, so long as it 'arouses anger, alarm, or resentment in others'* based on race, color, creed, religion or gender."

And as for racist messages, "if the St. Paul ordinance had been in effect in the South during the 1950s, it could have been used to prosecute a black family for putting a sign on their front lawn demanding: 'Integrate all-white schools now!' That speech would certainly have 'arouse[d] anger, alarm, or resentment in others on the basis of race.'"

In 1992 and beyond, if the Supreme Court had upheld the St. Paul ordinance, anyone with strong opinions would have been in peril. In the December 1991 *St. Paul Pioneer-Press,* Steven Thomma of that paper's Washington Bureau looked ahead:

"...what if the same ordinance were used to prosecute a rabbi whose Star of David angered Arabs who saw it as a Zionist symbol? Or a priest whose crucifix caused resentment to devoted atheists? Or an abortion foe whose picture of an aborted fetus alarmed abortion-rights advocates?"

Or the other way around. What if a pro-choice advocate placed on the lawn of her or his own home a "symbol, object, appellation or characterization" that accused the Catholic Church of cruelly and viciously enslaving women through its aggressive opposition to abortion rights? That would cause anger, alarm, and resentment in a lot of people who—under this ordinance—could bring charges of disorderly conduct against the pro-choicer.

Faced with this dangerous dragnet law, one might have expected those organizations known for their resistance to government suppression to unite against the St. Paul ordinance—and to send bristling briefs to the Supreme Court showing how this ordinance threatens their own constituents.

That's not what happened, and this deep split concerning the First Amendment is going to help censors of all kinds in Congress as well as in cities and states because it fragments groups that are often in alliance. The division will continue long after the Supreme Court decision in the St. Paul case, and I don't think anything can be done about it because the split is caused by the inability of one side to learn from history.

Submitting briefs to the Supreme Court against the St. Paul ordinance and its evisceration of the First Amendment were: the American Civil Liberties Union, the American Jewish Congress, the Center for Individual Rights, the Association of American Publishers, the Freedom to Read Foundation, and the conservative Patriots Defense Fund of Texas.

On the other hand, there was this long dismaying list of organizations that support the St. Paul ordinance, and to hell with the First Amendment.

The Asian-American Legal Defense Fund; the NAACP (the NAACP Legal Defense Fund would have been on the list but didn't have time to file a brief); the Anti-Defamation League of B'nai B'rith (two of whose lawyers helped the prosecutor prepare for the Supreme Court); People for the American Way; the Young Women's Christian Association of the USA; the Center for Constitutional Rights; the Center for Democratic Renewal; the National Council of Black Lawyers.

Also, the National Council of La Raza; the International Union, United Automobile, Aerospace and Agricultural Implement Workers of America—UAW; the National Organization of Black Law Enforcement Executives; the National Lawyers Guild (of course); the United Church of Christ Commission for Racial Justice; the National Institute Against Prejudice and Violence; the Greater Boston Civil Rights Coalition; the National Coalition of Black Lesbians and Gays; and the National Black Women's Health Network (that brief was written in part by Catharine MacKinnon).

Weep for the First Amendment. The members of every group in that list of supporters of the St. Paul ordinance would have been vulnerable if the Supreme Court had followed their lead.

On December 1, 1991, the *Minneapolis Star Tribune* reported: "Attorney William Kunstler, who represented defendants in the recent flag-burning cases before the U.S. Supreme Court, is siding with the prosecution in the St. Paul case."

That seemed likely. Kunstler is a founder and vice-president of New York's Center for Constitutional Rights, and since the Center went against the First Amendment in this case, I figured Kunstler might too. Still, I called him.

The *Minneapolis Star Tribune* was wrong. "I'm opposed to any ordinance like this," Kunstler told me. "That puts me in conflict with a lot of my constituencies." (His client in the flag-burning case, Gregory Lee Johnson, for instance, had sided with the St. Paul prosecutor.)

"In the St. Paul case," Kunstler said, "I'm a strict First Amendment supporter. If this ordinance stands up, the First Amendment will be in shambles."

As for why his usual allies are on the other side, Kunstler said of the black groups in particular, "You tell a black person that a cross has been burned and all he or she sees is that burning cross."

But there was more to it than that. Some of the groups, like the National Lawyers Guild, have traditionally had what I would call an ideologically elitist view of the First Amendment. Guild members will support your First Amendment rights if they agree with your views. Otherwise, if you're not part of their beloved elite, go to the ACLU for help.

Nearly all the groups—including the Guild—on the anti-First-Amendment list in this case are obsessed with the need to smite hate speech, hip and thigh. Most have supported the punishment of "hate speech" codes on college campuses and in bills before state legislatures. The Anti-Defamation League's model "hate crimes" statutes or variations of it have been adopted in many states. (These statutes increase the penalties for crimes—like physical assaults—if the perpetrators use bigoted speech.)

The NAACP has pushed for "hate speech" laws in various cities and states, and the other organizations believe in "balancing" the First Amendment against the hurt and harm caused by offensive speech. The First Amendment always loses.

By contrast to these smiters of the First Amendment, there was a letter in the January 4, 1992 *New York Times* that distills the other side of this argument for "balancing" the First Amendment against "hate speech." The Lost-Found Nation of Islam had recently been denied permission to hold a meeting at a public elementary school in Harlem once officials at the Board of Education found out there were posters proclaiming the title of the main speaker's address: "Are Jews Hiding the Truth?"

Thereupon, James Vlasto, Chancellor Joseph Fernandez's spokesman, said the meeting had been canceled because "We cannot have hate or propaganda of any kind emanating from our schools."

Michael Meyers (black) of the New York Civil Rights Coalition and Norman Siegel (Jewish) of the New York Civil Liberties Union protested to the Board of Education and to Fernandez. In addition, Siegel wrote to *The New York Times*:

"It is understandable that government officials should be concerned about the increase in hatred, racism, and anti-Semitism that seems to have engulfed our city. We share this concern. However, government officials must be scrupulously vigilant in guaranteeing that constitutional protections are not discarded.

"It is well-established constitutional doctrine that whenever government permits private groups and individuals to use publicly owned facilities, such permission cannot be conditioned on the content of the speech or determined by whether government approves or disapproves of the group's political message. To do so is to violate the principles in the First Amendment of the Constitution.

"This month, Associate Justice Sandra Day O'Connor, speaking for a unanimous Supreme Court [the 'Son of Sam' case concerning the proceeds of books written by people convicted of a crime] stated:

"'The Government's ability to impose content-based burdens on speech raises the specter that the Government may effectively drive certain ideas or viewpoints from the marketplace.'"

This is not in Siegel's letter to the *Times*, but Justice O'Connor added: "The First Amendment presumptively places this sort of discrimination [concerning the content of speech] *beyond the power of government*... 'The fact that society may find speech offensive is not a sufficient reason for suppressing it. *Indeed, if it is the speaker's opinion that gives offense that consequence is a reason for giving it constitutional protection.*'" (Emphasis added.)

Returning to whether a public school should be the after-hours site of a group asking "Are Jews Hiding the Truth?" Norman Siegel ended his letter to the *Times*:

"Denying the use of Public School 154 to the Lost-Found Nation of Islam for Mr. Vlasto's rationale is in direct violation of the Constitution."

As usual, people and organizations who take the side of the First Amendment in controversial cases are rare. One of those in opposition to the St. Paul "hate speech" law was David Cole, long associated with the Center for Constitutional Rights and who is now also a professor at the Georgetown University Law Center.

Cole, like just about everybody at the Center for Constitutional Rights, has spent his career litigating against racism and other forms of discrimination, including the punishing of speech spoken or printed by those on the Left. (He was deeply involved in the flag-burning case.)

Of the St. Paul ordinance, Cole told me: "It is dangerous to empower the government to make these kinds of judgments—that is, which groups' speech should be protected and which should not.

"Giving the state the power to suppress speech is always more dangerous to those who want to change society."

Yet the prosecutor in the St. Paul case, Tom Foley, told the Supreme Court of the United States:

"Given the historical experience of African Americans, a burning cross targeted at a black family under the circumstances outlined, is an unmistakable threat. Terroristic conduct such as this can find no protection in the Constitution."

Foley also claimed that the Minnesota Supreme Court had sufficiently "narrowed" the ordinance to make it constitutional. But it still remained dangerously overbroad. At oral arguments before the United States Supreme Court, the Justices did not seem impressed by this "narrowing."

Defense attorney Ed Cleary kept on saying that there are other ways to punish cross-burning without endangering everybody's free speech.

Russ and Laura Jones—who, with their five children were the targets of the cross-burning—do not agree. Being Jehovah's Witnesses, as Ruth Marcus noted in the *Washington Post*, they "are especially sensitive to free-speech arguments."

But they do not see *R.A.V.* v. *St. Paul* as a First Amendment case. "If it was just a view," says Laura Jones, "it would be fine. But we took this as a threat, and all black people take a cross-burning as a threat, just as all Jewish people take a swastika splattered across the wall as a threat."

But the seriousness of the cross-burning, which is indeed a threat, is not disputed by the First Amendment side. Under the St. Paul "hate speech" ordinance, if Russ and Laura Jones were to put on their lawn a message praising children who refuse to salute the flag because of their religious convictions, that message would arouse anger, alarm and resentment in some passers-by. And that could result in the arrest of Russ and Laura Jones.

On June 22, 1992, the Supreme Court unanimously struck down the St. Paul ordinance. And five of the justices—in a landmark decision—went further. They greatly expanded the First

Amendment's protection of "hate speech" throughout the country.

Said Justice Antonin Scalia for the majority: "The point of the First Amendment is that majority preferences must be expressed in some fashion other than silencing speech on the basis of its content.... Let there be no mistake about our belief that burning a cross in someone's front yard is reprehensible. But St. Paul has sufficient means at its disposal to prevent such behavior without adding the First Amendment to the fire."

As the *Washington Post* pointed out in an editorial: "The ruling will force reconsideration of hundreds of laws and speech codes in public universities. All regulations that impose content-based restrictions on speech are in jeopardy. " Presumably this jeopardy extends to the laws, in nearly all the states, that increase prison sentences for crimes committed out of racial, religious, or other forms of bias.

The crucial importance of this decision—in a time of continual attacks on the First Amendment from the Right and the Left—was underlined by the *Washington Post*: "The preservation of a forum in which even insulting, hurtful, and outrageous ideas can be expressed is an essential price of our system; without it, free speech would be fatally undermined."

"The Klan is in effect a persecuted group...."

> Privacy in one's associations.... may in many circumstances be indispensable to freedom of association, particularly where a group espouses dissident beliefs.—JUSTICE JOHN HARLAN, DELIVERING THE DECISION OF THE SUPREME COURT, *NAACP* V. *ALABAMA* (1958)

Many people say they believe that everybody is entitled to his or her rights under the First Amendment. But then come the exceptions—depending on whom you're talking to.

There are those who say everyone is protected by the First Amendment except Jesse Helms or Louis Farrakhan or the Ku Klux Klan. There have to be some limits.

Consider the Ku Klux Klan's test of the First Amendment and its supporters in Mississippi in the 1970s. They wanted to hold a rally proclaiming the glories of segregation. They wanted to hold it—after hours—in the yard of a public elementary school that was under a court order to integrate. When they were turned down by the board of education, the Klan went to the state's American Civil Liberties Union affiliate. The schoolyard was a public place, they said, and they had a First Amendment right of association and assembly there.

There was a bitter fight inside the Mississippi ACLU, which eventually involved officers of the national ACLU, who—as was to happen later in Skokie, Illinois—understood that the First Amendment is indivisible. Once it starts to be applied selectively, no one, ultimately, will have a safe place to speak or associate.

Finally, the Mississippi ACLU—at a high internal cost— acknowledged the Klan's right to have that permit to demonstrate in the schoolyard. In the wake of that decision, ten of the twenty-one board members resigned, including the seven black members.

The Klan clasped the First Amendment in its odious embrace again recently in Georgia in 1990, thereby infuriating a goodly number of civil rights workers and civil libertarians. Especially since this case had to do with a member of the Klan deliberately breaking a 1952 Georgia law that forbade the wearing of masks or hoods in public. That law had been aimed at the Klan because, as a vintage Klan watcher says: "A Klansman in a Klan mask does have an organizational history of violence."

Defying that law last February was Shade Miller, Jr. He was unemployed, and a member of the Invisible Empire, Knights of the Ku Klux Klan. Miller believed that the Constitution was being violated by the 1952 statute that prohibited him—or anyone else in Georgia—from wearing "a mask, hood, or device by which any portion of the face is so hidden [as] to conceal the identity of the wearer."

The intent of that law was to diminish the violence perpetrated by men in masks on the theory that once the protection of anonymity was removed, unmasked bigots would slink away.

On the other hand, Shade Miller's position was that members of the Klan who were forced to show their naked faces while on parade would become pariahs in the community. They might even run some physical danger.

So, on the fateful day of his civil disobedience, Shade Miller, Jr., drove his pickup truck to the county courthouse in Lawrenceville, and ceremoniously put on his mask and hood. Miller, as he had desired, was arrested. If convicted, he would be subject to a thousand-dollar fine and a year in prison. As they say in the trade, this was a test case.

To obtain a lawyer, Miller went to the president of the Georgia affiliate of the ACLU, Michael Hauptman, who is a man of passion, extensive skills, and just as extensive a sense of irony.

This was not to be, however, a defense with the imprimatur of the Georgia ACLU. Hauptman told me he had decided to do it alone because he anticipated some resistance if he proposed that Shade Miller become a client of the Georgia affiliate of the ACLU.

Not all ACLU members, including board members, can bring themselves to defend the First Amendment rights of racists, anti-Semites, and the like. For instance, the three California ACLU affiliates—Southern California, Northern California, and San Diego—advocate punishing the use of racist or sexist speech on college campuses—despite the national ACLU board's opposition on First Amendment grounds. This is known as "feel-good civil libertarianism," since it's guaranteed to make your friends congratulate you for caring more about combating prejudice than for sticking to First Amendment "technicalities."

Michael Hauptman is a civil libertarian, period. And he is the kind of lawyer about whom a movie ought to be made—exemplifying the advice of Ben Webster, the powerfully intimate tenor saxophonist who used to say, "When the rhythm section ain't going right, go for yourself."

Hauptman defends those he wants to defend, no matter what anyone else thinks. He has been the lawyer for witch doctors, the homeless, the outspoken civil rights loner Hosea Williams, and, as described by the *Atlanta Constitution,* "a parade of candidates for the electric chair."

Hauptman puts it this way: "I've represented all kinds of bad people.... I even once represented an insurance company and a bank."

When I talked to Hauptman during the case of Shade Miller, the lawyer had no doubt that the Constitution was on Miller's side.

The rights and liberties in the Constitution belong just as fully to Shade Miller as they do to board members of the ACLU. And the forced unmasking of Miller endangers his rights of speech and assembly—let alone him. That 1952 law cannot stand, said Hauptman.

At first, the Georgia law forbidding the public wearing of masks and hoods was struck down by Judge Howard Cook of the Gwinnett County State Court. Said the judge:

"... even though the 'Klan' may represent controversial ideas, even hateful ideas, such ideas are still entitled to... protection.... Prohibiting the wearing of masks under the Georgia statute in question interferes with the right to symbolic speech as well as the rights to assembly and free association."

In a section of his decision that particularly infuriated long-term civil rights advocates, the judge said that the Klan "is in effect a persecuted group in that its beliefs may be so abhorrent to most members of society that the Klan members and their families may be in the same amount of danger as... the black members of the NAACP in *NAACP* v. *Alabama.*"

What does this classic 1958 case—protecting the rights of black civil rights workers—have to do with the Klan that so often savaged those rights and those people?

NAACP v. *Alabama* concerned the attempt of that state to force the NAACP to produce many of its records, including the names and addresses of all of its members and "agents."

The NAACP strongly objected because exposing its members' names and addresses could well have endangered those members.

A lower court, however, ordered the membership lists—and other records—turned over. The NAACP complied, except for the membership lists. The Circuit Court thereupon held the NAACP in contempt and fined it $100,000.

The Supreme Court ruled that the NAACP had a constitutional right to withhold its membership lists. The order to produce the lists, said Justice John Harlan, entailed "the likelihood of a substantial restraint upon the exercise by the [NAACP's] members of their right to freedom of association."

The NAACP, Harlan continued, "has made an uncontroverted showing that on past occasions, revelation of the identity of its rank-and-file members has exposed these members to economic reprisal, loss of employment, threats of physical coercion, and other manifestations of public hostility."

If the membership lists were turned over, Justice Harlan said, "members may withdraw from the association and dissuade others from joining it because of fear of exposure of their beliefs shown through their association...."

The lower-court judgment of civil contempt and the $100,000 fine were revoked.

As for the Georgia Ku Klux Klan case, an appeal was taken by the state of Georgia to the Georgia Supreme Court. Rooting for the state were such critics of Judge Howard Cook and Michael Hauptman as the regional NAACP (notwithstanding *NAACP* v. *Alabama*), the Anti-Defamation League, and the Southern Poverty Law Center. They hardly see the Klan as "a persecuted group," and they see no reason for *not* stripping Klan members of their anonymity.

Also outraged is David Fuller, the assistant Gwinnett County solicitor, who defended the 1952 Georgia law at the trial. Said Fuller to the *Washington Post:*

"When this statute was enacted, there were a lot of people being murdered and terrorized. There was vandalism of property and this act stopped that.... The Klan is not deserving of the anonymity the mask would afford it."

Many people believe, as does Fuller, the assistant solicitor, that it's necessary to be "deserving" of constitutional rights to be protected by them. But nowhere in the text of the Bill of Rights is there a sliding scale by which "decent" folks get more of those rights, and "awful" folks get hardly any.

Assistant Solicitor Fuller also insisted that Judge Cook's ruling, unless it is overturned, would give the Klan "carte blanche to revert to how it operated in the '30s and '40s."

If this prediction is in any way accurate, it is a startling indictment of Georgia's law-enforcement and judicial personnel. In the 1930s and 1940s, there were cops and judges who had kinship with the Klan—some of it literal. But if the slightest residue of judicial and police collusion with the Klan remains, the answer is not to bend the Constitution and keep the anti-mask law, but rather to engage in a pitilessly thorough investigation of Georgia's justice system.

Even before that investigation, why didn't the assistant solicitor offer specific evidence to back up his claim that the Klan, if its anonymity is protected, would be given "carte blanche" to go back to the whippings and killings of the thirties and forties? If he had *any* such evidence, as an officer of the court, he was obligated by law to produce it.

In September 1980, in Gainesville, Georgia, the Klan held its annual Labor Day rally. Some of the Klansmen wore hoods covering their faces as they celebrated their lower court victory.

But in December, the Supreme Court of Georgia overturned the judgment of the trial court, and held the Georgia anti-mask law to be constitutional.

The case was sent back to the trial court in Gwinnett County, and there the jury ignored the state Supreme Court ruling and acquitted Shade Miller anyway. The law remains constitutional in the state of Georgia, but Shade Miller had successfully defied it with the help of an exultantly independent civil liberties lawyer.

IX

When Decent People Try to Ban Speech for the Common Good

"How far can an artist go?"

> The law unfortunately, in my opinion, now says the pre-born, the fetus, is not human and is, therefore, not entitled to the full protection of the Constitution.—CONGRESSMAN JOHN ERLENBORN, IN HOUSE DEBATE, FEBRUARY 2, 1984

> I am aware, as you are, of the extreme importance of the protection of our constitutional right to freedom of speech—a right which is all the more precious within an intellectual community whose very reason for being hinges upon the ability to inquire, to investigate, to think, to speculate, and to express one's views freely, irrespective of how unorthodox or unsettling those views may seem to others. The intellectually stifling results of censorship—while deplorable in any setting—would be all the more abominable if allowed to exist within the college environment.—WILLIAM M. ANDERSON, JR., PRESIDENT OF MARY WASHINGTON COLLEGE, IN A DECEMBER 7, 1983, RESPONSE TO FACULTY CONCERN THAT THE ADMINISTRATION HAD BANNED A PAINTING BY MARY CATE CARROLL FROM A CAMPUS EXHIBITION

How far can an artist go? Where is the limit of license?—BAR-
BARA MEYER, CHAIRMAN OF THE ART DEPARTMENT, MARY WASH-
INGTON COLLEGE, *FREE LANCE-STAR*, FREDERICKSBURG, VIRGINIA,
OCTOBER 25, 1983

I have covered many censorship cases, and read of many
more; but this one, as Duke Ellington might have said, is
beyond category. For some people, especially liberals, it is also
extremely irritating. I tried it out at a conference on censorship in
Key West, and the participants, all fierce supporters of free expression, listened in sullen silence. Only later, in one-on-one conversations, did some members of the audience tell me that I had shown
"poor taste" in bringing the matter to their attention.

Hal Davis of the *New York Post* started me out on this story by
sending a clipping of a December 29 piece in the *Baltimore Evening
Sun* by Carl Schoettler ("Artist Is Free, but Her Painting Is Under
Arrest").

I called Schoettler and he gave me additional leads. I found
the embattled painter, who turns out to have some of the quality of
Bartleby the Scrivener, though she is more cheerful and vastly
more self-reliant. And I also found some of the Mary Washington
College faculty members who have been engaged in combat over
whether the expulsion from campus of Mary Cate Carroll's painting, *American Liberty Upside Down,* was an act of censorship or rather
had been absolutely necessary to prevent the college from being
prosecuted for violating Virginia laws concerning the distribution
of, and trafficking in, dead human bodies.

Mary Washington College, in Virginia, is halfway between
Washington and Richmond. It is state-supported (thereby bringing
the First Amendment into play if there has been any censorship)
and coeducational. It emphasizes the liberal arts, and has a full-
time student body of close to 2,500. The college was once part of
the University of Virginia, so there is a link between it and Thomas
Jefferson.

In 1977, there came to Mary Washington College one Mary
Cate Carroll, who had already studied at the Corcoran School of
Art in Washington and, after being awarded a bachelor of arts
degree at Mary Washington in 1980, went on to get a master's
degree in fine arts at the Maryland Institute of Art in Baltimore,

where she lived at the time of this strange controversy.

While at Mary Washington College, Carroll had revealed a number of abiding characteristics. She likes to think things through, and when she finally figures out where she ought to be, she will not be moved. She believes in equality, right across the board. In her senior year, for instance, she did a painting of a bride. In the painting, there was a real shelf on the bride's stomach, and on that shelf, with its kitchen wallpaper, you could see a sort of cupboard with cleaning supplies in it. She was making a comment in that painting. It was not the kind of comment Phyllis Schlafly would make.

At first, while at Mary Washington College, Carroll did not believe there was anything wrong with abortions. She is, after all, as she puts it, a child of the sixties. But after a couple of years, she changed her mind. Why? Well, she'd been studying fetuses in the biology lab and she'd sketched a number of them and well, if you looked at them, really looked at them, I mean, they looked human, you know.

Something else happened to Mary Cate Carroll while she was an undergraduate. She told about it in the Fredericksburg *Free Lance-Star* in October 1983, after her painting had given the willies to the administration of Mary Washington College:

"When a student at... the college, I saw slides of reliquaries in Mrs. Meyer's art history class—they were identified as art. A reliquary is a peculiar art form because the artist's job is to create a work of art to enshrine the remains of all or part of a human being—usually a martyr. In essence the artist creates a work of art where the focal point is something which he has not created—the relic.

"For example, when in Rome this summer, I saw the entire body of a saint enshrined in a glass reliquary. But what particularly comes to mind is the reliquary of St. Foy, from the tenth century, which was presented by slide in Mrs. Meyer's class. In this piece, the unknown artist has fashioned of gold and wood the figure of a man. In his middle is a tiny door. Enshrined within are relics of his body."

It must be satisfying to a professor when a student tells, with such specificity, of having been greatly influenced by something taught by that professor. And Mary Cate Carroll sure was influenced by those slides of reliquaries. Yet, as we shall see, Professor Meyer, chairman of the Art Department, wishes she had been spared this particular student, then and forevermore.

Mary Cate Carroll has been a quite impressive alumna of Mary Washington College. But who would have expected anything else? While at the school, she was elected to Phi Beta Kappa. And she was graduated with a Certificate of Highest Distinction (the equivalent of summa cum laude). And after graduation, there were scholarships, including one on which she traveled to Italy, and various career-enhancing exhibitions.

Naturally, when Mary Washington College, as part of its seventy-fifth anniversary celebration, decided to hold a major exhibition of work by alumni of the school's Art Department, how could they leave out Mary Cate Carroll? Of course, they couldn't. She was invited, and told to select whatever she'd like to have in the show— with a limit of five paintings.

One of the paintings Carroll chose was *American Liberty Upside Down*. It is an American family scene—a man and a woman sitting on a couch, and a child on the mother's lap. Ah, but the baby is not really there. She has drawn the baby only in outline, in dotted red lines, and it has no features. But in the middle of that child, there is a little door. Go ahead, you can pull it open. And when you do, you will see inside what reporter Jennifer Strobel in the Fredericksburg *Free Lance-Star* has nicely described as "the actual remains [in formaldehyde] of a saline abortion; a tiny, greenish [male] fetus, its arms, legs and head well-formed and curled up in a jar." A real jar.

Where had Mary Cate Carroll gotten that fetus? From a professor in the college biology department who had seen a lot of fetuses, and had been thinking about how human they look for a long time.

Before the alumni exhibition opened, and therefore before it was possible to offend any art lovers, an emissary of Mary Washington College ordered Mary Cate Carroll to remove that painting, and that thing in it, forthwith.

The artist was surprised. She had expected some intensity of response to her painting, but not plain old straight-armed censorship. Not on a college campus. "I thought a college was a place for the free flow of information," she says. "They objected to there being a fetus, a real fetus, in the painting. But if a fetus can be studied for physical properties in a biology class, why can't it be looked at on a social, on a moral, level in an art show? Especially in an art gallery on a college campus!"

According to Mary Cate Carroll, she was initially told that her painting had been thrown off campus because it was too "controversial," "inappropriate" for a college art show, "in poor taste," and "irreverent." Later, Barbara Meyer, chairman of the Art Department, expanded on that last criticism in an article in the Fredericksburg *Free Lance-Star*. The use of a real fetus in this painting, said Professor Meyer, showed the artist's contempt of the fact that "reverence for life is an essential component of the human condition."

It was not until two days after the fetus got its marching orders, however, that Mary Cate Carroll was informed that the true reason for the banishment of *American Liberty Upside Down* was that there had been "legal problems" with the painting. That greenish fetus— "bilious green," as Professor Meyer described it to me indignantly—had been on campus in violation of the Virginia Code. Specifically, in violation of those parts of the Code that have to do with dead human bodies, their transportation across state lines, the sale and purchase of said bodies, and "their lawful exhibition in only those public places where they are to be used for public scientific education and training in health and related subjects."

Representatives of the college noted somberly that if they had not acted swiftly to get that fetus off campus by sundown, Mary Washington College might well have been charged with a Class One misdemeanor, fined $1,000, or incarcerated for a year for being a party to violations of the Virginia Code.

Said Mary Cate Carroll:

"I took this five-month-old Johnny Doe out of the biology lab where it was a specimen and made him into a human being. I introduced this victim into the conversation."

...the word "person," as used in the Fourteenth Amendment, does not include the unborn....

—Supreme Court Justice Harry Blackmun, speaking for a 7–2 majority of the Court, *Roe* v. *Wade*, 1973

* * *

On January 23, 1984, Mary Cate Carroll, the censored artist, gave her version of what had happened at Mary Washington College in Virginia to an interviewer for National Public Radio.

She said she had had no objections to abortion when she first came to Mary Washington College as a student in 1977. "At the time," she went on, "I thought women's rights were paramount. I had not considered the child's rights." But working with fetuses in the biology lab, and sketching them, planted a seed in her mind. And in two years, she was no longer pro-abortion.

There came a time when she felt impelled to do a painting about abortion. "It seemed logical to me," she says, "to find a fetus and put it in that painting. Since a seed had been planted in me by the fetuses I had seen, perhaps a seed could be planted in someone else through my painting."

Mary Cate Carroll was also thinking about *Roe* v. *Wade* while she was conceiving that painting, *American Liberty Upside Down*.

"The Supreme Court has said," Mary Cate Carroll points out, "that this fetus, the one in the painting, whom I call Johnny, has no recourse under the law, has no voice, has no right to petition. So since I *do* have a voice and a right to petition under the law, I am petitioning for Johnny by doing this painting."

Before the alumni exhibition began, Mary Washington College told Mary Cate Carroll that *American Liberty Upside Down* could not be shown unless she replaced the real fetus with a drawing of a fetus, or some other artificial substitute. But the whole point of her painting, said the artist, was to enable the viewer to see Johnny. The real Johnny, not an equivalent made out of margarine.

The college kept insisting it was not censoring the painting at all, just Johnny. It had to kick him off campus because the presence of this dead thing on campus violated the Virginia Code. But from talking to various Mary Washington College faculty members, pro and con, it's clear to me that the quintessential, visceral reason was that some folks found Johnny disgusting. Why, even in the *Village Voice* newsroom, in just describing the story, without a photograph, I have had several colleagues react with quite visible disgust when I tell them who is lurking behind the door in the middle of the mother in the painting. As Mr. Eliot said, "Human kind cannot bear very much reality."

To hear the other side at Mary Washington College, I spoke to Professor Barbara Meyer, in whose classes Mary Cate Carroll used to sit. In an interview in the *Free Lance-Star,* Meyer conceded that the painting can be considered a work of art.

, "However," she went on, "the contents of a bottle that was placed on a shelf within the framework of the painting, namely a second-trimester fetus, cannot by any standard be called a work of art. Had we allowed this flagrant and crass exploitation of this pathetic form, we would have flouted a moral as well as a legal obligation to treat it with dignity. Reverence for life is an essential component of the human condition."

Meyer added that she, of course, affirms the right of artists to express themselves freely. But "should an artist assume the posture that he or she is the sole arbiter of what the public 'should see' or when, where and if the public 'needs to be shocked'? How far can an artist go? Where is the limit of license? What would be the next step following the display of a human fetus in a painting today? *Would it be perhaps placing some other offensive morsel of human tissue, chosen by the whim of the artist, in a painting tomorrow?*" (Emphasis added.)

In a letter to me, Professor Meyer made another point: "The fetus was meant to shock, that is why Carroll would not remove it in lieu of a drawing of a fetus. The fetus, as well, depending on your personal interpretation of its status, had a potential for human life. But many believe deeply and sincerely that *it was already a human being.* Is this not the primary rationale for banning abortion? As such, did it belong in a mason jar inside an ambivalent painting on public display?"

There's a failure of communication here, all right. Barbara Meyer seems to me to be making Mary Cate Carroll's point. But not entirely. In a phone conversation we had, Professor Meyer said, "I do not consider human tissue to be an article of mixed media." But then again, is Johnny only "human tissue," or more than that? Or, as Mary Cate Carroll said in an interview in the *Free Lance-Star,* "When you first see it, you're shocked....It's hard to say that's not a human being when it's right there staring you in the face."

Mary Cate Carroll's answer to Barbara Meyer appeared in the Fredericksburg *Free Lance-Star.* One part told of how Carroll had learned about reliquaries while a student of Barbara Meyer. (Meyer's tart comment about reliquaries to me was "We are no longer living in the social environment of the thirteenth century.") But *American Liberty Upside Down* is a reliquary of our time, the remains, says Carroll, "not of one killed for his beliefs, but of one killed because his life was deemed inconvenient.

"I can imagine," Mary Cate Carroll wrote, "that had I been an artist in wartime Germany and had attempted to show a painting/reliquary which enshrined the body of an Auschwitz victim, there might also have been censorship with the excuse that the artist was not showing reverence for human life...."

"Once you open the door of Johnny's reliquary," Carroll went on, "the artist is no longer important. What is important is the conversation, the communication, the silent appeal that Johnny makes to you, the viewer. Johnny speaks more effectively than any artist or writer. What Mary Washington College has done by censoring this painting is to deny to each and every one of you the opportunity of having that conversation with Johnny."

Some members of the faculty at Mary Washington College were still much troubled about Mary Cate Carroll's charge that she had been censored. One faculty member in particular, Paul Slayton, chairman of the Education Department and a longtime battler against censorship, had no doubts about the matter. He was Carroll's primary champion on campus. It was largely because of Slayton and, of course, Mary Cate Carroll herself, that the college administration had been on the defensive since October, when Johnny was told to leave the campus.

A faculty committee began looking into the matter. Meanwhile, the college president, Dr. William Anderson, Jr., spoke of the sacredness of free expression, especially in a college environment, with the passion of a Thomas Jefferson. But, he said, as did Barbara Meyer and other college administrators, this was not a case of censorship. A college is obliged to obey the laws of the state, and having Johnny in an art exhibition was an offense to those laws.

No college official could give me a clear idea of which laws were being abused, so I called the office of the attorney general of Virginia. There I was told that the local commonwealth attorney in the Fredericksburg area had been thinking of bringing action against Mary Cate Carroll and the science professor who had given the fetus to her. On what grounds? Well, no one in the attorney general's office was quite sure. Maybe that's why the commonwealth attorney dropped the idea.

I was sent a copy of the possibly relevant sections of the health section of the Virginia Code. One part of the Code dealing with fetuses has to do with medical certification of a fetal death. But that was taken care of long before Mary Cate Carroll ever saw Johnny. Then there's a requirement for a transit permit for a fetus leaving the commonwealth of Virginia. Or, if the fetus is from another state, said fetus has to have an entry permit from the district where it was discarded. Well, Johnny was given to Mary Cate Carroll in the state of Virginia, and my information is that he and the painting have not lately left the state. So that section doesn't apply, nor do any of the other provisions about fetuses.

I went back to the notes of my conversation with the attorney general's office, and I noticed that all the sections read to me over the phone had nothing to do with fetuses. They were about dead human bodies. They can't be exhibited, as it were, except in medical schools and places that teach health science. And they can't be bought and sold. *American Liberty Upside Down* was for sale, a college administrator gleefully reminded me. (The college did seem to base its fear of being prosecuted, had it not censored the painting, on the laws concerning dead human bodies.)

Remember, we're talking about dead *human* bodies. Aha, said Mary Cate Carroll when she was first told of the laws she may have broken. It's legal to kill a fetus because it's not a human being. But, Carroll notes, once a fetus is dead, according to Mary Washington College's interpretation of the Virginia Code, it *is* defined as a human being.

Well, which is it?

"I don't think Mary Washington College should be allowed to walk on both sides of the fence at once," says Mary Cate Carroll. "On the one hand, they say this is a dead human being. And then, on the other hand, they say it's a disgusting morsel of human tissue."

In 1985, Mary Cate Carroll was invited by Mary Washington College to participate in an exhibition. Six of her paintings were included. One of them was *American Liberty Upside Down.*

The college, largely because of the acute dissonance caused by Carroll's first attempt to show the painting there, was developing a policy on academic freedom. By 1987 the policy had been adopted by the faculty and then by the Board of Visitors. It declared, among other things, that "artists and other guests invited by the institution and/or by recognized student, faculty, and institutional organizations shall be protected from any form of censorship or disruption, and shall be afforded the same freedom of expression in the chosen medium as is guaranteed members of the Mary Washington College community."

The "disgusting morsel of human tissue" had brought freedom of expression to the college.

"I'm sorry that you had no subscription to The Progressive *just when you needed to cancel one," said the editor.*

The Progressive was founded in 1909 by Robert M. La Follette, a political reformer and a particularly effective muckraker, who was governor of Wisconsin and then a senator from that state. The June 1985 issue of the magazine was very much in his spirit. There was a piece on how the leadership of the AFL-CIO, while getting itself arrested in anti-apartheid demonstrations in this country, was actually striving to constrict and coopt the black union movement in South Africa. Another article analyzed the long-term multiple costs to Israel of the worst self-inflicted wound in its history, the invasion of Lebanon. Also in the issue was an attack on certain dishonest tactics of part of the right-to-life movement.

And, as often happened, there was a wholly unexpected article, this one on the current state of the Wobblies, the Industrial Workers of the World, whose free-speech wars on the West Coast in the early part of the century are among the more inspiring battlefield encounters in American history—when the Wobblies defied local ordinances prohibiting public speech and assembly. Those wars, are not, alas, taught in our schools. But how grand it would be to see a high school glee club, in full cry, before a beaming principal and board of education, singing from the Wobbly *Little Red Song-book:*

"Out there in San Diego
"Where the western breakers beat,
"They're jailing men and women
"For speaking in the street."

Anyway, according to *The Progressive,* there are still Wobblies in the land, and some were even engaged in a strike right now—against the Keller Fish Company on Long Island.

Also in the June issue was the customary full-page "Memo from the Editor," Erwin Knoll. As has happened before, it concerned certain disagreements between some readers and the editor, but this time there was a new player—a foundation that had canceled its own subscription to the magazine and had further indicated it would no longer help *The Progressive* get financial support.

What terrible thing had Erwin Knoll done? In what way had *The Progressive* gone beyond the pale of decent liberal orthodoxy? For this was no ordinary foundation. This was a network of the most liberal foundations in the nation, committed to social change and to the grass roots and all the other nutritious political values. Founded by socially conscious children of the rich, it's called The Funding Exchange, and its executive director, June Makela, had stricken *The Progressive* from its list of the deserving poor. The charge: heresy.

Earlier in the year, *The Progressive* had run a small ad—two inches by two columns—in the back of the magazine. It was from Feminists for Life of America in Kansas City, Missouri. The organization's president, Rachel MacNair, has been imprisoned for protesting nuclear power and abortion. She is also a member of the War Resisters League.

When they can get the money together, Feminists for Life of America puts out a newsletter. A recent issue dissected pro-lifer Ronald Reagan's relentless war on the WIC program, "which provides healthy food to pregnant women, nursing mothers, and children under age five." There was also a reprint of a stunning letter from prison by Elizabeth McCalister. (She was serving a three-year term for damaging one of the government's nuclear death machines.)

Said [McCalister] of some of the hierarchy of her Catholic faith: "…a number of our own bishops march in lockstep with the Ronald Reagans and the Jerry Falwells…narrowing political choices, cherishing the unborn even while they damn the born to the Gehenna of war, violence, social and personal neglect—the expression of utmost contempt for the living."

Well, you can see how dangerous a group Feminists for Life of America is. They gave a forum to a convicted, blasphemous felon. But even worse was the advertisement they perpetuated in *The Progressive* in three consecutive issues.

On the left-hand side of the small ad was a picture of an eight-week-old fetus. He or she was unmistakably of the human species. The headline on the ad was: "This Little Girl Deserves Protection…So Does Her Mother."

Then came the text, an act of utter heresy, an affront to the orthodox theology of the left:

[The mother of the eight-week-old fetus needs protection from:]

• Judges who patronizingly decide she doesn't need to know what is going on inside her body in order to make her decisions.

• Doctors who make high profits (even by medical standards) if they can talk her into letting the child be killed.

• Social attitudes that are negative about her pregnancy, and cheat her out of the help she needs.

A number of *Progressive* readers were grossly offended by the ad. Wrote David Katz of Hermon, New York:

"…What's next—American Nazi Party advertising? The Ku Klux Klan?

"I thought I was subscribing to *The Progressive?*"

Then there was a letter from Michael Ratner of the Center for Constitutional Rights in New York. I know Michael Ratner. If the FBI has a hit list, Ratner is on it because as a Bill of Rights lawyer, he has considerably embarrassed the Bureau at legislative hearings, in court, and by what he has released to the media. And Ratner has done other valuable work on behalf of liberty of conscience, speech, and travel, and other American basics.

Yet Ratner, the civil libertarian, wrote to Erwin Knoll, editor of *The Progressive:*

"Happily I am not a subscriber so I needn't cancel my subscription. I would surely do so after seeing the anti-abortion ad of the Feminists for the Life of America...."

Erwin Knoll was concerned that Ratner had left in such frustration. So Knoll gave Ratner some of his customary wise counsel:

"I'm sorry that you had no subscription to *The Progressive* just when you needed to cancel one. It's a good idea to subscribe so you won't be caught in that sort of predicament."

It is one thing to lose readers. But for a magazine on the left—that is not subsidized by a rich publisher or editor-in-chief or through other means—losing foundation support is even more of a blow. Especially if you lose The Funding Exchange, which acts as a kind of matchmaker for donors, some of them anonymous, who want to give some money to virtuous forces working for social change.

There came to Erwin Knoll a letter from June Makela, executive director of The Funding Exchange. It was sent in March.

"In all of the 1985 issues of *The Progressive* to date, an ad appeared which was apparently placed by a group called Feminists for Life of America. We were greatly offended by your decision to run such an advertisement. Although we respect the integrity of your magazine in setting its own policies, we are surprised and shocked over the apparent lack therein with regard to advertisements.

"The staff of The Funding Exchange has decided not to renew its subscription and I am afraid that this inconsistency will also make it difficult for our staff to lobby for funding for your publication."

That's exactly the kind of letter a right-wing foundation would send to one of its kept journals if the editor there had printed a piece critical of America's "free market" economy.

On March 22, Erwin Knoll answered June Makela, the executive director of the most "progressive" foundation conduit in these United States:

"I am dismayed and deeply distressed by your letter of March 20.... It does not surprise or trouble me that you found the contents of the ad offensive. So did many—perhaps most—of *The Progressive*'s subscribers. So did many—perhaps most—of *The Progres-*

sive's staff. So did I." (Knoll is pro-choice, as is the editorial policy of the magazine.)

"But your letter does not state that you were offended by the message of the ad; what offended you was our 'decision to run such an advertisement.' What dismays and distresses me is your intellectual intolerance....

"Your interest is not in rational discourse but in censorship. You find it intolerable that *The Progressive*'s readers should be exposed to a point of view you deem obnoxious.

"We have more confidence than that in our subscribers. We believe they are mature, thoughtful, and intelligent human beings, capable of thinking for themselves. We believe we can expose them to any thought without jeopardizing their minds, their bodies, or their immortal souls.

"For that reason, we never want to say to an advertiser, 'We find your message so frightening that we dare not present it to *The Progressive*'s readers.' The editorial columns of *The Progressive* are *our* turf where we, as writers and editors, have *our* say. The advertising columns are there for anyone within the law who wants to buy space to talk to our readers.

"I'm sorry you find that policy repugnant. You're not the only one, of course. The ad to which you take exception has probably already cost us more in lost subscription income than it has produced in advertising revenue. We expected that when we accepted the ad. It wasn't the first one we have accepted in full awareness of its potentially negative impact on our extremely limited resources, and it won't be the last....

"So we regret, of course, your staff's decision not to renew its subscription, because we need and value every subscription to *The Progressive*. And we regret that you will find it difficult 'to lobby for funding' for *The Progressive*, because you have rendered generous assistance to us in the past, and we had anticipated calling on you again for help with important projects.

"But we will do our best to get along without your subscription and without your financial help, because much as we prize both of them, they don't mean nearly as much to us as integrity and our commitment to freedom of speech.

"I hope you will share this letter with the members of your staff (who presumably think of themselves as staunch defenders of human rights and free expression)...."

Erwin Knoll told me that in time, the mail to the magazine became quite supportive of the notion that its liberal readers are strong enough to cope with ideas they don't like. And in reaction to those who had shunned *The Progressive* because of that subversive ad, there have been some advance renewals, and a couple of hundred dollars in contributions.

A reader wrote to me (I write for *The Progressive*): "Sometimes in the late '60s, a good many liberals began to lose their interest in other people's freedom of speech, and I think that has something to do with the declining appeal of liberalism."

And another reader wrote to *The Progressive:*

"It is unconscionable for individuals on the left to be calling for censorship because an advertisement or a point of view doesn't reflect current left orthodoxy.

"Furthermore, a significant number of us maintain our political and social orientation to the left but oppose abortion. We are Catholics who have been left-wing activists for years and base our values on respect for the sanctity of life. This value has moved us to oppose war and work for peace, to strive for equal access to resources, to fight against poverty, hunger, and racism, to organize labor, to change profit-dominated economic systems, to work for justice—and to oppose abortion.

"Many of us believe fellow progressives have become rigid and dogmatic when they cannot permit expression of a view that dissents from their version of 'correct thinking.'"

Another letter said:

"I can't believe that some of your readers got so excited and bothered by the Feminists for Life advertisement. I worry about much of the so-called left. So many have become wimps that I can see how Reagan won.

"I want to hear both sides, or all sides (what was the last issue that had only two sides)..."

Wrapping it up was this comment from a reader:

"It is not particularly surprising that the pro-life advertisement caused some to react with such confusion. So-called liberals are just as intolerant as so-called conservatives."

"What Playboy, *the American Booksellers Association, and their cohorts... have done here will come back to haunt them—and all of us."*

John Spear is the editor of the *Orange County Post,* a 2,700-circulation weekly in upstate New York. In the summer of 1989, he became the defendant in a suit brought against him and others by the town of West Hartford, Connecticut, under the Racketeer Influenced and Corrupt Organizations Act (RICO). The suit ostensibly concerned the blockade of an abortion clinic in West Hartford on June 17 of that year. The town was asking for $43,000 to compensate it for extra police expenses incurred in arresting the protesters.

Since this was a RICO suit, the defendants, if they lost, would have had to pay three times $43,000—in addition to the town's attorney's fees. They had already, from the day of the indictment, been branded as "racketeers."

John Spear was not in West Hartford on June 17. So why was he in the dock? The answer requires looking at how RICO began, how it grew, and why it now can threaten almost any group of nonviolent protesters—as well as bystanders who criticize what is being done to those protesters.

Congress passed RICO in 1970. The legislative record leaves no doubt that the statute was directly aimed at organized crime, particularly at the Mob's infiltration of previously legitimate businesses. However, it is unconstitutional to pass a law aimed specifically at any one group. Therefore, the language of the statute is very broad—so broad and slippery that all manner of people in no way associated with organized crime have been caught in the quicksand of RICO.

The definitive exploration of the scope of RICO appeared in the May and June 1987 issues of the *Columbia Law Review,* along with a distillation in the January 11, 1989, issue of *Newsday.* The author of all these articles was then Columbia University law professor Gerald Lynch, who pointed out that RICO "makes it a crime for anyone to commit a 'pattern' of two or more 'racketeering acts' in conducting the affairs of an 'enterprise.'"

What, then, is a "pattern" of "racketeering acts"?

Says Professor Lynch:

"Because the definition of the crime is so abstract, just about any kind of crime can be prosecuted as a RICO violation. An enterprise can be anything—a company, a union, a government office, a Mafia family, or just a couple of guys who get together on a Saturday night to raise hell. And while the courts have struggled over what exactly constitutes a pattern, they are hard put to draw a line short of 'any two crimes' on the long list of violations defined as 'racketeering acts.'"

Accordingly, Texas Air filed a RICO suit against the machinists' union, which had publicly charged that Texas Air was violating airline-safety rules. That criticism, that use of speech, said the airline's lawyers, constituted a "pattern of racketeering activity." Landlords have used RICO to quell unhappy tenants who organized, through speech, for their rights. Agribusinesses have sued Cesar Chavez and the United Farm Workers under RICO for "inducing" the California Agricultural Labor Relations Board to issue "fraudulent" complaints against these warmhearted employers.

With regard to journalist John Spear, as a RICO defendant he paid a lawyer for many hours and hours of depositions and hearings—because the town of West Hartford charged that he had engaged in "extortion."

In his newspaper, Spear had excoriated police actions in pro-life "rescue" attempts at abortion clinics in West Hartford. "All civil rights of those arrested were suspended," he wrote, "when torture, physical injury, and abuse were the order of the day."

In examining the larger of the two demonstrations—the one on June 17—reporters on the scene agreed with Spear. And I saw videotapes of that police riot and read depositions and affidavits by people arrested at both events. Police in West Hartford used "pain-compliance" techniques on demonstrators who go limp—a traditional response to arrest used by all kinds of nonviolent protesters. The "pain-compliance" techniques inflict so much pain that the person under arrest eventually does what the police want him or her to do. And that is the basic definition of torture. The staff of the United States Civil Rights Commission staff also came to the same conclusions as John Spear.

So why is what he wrote "extortion"? By criticizing such police techniques, it was charged, John Spear had tried to intimidate West Hartford's guardians of the peace, thereby attempting to "extort" a different kind of police behavior the next time there was a nonviolent civil-disobedience protest in town.

Yet, obviously, Spear had a First Amendment right to expose what he considered to be police lawlessness.

He is a stubborn man, and I doubt that this costly experience will deter him from writing whatever else is on his mind about the West Hartford Police Department, or anything else. But other editors and reporters may take heed from what has happened to John Spear, and may mute their criticisms of the police in their towns. Few people, in or out of journalism, enjoy the costs of being a defendant.

Spear was eventually dropped from the RICO suit. He then sued West Hartford, among others, on the ground that the RICO charges had violated—had chilled—his first amendment rights. He not only lost that suit in the Second Circuit Court of Appeals, but he was also assessed $13,463 in lawyers' fees for the other side. In 1990, Spear and his wife, Mary, had an adjusted gross income of $10,641.

As several defense lawyers in RICO cases have told me, there are plaintiffs with deep pockets who bring RICO suits with no expectation of winning but in the hope of scaring their critics into keeping their complaints to themselves from then on.

Consider the case of Helen Cindrich of Pittsburgh. As executive director of People Concerned with the Unborn Child, she operates a hotline—a clearinghouse for information about anti-abortion meetings and other activities. It never occurred to her, she told me, that she would have to defend herself in court for reporting news, including news of arrests, some of which was taken from local papers.

Somehow, Cindrich did not see herself as a racketeer.

Nonetheless, she did become a RICO defendant. The owner of a building which, at the time, housed two abortion clinics was disturbed by having anti-abortion demonstrations at his property. The landlord's subsequent RICO suit against the pro-life demonstrators enveloped Helen Cindrich.

Why Cindrich? I asked the owner's attorney, Ellen Doyle, former executive director of the American Civil Liberties Union of Pittsburgh.

"All those demonstrators," Doyle explained, "were showing up at the building, and we're suing all those who are responsible for all those people showing up at the building." So much for the First Amendment rights of association, assembly, and dissemination of news.

After a good many months, Helen Cindrich's lawyer succeeded in having the suit withdrawn. But her sense of her free-expression rights has been dimmed. She told me she is much more careful now about what she puts on the hotline and in her newsletter. And there are certain speakers she will no longer invite. They might be advocates of civil disobedience, and if such acts occur, she may well be charged with being an accessory.

Helen Cindrich has come to believe that mere advocacy can be dangerous. Who knows when RICO will come after her again?

Since pro-lifers have been caught in the undertow of some of the RICO suits aimed at dissidents' First Amendment rights, a number of pro-choice groups have exulted over this fearsome statute.

When, for instance, the RICO conviction of a group of anti-abortion demonstrators in Philadelphia was upheld by the Third Circuit Court of Appeals, Patricia Ireland, executive vice president of the National Organization for Women, declared: "As long as anti-abortion extremists continue to behave like gangsters, it is wholly appropriate to treat them like gangsters under the racketeering laws."

On the other hand, some of the journals on the left have indicated an awareness that RICO can be used against *any* group of protesters—not just pro-lifers. *The Guardian* has editorialized in this regard, and in the *Resist Newsletter* (which reaches community organizers, feminist, and anti-racist groups around the country), Tatiana Scheiber has pointed out:

"Anti-abortion demonstrators argue that we should take advantage of the [RICO] law, as long as it's there, to keep clinics open. But that's exactly the process by which the right to dissent is worn away.

"When the RICO law was first passed, I remember gathering information about the dangers it presented, both in terms of the stripping away of pretrial presumptions of innocence, and the arbitrary definitions of terms like criminal conspiracy and extortion. I have only seen my fears confirmed as RICO's net has widened.

"Shouldn't we be organizing to *protest* repressive federal legislation rather than using it when it happens to serve our ends?... [RICO] could soon be used against any member of a group that engaged in any sort of confrontational tactic as a form of protest."

RICO is a powerful weapon, and as such it is dangerous. Unpopular defendants should not be targets for overkill.
—*Washington Post*

Protecting the First Amendment involves networking, as does most other enterprises. Those involved in nurturing free speech meet and exchange strategies at seminars and conventions of librarians, booksellers, and magazine distributors. You get to know the leading lawyers and other advocates.

For instance, I've known Burt Joseph, who represents Playboy Enterprises, for many years. I have considered him one of the most resolute of all First Amendment lawyers.

Max Lillienstein, counsel for the American Booksellers Association, has seemed to me to embody the Brandeis-Douglas-Brennan approach to free speech and press. And by reputation, and an occasional phone call, I am aware of Michael Bamberger's achievements in defending the First Amendment. He represents the Media Coalition.

In 1991, these three attorneys—with Bamberger the lead lawyer—engaged in a First Amendment war in Florida. They claimed the First Amendment was on their side. But they were using a weapon that the American Civil Liberties Union—and many other paladins of the First Amendment—regard as one of the most powerful threats to freedom of expression in the history of the republic.

So how come First Amendment lawyers Bamberger, Lillienstein, and Joseph were using RICO to protect [*sic*] the First Amendment in Florida? Well, they have told me, they needed "strong medicine" to be effective advocates of their clients. "And if

Congress gives us something stronger, we'll use that, too." The clients in this case included Playboy Enterprises; the anti-censorship American Booksellers Association (whose members should be ashamed of themselves for embracing RICO); the Council for Periodical Distributors Associations; the International Periodical Distributors Association; and the Duval-Bibb Service, a Florida wholesale distributor of books and periodicals.

And who were the defendants? One of the most unpopular figures in the First Amendment community is the Reverend Donald Wildmon of Tupelo, Mississippi. Through his American Family Association, he was one of the leading protesters against Martin Scorsese's film, *The Last Temptation of Christ.* The AFA also takes credit, with reason, for the fact that Madonna's Pepsico commercial, a rather bizarre act of irreligious revisionism, was taken off television.

Wildmon and his colleagues have been active as well in various states in boycotting retailers selling "leading softcore porn magazines."

Reverend Wildmon has also been much exercised about the current "anti-family" state of television. As executive director of Christian Leaders for Responsible Television (Clear TV), he helps plan boycotts and other purgative strategies to cleanse the airwaves.

Wildmon's American Family Association has some 525 local chapters in the nation, including Florida. In federal district court there, the First Amendment Good Guys filed a RICO suit against the American Family Association of Florida.

In the Florida RICO suit, the American Family Association was charged with acts of "extortion" because they tried to get magazine and book retailers to stop selling, as the plaintiffs say, "certain materials protected by the First Amendment." The AFA calls them "sexually explicit magazines."

Specifically, what acts of "extortion" did the American Family Association commit?

They were terrifying acts. Members of the American Family Association sent "numerous" letters and postcards. They picketed the home of an officer of a wholesale distribution company. They threatened boycotts. And in a particularly determined letter, they threatened to hold a press conference to expose to the public and to law-enforcement agencies those stores that were acting "illegally" under Florida law by selling magazines that carry ads for obscene videos.

Actually, as the American Family Association admitted, it was wrong about that Florida obscenity statute. The law applies to magazine publishers, not to stores. But making a mistake is not the same as racketeering. The Supreme Court has noted that you can't have free speech without allowing for a certain amount of error.

Now, as for the other dreadful things the AFA did—sending letters, picketing, threatening boycotts—Cesar Chavez is lucky that the First Amendment Good Guys approve of him. And approve of his urging that people write letters, picket, and threaten boycotts.

Another charge against the American Family Association of Florida by these First Amendment lawyers is that as a result of AFA's actions, 1,400 convenience stores tossed out the offending magazines. Now, boycotting and threatening a boycott—of companies doing business with South Africa, let's say—is protected First Amendment activity. Were these lawyers saying that the First Amendment no longer applies when the boycott is successful?

Or were they saying that some people are so obnoxious, so hostile in their very bones to the First Amendment, that they should not be considered fit for its protection? Reverend Wildmon, for example?

Oren Teicher, executive director of the grandly titled Americans for Constitutional Freedom—to which several of the plaintiffs in the Florida suit belong—said of Wildmon and his ilk:

"If they dislike a TV show or a magazine, they want to drive it out of the market. That's un-American, and we're going to stop them."

Verbal protest is un-American?

Now it must be said that at one point the American Family Association of Florida threatened a RICO suit against the distributors and retailers of magazines that apparently are of particular erotic interest to AFA members. But this was hardly an excuse for the First Amendment Good Guys to bring RICO onto *their* team.

After all, a fundamental tenet of consistent civil libertarians is that even defendants who hold the Bill of Rights in contempt are entitled to the Constitution's protection. That's why the ACLU had to defend the native Nazis in Skokie.

But what about these charges of "extortion"? If the plaintiffs and their attorneys really believed that there is evidence of extortion that was not really free speech, why didn't they try to get a local district attorney to file criminal charges of extortion?

"You couldn't get a local Florida D.A. to do that," Max Lillienstein told me.

Had anybody checked to see if in all the state of Florida there wasn't one D.A. who would file such a charge—*if* the evidence was there and not just part of RICO boilerplate?

Lillienstein said that nobody had checked.

What he and Burt Joseph and Michael Bamberger—along with their clients—have done is to give RICO a respectability in cases brought to punish speech that it had never had before.

If I had been the assistant corporation counsel for the town of West Hartford, criticized for bringing a RICO suit against newspaper editor John Spear, I would reply:

"RICO is by no means the threat to free speech and the free press that some have claimed. Why, a group of magazine publishers and distributors—together with the prestigious American Booksellers Association—have brought a RICO suit against extortionists in Florida. Do you believe that people who depend for their very livelihood on the First Amendment would use a statute they believe endangers the very foundation of our liberties?"

Gara LaMarche, former executive director of the Texas Civil Liberties Union, now a board member of the New York Civil Liberties Union and head of the Fund for Free Expression, said of the RICO suit:

"It is extremely shortsighted, and a sharp break with the tradition that you fight speech with more speech—not by muzzling your adversaries. *Playboy*, the American Booksellers Association, and their cohorts in this suit are powerful institutions with many means at their disposal to counter the American Family Association—and without lending legitimacy to an extremely repressive tool like RICO. What they've done here will come back to haunt them—and all of us."

Meanwhile, on the radio, I heard a statement by a representative of *Playboy* on the occasion of the first edition of the Hungarian version of the magazine:

"Hungarians can now enjoy the same democratic freedoms *Playboy* has always championed."

The suit finally was settled, with the American Family Association continuing to exercise, and even enjoy, their First Amendment rights.

It is always a mistake to believe that the only serious danger to the Bill of Rights comes from the likes of Jesse Helms, Strom Thurmond, the Reverend Donald Wildmon, or the Supreme Court.

X

The Dangerous
Free Marketplace of Ideas

*"It looks as if they're just throwing him off the back
of the sleigh."*

At the end of Albert Camus's *The Plague*, the doctor, listen
ing to the joy of those who had been spared, remembered
that "such joy is always imperiled" because "the plague bacillus
never dies or disappears for good." The day would come when it
would rise up again.

Attempts to crush someone whose speech and ideas have
offended a particular group are a recurrent plague in all countries,
certainly including this one. For all the shortness of its duration,
the ferocious campaign against Andy Rooney was especially omi-
nous; and although he has survived, an autopsy of that campaign—
and some of its precedents—may alert some people against helping
to spread the next plague.

In 1959, I was helping Robert Herridge—the most original and
most stubborn producer in television history—assemble a folk
music hour for CBS-TV. During a rehearsal, a page left the sponsor's booth with a message he delivered to Herridge, who was work-

ing with the lighting. Herridge read the note, and in full view of the sponsor's booth, he tore it up.

Later, I asked him what that was all about. "Cisco Houston," he said. Cisco—who had been in the Merchant Marine with his friend Woody Guthrie—sang mostly about life on the road, along with songs of the West. He was very low-keyed, personally and in his music, but the music and the man stayed in your mind. I had chosen Cisco for the show.

"They say," said Herridge, "that his name is on some goddamn list of people who knew Communists or sang for Communists or signed some letter or said something that got them in somebody's file. They say, if we keep him on the show, people will boycott the sponsor and go after CBS."

Cisco stayed on the show. There was no further word from the sponsor.

Herridge was very unusual in those days of *Red Channels* and letter-writing campaigns to protect America from Reds and Comsymps (a term much used then). Other producers caved in. Networks caved in. Hollywood studios caved in.

Hundreds of people—writers, producers, actors, reporters— lost their jobs because of pressure groups. And Paul Robeson's name disappeared from *Who's Who in America.*

In some key respects, those were different times. The government then was also involved in punishing speech—through congressional committees hunting subversives, and their progeny in state and city legislatures.

But what happened to Andy Rooney when CBS News surrendered to pressure groups because of what he said—and what he is said to have said—is not dissimilar in other key respects from the freezing of free speech in the 1950s and 1960s.

There was the organized letter-writing campaign following Rooney's December 1989 special, "The Year with Andy Rooney," in which he offended some gay people and gay organizations by saying:

"There was some recognition in 1989 of the fact that many of the ills which kill us are self-induced. Too much alcohol, too much food, drugs, homosexual unions, cigarettes. They're all known to lead quite often to premature death."

An avalanche of angry letters followed. Obviously, letters—whether written individually or orchestrated—are a time-honored form of rebuttal. And when they demand someone be fired for what he or she said, that's also time-honored.

The bottom-line test of whether speech is indeed free comes when the boss decides whether to yield to those who would defenestrate the speaker or writer. David Burke, then president of CBS News, did not cave in after Andy Rooney's December special; but he instantly surrendered his and the news division's independence when he suspended Andy Rooney in 1990 for three months without pay after Rooney allegedly told a reporter for *The Advocate,* a gay publication:

"Blacks have watered down their genes because the less intelligent ones are the ones that have the most children. They drop out of school early, do drugs, and get pregnant."

Rooney denies those are his words. I believe him. Not only because he—a chronically and bluntly truthful man—denies it, but also because the *New York Post* reported that the previous December, Rooney told one of its reporters—without mentioning any race—that school dropouts "are having the most children, and the people who got out of college are having the least."

Rooney knows about the schools in places like West Virginia. "It's a class thing," Rooney told me, "not a race thing." (Even as a class thing, poor parents with a lot of kids have some brilliant children and many decent kids, even if they don't go to Harvard. And some from privileged classes who do go to Harvard and wind up in the slammer. But in any case, this is Rooney's *opinion.*)

Rooney thinks the reporter for *The Advocate* made it a race thing—even after Rooney had mentioned to him the white dropouts in West Virginia—in order to get Rooney in trouble in retaliation for what Rooney had said about death-causing "homosexual unions" on the air in December.

The reporter for *The Advocate* says his notes are accurate, and his editor stands by the reporter. The reporter, Chris Bull, did not record the interview.

In the Madame Defarge stage of McCarthyism (guillotine first, proof of guilt afterward), the press in the 1950s did a great deal to start the flames reaching toward the heretics at the stake. Not only such insatiable soul-catchers as columnists Westbook Pegler and George Sokolsky, but often the very news columns functioned as indictments. After all, even *The New York Times* fired some of its reporters in those years for exercising their Fifth Amendment rights.

On the Rooney story, the press, in 1990, did not intentionally act as executioners. But the headlines and the reporting gave the swift impression that all the charges against Rooney's wayward speech had been verified, despite his denials—which were seen as pro forma. This led Rooney's daughter, Emily, who was a journalist working in London, to say that "news is the new McCarthy."

Except for a relatively few papers, news has always been a potential destroyer—before and after Tailgunner Joe. The headlines, the way a story is played, the positioning of the denials—all this can create a heavy presumption of guilt.

But fair-minded, sophisticated readers are supposed to wait until the evidence is in before joining the celebrating throngs on the way to the auto-da-fé. Not the mayor of New York, David Dinkins. Rushing to condemn Rooney on the basis of raw news reports, the mayor telephoned CBS to "register shock." Dinkins also said: "Before [Rooney] is reinstated, CBS News ought to be certain it will not be embarrassed by Mr. Rooney in the future."

The only way to be certain of that was to terminate Mr. Rooney with extreme prejudice.

Rooney got into further trouble at CBS headquarters, Black Rock, because of a letter of apology, more or less, that he sent to *The Advocate.* What he said in it disturbed others besides news director David Burke, but it particularly offended him. In part, the letter said:

"Do I find the practice of one man introducing his penis into the anus of another repugnant? I do. Is it ethically wrong and abnormal behavior? It seems so to me, but if a person can't say what he thinks, he probably doesn't have a thought, so I'd settle for thinking it's merely bad taste."

Rooney did not say this on the air. He said it on his own time. Should a reporter or an editor or a commentator censor himself when he's not on the job? By what criteria?

David Burke suspended Andy Rooney. Yet there had been a vigorous exchange of ideas, which would have been even more vigorous if Rooney had read that passage on the air. And such an exchange of views is at the very core of the First Amendment. Granted, CBS is privately owned, but for a news division to censure one of its commentators for being controversial does go against the *spirit* of the First Amendment.

But where were the protests from civil libertarians and/or liberals about Rooney's suspension? They had been vividly aroused in support of Martin Scorsese's *The Last Temptation of Christ.* It gravely offended many Christians who were convinced, beyond any doubt, that Scorsese had deliberately desecrated their Savior. The protesters wrote letters. They picketed, and some theater chains and individual movie houses did refuse to show the film. But Scorsese had help. Many civil libertarians and liberals loudly decried these attempts to silence *The Last Temptation of Christ,* and in some areas, they got exhibitors to lift the ban.

The great majority of these champions of free expression, however, refused to criticize the censorship of Andy Rooney. They were afraid of being called racists and homophobes.

And then there was the dependably respectable *New York Times,* which, in a February 13, 1990, editorial, praised the CBS News president who had punished Andy Rooney: "Score 10 on the common-sense scale for David Burke... for his handling of the newest outbreak of slighting words." Along with "fighting words" (whatever they are), the words attributed to Rooney, said the *Times,* do not have "a place in civil public discourse."

But Stuart Kellogg, editor of the gay magazine *The Advocate,* revealed a much deeper understanding of our free-speech traditions. "We did not want to get Rooney punished for what he said in our magazine," Kellogg told me. "You don't throw out the whole person for something he said that you don't like." As for CBS, "it looks as if they're just throwing him off the back of the sleigh."

In 1987, the Writers Guild of America set up picket lines in front of CBS. Andy Rooney not only gave verbal support to the striking writers and editors; he refused to cross their picket lines and refused to do any new segments for "60 Minutes" while the strike was on. After a month, with the strike still not settled, he threatened to leave CBS. In tribute to his solidarity with the labor movement, the bosses suspended his $7,700-a-week salary.

He was the only CBS star to put his job on the line. Rooney believed CBS workers without marquee names were getting a raw deal.

A former CBS official told me that Rooney's "disloyalty" to CBS during the strike was no small factor in his later suspension over his use of "slighting words."

Before his notorious conduct during the Writers Guild strike, there had been the firings of more than two hundred people in the news division, including a startling number of long-term correspondents who had shown exemplary loyalty to CBS News for decades.

In her book, *What I Saw at the Revolution* (Random House), Peggy Noonan, who was working for Dan Rather at the time, writes:

"CBS saved money, but it spent loyalty as if it was going out of style, which perhaps it is. [Dan] Rather captured it. An executive was wondering aloud about the effect of the cuts on office morale and the sense of tradition. 'Listen,' Dan said, 'this place has all the tradition of a discount shoe store.'"

Around the same time, in his syndicated newspaper column, Andy Rooney wrote about his employers: "CBS, which used to stand for the Columbia Broadcasting System, no longer stands for anything. They're just corporate initials now."

If that judgment needed confirming, David Burke, president of CBS News, did just that by suspending Rooney on February 8, 1990, and by the language of the suspension, which should have led—the Rooney issue aside—to the loud, public dissent of any self-respecting journalists in the CBS News division. Or anywhere else.

Referring to Rooney's words, both actual and only alleged, which led black and gay groups to call for his head, Burke declared:

"I have made it clear that CBS News cannot tolerate such remarks, or anything that approximates such comments, since they in no way reflect the views of this organization."

There was no further explanation about "anything that approximates such comments." This is the news division that proudly declares it is in the tradition of Edward R. Murrow. And how is anyone—reporter, editor, anchor—to know if he or she has "approximated" speech that could lead to his having to clean out his desk by five o'clock?

And where is such speech prohibited? At home? During a lull at a PTA meeting? At a bar?

The clear intent of this threatening fog was to strike fear into all the employees of CBS News. From that very day, the big chill was on. That afternoon, I called someone at "60 Minutes" who has helped me on stories, and whom I've helped. He is a man of no little courage when out in the field, and, until now, he has always been forthright in our conversations. This time, he would not say a word about what had happened to Andy Rooney. He was clearly uncomfortable in censoring himself, but that's what he had been told to do.

Indeed, nobody at CBS News, so far as I know, publicly supported Rooney. Walter Cronkite, no longer on the staff, did, but not even Burke would dare retaliate against the George Washington of CBS News by trying to get him removed from the board of directors.

Also publicly expressing dismay at what Burke had done to Rooney were three former presidents of CBS News—Fred Friendly, Dick Salant, and Ed Joyce.

Privately, Mike Wallace and Don Hewitt, the orchestrator of "60 Minutes," did push Burke hard for the removal of the suspension.

And Rooney told me that on the day he was suspended, some of his colleagues—Ed Bradley, Mike Wallace, and Don Hewitt—came over to him with warm expressions of support.

But publicly, what Wallace said—on "60 Minutes" the Sunday following the suspension—greatly surprised Andy Rooney.

"A personal note" was how Wallace's public threnody began:

"Andy Rooney, to his credit, acknowledges that he owes an apology to gays and blacks who were offended by statements attributed to him."

It's true that Rooney subsequently apologized, in the sense that he said he had not intended to offend, and was sorry if he had.

The basic question—ignored by Wallace—is why those opinions by Rooney merited his suspension and public humiliation.

After all, as Fred Friendly told me, Rooney has "insulted at least four Presidents of the United States, the head of the National Rifle Association, the heads of the tobacco industry, and scores more."

Why didn't he have to apologize to them? Because the previous news directors he worked for were not prone to panic.

On that February 11 "60 Minutes," Wallace went on to say:

"He [Rooney] firmly denies having made any such statements about blacks.

"Even though the remarks attributed to Andy Rooney were not made on '60 Minutes'—*and indeed could never have been made on '60 Minutes'*—this is the broadcast with which he has been most closely associated." (Emphasis added.)

This is known as isolating the pariah from his decent colleagues. Dr. Jekyll works here, but not, Lord's sake, Mr. Hyde.

Wallace closed this way:

"After his three-month suspension, which he himself has acknowledged is understandable, we who have been his colleagues through the years surely look forward to his return here."

Look again at the slippery claim that Andy Rooney "himself acknowledged" that his suspension was "understandable."

What Andy Rooney did, in truth, say in the public prints (*New York Times*, February 9) was: "I am accepting his [David Burke's] offer of suspension rather than to permanently end my career at CBS."

Rooney took the three-month sentence because he didn't want to be fired. Wallace twisted Rooney's real reason to make it appear as if he took the punishment in contrition for his abominable sins.

And what did the rest of Andy Rooney's admiring "60 Minutes" colleagues have to say on the air or to reporters about the silencing of Andy? Not a word.

"These million-dollar babies!" a former worker at the CBS News division said to me. "Actually, Mike is a three-million-dollar baby. They all have principles, but not when it comes to risking their money to stand up for Andy publicly."

There are others who abandoned their principles—not for money, but for political expediency. Tom Stoddard, then executive director of the Lambda Legal Defense and Education Fund, used to be a civil libertarian. He was a very able staff lawyer for the New York Civil Liberties Union. But in the February 8 *New York Post,* Stoddard delivered this verdict on Andy Rooney before trial:

"This is Bull Connor without the dogs and the fire hoses."

Surely that's not the quality of due process that Stoddard demanded for his Lambda clients.

While the guillotine was being jubilantly prepared for ex-citizen Rooney, I got a call from the legal director of an ACLU affiliate in another state. "I'm writing to the national office," he told me, "to ask why the ACLU has been silent. Sure, there's no government action involved, but the ACLU has spoken out before when a private institution has violated the spirit, if not the letter, of the First Amendment."

And where was the New York Civil Liberties Union? Was it afraid of being called racist and homophobic if it stood by its principles in this case? A good many silent white liberals and libertarians were indeed afraid of being stigmatized if they spoke up.

Meanwhile, His Honor, the otherwise fastidious mayor of the City of New York, continued to refuse to concede that he might have rushed to condemn Rooney without waiting to find out what Rooney had actually said. By contrast, Benjamin Hooks, after the NAACP had conducted its own investigation, said publicly: "Rooney has an excellent reputation. We're satisfied he's not a racist...." But after Hooks's statement, all that gracious Mayor David Dinkins would say was: "This is pretty much ancient history. Now it's a matter between CBS and Rooney."

But part of that ancient history was a record of egregious unfairness, and Dinkins contributed to that. Indeed, on February 11 on WNBC-TV, Gabe Pressman asked the mayor: "Do you think Andy Rooney can be rehabilitated, assuming he said what he said?"

"Well, we'll see," said David Dinkins.

Only one journalist, so far as I know, tried to check the track record of the reporter, Chris Bull, who did the incendiary interview of Andy Rooney for *The Advocate.* In his weekly column for *U.S. News and World Report,* John Leo noted that two previous Bull subjects—*Newsday* AIDS reporter Catherine Woodard and Chuck Orleb, publisher of the gay newspaper *The Native*—claim to have been badly misquoted by Bull.

According to Leo, Woodard says she "never said *The New York Times* was biased against gay activists, as Bull had her saying and…when that and another statement she never made were attributed to her, Bull said he may have made a mistake and confused her remarks with those of someone else in his notebook."

Orleb, saying he was "reworded" by Bull, adds: "I felt he had an ax to grind." (It took John Leo all of fifteen minutes to get this illuminating information.)

When the press leaps into a story—without really looking into it—and when corporate executives are frightened by pressure groups who believe what they see in the press, the right to free speech gets badly mauled.

As for Rooney's apparent victory in being reinstated after less than a month, it had nothing to do with recognition by CBS or by most of his gay and black critics that suppressing speech cuts more than one way.

What rescued Rooney was not the sudden revelation that free speech is indivisible. It was rating points. Revenues from "60 Minutes" are a crucial element in the network's profits, and the show lost about 20 percent of its audience during the three weeks Rooney was off the air. Network brass aren't sure that the decline was attributable to the departure of viewers who pined for Andy Rooney, but they didn't want to take the chance that Rooney's absence might, indeed, be the cause.

So CBS's was a free-market decision, hardly one based on concern for the other free marketplace—that of ideas.

What disturbed Rooney most was that many people—he had no idea how many—believed what was said about him by the black and gay organizations. He is afraid, he told me, that for the rest of his life he'll be tagged as a racist by those who know only what they saw in the newspaper headlines.

"How can I now say," Rooney asked in frustration one day, "'I am not a racist.' It's like saying, 'I am not a crook.'"

As for his colleagues, even now that Rooney is back from exile, everybody on that program is going to watch what he or she says— off the air—for fear of having to go through what Rooney did. And Rooney is going to be a lot more careful from now on.

Indeed, in May 1990, he told a meeting of the Constitutional Rights Foundation in Los Angeles: "You may have wondered if my experience has caused me to be more careful. I guess I have to confess it has."

Later, Andy Rooney censored himself. He was going to criticize the concept of all-black colleges on "60 Minutes." But the integrationist killed his own piece because Ed Bradley objected. Rooney still feels all-black or all-male colleges are a bad idea but he won't say so on "60 Minutes."

"The Constitution leaves matters of taste and style... largely to the individual."

The headline in the May 7, 1990, *New York Times* proclaimed: "Breslin Suspension Called a Victory for Minority Journalists." In the story, Helen Zia, managing editor of *Ms.* and president of the New York chapter of the Asian-American Journalists Association, was quoted as saying that if *Newsday* columnist Jimmy Breslin had not been suspended, they would indeed have suffered a defeat, and "there would have been a great outcry."

The battle had been won, however, *before* Breslin's suspension—and that punishment obscured the victory. The people at center stage and those journalists covering the story were not aware of how significant a victory had already been achieved in proving that the most effective way to deal with outrageous speech is with more speech, more compelling speech.

Nothing happens entirely for the first time. That's the first thing I would tell my students if I were teaching the Breslin case in the public schools. (Having spent some time with fifth-graders in the past year, I now realize that you don't have to wait until high school to examine, in detail, the mine fields and triumphs of free speech. These kids, being very opinionated, are much intrigued by this sort of thing.)

I would go on to say that arguments about the limits of speech go back before the Revolution. In some of the colonies, you could be banished, or worse, for blasphemy. And only seven years after the ratification of the Bill of Rights in 1791, President John Adams and the Federalists pushed through Congress the Alien and Sedition Acts under which a number of reporters and editors were imprisoned for bad speech—speech disrespectful of the President and Congress.

And not only journalists were put away for not holding their tongues. In a New England town, a citizen, having partaken freely of certain spirits, watched President Adams make a grand appearance accompanied by a sixteen-gun salute. The citizen said, aloud, "I do not care if they fired through his ass." The citizen was clapped in jail.

And so it has been throughout our history. Bad speech, disgusting speech—public or private—had its punishments. From the stocks to prison to harsh money damages in defamation cases.

From the beginning, however, there were those who advocated a different approach to demeaning, hurtful speech. Beginning with James Madison and including, in our time, Justice Hugo Black, the idea was that so long as there is room and time to reply to bad speech, counterspeech would provide the punishment that was needed. Not money damages, not imprisonment, but the shining of a pitiless verbal light on the lies and distortions and sheer meanness of the awful speech in question.

Joe McCarthy, for instance, received his terrible punishment not in his eventual censure by the Senate, but before that, from devastating counterspeech: Ed Murrow on television and Boston lawyer Joe Welch during the Army-McCarthy hearings. ("Until this moment, Senator, I think I never really gauged your cruelty or your recklessness... Have you no sense of decency, sir, at long last? Have you no sense of decency?")

Having gone over that ground with the fifth-graders—who are more open to history than those adults who are under the illusion they remember it clearly—I would move on to the Breslin story.

It is a classic illustration—except for the end—of good speech pursuing and driving out bad speech. What Breslin said in the *Newsday* newsroom about Ji-Yeon Mary Yuh, a reporter for the same paper, was clearly speech the intent of which was to verbally batter its target. From "yellow cur" to "slant-eyed" to what *The New York Times* demurely called "an obscene anatomical reference." (A word no *New York Times* reader has ever heard or used. The word is "cunt.")

In that soliloquy, which will dog him the rest of his days, Breslin also railed at her for having the nerve to send him a computer message that called a column of his "sexist." She had no right, he more than implied, to criticize *him*, because she was inferior, in more ways than one. She did not deserve free speech.

So what happened? Breslin was battered with so much free counterspeech—from Ji-Yeon Mary Yuh and the Asian-American Journalists Association to black and Hispanic journalist organizations—that he was overwhelmed. And he suffered considerable damage. Not from the suspension, but from what this did to his reputation as a journalist.

Despite his novels, a play, and a nonfiction book, Breslin defines himself as a reporter. It is his reason for being—a chronicler of his times who doesn't get his news from press conferences, but in the streets.

In a column in the May 9 *Washington Post* ("The Real Jimmy Breslin"), Tony Kornheiser recalled just a couple of the obsessions that have made Breslin an invaluable guide to the plague years:

"A while back, when New York was in a blood lust about the heroism of subway vigilante Bernhard Goetz, it was Breslin who asked whether all the black-slappers would feel as full of affection had it been a black man shooting four white youths.

"When everyone was running scared from AIDS, preaching that it was a plague and deriding its victims as subhuman, Breslin went to their homes and talked to AIDS patients so New Yorkers could see these were real people, sons and daughters, to care about and feel compassion for...."

Breslin has gone into neighborhoods that have never seen a journalist before. And the people there are not just stories to him. They are indictments of those public officials who are concerned only about themselves—and his contempt for those official parasites is savage.

But this extraordinary record of showing those in power the naked lunch at the end of the fork—in William Burroughs's phrase—now became blurred. Not to those who had read him for a long time but to those who had never read him or had picked him up only recently. And many young readers—knowing him now, because of his explosion in the newsroom, only as the kind of caricature who appears in *Doonesbury*—are not likely to even begin to look at his columns. Except maybe to see if there's a sentence or two that will further fit their stereotype of him.

Much of this will fade away in time, but not all of it. It has been a national story. And worst of all, it will stay in Breslin's own mind. He blew it.

So, I would tell the fifth-graders, you can see what happened to bad speech once it was attacked by more speech. The bad speech got chased out of the arena. Exactly what James Madison, the architect of the First Amendment, had in mind.

Was that sufficient punishment for Jimmy Breslin? More than sufficient, I think, but not enough for those who wanted the further humiliation that attends being suspended. And Breslin played right into their hands by getting on the Howard Stern radio show, where he did indeed make light of his apology and the hurt he had caused. He had not been suspended at that point.

I do not know Breslin at all well, but I suspect that his performance on the Stern program was a way of showing himself that he had not been brought down, that he still had his pride. Unlike Lyndon Johnson, he was not about to show his scars in public.

That Breslin move allowed the brass at *Newsday* to appease the various groups that wanted Breslin suspended. He had been insufficiently contrite, said the brass.

They, too, had missed the point. When you let free speech have its way—when all sides can get their say—then official punishment is unnecessary. Workers on newspapers, even those in charge, ought to know that better than most.

So we come back to that May 10 *New York Times* headline: "Breslin Suspension Called a Victory for Minority Journalists." Not really. The day may come when some of them—being forceful journalists like Breslin—will say or write something that will inflame an organized group. And even though that group will have plenty of space and time to respond, that won't be enough. They'll want more punishment inflicted on the offender. And since newspapers increasingly yield to such pressure, the protesters will get what they want.

That's what happened, for a time, to Andy Rooney. Having

experience in being a target, he was invited on the May 11, 1990, *Nightline.* When he was asked what he thought of the suspension of Breslin, Rooney said:

"Probably they did the right thing." But, he added, the suspension made sense as being for "bad taste." This was "not a matter of free speech."

But "bad taste" and "free speech" are inextricably bound to each other. Yet here is Andy Rooney—who has learned more than he cares to know about the dangers of engaging in free speech—adding to those perils by saying that speech should no longer be free when it's in "bad taste."

Bad taste to whom? I commended to Andy Rooney the opinion by Supreme Court Justice John Harlan in *Cohen* v. *California.* (Cohen had appeared in a corridor of the Los Angeles County Courthouse wearing a jacket bearing the words "Fuck the Draft." And women and children were present, the prosecutor emphasized.)

Said Justice Harlan: "While the particular four-letter word being litigated here is perhaps more distasteful than most others of its genre, it is nevertheless often true that one man's vulgarity is another's lyric." Harlan went on to say that "the Constitution leaves matters of taste and style...largely to the individual."

The case of Jimmy Breslin was surely one of free and offensive speech that might be Andrew Dice Clay's lyric, but that speech should not have been punished officially. Left to defend itself in the open exchange of more free speech and ideas, it was knocked out. And that should have been the end of it.

The Day They Came to Arrest the Painting

In 1988, not long after the death of Harold Washington, mayor of Chicago, a painting was arrested in that city on the charge that its continued display might very well incite a riot. The painting was a satiric portrait of Washington himself. Its forced departure from the School of the Art Institute of Chicago is a classic illustration of what Judge Learned Hand had in mind when he said:

"Liberty lies in the hearts and minds of men and women; when it dies there, no constitution, no law, no court can save it."

As for Harold Washington, he became known nationally as the embattled mayor of Chicago, largely thwarted for much of his first term by a City Council majority of white racist descendants of the ancient regime.

Smart, resourceful, Washington eventually prevailed and he was beginning to bring some degree of racial understanding—and even comity—to that bristling city. But in November 1987 Washington died suddenly, leaving an enormous vacuum. The city began building racial walls again, and what happened in the aftermath of the offensive painting has made the walls higher.

Few people outside of Chicago knew much about Harold Washington's protection of the Bill of Rights while he was in Congress. In the Illinois legislature, he had had an excellent record on civil liberties legislation, and he kept that up as a member of the House.

I became aware of the intensity of Washington's concern with freedom of expression, among other Constitutional guarantees, through Congressman Don Edwards of California. A former FBI agent, Edwards has long been chairman of the House Subcommittee on Civil and Constitutional Rights and is a passionate civil libertarian. Edwards's committee has oversight jurisdiction over the FBI, and in other ways gets involved in reminding government agencies that this was not intended to be a police state. Over the years, Don Edwards has sent me transcripts of some of the subcommittee's public hearings.

I have referred, on occasion, to Edwards as "the congressman from the Constitution." The same could be said of Harold Washington. A man of swift, probing intelligence, he would ask government officials the kinds of questions that William O. Douglas or William Brennan might have.

When the story broke that a painting of Harold Washington had been busted on the ground that it insulted his memory, I asked Don Edwards for his reaction.

"Harold would have howled at the arrest of that painting of him," said Edwards. "He would have thought it was hilarious to arrest a painting, including one making fun of him. And he would surely have protected the right of the painter to do what he did."

That's not just speculation. When Washington was mayor of Chicago, there was a long period when, encircled by hostile aldermen and other enemies, he was hard put to keep the city running. In the midst of all this, there erupted what some have called the dial-a-poem war. The city's Department of Fine Arts had made it possible for anyone to dial a number and listen to a poem read aloud by its creator.

One week, a very angry black poet, who was on the tape that week, used an accusatory obscenity that some white folks took very personally, and there were cries that the poet be disconnected permanently.

Harold Washington, annoyed that he had to deal with this furor at a time when far more vital controversies were threatening to bring him down, nonetheless refused to have the city throw the poet off the line.

"We're not in the business of censorship," Washington told an associate. "If you scratch one word, where does it stop?"

Later on, a young white artist was commissioned to paint a mural on the wall of a new public library in a white North Side neighborhood. The painting included what might be called vivid fertility symbols. Some of the residents in the area were not pleased. Indeed, they wanted the mural destroyed. Instantly.

Aldermen from that part of the city saw a chance to embarrass the mayor who was still entangled in ferocious councilmanic wars. As with the inflammatory poem, Washington could have done without the painting. But something in the mayor could not let him endanger the mural. He protected it and the artist.

Washington, a colleague of his told me, was very much aware that in the case of a mural commissioned by public funds for a public place, the feelings of the people who would have to live in its proximity troubled him, but while their concerns ought to be taken into account, he could not come down in favor of suppression.

Harold Washington firmly believed—as he used to tell his press secretary, Alton Miller—that an artist must be protected, including his right to make a fool of himself.

But after his death, a lot of people in Chicago, who claimed they were preventing Harold Washington's memory from being desecrated, did something in his name that he would never have done. They became censors.

At 8:00 A.M. on May 11, 1988, an exhibition went up of works by graduating students at the School of the Art Institute of Chicago. The show was closed to the public. One of the paintings was twenty-three-year-old David Nelson's *Mirth and Girth.*

As described by Michael Brenson in the May 29 *New York Times,* the painting "is about four feet tall and three feet wide. It is a frontal view of Mayor Washington, with a resolute yet benevolent expression on his face and an ample paunch. He is naked except for a bra, bikini underpants, garter belt and stockings."

Word of the painting traveled fast, and the city council rushed through a resolution, sponsored by black aldermen, threatening to withdraw municipal funds ($5.3 million out of $44 million of the school's revenue last year) unless the painting was removed from the School of the Art Institute.

By three-fifteen that afternoon, direct action had been taken. Two aldermen appeared at the school, took the painting off the wall, and tried to leave with it. (Presumably an execution would have followed.) Students, however, blocked them, and rehung the painting.

More aldermen arrived. They too tried to make a citizen's arrest of the painting, but were stopped by security personnel who suggested they see Anthony Jones, president of the school. Jones had been brought to Chicago sixteen months before from his post as president of the Glasgow School of the Arts in relatively serene Scotland.

At the meeting with Jones, police were also present, and they announced that they were taking the painting into protective custody.

In the May 12 *Chicago Tribune,* Jerry Crimmins and Robert Davis quoted Anthony Jones as saying: "The police were very concerned that [exhibiting] this work would lead to riots. 'Incitement to riot' was the phrase they actually used." The story added that according to school officials, Jones was "required by the aldermen to sign a statement indicating that the work would not be exhibited further."

Still, the aldermen did not trust the school to keep *Mirth and*

Girth under lock and key. (By this point, the painting had a vertical gash four to six inches long. The perpetrator is unknown.) So, Jones reported later, "[Police Superintendent Leroy Martin] said in order to calm the situation, they would take it away and lock it up in the central police station."

At first, before that meeting, school president Anthony Jones had brandished the First Amendment. Many found the painting in bad taste, he said, "but the First Amendment is not a remote issue for us here in a school on the cutting edge of art and design."

So why did he let the painting be handcuffed and booked, and then swear never to show it again? Well, as he told *The New York Times:* "When the aldermen tell you there will be major civic unrest, with marches on the Institute and bombings, and people ask me if I believe them, I absolutely believe them."

In addition, Marshall Field, head of the Art Institute, apologized to the city of Chicago for the Institute's having given space—and its imprimatur—to this act of irreverence toward the late mayor.

Threats by public officials of physical harm to the school—and, by inference, to its staff and students—actually caused the censoring of a painting in a major American city. Worse yet, the police gave their encouragement to the censorship by declaring there would be riots if the painting were not imprisoned.

Because cops and public officials are involved, this is a particularly raw example of "the hecklers' veto."

The use of the "hecklers' veto" was as unconstitutional in Chicago as it had been in Albany, New York, with the South African rugby team.

Whites, threatening disruption and violence, tried to use the "hecklers' veto" to block marches by blacks demonstrating for civil rights in the 1960s and after. In decades past, it's been used against labor unions and women's rights activists. It is the kind of clubbing of the First Amendment that would have infuriated Harold Washington.

In this instance, as Jay Miller, executive director of the Illinois ACLU, told the *Chicago Sun-Times:* "If there was a threat, the way to prevent a riot would have been to protect the painting and arrest the rioters and hecklers. What they did was arrest the painting."

The painting was returned to David Nelson. It was not likely to be seen in Chicago again in the near future. Nor were other works regarded as too controversial. The *Chicago Tribune* reported (May 14):

"A group of clergymen led by the head of Operation PUSH...vowed to impose 'sanctions' against the Art Institute of Chicago unless it implemented a review policy *to prevent offensive portraits from being exhibited in the future by its students or by contributing artists.*" (Emphasis added.) The statement resulted from a "unity" meeting of the "One Hundred Pastors for Peace and Tranquility in Our City."

And Alderman Allan Streeter warned the Art Institute of Chicago that it has "a moral obligation" to determine what works will be displayed on the basis of how "Jews or Croatians or Poles will respond to it." What about Italians, Irish, and Arabs?

In a lead editorial, the *Chicago Sun-Times* thundered: "...By what right do [the black aldermen] coerce an official of a private institution to sign a statement promising to do or not do something, like hang a particular painting? No one in the United States—not the President, not the Supreme Court, not a unanimous Congress—has such power....

"By what right do they order the seizure of private property, without warrant, without due process? Why stop at this private school? Do roving bands of aldermen have the right to storm private homes, grabbing whatever offends them?

"By what right do they decide that this painting, any painting, ought to be confiscated, locked in custody, burned or otherwise destroyed? Do aldermen offended by books in the public library think they have the right to organize a posse to purge the bookshelves?"

Harold Washington could have written that editorial.

But why did David Nelson do what he did? "In Chicago at this time," he said on radio station WLUP, "Harold Washington is like an icon. He's like a deity...Last week I saw [a poster] they're selling. It shows the skyline of Chicago with the clouds swirling above Chicago, and on one side there's Jesus looking down on Chicago and on the other side Harold Washington is looking down on Chicago, and I said, 'Oh, come on, this is ridiculous.'"

XI

Obscenity, and How It Did In Lenny Bruce

"There are as many different definitions of obscenity as there are human beings, and they are as unique to the individual as his dreams."

Hardly noted during the bicentennial of the Constitution in 1987 was a heartfelt tribute to the Framers of the Constitution by the Supreme Court of Oregon the year before. That body, the highest court in the state, ruled unanimously that from then on, there can be no prohibition of any form of expression in Oregon on the ground that it is obscene. Obscenity is no longer recognized as a term in law in that free state.

The state's Supreme Court did what Justice William Brennan has been advocating for years. When the United States Supreme Court, he said, is crabbed and cranky when dealing with basic liberties, the courts of the individual states should look to their *state* constitutions, which sometimes are as protective—and even more protective of liberties in certain areas—than the United States Constitution.

315

Not everything the nation's highest court decides need be agreed to by the individual state courts. The United States Supreme Court does set the *minimum* constitutional protections for every American, from sea to shining sea. And no state court can make a ruling that is *weaker* than those bottom-line protections. For instance, no state court can get away with deciding that local district attorneys have a right to prevent the press from attending a trial. And no state court could uphold a municipal ruling forbidding the flying of red flags. (Earlier in this century—before the United States Supreme Court said that the Bill of Rights applied to the individual states as well as to the acts of Congress—twenty-eight states criminalized the flying of flags that were red.)

On the other hand, state constitutions and state courts can provide stronger protections to the liberties of their citizens than do the federal courts or the Congress. And that's why Justice Brennan kept advising constitutional lawyers to try to bring certain cases into the state rather than the federal courts.

In Oregon, Article I, Section 8 of the state constitution states with admirable clarity and conviction:

"No law shall be passed restraining the free expression of opinion, or restricting the right to speak, write or print freely on any subject whatever."

Now, it could be said that the First Amendment to the United States Constitution, while not as muscular in its language, is also clear and broad: there shall be "no law....abridging the freedom of speech or of the press."

Unfortunately, however, the U.S. Supreme Court has muddied that once clear stream of free expression and has created exceptions that do abridge the freedom of speech and of the press: defamation and obscenity, among them. And with regard to obscenity, the Supreme Court's definitions have become murkier and murkier until it is often very difficult for someone to know he is breaking the law until he has been fined and/or imprisoned.

At last, the Oregon Supreme Court rebelled against the limitations on expression set by the nine Justices in Washington. Once it decided—on the basis of its *state* constitution—to give the citizens of Oregon more, not less, protection concerning freedom of expression, then that state court was free to simply brush aside all of the Supreme Court decisions penalizing obscenity.

Moreover, in the bicentennial year, the unanimous court—in a decision written by its most conservative member, Robert E. Jones—took manifest delight demonstrating that by ignoring the tortured route of the United States Supreme Court, these Oregon jurists were following the original intent of the Framers.

Duly and, one might say joyously, noted was the fact that, as William O. Douglas used to say, "the First Amendment was the product of a robust, not a prudish age." They might have added that James Madison, the principal creator of the First Amendment, and a very serious, studious man, was also known for his considerable reservoir of Rabelaisian anecdotes. In the libraries of many of the Framers, as well as those of other colonists, were such erotic classics of the time—some of them likely to get their sellers busted two centuries later—as John Cleland's *Memoirs of a Woman of Pleasure,* Ovid's *Art of Love,* the stories of Rabelais, and especially two sexually graphic works by Framer Benjamin Franklin, *Advice to a Young Man on Choosing a Mistress* and *Polly Baker.* (Thomas Jefferson wrote approvingly of *Polly Baker.*)

Going to the historical roots of the naturalness with which the Framers regarded the kinds of sexual expression that lead modern law-enforcement personnel to raid bookstores and movie houses, the Oregon Supreme Court quoted from Harvard law professor Laurence Tribe's book *American Constitutional Law.* He notes that in the colonies at the time of the Revolution, "only one state (Massachusetts) had any... law" punishing obscenity. And that law had to do with sacrilegious—blasphemous—speech. Not secular speech.

It wasn't until the nineteenth century that the United States Supreme Court, ignoring the intent of the Framers and preferring instead to listen to the arguments of such as Anthony Comstock, began to punish "dirty" speech.

Significantly, the case that the Oregon Supreme Court used to free its state of the United States Supreme Court's strictures on speech was a classic "dirty books" bust. None of the works involved are in the Modern Library or are taught in literature courses. So the issue here was not any kind of exculpatory "serious political, literary, artistic or scientific value." The issue was expression, anybody's and everybody's right to say and read what he or she wants to, no matter what Phyllis Schlafly or Catharine MacKinnon think.

In Redmond, Oregon, Earl Henry was the proprietor of what is euphemistically called an "adult bookstore." He was charged with possessing and disseminating obscene materials, thereby breaking a law of the state of Oregon that prohibits such activities.

Mr. Henry has become a figure in the history of American free expression because the raid on his bookstore led to Oregon becoming the first state in the nation to abolish the offense of obscenity.

In doing so, the state court proudly recalled the history of Oregon itself, emphasizing that "most members of the [Oregon] Constitutional Convention of 1857 were rugged and robust individuals dedicated to founding a *free society unfettered by the governmental imposition of some people's views of morality on the free expression of others.*" (Emphasis added.)

And the Oregon court made it utterly clear that at least in Oregon, "obscenity" is speech; and all speech is protected.

The ruling does not mean that an "adult" bookshop, for instance, can be set up anywhere at all. Regulations, says the Oregon court, are permissible "in the interest of unwilling viewers... minors, and beleaguered neighbors." However—and this is the key to Oregon's newly expanded freedom of expression—"No law can prohibit or censor the communication itself."

Among other things, the Oregon state court's historic decision is a reaction against the quagmire that the United States Supreme Court has made of its "obscenity" rulings. The nine Justices don't know what obscenity is even when they see it, but they still keep trying to suppress it, despite the First Amendment.

How did the modern High Court slide into this quicksand? As Michael Kent Curtis points out in an illuminating analysis, "Obscenity: The Justices' Not So New Robes" (*Campbell Law Review,* Campbell University, North Carolina, Summer 1986), the descent began in 1957. The case was *Roth* v. *United States.*

Justice William Brennan, writing for a majority of his colleagues, said flat out that "obscenity is not within the area of constitutionality protected speech or press." (He was new to the Court, had not thought through this issue, and was later to regret his decision.)

This is judge-made constitutional law. You cannot find it in the

Constitution or in the debates leading up to the framing and adoption of the Constitution.

What is this form of speech so dangerous as to be explicitly cast out of the First Amendment in *Roth?* Why, said Brennan, it's material that appeals "to prurient interest... having a tendency to excite lustful thoughts."

Seeing that, Benjamin Franklin might well have wondered what pinched nation this was that had supplanted America.

Brennan went on to set up the criteria by which courts could decide that unfettered lustful thoughts were loose in a town: A work is obscene if, to the "average person, applying contemporary community standards, the dominant theme of the material taken as a whole appeals to prurient interest."

Every phrase in those guidelines is so overbroad and vague as to invite the confusion that ineluctably mounted through the years.

Even then, Brennan was worried that his decision might wind up making "good" books illegal, along with volumes teeming with lustful thoughts. So, in the *Roth* decision, he cautioned that "the door barring federal and state intrusion" into the First Amendment area "must be kept tightly closed and opened only the slightest crack necessary to prevent encroachment upon more important interests."

The warning was useless. The crack kept widening and widening until, in 1973, Brennan, in an agonized dissent (*Paris Adult Theater I* v. *Slaton*) gave up trying to draw a line between "obscenity" and speech that is protected by the First Amendment. He emphasized that "such indefinite concepts as 'prurient interest,' 'patent offensiveness,' [and] 'serious literary value' result in utterly intolerable" uncertainty that "invites arbitrary and erratic enforcement of the law."

His colleague, William O. Douglas, had not been fooled from the start that it was possible to lasso "obscenity" without also crippling the First Amendment. At the beginning, in *Roth*, Douglas had insisted that the notion of "community standards"—which the Court was to hold onto through the years as an illusory way out of the quicksand—was wholly unconstitutional.

"If the First Amendment guarantee of freedom of speech and press is to mean anything," Douglas said, "it must allow protests even against the moral code that the standard of the day sets for the community."

That's what James Madison used to say.

Furthermore, as "community standards" inevitably meant that *different* communities—hamlets, counties, cities—could set *different* standards, there was no longer a national First Amendment. Material that would escape arrest and conviction in New York could be busted in Wichita, Kansas. The affirmation by the Supreme Court of this balkanization of the First Amendment means that its protections in this area of the law vary according to where citizens live. It is one thing for state courts to make guarantees of liberty stronger than the federal standard, but to have no national standard at all is to insure arbitrary enforcement of the law based on what the majority in any given jurisdiction wants.

This is majoritarianism, and the Bill of Rights was clamorously insisted upon as an addition to the Constitution so that individual Americans were not trampled upon by an offended majority.

But the Supreme Court goes on trying to make criminal sanctions against "obscene" speech constitutional. In yet another dissent (*Pope* v. *Illinois*), Justice Brennan tried once more to convince his colleagues that they keep going deeper and deeper into a sinkhole:

"...*any* regulation of such material with respect to consenting adults suffers from the defect that 'the concept of obscenity' cannot be defined with sufficient specificity and clarity to provide fair notice to persons who create and distribute sexually oriented materials [that they're breaking the law]."

Not only is it impossible to draw a bright line—or even a discernible faint line—between criminally punishable "prurient" speech and protected erotic literature, but each attempt further undermines the First Amendment.

Throughout the history of the Court, William O. Douglas understood the indivisibility of free expression in this area far more clearly than any other Justice. At the beginning, in the 1957 *Roth* case, Douglas said (and he never altered his conviction):

"The standard of what offends 'the common conscience of the community' conflicts ... with the command of the First Amendment.... Certainly that standard would not be an acceptable one if religion, economics, politics or philosophy were involved. How does it become a constitutional standard when literature treating with sex is concerned?

"Any test that turns on what is offensive to the community's standards is too loose, too capricious, too destructive of freedom of expression to be squared with the First Amendment. Under that test, juries can censor, suppress, and punish what they don't like, provided the matter relates to 'sexual impurity' or has a tendency to 'excite lustful thoughts.' This is community censorship in one of its worst forms..."

Douglas was never able to convince the other Justices that "there are as many different definitions of obscenity as there are" human beings "and they are as unique to the individual as his dreams.... Whatever obscenity is, it is immeasurable as a crime.... It is entirely too subjective for legal sanction."

At last, however, a state court has embodied the Douglas clarity of constitutional vision into law. The Oregon Constitution guarantees everyone in that state the "right to speak, write or print freely on any subject whatever."

It does not say "except for obscenity."

"What I want people to dig is the lie."

> Lenny said, "You don't understand. I'm not a comedian."
> I said, "Oh, you're not?"
> He said, "Do comedians get arrested? All the time?"—SALLY MARR, LENNY BRUCE'S MOTHER, ON "INSTANT RECALL," A SYNDICATED TELEVISION SERIES, DECEMBER 1990

Very bright, with wide-ranging curiosity, she works on the editorial and op-ed pages of the *Washington Post*. I asked her what she thought of Lenny Bruce.

She knew the name, but that was about it. After all, he had died two years after she was born. There was very little she could have seen of him on film. He had been a guest on some Steve Allen programs but the dictates of the Standards and Practices desk at the network made it impossible for Lenny to be Lenny on those shows.

There were a few other TV bits here and there, and one bizarre interview I did with Lenny for Canadian television that is shown every few years or so. (More of that singular event in the history of television later.) And there was, in December 1990, a section on Lenny in the syndicated television series "Instant Recall," but that was shown on Channel 4 in New York City at four o'clock in the morning, and at other odd hours in other cities.

So Lenny Bruce is largely unknown to the young. And if you're older and didn't frequent certain clubs in San Francisco, Chicago, and New York in the late fifties and early sixties, he may not be much more than a name to you either.

Yet, as Ralph Gleason, then of the *San Francisco Chronicle*, and the most honest and knowledgeable historian of Lenny's career, put it:

"So many taboos have been lifted and so many comics have rushed through the doors Lenny opened. He utterly changed the world of comedy." And of other dimensions of free thought, as well as free expression.

Sure, among his contemporaries were Mort Sahl, Jonathan Winters, Nichols and May, Bob Newhart, and Shelly Berman. But, as Gleason said, "they generally took on the thick outer skin of America... but even Jonathan Winters [who was and is a truly original comedian] did not strike out as a social critic challenging the values, priorities, and assumptions of the whole American way of life as Bruce did."

There's something wrong, Lenny said, about a society that gives more respect to a gunner's mate than to a whore. "It's perverse," Lenny would point out, "to give more respect to men who kill than to ladies who at least play at loving you."

One night, in a New York club, the audience was roaring at a series of Lenny Bruce "bits" parodying organized religion and the criminal justice system when he stopped, as he often did, because he'd just thought of something else.

He spoke as a Jew, hooked on the Jewish tradition of justice. How, Lenny asked the audience, which was now still, could a Jew mourn the murdered in the concentration camps while having no sense of personal guilt at all those human beings killed by us, long-distance, in Hiroshima?

An audience never knew what to expect from Lenny, because he didn't.

He liberated a lot of comedians—and audiences—in terms of the language they can use in public. But he took the fall for that, being busted and convicted for words you can now hear in movies, on cable, in clubs (though watch out for Cincinnati, despite the Mapplethorpe victory).

Because of Lenny Bruce, Eddie Murphy, Andrew Dice Clay, Richard Pryor, Sam Kinison, and many other performers can work, most of the time, without fearing that an undercover cop, sitting in the dark, will be taking notes on their acts. And they don't have to fear that the hidden cop will then stumblingly read from those blurred notes in court as evidence that an obscene performance had been given.

That's what used to happen to Lenny.

But only Richard Pryor, in his early work, used to take the covers off the way we live—with bitingly hilarious disdain for sentimentality. Pryor's view was from way outside. Lenny was an outsider, too, but he knew there were those who lived even more on the edge. Like blacks, I would have liked to see him and Pryor on the same stage.

The other beneficiaries of Bruce have almost none of his dangerous depth of vision. Andrew Dice Clay cultivates the lumpish humor of chronic boorishness. (There are few things more deadly than an utterly shallow solipsist.) Eddie Murphy has equated success with a license for embarrassing self-indulgence. He has become the very model of hubris without a cause.

Sam Kinison does have flashes of wit that go beyond his own limited life, but, unlike Lenny Bruce, he has no sustained, coherent view of the world, even his own world.

Lenny wanted to open the doors, just about all the doors. He had this nutty idea that if people didn't use language to conceal from themselves what they actually do and want to do, life would be a lot more open and flowing. And there'd be a lot more pleasure, even for those to whom the word has only been a word for most of their lives.

By opening the doors, Lenny Bruce convinced the authorities that he was a clear and present danger to community standards and values. They were right, and so they didn't let the First Amendment stand in their way.

When Lenny Bruce came up for sentencing—on a charge of public obscenity—in New York in 1964, then–assistant district attorney Richard Kuh, who had prosecuted Bruce as if he were a serial murderer, told the three-judge panel that this perpetrator must serve time.

The reason? In addition to the outrageous words that Bruce had used in his act, "the defendant Bruce, throughout the trial—and since the trial—has shown by his conduct complete lack of any remorse whatsoever."

Lenny had indeed shown no remorse for saying—actually saying in public in New York City—cocksucker, tits and ass, fuck, and other words that also infuriated prosecutors in a number of other cities, as well as church officials and the police dispatched to dispose of this subversive force.

During a bust in San Francisco for the use of "cocksucker" in a performance, a cop said to Lenny, "Do you really think it right to use a word like that?"

Such was the official culture of the time.

During the same bust, a police sergeant said to the disturber of the peace: "I can't see any way you can say this word in public. Our society is not geared to it."

The unremorseful Bruce looked at the sergeant and said: "You break it down by talking about it."

His tone was not hostile or aggressive. Lenny was trying to explain that he was digging beneath the words to get at why some people, like these cops, panicked when they heard these words in public. As usual—in his act, and as a defendant in courtrooms—Lenny saw himself as a sort of teacher. And you couldn't teach someone if you put him down.

The way he looked confounded some cops. Unlike the saturnine, all-knowing Mort Sahl, for instance, Bruce could have come out of a photograph of a prewar ghetto in Poland—his dark eyes innocent of guile and reflecting his yearning to excel at the Talmud.

After one of Lenny's performances in New York, a woman in the audience said, "He looks like such a nice Jewish boy—until he opens his dirty mouth."

Some of the words were Yiddish, as might have been expected from someone with the look of a nice Jewish boy. The key phrase was "the *zug gornischt* culture." The term means "say nothing." To Lenny, the culture at the time was afraid to acknowledge sexual pleasure. There were also the lies told repeatedly, like a gong, by government officials and religious leaders. And a hidden obbligato was the anguished frustrations of so many people, silent and alone, in that *zug gornischt* culture.

"What I want people to dig," Lenny said, "is the lie." And certain words, he noted, were suppressed to keep the lies going. "But," Lenny insisted, "if you *do* them, you should be able to *say* the words."

You should be able to use words that tell the truth. "An out-of-town buyer checks into a hotel," Lenny would say on stage, "goes up to his room, and decides he wants a hundred-dollar prostitute. He makes the call. A few minutes later, there's a knock on the door, and a bearded writer comes into the room."

In addition to the fear of saying out loud what you actually do and want, there were all the other kinds of "respectability." Just what is "respectability"? It means, said Lenny, "under the covers. So the crime I committed was pulling the covers off."

Some of the words that got him into deep trouble were not "dirty" in that they celebrated the pleasures of sex. Frank Hogan, the revered district attorney of Manhattan for many years, and a very religious man, was profoundly offended by what he regarded as Lenny's attacks on certain inconsistencies of the Catholic Church. Lenny, however, felt he was simply illuminating anything bogus wherever he found it.

In one of his "bits," Christ and Moses had returned to earth and were standing in the back of St. Patrick's Cathedral. Christ, looking at the altar where then-Cardinal Francis Spellman was officiating, says to Moses: "My visit took me through Spanish Harlem where there were forty Puerto Ricans living in one room. What were they doing there when this man"—he pointed to the Cardinal—"has a ring on worth $10,000?"

"I do this bit in Milwaukee," Lenny said, "and in the middle of the night, a bang on the door and it's 'OPEN UP!'"

There were rabbis who also thought Bruce went too far, as

when he took the role of a Reform rabbi preaching to his congregation:

"There has been a lot of talk about whether or not God is dead. We're not here for that. We're here to build a new Jewish center."

Because of his various busts, Lenny had become a scholar of the First Amendment. It was his Talmud. He had utter faith that whatever happened to him in the lower courts, he and the First Amendment would be redeemed on high. But the one place he didn't want a lower-court conviction was New York.

"Club owners around the country," he told me, "will figure that if I've been convicted in the most sophisticated city in the country, prosecutors will be waiting for me everywhere. So who needs that?"

It was tragic to see arguably the most brilliant comedian of our times destroyed by the society whose freedom he was vainly trying to protect.
—Lester Block, letter to the editor, *The New York Times*, October 10, 1990

You don't know anything about anybody but you. Just you live in that thing. You always live alone. You're always in there, even with your wife. That's why I can't sell out. That is, so long as I stay honest with myself. And that's why I'm somebody different each time out. I keep changing. I'm not bragging about this but—well, it exists, that's all I'm telling you.
—Lenny Bruce

I first heard about Lenny Bruce from Ralph Gleason, who was writing for the *San Francisco Chronicle* and *Variety*. Ralph was a jazz critic, but he covered everything that interested him—from politics to comedians. He was also the first jazz critic to enjoy rock music, and say so publicly (a heresy among his colleagues then).

Ralph was a passionate man. In letters and phone calls, he enthusiastically tipped me to performers about to break through, and he lashed out at phonies and exploiters in and out of show business. He wrote with great love and anger, depending on the subject of the day.

There was this guy, this comic, he told me, working strip joints on the coast as well as some clubs in San Francisco. He was coming East. There is nobody like him. Nobody. He's going to have the impact that Louis Armstrong and Charlie Parker had on jazz.

So, in April 1959, I went to the long-vanished Den of the Duane Hotel in Manhattan. It had as much charm as the corridors of the Motor Vehicles Bureau. But once Lenny Bruce began to swing, the surroundings slipped out of mind.

Ralph Gleason's jazz analogy was apt. Lenny was a pulsing, zooming, crackling, joyful comic force. Moreover, he knew a lot about jazz, and the players dug him, too. Whenever there was a jazz group on the bill with him, most of the musicians would stay to hear his act rather than go out for a break at intermission.

Lenny saw himself as a verbal equivalent of a jazz musician in terms of improvising, dynamics, and time. You could really feel his beat, and there was a fair amount of bop in it. (The accents kicked in unexpectedly—but coherently.)

And in most of his "bits," he took on a number of roles and voices. So in that sense, he sometimes became a jazz combo—each character's individual textures and ways of shaping time fused into a swinging whole.

That night at the Duane, I was surprised to see Dorothy Kilgallen in the audience. She was a powerful columnist for Hearst's *Journal-American* and a considerable presence on radio and early television. A gossip columnist, she was also very political, very right-wing political. And like most gossip columnists, she could be a Cotton Mather–style moralist.

But there she was, laughing long and hard, as Lenny exposed and demolished such taboo words as "cocksucker" and "fuck" and talked of the "tits and ass" culture. And he did some "bits," in one of which some prelates of the Catholic Church came on like anxious hustlers. As an obbligato, he did variations on one of his basic themes: "sexual pleasure has become a dirty word."

Kilgallen wrote about Lenny in her column, as did others, and he began to work around town—with side trips to other cities. He was most comfortable at the Village Vanguard, as are many jazz musicians to this day. But Max Gordon, the owner, wanted to try him uptown at the Blue Angel, which Max co-owned.

The Blue Angel was a posh club, frequented by people who seemed mostly concerned with how they looked. They considered themselves very sophisticated, but actually the counterman at the nearby deli was much more hip.

Lenny was not all that comfortable at the Blue Angel, and he was delighted to go back downtown to the Village Vanguard. The audience there was largely composed of young liberals, much concerned with the civil rights movement and other—as they used to be called—"progressive" causes.

One night, Lenny landed on stage, looked at the integrated audience, and said:

"Any spics here tonight? Any kikes? Any niggers?"

The audience froze. Lenny had gone too far, much too far. What the hell had gotten into him?

They soon found out. He was trying to get them to look beneath the deeply wounding impact of certain words so those words would no longer have demonic, paralyzing power over them. And could be dealt with. Take the covers off. Bring taboos out into the open so you can break them down.

Except for some busts in a few cities, Lenny was moving right along. His records on Fantasy—which are still in print—were considered family treasures in some homes. And he was continually changing and growing as a performer. I'd sometimes hear him four or five nights a week at the Vanguard, and each time was like the first time.

There came to be intimations that Lenny was finally going to be busted in New York. It was those words, and the joyful irreverence about the Church. The word of the impending arrest worried him.

Lenny called me one Sunday morning. He'd been tipped that the bust would come that night at the Village Vanguard. Did I know a clergyman, a hip clergyman, who'd come down and be his witness?

I found one, and the man of the cloth did show up, and he became a fan. But the cops didn't make it.

The bust finally did come down on April 3, 1964, at the Cafe Au Go Go in the Village. As Lenny noted at the time:

"They said the shows [that led to his arrest] were the 27th,

28th, and the first of April. They viewed those shows, and they filed this information that it was an indecent show. It took them three days, three shows to decide that it was indecent, and it seems it's taken eight years—in the history of my performances in New York—Carnegie Hall, Town Hall, Basin Street East, Village Vanguard—for them finally, I guess, to understand what I was saying.

"And they found it was obscene enough to put me in a jail cell for the last 24 hours. What I wish they'd do is tell me what words are obscene."

In the dark, during Lenny's shows, there was a very attentive man named Herbert Ruhe. Formerly with the CIA, he was now engaged in less dramatic pursuits. An inspector for the city's licensing division, he was monitoring Lenny's act. As best he could understand it.

I talked to Ruhe during Lenny's trial for public obscenity. He was a conscientious public servant with no animus—that I could discern—toward either Bruce or his material. He was just, you know, doing his job.

Most unfortunately, Ruhe was not up to that job. Lenny had to endure hearing his act performed before a three-judge panel by a nonperformer who had more or less memorized it. Nobody, certainly not the judges—who had refused to let Lenny do his own act—thought any of Ruhe's surrogate act was funny. How could they? It not only wasn't funny. It was awful. I kept shaking my head.

"This guy is bumbling," Lenny kept saying, "and I'm going to jail. He's not only got it all wrong, but now he thinks *he's* a comic. I'm going to be judged on *his* bad timing, *his* ego, *his* garbled language."

The revered (though not by me) district attorney Frank Hogan had had difficulty finding someone to prosecute Bruce. I found that out from sources in his office. Lenny had fans among the assistant district attorneys, and others felt there was no basis for even an indictment. According to the Supreme Court standards of the time, Lenny's performance had to be without any redeeming social value to be legally obscene. For Christ's sake, so to speak, Lenny was Eugene Debs with an act.

But Hogan wanted this blasphemer. He wanted him bad.

In a *New York Times* article (later reprinted in the September 21

Los Angeles Daily Journal, a legal newspaper), former New York assistant district attorney Gerald Harris revealed how he ultimately refused to prosecute Bruce. First, he tried to persuade the hierarchy in the D.A.'s office to let the case go. That having failed, Harris presented it to a grand jury and, to his surprise, the jury voted to file charges.

Harris then went to Hogan and said he could not, in conscience, go on with the case.

So where, in Hogan's office, was there a prosecutor who recognized Lenny Bruce's clear and present danger to the community? Hogan found the perfect recruit—a humorless, ambitious assistant district attorney named Richard Kuh. And Kuh did indeed make a name for himself during the trial. No matter what else he does in his life, Kuh will be remembered in his obituary as the man who fearlessly secured the conviction of Lenny Bruce.

As for the choice of Lenny's lawyer, I made a terrible mistake. Lenny had asked my advice, and the best First Amendment lawyer I knew at the time was Ephraim London. He had argued successfully before the Supreme Court and other appellate courts and he was a scholar of the Constitution. He was also a man of utter self-confidence.

The problem was that he was essentially an appellate lawyer, an expert on transforming reversals in a lower court into triumphs up above. Lenny understood this from the beginning. After the first week of the trial, he told me: "This guy doesn't *expect* to win down here. Every day he's laying the groundwork for an appeal. But I've got to win down here—if I'm going to be able to work."

One of Lenny's star witnesses was Dorothy Kilgallen. She was treated with the utmost respect—by the judges, the court attendants, *et al.* Mr. Kuh, however, figured he had a way to break her down. He had assembled all of Lenny's "dirty words" during the performance in question, and with them festering in his busy mind, he approached the witness.

Kilgallen, demurely dressed, wearing white gloves, sat coolly in the witness chair. Kuh circled her and then pounced. "You say that Mr. Bruce is an artist of social value. Would you tell me your reaction, Miss Kilgallen, to these words he used in his act?"

Kuh, in a loud, accusatory voice, shook the courtroom with a machine-gun-like barrage of "cocksuckers," "fucks," "tits," "ass," and similar colloquialisms heard regularly in police squad rooms around the city.

Dorothy Kilgallen, unfazed, looked at her gloves and then at the prosecutor. "They are words, Mr. Kuh. Words, words, words."

At Lenny Bruce's 1964 trial for public obscenity in New York, I was one of the witnesses for the defense. I had come armed with recent Supreme Court decisions on obscenity, which should easily have cleared Lenny because his work surely had "redeeming social value." But the prosecutor, Richard Kuh—a dime-store Torquemada—would have none of that.

Kuh wanted to show the kind of subversive lowlife the defendant had recruited to testify for him.

Was it not true, the prosecutor asked me with disdain, that I had written a book praising a man who advocated draft resistance and other forms of active civil disobedience? Was it not true that the name of this lawbreaker was A. J. Muste?

A. J. Muste was a pacifist, much influenced by Mohandas Gandhi. Martin Luther King had told me that A. J. had been a key influence—when King was a theology student—in persuading him of the power of active nonviolence. And A. J. had become a major strategist of the anti–Vietnam War movement in the United States.

I owned up to having written a biography of A. J. Muste and of greatly admiring the man.

The trial proceeded with less subversive witnesses for Lenny, but it was no use. On November 4, 1964, the judges (two to one) found him guilty and sentenced him to a year in prison. The sentence was stayed pending appeal.

Work for Lenny dried up around the country. There were some gigs, but not at good money. So Lenny had a lot of time to spend researching his appeal.

I used to visit him at the Hotel Marlton—not exactly the Plaza—on Eighth Street in Greenwich Village. The tables, chairs, sofa, and floor were covered with legal briefs, trial transcripts, case books of constitutional law, and Lenny's own copious notes on his case.

The First Amendment would be his Excalibur, rising from the

lake of thickheadedness and releasing him from the spells of his enemies. Lenny was utterly convinced that the Constitution could make him whole again. And then the gigs would come flowing back and finally, he could look out into the dark without fearing that at some table, a plainclothes cop was taking garbled notes on his performance.

Maybe his case would go as far as the Supreme Court. Maybe he could do his act before the Justices. They certainly would understand the redeeming social value of his performances. They would understand that his act was speech protected by the First Amendment.

Well, Lenny *was* redeemed by the First Amendment. Posthumously. Lenny died in 1966 of an overdose of morphine. Or, as Phil Spector said, "an overdose of police." He had left New York. His act, when he did work, was usually about his trial, with Lenny taking all the parts. It was hilarious. Even prosecutors in the audience broke up.

A year or so before he died, I saw him in San Francisco. On stage and off, he talked about the trial. It was a dingy club. The dressing room was shabby, a syringe lay on a chair, there was a splotch of blood on the floor.

The energy was still there. It was feverish now. He hadn't given up. But the life force was running out. In his notes for "Lenny Bruce Live at the Curan Theater" (Fantasy), Ralph Gleason wrote:

"In the months before he died, Lenny Bruce couldn't get a job.... The gas company wanted to turn off the electricity and gas— and did for a while."

On August 3, 1966—according to an "Instant Recall" television program about him—Lenny found out he was going to lose his home. He took the overdose that day. Ralph Gleason was convinced the overdose was not deliberate. Lenny was still insisting that he and the First Amendment would win.

The cemetery wouldn't allow a public service to be held for fear of some kind of public demonstration that, like his language, might get out of bounds.

Two years later, an appellate court in New York reversed Lenny's public obscenity conviction, and two years after that, the state's highest judicial body, the Court of Appeals, affirmed the reversal.

Lenny had been right about the First Amendment. For all the good it did him.

Some time after, Richard Kuh, by then an interim district attorney, was running for a full term. He looked like a sure shot because there was no visible competition of consequence.

I started writing a series on Kuh for the *Village Voice*, interviewing former and present colleagues of his—and other members of the criminal justice establishment. After the third article appeared, I got a telephone call from Henry Morgenthau, whom I had never met or talked to. Having read about Kuh in my series, Morgenthau said he was now seriously thinking of running for district attorney. He did, and still is Manhattan district attorney. Kuh is in private practice.

Lenny's last years were grim. As Ralph Gleason noted, "He tried to perform in Australia but was evicted before he could perform." His "reputation" had preceded him. Even before his New York conviction, "he was invited to the Edinburgh International Drama Festival but the British government refused to let him enter the country."

In one sense, Lenny could understand being made a pariah. He was taking off the covers. But on the other hand, what *harm* was he doing? And to *whom?*

It hurt because Lenny was a romantic. Fundamentally, he believed in the perfectibility of us all. If you expose the lies of our lives and our government by making people laugh at the lies, then maybe we can move on from there.

Some people I've known have never lost their sense of rage. Lenny never lost his sense of wonder—and excitement at new signs of change, real change, in the way we live. One night, backstage, he started asking me about the then-rising civil rights movement. Who was this Bayard Rustin working with Martin Luther King? Who was this other guy in the Student Nonviolent Coordinating Committee? Lenny got more and more excited about the possibilities of it all, and wrote out a check for the March on Washington.

Offstage, Lenny was most at ease with night people like himself. Musicians, waitresses, bartenders, strippers, and others to whom sunlight is rather exotic. Although he enjoyed company, I often got the sense that essentially he was quite lonely. Or alone.

He was a caring friend, as I found out in a rather bizarre way. The Canadian Broadcasting Company asked me to do a television interview with Lenny at the Village Vanguard, where he was then appearing. We'd do it in the late afternoon. Just us, the crew, and the empty tables.

I thought I had told Lenny—or maybe I forgot to—that I'd had years of experience in radio and some in television. Lenny, however, thought that all I knew how to do was write so I'd be nervous on camera and then I'd be embarrassed because I was nervous.

Rather than letting me look bad, Lenny figured he'd have to carry me, and he got ready for the television interview by making sure his energy would be up. He swallowed, I found out later, a remarkable quantity of amphetamines.

That afternoon, I watched him come flying down the stairs. He was so up that he was literally hopping around the room. When the television lights went on, he seemed to be moving in several directions at once. As the interviewer, I had to follow Lenny wherever he went and at whatever careening speed he was impelled to go. (Otherwise, the sound would have been fragmented.)

So, I interviewed Lenny jumping up and down beside him, lying next to him on the floor of the bandstand, jumping with him on top of a table. At one point, we were racing around the bandstand like two of the Three Stooges.

The crew didn't know what to make of it all. I knew it was a disaster. But Lenny was pleased. He had carried me.

I was astonished when I heard that the CBC had actually put the show on the air. The critics from the larger cities in Canada praised our act as a new dimension in the art of avant-garde television. In the smaller cities and towns, the critics reported what was actually on the screen. One nut chasing another nut.

That show, in bits and pieces, is shown every once in a while during some of the television retrospectives of Lenny; but, like all of his other relatively few television shots, it's not Lenny as he was in clubs and concerts. For that, you have to listen to the Fantasy LPs.

Lenny had admirers in all kinds of places. Lawyers, teenagers, college professors, jazz players, even some club owners, Bob Dylan,

Jonathan Miller, the Beatles (especially John Lennon), and Grace Slick (who wrote the song "Father Bruce" for him).

When Lenny died, there was a *Washington Post* editorial:

"Lenny Bruce believed in free speech with a passion that was often masked by the jokes he told. He was a social satirist, one of the boldest and one of the best."

After Lenny was dead, there was a Broadway show, *Lenny*. Tom O'Horgan directed, with Cliff Gorman as Lenny. It reminded me of the licensing inspector giving Lenny's act at the trial.

The only interesting thing about the show was that Richard Kuh went backstage and congratulated the cast.

Lenny wouldn't have been surprised. He was an expert on chutzpah, high and low.

Once, in a club, a customer who didn't get it—but I guess that's wrong, he did get it—threw Lenny through a plate-glass window. Kuh was more civilized.

Lenny once got a note from an Episcopal minister:

"Thank you for caring so much about life."

And that, of course, was what did him in.

XII

The Gospel According to Catharine MacKinnon

"This is thought control. It establishes an 'approved' view of women, of how they may react to sexual encounters, of how the sexes may relate to each other."

> The First Amendment...then came into question, with Karen Santoriello asking why it was considered so sacrosanct. In her view, pornography is such a significant threat to women that the Constitution, by protecting it, is causing half the population to live in danger. Does this society consider the safety of the First Amendment to be of greater importance than the safety of its people?—FROM THE MAY 16, 1984, MINUTES OF THE HUMAN RELATIONS FORUM DISCUSSION "PORNOGRAPHY ON CAMPUS," UNIVERSITY OF MASSACHUSETTS, AMHERST

Madison, Wisconsin, is one of my favorite college towns. In the bars and restaurants, the college paper and the classrooms, ideas still matter, even if they don't have a direct connection to a job down the line. It's a lively, often contentious place, with some of the flavor, if not the exalted desperation, of the sixties.

As far as I can tell, most of the folks there, if you ask them, are opposed to censoring anything.

Censors do exist in Madison, though. In the 1980s, a brave bunch of radicals shouted down born-again Christian minister Eldridge Cleaver when he tried to give a scheduled talk at the university. The ex-radical and former Black Panther leader was too corrupt to be heard, they said. And if you wanted to hear him anyway, then clearly you were also full of bourgeois corruption.

Then there was the attempt by a feminist group to shut down an art exhibit at the university. They said it was sexist. I questioned whether it was art, but it sure was sexist. During a lecture there, I pointed out that picketing and counterexhibits were the way to deal with the provocation. Censoring it would just establish the precedent of shutting down controversial exhibits, and the university would eventually use that precedent to shut down some "offensive" feminist exhibition. In response, it was suggested that it was long past time for me to be shut down.

Feminists on campus were split on the matter of that exhibit. Feminists often are divided, though you'd hardly know it from the press, which views that movement as being conveniently monolithic.

Despite these exceptions to the free flow of ideas, the town had had the feeling of a good bar. You could get into a reasonably interesting argument almost any place, and nobody would call the law on you, no matter how outrageous your ideas and language.

Then, on Ted Koppel's "Nightline," I saw a march in Madison. The program was entitled "Women and Pornography," and near the top of the half hour, there was footage of Madison's annual "Take Back the Night" demonstration. The focus of the march that year was pornography and the overwhelming need to get rid of it because, as county supervisor Kathleen Nichols had told a rally earlier that evening, pornography is now 70 percent more violent than it was a decade ago, thereby being all the more dangerous to women.

Nichols had proposed a new law for the county that would make pornography into a civil rights, not a First Amendment, violation. Perpetrators would be guilty of sex discrimination. This approach is based on a theory developed by Catharine MacKinnon, professor of law at the University of Michigan, and Andrea Dworkin.

Professor MacKinnon had taken part in a symposium in Madison on the day of the march, and Andrea Dworkin was also in town.

On "Nightline," the marchers looked as if they had stepped off the canvas of a latter-day Norman Rockwell devoted to portraying the diversity of good, caring citizens. Students, elderly people, professionals, union organizers, bohemians, teachers, musicians. You could tell (and friends of mine in Madison later confirmed) that most of them were liberal, anti-racist, and regular listeners to "Morning Edition" and "All Things Considered" on National Public Radio.

Their faces were lit by street lamps, and by lighting crews. But there was also an inner illumination—the light of faith, the fire of conviction that you are part of a true solidarity of will that must triumph because it is so right. Had there been a plebiscite during the march that night on a civil rights statute that would censor pornography, that bill would have passed by acclamation.

Watching the zeal in those eyes, I wondered what would have happened if, in Madison—with its lively, free marketplace of ideas—a few of the marchers had been swept by their feelings to break into some of those pornographic bookstores en route and, well, reduce the vileness in them to ashes. Provided no clerks or customers had been injured, would those still in the line of march have cheered?

In a subsequent year, an "adult" bookstore was indeed largely destroyed in Madison. And there were cheers from the true believers in suppression of vile-free expression.

Meanwhile, the MacKinnon-Dworkin jihad against pornography and the First Amendment has had a greater impact throughout the nation than I first thought possible. While their followers do not burn down "adult" bookstores, except perhaps in their dreams, they are busy lobbying legislators, lecturing, and otherwise resembling latter-day Anthony Comstocks. And the spectrum of support for MacKinnon and Dworkin reveals, once more, that the Right is hardly the only force for censorship.

The history of this strategy also indicates that the growing division among feminists about whether the state should decide what we read and see can deeply affect the nature and future of feminism. As Cryss Farley, a feminist and executive director of the Iowa Civil Liberties Union, says of the spread of the MacKinnon-Dworkin credo: "Does the women's movement really want to lend its name to such repression?" Gloria Steinem already has.

First, the theory of this censorship in the name of civil rights—as it has been embodied in an actual law, the first MacKinnon-Dworkin statute to be passed. It was signed by the mayor of Indianapolis on May 1, 1984.

After holding hearings on women and pornography, the Indianapolis City Council declared that pornography "discriminates against women by exploiting and degrading them, thereby restricting their full exercise of citizenship and participation in public life."

The ordinance followed, and it further underlined the civil rights rationale first developed by MacKinnon and Dworkin:

"Pornography is a discriminatory practice based on sex because its effect is to deny women equal opportunities in society.... The bigotry and contempt it promotes, with the acts of aggression it fosters, harm women's opportunities for equality of rights in employment, education, access to and use of public accommodations, and acquisition of real property, and contribute significantly to restricting women in particular from full exercise of citizenship and participation in public life, including in neighborhoods."

What, then, is pornography? Under the MacKinnon-Dworkin law in Indianapolis—and ten cities or more were waiting to enact similar laws if Indianapolis's held up in court—the core definition is "the graphic sexually explicit subordination of women, whether in pictures or in words."

Off the drawing board and into real life: a woman walks into a bookstore or a movie house or past a newsstand and finds herself offended by some material that meets the minimal triggering criteria. She then files a complaint with Indianapolis's Office of Equal Opportunity, which thereupon sends out its investigators. A hearing is then held and if the agency finds the material is pornographic—and is upheld by a court—the material is removed and fines are levied. Moreover, the court would be asked to issue an injunction forbidding the further dissemination of the given book, magazine, or movie in Indianapolis.

This injunction is what is called in the First Amendment trade a "prior restraint." Pure censorship. The most direct and destructive suppression of speech that can be perpetrated by the state, short of what happened at Kent State.

There's more. A woman in Indianapolis is raped, and claims that a particular movie or television news report about a rape had incited her assailant. Under the ordinance, she can sue the film distributor, the owner of the movie house, or the television station for damages. Indeed, in this and other claims for damages allowed by this law, the plaintiff can go after the writer of a script, the publisher of a book—anyone in the production chain.

To win money damages, the plaintiff must prove "intent"— knowledge on the part of the person being sued that the material is pornographic under the MacKinnon law. As we shall see, that law is so broad and vague that God could be in the dock for passages in the Old Testament.

This "civil rights" approach to eradicating pornography was first introduced in Minneapolis. A bill similar to the Indianapolis statute twice passed the City Council there, and was twice vetoed by Mayor Donald Fraser because he would not defect from "our cherished tradition and constitutionally protected right of free speech."

Perhaps the most bizarre turn in the tumultuous history of the MacKinnon-Dworkin countertradition was a letter sent to the president of the Minneapolis City Council on the occasion of Donald Fraser's first veto of the MacKinnon-Dworkin bill. The letter was written—"in dissent and dismay" at Fraser's veto—by the justly celebrated First Amendment gladiator, Professor Laurence Tribe of Harvard Law School.

In the letter, Tribe chastised the mayor for "hiding behind the First Amendment" by not letting the courts decide, instead of unilaterally killing the bill by veto. The Dworkin-MacKinnon legislation, said Tribe, "is not obviously unconstitutional" and its supposed invalidity "follows surely from no clear precedent." Tribe added that while he is uncertain as to how a judicial test will come out, he felt the MacKinnon-Dworkin creation "may eventually be found to be the first sensible approach to an area which has vexed some of the best legal minds for decades."

Professor Tribe later acknowledged error and resumed his support of the First Amendment.

During that period in Minneapolis, a feminist member of the City Council, Kathy O'Brien, opposed the statute. "The status of women," she said, "is better in open societies than in closed, restrictive societies. This is censorship."

The woman with whom he had been living left in anger, and returned to her father's house—a long journey away. After four months, the man she had left went to visit her, hoping to persuade his former companion to go back with him. He succeeded.

They left her father's house, and on the road, as evening came, they stopped in a small town. There was no hotel, and no one offered to take them in for the night until an old man finally said they could stay with him.

During dinner, there was much pounding on the door and when the old man opened it, a group of men ordered him to send out his male guest, because they wanted to sodomize him. The guest preferred not to accommodate them, and instead offered to lend the men the woman he had just convinced to return to him. She had no voice in the matter.

The deal was struck; a lengthy gang rape took place. In the morning the traveler found the woman lying at the door of the house with her hands on the threshold. "Stand up," he said. "It's time to leave." There was no answer. The woman was dead.

He placed the woman across his horse and continued on the way home. Once he got there, he took a knife and cut the woman's corpse into twelve pieces. He sent one piece to each of the twelve family branches with which he, and his father before him, had nurtured close relations. With each piece of the corpse was a message. It can be distilled into a single word: "Vengeance!" And vengeance was taken on all the men who had raped the woman.

That story, and therefore the book containing it, was in violation of the letter and spirit of the anti-pornography law in Indianapolis designed by Catharine MacKinnon and Andrea Dworkin.

The Indianapolis ordinance, after all, defines pornography as "the sexually explicit subordination of women, graphically depicted whether in pictures or in words, that includes one or more of the following":

- "Women are presented as sexual objects who enjoy pain or humiliation; or
- "Women are presented as sexual objects who experience sexual pleasure in being raped; or
- "Women are presented being penetrated by objects or animals; or
- "Women are presented in scenarios of degradation, injury, abasement, torture, shown as filthy and inferior, bleeding, bruised, or hurt in a context that makes these conditions sexual;
- "Women are presented as sexual objects for domination, conquest, violation, exploitation, possession or use through postures or positions of servility or submission or display; or
- "*Women are presented as sexual objects tied up or mutilated or bruised or physically hurt, or as dismembered or truncated or fragmented or severed into body parts.*" (Emphasis added.)

The story I've just told you was clearly guilty of being pornographic under the Indianapolis ordinance, a civil rights statute aimed at material that cannot be prosecuted under obscenity statutes.

Any woman in Indianapolis, if the courts had allowed the law to be enforced, could sue to have the book containing this story removed from the city. She could also ask the court to issue an injunction forbidding the appearance of this material in the city forevermore. And she could sue the publisher, the editor, the writer—anyone in the chain of production—for damages if she could prove that they knew this stuff was pornographic under the city statute.

A plaintiff could have some trouble collecting from the writer because the story is from Chapter 19 of the Book of Judges in the Old Testament.

The scope of the material—in all forms of expression—that the MacKinnon-Dworkin guillotine would remove from all eyes was, as Thomas Emerson of Yale Law School put it, "breathtaking."

During his years at Yale, Emerson became the nation's most lucid and challenging analyst of the First Amendment. (See *The System of Freedom of Free Expression*, Vintage paperback.) In his commentary on the new censorship, Emerson noted that he agreed with MacKinnon that "pornography plays a major part in establishing and maintaining male supremacy in our society."

But, Emerson asks, is the solution to the harm done by pornography a law so "nearly limitless" in its scope that it "would outlaw a substantial portion of the world's literature"?

Among the works Emerson cites as being tossed into the tumbrils if the courts were to affirm the Indianapolis ordinance were William Faulkner's *Sanctuary* and those two venerable novels whose court appearances we thought were finally over, Henry Miller's *Tropic of Cancer* and D. H. Lawrence's *Lady Chatterley's Lover.*

But there were many more books, sculptures, movies, magazines, videocassettes, television programs, and newspapers that could be banished from Indianapolis and any other city persuaded by MacKinnon and Dworkin to protect their inhabitants from the pornography plague.

During the court battle in the U.S. District Court for the Southern District of Indiana, the American Civil Liberties Union and the Indiana ACLU filed a joint *amicus* brief. It included a very small sampling of what works would be banned under the Indianapolis ordinance. Among them: Nabokov's *Lolita*, Petronius's *Satyricon*, Fielding's *Tom Jones*, and Géricault's *A Nude Being Tortured.* The *amicus* brief also spoke of film scenes that would be stopped at the borders of any cities adopting this legislation: "....the shower scene in *Psycho*, the sexual subordination and debasement in *Seven Beauties*, the dramatization of Jack the Ripper in *The Ruling Class* and *Time After Time*, the rape scenes in *Looking for Mr. Goodbar*... domestic violation and domination in *The Godfather*...."

The ACLU court papers went on to point out that "On its face, the ordinance would prohibit much clinical sexual literature, from medical texts and scholarly studies to popularized works of sociology...."

Farfetched? Well, said the ACLU, "Since the key operative term, 'sexual subordination,' is inherently vague,... individuals who object simply to the neutral scholarly presentation of such material as inevitably perpetuating a climate of subordination will be empowered to object to such material."

The "linchpin of the ordinance," as the ACLU describes it, is the term, "subordination of women." To the writer of a book, the maker of a movie or a piece of sculpture who doesn't want to get banned in MacKinnon-Dworkin model cities, what kind of guideline is that term? What does it mean?

When a statute is made out of fog, it fails to give, as the Supreme Court has said, "the person of ordinary intelligence a reasonable opportunity to know what is prohibited, so that he may act accordingly." That's not all the destructive mischief that can be caused by vagueness in a law. There are no reasonably clear guidelines for the police and judges who have to enforce the law. The result is drumhead justice. Police and judges decide arbitrarily who gets taught a lesson.

Moreover, the MacKinnon-Dworkin way of strangling pornography leads to epidemic self-censorship, should their standards ever be adopted. If you're unclear as to what you're forbidden to write or paint or film, you—in the language of the Supreme Court— "steer far wider of the unlawful zone...than if the boundaries of the forbidden areas were clearly marked."

Keeping the boundaries of the forbidden areas imprecise has long been the delight of censors. Anthony Comstock, for instance, was responsible for the 1873 laws that bore his name and banned from the federal mails all publications of an "obscene" or otherwise indecent character. What did those terms mean? The Comstock laws did not say.

Later amendments made the Comstock laws even vaguer by prohibiting from the mails any "lewd and lascivious" or "filthy" stuff or anything with an "indecent or immoral purpose."

"The definition," historian William Preston has pointed out, "was broad enough to exclude discussion of birth control, marriage counseling, and abortion for years."

It is one of the marvels of censorship that its architects, no matter how disparate their intentions and their backgrounds, end up uncannily resembling each other. So it is that if Catharine MacKinnon looks into a mirror one day, she may see, staring sternly at her, Anthony Comstock.

In Des Moines, Iowa, every member of the City Council, I was told, would have considered it an honor and a privilege to vote for a MacKinnon-Dworkin bill. The then-mayor of that city, Pete Crivaro, admitted that there were people who would view such an ordinance as "censorship" and would contest it. But the mayor of Des Moines was unafraid. He says: "We must do what is in the best interest of the majority."

In a letter to Thomas Jefferson, James Madison warned of majoritarianism as the insatiable enemy of the Bill of Rights:

"...the invasion of private rights is chiefly to be apprehended not from acts of Government contrary to the sense of its Constituents, but from acts in which the Government is the mere instrument of the major number of the Constituents."

James Madison, however, did not have the right stuff for Des Moines. Patrice Sayre, president of the city's chapter of the National Organization for Women, understands America better than that Virginian ever did. She said of the gospel according to MacKinnon and Dworkin: "It is a civil rights issue when a group of citizens are being degraded. This is an issue where civil rights should supersede First Amendment rights."

Among the cities that agreed and were willing to pass the MacKinnon ordinance were Detroit, Des Moines, Omaha, Columbus, St. Louis, Cincinnati, and Madison, Wisconsin.

What the smiters of pornography ignore is that this kind of "civil rights" relief cannot be limited to only one group. If the courts do eventually approve the MacKinnon-Dworkin theory, then many other groups with strong claims of being harmfully discriminated against in books, films, and television will also start using these statutes. They will sue for an injunction to have certain offensive material forever banned from a town or a city. They will bring suit for damages against anyone involved in the making and production of that material.

As Cryss Farley, executive director of the Iowa Civil Liberties Union, says—with crunching logic—"Few would argue that sex discrimination, brutality against women, and oppression of women do not exist. Much in our culture also oppresses Indians, Hispanics, Asians, homosexuals, and others. Anti-Semitic literature is unarguably harmful to Jews, as is racist literature to blacks. Are we going to afford racial and ethnic minorities and religious minorities a similar civil right to suppress speech which denigrates these groups?"

I know of black educators who would surely go after an injunction to ban *Huckleberry Finn*. I can think of some Jews who would finally take care of *The Merchant of Venice* and *Oliver Twist*.

For the first time, books and movies and television will be as pure as country water. To maintain the peaceable kingdom, publishers and filmmakers will hire consultants trained by every group that has been offended by "pornographic" material, and those consultants will keep towns, cities, and minds clean.

And won't a result of this cleaning of the air be a marked decrease in crimes of rape and other violence against women? That's what the pro-censorship feminists have aggressively maintained.

A particularly useful analytical survey of the research in this field has been written by Marcia Pally and published by the Freedom to Read Foundation and the Americans for Constitutional Freedom. (Executive director of the Freedom to Read Foundation is Judith Krug, who is in charge of the Office of Intellectual Freedom of the American Library Association.)

In 1986, then–Surgeon General C. Everett Koop convened a Workshop on Pornography and Public Health, and the researchers reported—as Marcia Pally notes—that there is "no evidence that exposure to sexual material leads to sex crimes."

Pally also quotes Drs. Edward Donnerstein, Daniel Linz (University of California), and Steven Penrod (University of Wisconsin) in a 1987 book, *The Question of Pornography: Research Findings and Policy Implications:*

"Should harsher penalties be leveled against persons who traffic in pornography, particularly violent pornography? We do not believe so. Rather, it is our opinion that the most prudent course of action would be the development of educational programs that would teach viewers to become more critical consumers of the mass media.... The legal [punitive] course of action is more restrictive of personal freedoms than an educational approach...."

In 1990, Donnerstein and Linz added:

"Despite the Attorney General's Commission's report [the Meese Commission] that most forms of pornography have a causal relationship to sexually aggressive behavior, we find it difficult to understand how this conclusion was reached....

"Most social scientists who testified before the commission were also cautious... when making statements about causal links between pornography and sexually aggressive behavior. *Any reasonable view of the research would not come to the conclusion that... pornography conclusively results in antisocial effects.*" (Emphasis added.)

And in 1986, Drs. Neil Malamuth and Joseph Ceniti (University of California) found (Pally reports) "no increase in aggression toward women in men who had watched sexually violent material."

The causes of rape and other violence against women are deeply rooted. Those women who believe that outlawing pornography will lessen violence against women might focus more on the family backgrounds and childhood experiences of violent males.

Roland Johnson, a social worker at a Minnesota treatment center for adolescent rapists, pointed out (*New York Times*, August 28, 1984) that most of them "have had no exposure, or very little, to pornography." More than 90 percent, however, were sexually abused as children. "I don't think pornography has that much influence on those who rape," Johnson said. "More important is what's happened to them in their past."

Still, it is possible, some would say, that along with a number of other influences that shaped the man, pornography might have had something to do with an act of violence against a woman. In that event, if the rapist were caught and it was alleged that a particular magazine, movie, or book had incited him to commit the rape, should that magazine, movie, or book be banned lest it be culpable, in some way, for another rape by some other perpetrator later on?

The assumption, then, would be that many men with certain propensities would react to the material the same violent way. Yet, as Dr. Edward Donnerstein emphasizes, it is impossible to determine, with any accuracy, what will actually trigger someone to violence.

"Certain people," says Donnerstein, "are influenced by who knows what.... It is very difficult to say what type of stimuli are going to take those individuals on the fringe... and cause them to act in a certain way."

In 1966, William O. Douglas, during a concurring opinion in *A Book Named "John Cleland's Memoirs of a Woman of Pleasure"* v. *Attorney General of the Commonwealth of Massachusetts,* observed in a footnote that "It would be a futile effort even for a censor to attempt to remove all that might possibly stimulate antisocial conduct."

Everything, and anything, said Douglas, is capable of triggering violence, and he quoted from a study on the subject in the *Wayne Law Review* (1964):

"Heinrich Pommerenke, who was a rapist, abuser, and mass slayer of women in Germany, was prompted to his series of ghastly deeds by Cecil B. DeMille's *The Ten Commandments.* During the scene of the Jewish women dancing about the Golden Calf, all the doubts of his life came clear: Women were the source of the world's trouble and it was his mission to both punish them for this and to execute them.

"John George Haigh, the British vampire who sucked his victims' blood through soda straws and dissolved their drained bodies in acid baths, first had his murder-inciting dreams and vampire-longings from watching the 'voluptuous' procedure of—an Anglican High Church service."

A visitor to Indianapolis in the summer of 1984 expressed concern that a Reagan appointee to the federal bench was going to make the first constitutional judgment anywhere in the nation on a wholly new approach to banning alleged pornography.

The ordinance, passed by the Indianapolis City Council, claimed to be a civil rights measure. Certain forms of pornography, said the Council, discriminate against women by degrading them. Accordingly, there was a compelling government interest in purging the city of this deeply invidious discrimination.

The federal judge hearing the case was even newer than the "civil rights" theory at issue. Sarah Evans Barker had been sworn in on March 30 of that year, the first woman to serve as a federal district court judge in Indiana. She had previously been a United States attorney, and before that had been active in Republican politics.

In her few months on the bench before her first historic case, Barker struck observers as quite unassuming, sometimes witty, and having, as one litigant put it, an overwhelming smile. She also became known for asking attorneys very hard questions and not allowing them to sidestep those questions.

On July 30, during a hearing in the anti-pornography case, the judge so kept after an assistant Indianapolis corporation counsel that the young woman fainted away. Barker called a ten-minute recess, and, when the arguments resumed, the judge took care to put the revived attorney for the city at ease.

When months passed without a decision by Barker, some Hoosier civil libertarians became uneasy. But on November 19, in a fifty-eight-page finding, Sarah Evans Barker, with precise and ordered passion, demolished the "civil rights" approach to suppressing speech designed by Catharine MacKinnon. In various cities, that approach had created political coalitions of fundamentalist religious groups and some feminists. Had Barker not struck down the Indianapolis ordinance, at least ten other municipalities might well have passed similar laws by the next summer, with more to follow.

Judge Barker noted that if free speech can be regulated on the basis of "protecting women from humiliation and degradation," other "legislative bodies, finding support here," could also act to suppress other degrading material on the ground that it discriminates against particular ethnic or religious groups, or the handicapped. The First Amendment, she pointed at, could hardly survive such mercilessly tenderhearted narrowing of protected speech.

Barker then directly addressed those feminists who have heralded the Indianapolis ordinance as an emancipation proclamation: "In terms of altering sociological patterns, free speech, rather than being the enemy, is a long-tested and worthy ally. To deny free speech in order to engineer social changes in the name of accomplishing a greater good for one sector of our society erodes the freedoms of all."

She also spoke, as James Madison had, of our greatest enemy— us. That is, majoritarianism. "To permit every interest group, especially those who claim to be victimized by unfair expression, their own legislative exceptions to the First Amendment so long as they succeed in obtaining a majority of legislative votes in their favor demonstrates the potentially predatory nature of what defendants seek through this Ordinance."

In 1985, the Seventh Circuit Court of Appeals also threw out the statute as unconstitutional. Judge Frank Easterbook, a Reagan appointee, said it was not a very good idea to put "the government in control... of which thoughts are good for us."

Easterbrook also noted: "Under the ordinance, graphic sexually explicit speech is 'pornography' or not depending on the perspective the author adopts. Speech that 'subordinates' women and also, for example, presents women as enjoying pain, humiliation or rape, or even simply presents women in 'positions of servility or submission or display' is forbidden, no matter how great the literary or political value of the work taken as a whole.

"Speech that portrays women in positions of equality is lawful, no matter how graphic the sexual context. This is thought control. It establishes an 'approved' view of women, of how they may react to sexual encounters, of how the sexes may relate to each other. Those who espouse the approved view may use sexual images; those who do not, may not."

And Easterbrook quoted from Supreme Court Justice Robert Jackson's opinion in *West Virginia State Board of Education* v. *Barnette* (1943):

"If there is any fixed star in our constitutional constellation, it is that no official, high or petty, can prescribe what shall be orthodox in politics, nationalism, religion or other matters of opinion, or force citizens to confess by word or act their faith therein."

In 1986, the U.S. Supreme Court summarily affirmed—without hearing oral arguments—both decisions below. (Justices Burger, Rehnquist, and O'Connor wanted to hear oral arguments before making a decision.)

So much, it seemed, for this ingenious approach to annihilating pornography. But toward the end of 1988, the battered concept took on new, vigorous life in Bellingham, Washington. A determined group called CROW (Civil Rights Organizing for Women), composed in part of students at Western Washington University, placed virtually the same ordinance as the MacKinnon-Dworkin statute on the November ballot. The citizens of Bellingham approved it by a 3–1 margin.

The ordinance was then attacked in a court suit by such customary co-conspirators for free speech as the ACLU, the American Booksellers Association, the Washington State Library Association, and, from Bellingham, bookstore owners, an artist, and a writer.

In an affidavit in the lawsuit, Dana Johnson Verhey, a librarian at Western Washington University, was concerned about the fate in Bellingham—if the statute were to stand—of such works as Nabokov's *Lolita*, Chaucer's "Miller's Tale," Joyce Eyman's *How to Convict a Rapist*, and the *Commission on Pornography: Final Report*, issued by former attorney general Edwin Meese.

It should be noted that the Bellingham ordinance, like the one in Indianapolis, makes no exception for material with serious literary, artistic, political, or scientific value.

The city of Bellingham was embarrassed by all of this. Once it was informed of the previous court history of this legislation, the city announced it would not defend the ordinance. At that point, three women moved to intercede as defendants in place of the city so that the court battle could go forward.

The strategy of CROW and their allies was to keep bringing this ordinance into court until, eventually, the Supreme Court would agree to give it a full hearing. Then, seeing the blinding light, the court would reverse itself and smite the pornographers from coast to coast.

The Bellingham statute eventually failed—despite Andrea Dworkin's presence there to cheer it on. But it surely will emerge again in some other town or city.

In December 1990 in Washington, D.C., I was on a Smithsonian Institution panel concerning many varieties of free speech and those who would restrict it. Sitting next to me was Catharine MacKinnon herself. I asked her if the defeat in Bellingham had lessened her confidence that her civil rights approach to anti-pornography legislation would yet prevail.

"Not at all," she said. "We'll be in the courts again and again until we win."

Whenever she and her supporters do appear in court to suppress pornography, among those in opposition, as in the past, will be free-speech feminists. For instance, the Feminist Anti-Censorship Task Force, which—throughout the national debate over the MacKinnon ordinance—appeared before city and state legislatures and in the press to counter those arguing for censorship in the name of women's rights.

In the various court battles, the most powerful brief to the Seventh Circuit Court of Appeals—against the MacKinnon position—was by the Feminist Anti-Censorship Task Force. Written by Nan Hunter, now a professor at Brooklyn Law School, it stated:

"The range of feminist imagination and expression in the realm of sexuality has barely begun to find voice. Women need the freedom and the socially recognized space to appropriate for themselves the robustness of what traditionally has been male language. Laws such as the one under challenge here would constrict that freedom....

"[We] fear that as more women's writing and art on sexual themes emerge which is unladylike, unfeminine, aggressive, power-charged, pushy, vulgar, urgent, confident and intense, the traditional foes of women's attempts to step out of their 'proper place' will find an effective tool of repression in the Indianapolis ordinance."

In Indianapolis, MacKinnon and Andrea Dworkin could not have prevailed at the City Council had it not been for the backing of a number of right-wing members of the council and similar support elsewhere in the city.

In other cities and states, pro-censorship feminists have sometimes allied themselves, as in North Carolina, with the religious as well as the political right to get anti-pornography laws enacted.

For the feminists, it is a perilous alliance. Harvard law professor Alan Dershowitz, writing about Andrea Dworkin's explicit sexual language in some of her works, tells of being in a debate with "a fundamentalist minister who has joined forces with feminist censors in their war against pornography." Dershowitz asked the minister "whether he would, if he had the power, ban Dworkin's writings. He answered without hesitation: 'We would most certainly ban such ungodly writings.'"

During the debate on the MacKinnon-Dworkin ordinance in Minneapolis, June Callwood, a prominent feminist, emphasized:

"Mistrust of civil liberties reveals a lack of historical perspective. The freedom enjoyed by today's feminists owes everything to civil liberties groups who fought for the right of marginal organizations and minorities to disagree with the majority.... Feminism and civil liberties are inextricable. The goal of both is a society in which individuals are treated justly. Civil libertarians who oppose censorship are fighting on behalf of feminists, not against them."

Catherine MacKinnon has characterized civil libertarians opposing censorship as "First Amendment wimps."

Among the supporters of the MacKinnon ordinance in various cities have been chapters of the National Organization for Women. It's all the more instructive, then, to see how certain members of NOW came to a more direct and personal understanding of the vagaries of censorship of sexual materials.

In Framingham, Massachusetts, the public library sets aside two rooms where local groups can present programs. There is no requirement that the library be informed of the content of the program beforehand. A regular user of this public forum is the South Middlesex Chapter of the National Organization for Women. It has shown films and held discussions on a wide range of issues, including the right of homosexuals to adopt children.

"We've never had any trouble from the board of trustees," a member of NOW told me in 1988, "until we advertised we were showing that movie." It is a British film, she added, and it has to do with sexual politics and alienation. "In a decaying sector of London," she said, "you see the alienation of blacks from society, and the alienation of intellectuals watching riots as voyeurs. And you see women being used by men, and by one another. We thought there was a lot to talk about."

When released in the United States, the film was treated, not always enthusiastically, as a serious movie. It is called *Sammy and Rosie Get Laid.*

After seeing a newspaper ad by NOW announcing the film's showing at the library, the board of trustees voted to ban it and, according to court papers, instructed the library's director, "to do everything in his power to prevent the showing of the movie."

NOW held its meeting in the library on the appointed date. Instead of the movie, the subject of discussion was censorship. NOW also sued the board of trustees for, among other things, violating the free-speech rights of its members in the "quintessential public forum" that is a public library.

Bella English, a columnist for the *Boston Globe* who relishes the universals in everyday ironies, saw a brief notice of the suit in a suburban paper and called George King, the chairman of the library's board of trustees. She wanted the minutes of the meeting at which *Sammy and Rosie Get Laid* was banned. King said the written minutes wouldn't tell her much. Ah, then, was the meeting taped? Yes, it was, and he supplied the transcript.

"I had to give it out to her," King ruefully explained to me. "Under Massachusetts law, it was a matter of public record."

Thereupon, readers of the *Boston Globe*—including the stunned members of the board of trustees of the Framingham Public Library—read excerpts in Bella English's column of the meeting at which *Sammy and Rosie*'s library cards had been canceled. George King assured me that the quotations are "totally accurate."

After establishing that "not one of the trustees has seen the film," Bella English let the trustees speak for themselves:

Karen La Chance: "I certainly concur that it's totally vulgar and inappropriate and I'm embarrassed about it."

Henri Fortier: "The title is actually sexually arousing."

John Flinter: "I really think it's rather demeaning of women. We don't use this conversation at home, at least in my home. If I ever hear my kids use these vulgar words, I just say 'knock it off, garbage-mouth.' It's not accepted at home; it's not going to be accepted here."

Jane Bell, a member of NOW who was admitted to the trustees meeting after it had begun, told them: "The title of the movie, as well as its content, has not been deemed to be obscene by law."

George King: "Well, I don't think obscenity is our concern here. Image, appearance is the problem.... It's just a very vulgar title. I think it's a term that's insulting to women, to be honest with you."

The vote was 6–4 against showing the movie. "It wasn't censorship," chairman King informed me. "We didn't ban the movie on the basis of content. It was a difference of opinion as to whether a title that would offend many users of our library should be advertised as being part of a library program."

I suggested that those offended were not compelled to see the movie. This seemed to be a new idea to Mr. King.

On the evening before the scheduled court hearing on NOW's motion for a preliminary injunction that it not be prevented from showing *Sammy and Rosie Get Laid* at its next meeting in November, the library's board of trustees reversed its decision to banish the movie.

They did not wish to see themselves in print, as censors, again.

In a response, a few years before, to Catharine MacKinnon, Nan Hunter and New York University law professor Sylvia Law said: "Without free speech, we can have no feminist movement. And if the anti-porn censorship is enacted, it is the right-wing-packed courts. . . who will decide what materials are printable in the United States."

XIII

Bringing the First Amendment (Live!) into the Schools

"Tell them stories," Justice Brennan said. "Tell them stories!"

In his farewell address to the American people, Ronald Reagan said, "If we forget what we did, we won't know who we are. I am warning of an eradication...of the American memory that could result, ultimately, in an erosion of the American spirit."

That erosion is already taking place, particularly among schoolchildren. Every year for the past quarter century, I have been spending a fair amount of time as a guest speaker in high schools, junior high schools, and some elementary schools around the country—from rural classrooms in Pennsylvania to big, fast-track high schools in Colorado. I've been in most of the states, and from time to time I also talk with students from various cities on radio call-in shows.

Most American kids are ignorant of their history as a free people. They know very little of what's in the Bill of Rights and the Fourteenth Amendment, and they know less of what it took to secure these liberties and rights. And if they leave school with such

356

ignorance, they are hardly likely, as adults, to fight to preserve their own liberties—let alone anyone else's. The young have not forgotten what Americans have done. They have simply never known.

For instance, not long ago at a middle school near Harrisburg, Pennsylvania, we were talking about the extent—and limitations—of the power of the police. I asked the students what they knew about the Fourth Amendment. Heavy silence. Finally, a brave youngster informed me that the Fourth Amendment was about the right to bear arms.

"Okay," I said, "let me tell you the story of the Fourth Amendment." (When I once told Supreme Court Justice William Brennan that I occasionally try to bring the words of the Constitution off the page and into the inner thoughts of the young, he said, "Tell them stories! Tell them stories!" And I always do.)

That morning, I told the future voters—and maybe some of the future legislators—of Pennsylvania about the writs of assistance (the general search warrants) that British SWAT teams used as they smashed into colonists' homes and turned everything upside down, including the colonists, to pry into cupboards and under beds for goods on which taxes had not been paid. These were random searches. The British troops did not need to have any reason to believe there was contraband in the home. They battered their way in when and wherever they pleased.

The faces before me grew indignant. I told them of fiery James Otis arguing long and fiercely against those writs in a Massachusetts court in 1761. And I told them of a young lawyer, John Adams, watching spellbound in that courtroom and then writing later that "the independence was then and there born."

The kids thought that was a neat story. They wanted to know more. They always do. I have yet to be in a classroom where—once the Constitution becomes inhabited by actual people—students are not eager to search further into that suddenly compelling document. Some of them look as though they've just discovered America.

In a few schools, I have found kids to whom the Constitution had already become something personal. That is, they actually felt it belonged to them. And some had used "the living Constitution" as an Excalibur against their principal or school board. Invariably, these students had come to their familiarity with the Constitution because a teacher had made those rights and liberties stay in their minds long after classes were over.

There are not nearly enough such teachers, but where they exist, they can have a lot of impact. For example, at Lindbergh High School in the Renton School District in the state of Washington, a teacher of civics had included Supreme Court decisions on student rights in his course. Five of his students had been particularly taken with the 1969 *Tinker* v. *Des Moines Independent School District* decision. Justice Abe Fortas, writing for a 7–2 majority of the Court, had stated: "It can hardly be argued that either students or teachers shed their constitutional rights to freedom of speech or expression at the schoolhouse gate."

That decision affirmed the right of thirteen-year-old Mary Beth Tinker and other students protesting the war in Vietnam to wear black armbands to school. But *Tinker* also came to be applied to protecting student expression in school newspapers—with certain limitations. Student expression can be curbed, for instance, if it may immediately create substantial disorder in the school, or if an article was obscene or defamatory. But the burden was on the principal to prove it was—under state law. Nor could an article invade the rights of others. Still, much freedom remained for student journalists.

But in 1988, these student rights were severely circumscribed by the Supreme Court's decision in *Hazelwood School District* v. *Kuhlmeier.* This decision gave school officials virtually unchecked power to censor any student expression that is school-sponsored or appears to have the school imprimatur.

The five Lindbergh High School students who had been turned on by the First Amendment in their civics class decided to publish a paper that had no connection with the school. It was produced outside the school and with no financial support from the school. But they did want to be able to distribute it on campus.

They distributed the first issue at a senior-class barbecue, and that led the principal to place letters of reprimand in their permanent school records. The five new journalists, he said, had defied him, because he had told them they could not distribute the paper until he had had an opportunity to review it.

The students took the principal and the school board to court, where they filed their own extraordinarily comprehensive brief on all the pertinent cases in the country concerning student press rights. They lost in Federal District Court, but a three-judge panel of the Ninth Circuit Court of Appeals unanimously ruled that the *Hazelwood* decision does not cover "underground" or "non-school-sponsored" papers. At least within the Jurisdiction of the Ninth District (most western states), those irreverent journals can be distributed in schools without prior review by the principal.

This was the strongest and clearest signal to kids all over the country that despite *Hazelwood*, they still have some First Amendment rights in school. And although an American Civil Liberties Union attorney represented the five young paladins of the First Amendment, it was their courage, determination, and research for their own brief that have helped keep alive at least part of the spirit of *Tinker* in American public schools.

There's another way to protect public school journalists from the *Hazelwood* blight. In 1989, the Iowa legislature passed a law—signed by the governor, Terry Branstad—that declares public school students have First Amendment rights unless student expression disturbs school operations. Also, students may not print "obscene, libelous or slanderous material." Except for those requirements, "there shall be no prior restraint" of student journalists in Iowa.

This law, even with its limits, is far less sweeping and authoritarian than Justice Byron White's ruling in *Hazelwood* that principals or school boards can cut out of the student paper, play, or speech anything inconsistent with a school's "basic educational mission" (the latter to be defined at will by the principal).

The successful lobbyists for this restoration of *Tinker* were the Iowa Civil Liberties Union and the Iowa High School Press Association (a group of high school student journalists and teachers).

There was little coverage of this First Amendment victory for students in the Iowa daily press—and no editorials in favor of the bill.

The indifference of much of the adult press to the very idea of student First Amendment rights is hardly limited to Iowa. Newspapers, increasingly worried that fewer of the young read the daily press, keep trying to figure out what to print that might atttact students. Some news about First Amendment wars in student newsrooms might help.

As of the bicentennial year of the Bill of Rights, California, Massachusetts, and Colorado had also made it clear that they were not relinquishing *Tinker.* With other states considering similar emancipation bills, there is a section of the Iowa law that may make a rejection of *Hazelwood* more attractive.

School boards and principals regularly complain that if students were to get more First Amendment rights, the school board or the school system would have to pay damages for any lawsuits resulting from what the students print. The Iowa law frees school officials or other school employees from any liability "for any student expression made or published by students."

But if school officials or other school personnel have "interfered with or altered the content" of the student expression, they are no longer free of liability—a compelling incentive for principals and others to resign their roles as censors.

Iowa state senator Rochard Varn, principal sponsor of the Iowa bill, sounds like Abe Fortas: "Students can't learn about fundamental rights and freedoms unless they are allowed to use those rights."

By contrast, under Justice Byron White's educational philosophy—as *Boston Globe* cartoonist Dan Wasserman had a student say in his strip right after the *Hazelwood* decision came down:

"According to the Supreme Court, the First Amendment guarantees freedom of speech and the press, except in real special cases like schools, where it could interfere with kids learning to be good citizens."

None of these laws exiling the *Hazelwood* decision from an individual state will be without some restrictions, including the prohibition of expression that disrupts the learning process in a school.

But there are times when what at first appears to be a potentially disruptive school experience can turn into what Oliver Wendell Holmes once described as the core of our system of free expression:

"If there is any principle of the Constitution that more imperatively calls for attachment than any other, it is the principle of free thought—not free thought for those who agree with us, but freedom for the thought we hate."

Belief in this principle hardly comes naturally, and it has not been learned by the vast majority of American adults or by their children. But it *can* be taught, as was demonstrated in 1988 at the North Garner Middle School in a town near Raleigh, North Carolina.

One morning, Mark Vice, Jr., a ninth-grader, came to school wearing a Confederate flag sewn onto the back of his denim jacket. The flag had been a Christmas present from his father, who has a Confederate flag tattooed on his forearm. The school's principal, Dr. Janet Stevens, who had asked Mark not to wear the jacket in school, forbade him to enter if he persisted.

Mark's parents went for help to the North Carolina Civil Liberties Union. ("These are his rights they're messing with," his father said.) One of its attorneys, William Simpson, together with the school's principal and the superintendent of schools, agreed that rather than get into a court battle, they would hold an assembly and let the kids hear the conflicting points of view. About 30 percent of the 850 students are black, and many had bristled at the sight of the jacket. There had been black-white tensions, including fisticuffs, at the school before.

A number of people spoke at the assembly, but Simpson's talk made the most lasting impression on the students. He told them that "today the Confederate flag is not very popular with school officials. Twenty years ago, the symbols of the civil rights movement were not very popular with many school officials.

"In the 1960s, black people marched in all parts of the South to bring down legalized racism.... Everywhere they marched they offended many white people who believed things were fine just the way they were. Those marchers faced angry white crowds who were disturbed by the marchers' message. If the hostile reaction of those crowds had justified bans on demonstrations and marches, there would be no Civil Rights Act or Voting Rights Act or integrated restaurants and motels.

"Instead of going to school and working together, black and white people would be at odds—much like they are today in South Africa, where for so long there was no freedom of speech."

In addition to the assembly, the principal had debates in each classroom, and then in a schoolwide meeting of representatives of each classroom, on whether hateful speech should be protected. Out of all this robust exchange of views throughout the school, there came an understanding on the part of most of the kids— from hearing viewpoints other than their own—that maybe this free-speech thing should apply to everybody. Mark Vice, Jr., came back to school, the Confederate flag still stitched to his jacket, and there were no disruptions—even though about a dozen other students started wearing Confederate flags to school.

(Originally, the North Carolina Civil Liberties Union had said in taking the case: "Even though we as an organization do not agree with the values represented by the symbol, he has the right to wear the symbol so long as he is not disrupting the educational process.")

Dr. Janet Stevens made a point of telling me: "I lifted the ban without Marc or anyone else knowing I was going to do it. I didn't want any group, including the ACLU, to think they can control this school."

Summing up the testing at the North Garner Middle School of Oliver Wendell Holmes's definition of true free speech, Dr. Stevens said: "Well, there was a real exchange of ideas. For the first time, they, black and white, have heard each other—however reluctantly."

From the beginning, the *Raleigh News and Observer*, a much-respected newspaper, had become involved in the dispute. In an editorial, the paper quoted, with ringing approval, from the Supreme Court's 1969 *Tinker* decision:

"Undifferentiated fear or apprehension of disturbance is not enough to overcome the right to freedom of expression.... It can hardly be argued that either students or teachers shed their constitutional rights to freedom of speech at the schoolhouse gate...."

But what about the 1988 *Hazelwood* decision? Didn't that give Dr. Stevens the absolute right to banish the jacket, the flag, and Marc because *Hazelwood* said a principal can censor anything he or she says is in conflict with the school curriculum or appears to be sponsored by the school?

That's true up to a point, said the *News and Observer*, but Marc

Vice's jacket with the flag on it is not part of the curriculum, and no one would ever suspect Dr. Janet Stevens of sponsoring it. So the *Hazelwood* decision, said the editorial, had nothing to do with Marc Vice, Jr.'s, emblazoned jacket.

Whether Janet Stevens did indeed have the legal power to keep Marc out of school—until he returned in other garb—was never determined in court. And that was all to the good in view of what finally happened in the school.

Before it was all over, a reader, Samuel McClintock, wrote the *News and Observer* and said he supported Mark Vice, Jr.'s, right to wear the Confederate flag on his back, but did not think the boy would be able to exercise that right "because we live in a country where educated adults do not respond rationally to freedom of speech.... Yet we expect our young to respond in calm restraint when confronted with a racist symbol."

As it turned out, however, some of the young, once they got to think about it, did respond rationally to a racist symbol.

In the summer of 1964, history was made twice in the small town of Philadelphia, Mississippi. On June 21, the Congress of Racial Equality became aware that three civil rights workers were missing. The three had been investigating the burning of a black church. Their names were James Chaney, Andrew Goodman, and Michael Schwerner.

On August 4, news went around the world that the bodies of the murdered civil rights workers had been discovered in an earth-fill dam near Philadelphia, Mississippi. They had joined the martyrs of the civil rights movement.

The other event coming out of the town in the summer of 1964 was a rebellion in a high school that led to a court case. It was simultaneously about civil rights, about student rights, and about the First Amendment. The ultimate decision greatly influenced the 1969 landmark Supreme Court ruling in *Tinker* v. *Des Moines Independent School District*—long the Magna Carta of student rights throughout the country.

The case, *Burnside* v. *Byars*, started in Philadelphia a month and a half after the bodies of Chaney, Goodman, and Schwerner were found.

The facts of the case are taken from the opinion of Judge Walter Gewin of the Fifth Circuit Court of Appeals. A resident of Tuscaloosa, Alabama, Gewin was a conservative, and it took him awhile after his 1961 appointment to the bench to understand why blacks in case after case before him were so aggrieved. Gewin was not a racist, but he was not a judicial hero in the mold of such southern judges of that time as Frank Johnson and J. Skelly Wright.

In his invaluable book, *Unlikely Heroes* (Simon and Schuster 1981)—about Johnson, Wright, and other judges of the Fifth Circuit who transformed the civil rights revolution into the rule of law in the South—Jack Bass says that Gewin's turning point was a 1970 case, *Miller* v. *Amusement Enterprises.*

A place called Fun Fair ran ads, urging "Everybody come!" A black woman, Mrs. Miller, took her two children there to ice skate. One, Denise, was light enough to pass, and the attendant gave her a pair of skates. Denise's brother, Daniel, twelve, who was dark, came to the counter afterward. Looking at him, the attendant scurried off to find the manager who came forth and informed Mrs. Miller that "Everybody come!" certainly did not mean people of color.

In his decision in that case, Judge Walter Gewin wrote: "The people standing in line waiting to rent skates began to giggle, and Denise, frightened and disappointed at not being allowed to skate [because the family was going to leave], started crying. As Denise stood there crying, others in the line appeared to be amused. Mrs. Miller and her children quickly left the park."

Judge Gewin ruled in favor of Mrs. Miller and her children, thereby further extending the public accommodations section of the 1964 Civil Rights Act.

Clearly, Gewin was moved by the humiliation suffered by that black family, but I think the turning point for him on civil rights matters may well have occurred four years before in *Burnside* v. *Byars.*

These are the facts of the case:

At the Booker T. Washington High School in Philadelphia, Mississippi, the principal, Montgomery Moore, learned in mid-September 1964 that a number of students in the all-black school were wearing "freedom buttons." The kids had gotten the buttons from the headquarters in Philadelphia of COFO (the Council of Federated Organizations), a coalition of civil rights groups.

As described by Judge Gewin: "The buttons were circular, approximately one and one-half inches in diameter, containing the wording 'One Man One Vote' around the perimeter, with 'SNCC' inscribed in the center." (SNCC was the acronym for the Student Nonviolent Coordinating Committee.)

The principal informed the entire student body that any such button was prohibited in class and, for that matter, anywhere in the building.

At the subsequent trial, the principal explained his order by saying that the buttons "didn't have any bearing on their education." Furthermore, those buttons "would cause commotion, disturbing the school program, what with kids passing them around, talking about them, and explaining to the students in the next row why they're wearing them."

On September 21, four kids defied principal Moore, showing up at school wearing the SNCC buttons. They were given a choice: off with the buttons or go home. Three of the four students left school.

The next day, the four returned, all of them without their SNCC buttons. So much for that black revolt, thought Moore.

But on the morning of September 24, there was what Mr. Moore called "a commotion." Thirty to forty children had showed up with the SNCC buttons, passing them around in the hall, he said, before they went into class.

The principal herded the kids into his office and gave them the choice: no button or no school. The great majority said goodbye and were suspended for a week. Meanwhile, the principal wrote a letter to the parents of each erring child:

"This is to inform you that your child has been suspended from school until you can come and have a talk with me. It is against the school policy for anything to be brought into the school that is not educational."

The parents agreed to curb their children, except for three women—Mrs. Burnside, Mrs. English, and Mrs. Morris. They went to court to enjoin the school officials from enforcing the suspension of their children on the basis of those buttons.

At trial, the parents claimed that the school regulation forbidding "freedom buttons" on school property abridged their children's First and Fourteenth Amendment rights to freedom of speech. The principal and other school officials contended, on the other hand, that the prohibition of the button was a reasonable exercise of school discipline.

The Federal District Court agreed with the school authorities and refused to issue a preliminary injunction against the anti-button rule.

On appeal, the case went to a three-judge panel of the Fifth Circuit, with Judge Gewin delivering the decision. Said Gewin:

"The Negro schoolchildren who attended an all-Negro high school wore the 'freedom buttons' as a means of silently communicating an idea and to encourage the members of their community to exercise their civil rights."

In a footnote, Gewin quoted from the trial testimony of two of the children. (Henry Aronson was their lawyer.)

"Mr. Aronson: What kinds of things would you like to do?"

"Miss English: Go uptown and sit in the drugstores and wherever we buy things uptown we can sit down and won't have to walk right out at the time we got it."

"Mr. Aronson: What else?"

"Miss English: And to register and vote without being beat up and killed."

"Mr. Aronson: It says 'One Man One Vote.' What does that mean to you?"

"Miss Jordon (age 16): I wanted to try to help the people to make them understand why I wore this pin, because I wanted them to go to the courthouse and register to vote."

"Mr. Aronson: What people?"

"Miss Jordon: The colored people in our community."

"Do they vote in Philadelphia?"

"Miss Jordon: No, sir."

Judge Gewin continued:

"The right to communicate a matter of vital public concern is embraced in the First Amendment right to freedom of speech and therefore is clearly protected against infringement by state officials...."

"Particularly, the Fourteenth Amendment protects the First Amendment rights of schoolchildren against unreasonable rules and regulations imposed by school authorities.

"The Fourteenth Amendment, as now applied to the States, protects the citizen against the State itself and all of its creatures—Boards of Education not excepted...."

The judge added that the free-expression rights of students while in school are not absolute. The principal and other officials can formulate rules and regulations necessary for orderly learning. But the rules have to be reasonable.

In this case, however, there was no evidence that the wearing of the buttons in any way disrupted orderly learning at the Booker T. Washington High School. Judge Gewin emphasized that "Even the principal testified that the children were [suspended] not for... disrupting classes but for violating the school regulation."

Absent any student disturbance, the court struck down the principal's rule as "arbitrary and unreasonable, and an unnecessary infringement on the students' protected right of free expression."

And, in a passage that would greatly influence the United States Supreme Court three years later in the *Tinker* student rights case, Judge Gewin declared:

"School officials cannot ignore expressions of feeling with which they do not wish to contend. They cannot infringe on their students' right to free and unrestricted expression as guaranteed to them under the First Amendment to the Constitution where the exercise of such rights in the school buildings and schoolrooms do not materially and substantially interfere with the requirements of appropriate discipline in the operation of the school."

The events at Booker T. Washington High School and their subsequent influence on First Amendment law were largely unnoticed then. And they have continued to be. But the courageous black kids and their parents who would not yield their First Amendment rights in the racist, murderous town of Philadelphia deserve to be remembered. Often.

Judge Gewin's decision in the case—and he was a much better writer than most judges—is readily available in a book, *Freedom of Expression,* that is one of a series of superbly produced volumes for the classroom. But actually, every book in the series is for anyone who wants to learn the key First Amendment cases in the Supreme Court and in the lower courts through the years.

The overall series, edited by Haig Bosmajian, is called *The 1st Amendment in the Classroom*. And the titles are: *The Freedom to Read Books, Films and Plays; Freedom of Religion; Freedom of Expression; Academic Freedom;* and *The Freedom to Publish*.

The publisher is Neal-Schuman Publishers, 23 Leonard Street, New York, NY 10013.

I hope some legal historian writes an article or even a book on the evolution of Judge Walter Gewin, described by Jack Bass as "a quiet, patient, unassuming man who lived in a modest frame house [in Tuscaloosa] in a middle-class neighborhood.... As a judge, Gewin drank coffee regularly at a Tuscaloosa cafe with a blue-collar clientele, because he believed working people and judges needed to see one another."

There are appellate judges who, because they do not see the actual people in the cases before them, regard laws and constitutional principles as abstractions. By contrast, there are judges, like William Brennan, who believe that "sensitivity to one's intuitive and passionate responses and awareness of the range of human experience" is a desirable part of the judicial process.

Walter Gewin, cautiously, might have agreed.

Of all the experiences I've had with students in trying to bring the words of the Constitution off the page, the most illuminating took place in Charleston, West Virginia, on a crisp October day in 1981. It was so striking that I can relive it, in detail, at will. And I often do.

The West Virginia Civil Liberties Union, a Charleston minister, and several unaffiliated friends of the Constitution had decided to hold a Bill of Rights Day for high school students—beginning early in the morning and lasting until evening.

For a week before the designated day, the high school students were assigned readings and engaged in class discussions of freedom of speech and press; the tangled relationship between the free-exercise-of-religion and the establishment clauses; cruel and unusual punishment; the occasional collisions between the demands of the free press and a fair trial; and other dilemmas of liberty. But these preliminaries were far less important than what happened on the day itself as the students plunged into specific issues involving the Constitution.

As the sun rose, the youngsters—150 of them—came to a large central site. They came from the city itself and from the rural enclaves within the steep hills outside Charleston. They were separated into twelve groups, each led by a teacher or by various outside workers in the constitutional vineyards. I was one of them.

Each group of youngsters was given both actual case histories and hypothetical situations. And the students took different roles, as participants do in Fred Friendly's Public Broadcasting System series on the Constitution and other subjects.

During the course of the day, some students imagined themselves cops confronted by deliberately provocative demonstrators advocating—but not engaging in—violence. Others became parents insisting that certain books must be removed from the schools because they were flagrantly obscene, unpatriotic, blasphemous, or contemptuous of the family. Still other students turned into librarians trying to point out that *if* library books were purchased solely according to the majority vote of the community, the kids would be growing up pathetically ignorant in a good many vital areas.

In the group I was working with, the main focus was on a real case—whether a group of utterly repellent American Nazis should have been allowed to demonstrate in Skokie, Illinois, where many Jews lived, including survivors of the Holocaust. The exchanges among the students were continually intense, not only during the group discussions but also during the breaks for soft drinks and sandwiches. Looking around, I saw much the same level of intellectual and emotional energy crackling in the other groups scattered around the meeting place.

By late afternoon, our group, having worn itself out, put the question to a vote. By a thin margin, the vote sustained Oliver Wendell Holmes. It was decided that the Nazis' placards and insignia, hateful as they were, fell under the protection of the very First Amendment those Nazis would destroy if they ever came to power.

Elsewhere in the room, some of the other units were still trying to make sense out of the Constitution and each other. I walked over to one. The students there were being told by a teacher leading the discussion that a bunch of West Virginians, members of a Communist splinter group, had decided to march up and down the streets of Charleston, brandishing red flags. They were going to carry inflammatory signs denouncing and insulting the President, the First Lady, the Constitution, and calling for the overthrow of the government.

The question was then posed by the teacher: Do these Communists, even under the First Amendment, have the right to so grievously offend decent people, including children, on the streets of Charleston? And since they will be calling for the overthrow of the government, was the Constitution intended to be a suicide pact? Was it intended to give the sworn enemies of our liberties the freedom to gain converts who would help destroy that liberty?

Furthermore, if the march were allowed, some of these Communists—as had actually happened during an aborted demonstration by the Communist Workers Party in Charleston a year before—would surely be beaten up. With the high probability of violence, including violence likely to spill over onto innocent bystanders, is it not more crucial to protect the public peace by prohibiting the march than to allow it?

The students argued long and loudly. I was particularly watching a slight young woman, looking like a young Sissy Spacek, with thin brown hair, maybe seventeen, who had not yet said a word during this explosive discussion. As she listened, she was biting her lip and suddenly, in a soft voice—which somehow silenced all the others—she started speaking, very slowly, more to herself than to the rest of us.

"Well," she said, rubbing her nose, "I was there last year when they beat up those Communists. I didn't think much about it, one way or another." She bit her lip again. "If I had, I guess I would have done some beating up myself. But now"—she screwed up her face—"well, now, after all I've been hearing and thinking today, well, maybe, they do have a right to go out there and march."

She paused, and then said, even more slowly, "And I guess they got a right not to get beat up doing it. No matter what they say. No matter what their signs say." She shook her head. "It's hard. But I guess I don't see no other way."

The young woman slipped into the background as another student, shaking his head in vigorous disagreement, shouted, "No, I don't see that at all! Communists have no rights. They want to take away our rights. It's just plain stupid to let them go around doing that. What I say is, let them go back where they came from!"

"But they're all West Virginians, remember?" said the teacher who was leading the discussion.

The student frowned and countered, "Well, let's kick them out of West Virginia. Send them to New York or some place like that."

The debate grew more fiery until finally there was a vote. A majority of the unit sided with the hard conclusion of the shy young woman who had not said another word.

I was standing next to a woman who lived in Charleston and had helped organize the Bill of Rights Day. "You see," she told me, "if you just give kids a chance to think about these things and work them out inside their heads, this liberty stuff comes alive for them. Of course, one day isn't enough, but you start any way you can. Why isn't this, or something like it, going on all over the country? Why isn't it a regular series on television?"

Why indeed? This "liberty stuff" will never come alive for most of the young if the Constitution continues to have as much personal meaning to them as the average annual rainfall in Wichita. And if the Bill of Rights does not become of passionate interest to them—and to their children—it will eventually dissolve into a charming legend of the early years of the Republic when individual liberty—rather than the will of the majority in all things—was actually considered the core of democracy.

"If being true to the First Amendment means that I am free to warp young people's minds in the name of intellectual freedom, is that what I should be doing?"

Rhode Island

I was once invited to be one of two speakers in a program concerning censorship at a graduate school of library science in Rhode Island. The first speaker was a young woman who had earned an impressive reputation in the New England area both as a librarian and as a persistent battler for children's right to read—and the right of librarians to select books for children according to their criteria as professionals. She had helped raise support and funds for a librarian in Massachusetts who had been forced out of her job because the local school board charged she had kept "unsuitable" books in the library.

As soon as she began to speak, she looked and sounded as if she were primarily involved in an inner dialogue. We were eavesdroppers. Clearly, she had been agonizing for a long time whether censorship was necessarily bad—in every possible circumstance. Maybe, she said, she had been emphasizing freedom at the expense of responsibility.

"Do I," she went on, "have the right to make available to children a book that might do them harm? Suppose, for instance, there is a nonfiction book about the Ku Klux Klan that makes the Klan appear to be noble, brave and an example of true Americanism? Well, since this is a nonfiction book, I can also make available another nonfiction book about the Klan that exposes its aims and its actions with specific illustrations from the past and the present. That way, the children will be able to compare the propaganda with the facts.

"But what if it were a *novel* about the Klan? Novels can be very dangerous. Novels can make bad ideas, damaging ideas, seductive. A novel can turn a youngster's mind around. Should I—do I have a right—to have on my shelves a novel that romanticizes the Klan? A novel in which the reader can make heroes of those hooded bullies and murderers in the Klan?"

She was still speaking softly, as if to herself. "Suppose," she went on, "a woman novelist—a fine, compelling writer—were to write a vivid, powerful novel against a woman's fundamental right of privacy to choose to have an abortion. A beautifully written novel in which the pro-life characters were so attractive they could make you cry, and the pro-choice people were cold and selfish. And in which the writer repeatedly calls abortion 'murder.'

"Should I allow such a novel to poison the minds of young people, to give them so misleading and distorted a sense of what's at stake in a woman's right to decide so deeply personal a question?"

She paused. "If being true to the First Amendment means that I am free to warp young people's minds in the name of intellectual freedom, is that what I should be doing? Maybe I could do with a little less freedom."

There was no doubt that this young woman—after long and painful reflection—had decided, in all honesty, that at times, a little, just a little, censorship was the right thing to do. The necessary thing to do.

During her talk, I was taking notes as fast as I could, having decided to scrap my own speech and use my time to answer hers.

But before I was to go on, the schedule called for questions from the audience addressed to the first speaker. A woman in her fifties rose. I later found out she had been a librarian in the Rhode Island public school system for many years.

"I want to make sure," the woman said to the first speaker, "that I understand what you're saying. Are you saying that we should put limits on what children learn and think and explore—so that they will be able to think for themselves when they grow up? So that they'll be more free when they grow up?"

I put away the notes I had just written. The woman had said in so few words what I had wanted to say. In response, the young librarian repeated what she had said in her speech—that certain ideas were too dangerous for middle-school or high school readers. But she had lost her audience, although I gathered—from conversations after the program was over—that the librarians there were grateful to her for reminding them what their job was.

Not long after, in upstate New York, a library center decided to do something about books that might be harmful to young readers. The center provided books, materials, and curriculum support to a number of school districts, including school libraries. It covered Albany, Schoharie, and Schenectady. In one of its newsletters, the following advice to other librarians appeared:

"Place a warning label on biased material:

"'WARNING: It has been determined that these materials are sex-stereotyped and may limit your sense of freedom and choice. (These labels can be typed and reproduced as a student project.)'"

A more interesting and educational student project might have been:

Who determined that these materials are "sex-stereotyped"? By what criteria? If, for the sake of argument, the books on this X-rated list are sex-stereotyped, do students learn more by not reading them at all or by reading them and figuring out how those stereotypes came to be?

Also, when the librarians in this upstate New York center proclaimed that these books "may limit your sense of freedom and choice," who actually was limiting the students' freedom of choice?

The newsletter went on to urge that librarians in the region "keep teachers well stocked with catalogues of bias-free materials."

Were there to be hearings for books that had been banned? Were authors of the condemned materials not to be allowed to defend themselves and to confront their accusers?

The librarians in that center—supplying advice as well as books to libraries in the region—surely considered Phyllis Schlafly and Jerry Falwell to be the very models of enemies of intellectual freedom.

"Why Teach Us to Read and Then Say We Can't?"

Children in many American schools are instructed early in thought control. This is not the term used by their school boards and principals. They call it the removal of "inappropriate" books.

For a long time, a book near the top of the hit list has been J. D. Salinger's *Catcher in the Rye*. In Boron, California, in 1990, a parent noted in alarm that the book "uses the Lord's name in vain two hundred times. That's enough reason to ban it right there," she explained. "They said it describes reality. I say let's back up from reality. Let's go backwards. Let's go back to when we didn't have an immoral society."

That parent is more candid than most of those on the political and religious right who object to certain books on their children's required or optional reading lists. They genuinely fear that forces—some say satanic forces—beyond their control have taken over the majority culture. And their responsibility, as parents and as Christians, is to protect their children—and all other children—from the infectious permissiveness of the larger society.

Strategically, it is a mistake to underestimate the seriousness of purpose and strength of will of these book police. I've spoken to many of them. They are not "kooks."

The resolution of the *Catcher in the Rye* furor in Boron, North Carolina, was the removal of the book from the high school language arts supplemental reading list.

In Clay County, in north Florida, school officials banished *My Friend Flicka* from the optional reading lists of fifth- and sixth-grade kids. The book has become an outlaw because in it, a female dog is described as a "bitch."

The harm that can be found in writing that has previously been considered free of malignities has also been exposed by school officials in Citrus County, Florida. As reported by Howard Kleinberg in the Los Angeles legal newspaper, the *Daily Journal*, a school cultural contest in Citrus County was canceled in 1990 "on the grounds that Joyce Kilmer, whose poem was part of the project, used the words 'breast and bosom' in it."

Attempts to control what children read, and thereby think, have been increasing across the country, according to annual accounts by the American Library Association and People for the American Way. There is a great deal of underreporting, however, as I've discovered in interviews with teachers and librarians through the years.

Many principals, for instance, yield immediately to complaints rather than have to deal with the controversy that comes with review committees and public hearings. And once there has been trouble in a school, some librarians do their own self-censoring of books they decide not to order.

Judy Blume's books, for example, are widely popular, especially among girls, but because they deal with real problems familiar to real youngsters, they are often attacked. At a meeting of librarians a few years ago, two of them from Minnesota told me how much they admired Judy Blume's ability to understand what's troubling kids. Then one of them added: "But we're not going to buy another book of hers. Too much damn trouble."

An increasing preoccupation of many fundamentalist Christians—to whom the Devil is no abstraction—has to do with satanism in books for children. Since the Devil can take on many forms, one has to sniff very carefully for the scent of brimstone. In Yorba Linda, California, parents insisting that satanism be removed root and branch filed objections to the presence of Old Nick in, among other books in the school, *Romeo and Juliet,* Maurice Sendak's *Where the Wild Things Are,* and a story by Nathaniel Hawthorne.

In response to the complaints, most of the children of the Satan-detectors were moved to safe classrooms in which those works were not taught.

Not all the putative censors win. By and large, those schools with a clearly worded and structured review procedure can often withstand these attacks. The parent or other complainer has to fill out a form specifying his or her objections. Faced with the form, some parents let the issue drop. But others go on. The review committee—consisting of librarians, teachers, and sometimes members of the community—usually provide some due-process protections for both the objecting parents and the accused books. And then there is the school board for final review. That being a political body, it can be more concerned with the next election than the First Amendment. But not always.

Here's how this review procedure worked in Watanga County, North Carolina. A philosophy professor and father of a child in kindergarten challenged a 1901 edition of Rudyard Kipling's *Just So Stories.* In one of the stories, "How the Leopard Got His Spots," the word "nigger" appears. A five-member review committee decided to remove the book.

Two librarians, however, appealed to the school board to reverse the sentence. The chairman of the school board—as reported in the American Library Association's *Newsletter on Intellectual Freedom*—said: "Freedom of speech is the vehicle through which can come the defense against those who would use words to harm human beings."

But the philosophy professor disagreed: "There are two things I very much want my daughter not to become. I don't want her to be a drug addict, and I don't want her to be a racist."

One of the librarians, however, carried the day: "In the end the only way we learn there are such issues as racism is by discussing them with our children. We ask that you vote to leave this book on the shelf."

The vote was unanimous. Rudyard Kipling's stories still have a home in the Watanga County elementary school library.

Another victory for free expression took place in Colonie, New York. At issue was the future in the Shaker High School Library of *The Progressive* magazine, a national liberal political journal. A sophomore—complaints do come from students as well as from all manner of school employees—wanted the magazine banned because it has contained ads for *The Anarchist Cookbook, Women Loving Women,* and *Prove Christ Fictional.* Also offensive to the student was a full-page ad by the Jewish Committee on the Middle East.

The student saw no reason that his family's tax dollars should be spent to enrich this offensive magazine. And 123 of his fellow students signed a petition agreeing with him. On the other hand, the library director brandished a petition signed by 395(!) students supporting the magazine: "Libraries should provide information on all points of view."

A review committee of school employees noted that *The Progressive* "would have to be of little value as a library source or be incendiary in nature to warrant a recommendation for its removal. There is no support for either conclusion."

The review committee also pointed out that the magazine had been part of the media center collection for ten years, and it would stay there. "We do students a disservice," said the committee, "if we feel they will succumb to every enticement they encounter. They are fully capable of ignoring the advertisements [the student] cites as objectionable."

Sooner or later, however, a very careful reader may come across the numbers 666 in an issue of *The Progressive* or in some book. That is the Devil's number, and in some other town, another review committee may be formed to banish the devil from the school library. In Wilton Manors, Florida, an elementary school play—with the number 666 in it—was denounced by parents and a local minister. The play was then revised, but by then, it was too late in the school year for it to be produced.

There once was a school—the Mowat Middle School in Florida—where everybody was an exultant reader. The school had become so lively a center of learning—where kids actually read books they didn't have to—that in 1985 it was one of 150 American and Canadian secondary schools designated a Center of Excellence by the National Council of Teachers of English.

In each classroom, there were libraries from which students could choose what they wanted—though no one had to read anything, including in class, that he or his parents objected to. By 1986, the ninth-graders at Mowat were scoring on the high-twelfth-grade reading level. As a parent said, "I've caught my son reading sometimes on weekends. I also caught him writing a letter to his grandmother without my telling him to do it."

Then came the affair of *I Am the Cheese*, by Robert Cormier, one of the most honored of all young adult novels (and a 1977 Library of Congress Children's Book of the Year). A parent didn't like some of the language, and the district superintendent, Leonard Hall, didn't like its negative attitude toward government. (The boy in the book is part of a family in the not-always-caring Witness Protection Program.)

I Am the Cheese was immediately removed from the curriculum, the superintendent having ignored the usual review procedure when there is a complaint about a book. Other books began to be cast into darkness.

Superintendent Hall commanded teachers to examine classroom books closely and separate them into three categories. In the first would be books without "vulgar, obscene or sexually explicit material." In the second category would be those with "very limited vulgarity and no sexually explicit or obscene material." In the dread third category would be books with "quite a bit of vulgarity or obscene and/or sexually explicit material."

"Quite a bit" was not made more specific—nor were any of the other terms in the formula. Teachers in the district's two high schools pored over the books and presented Hall with sixty-four titles that were flagrantly impure by his standards and so belonged in category three. Hall removed them all from the reading lists. Among the titles:

The Red Badge of Courage, Intruders in the Dust, Oedipus Rex, Animal Farm, Twelfth Night, The Autobiography of Benjamin Franklin, The Canterbury Tales, John Ciardi's translation of *The Inferno, Hamlet,* and, of course, *Fahrenheit 451,* Ray Bradbury's novel about a future time when the only way to keep certain books alive is to go into hiding and memorize them, for otherwise they would be burned by the state.

At a crowded school board meeting to consider this remarkable new way of grading Western literature, students and teachers wore black armbands. Outside the room, a number of kids held up posters: "Why Teach Us to Read and Then Say We Can't?"

The school board put most of the books back on the classroom lists (*I Am the Cheese* excepted). But the superintendent and the principals under him retained the power to remove "unclean" books.

Subsequently, a number of books were banished from the Mowat School by its principal, including a young-adult novel of mine, *The Day They Came to Arrest the Book*. It's about attempts in a high school by black parents, fundamentalist Christian parents, and feminists to ban *Huckleberry Finn*. My novel was exiled because it has a "goddamn" in it.

Gloria Pipkin, a brave teacher at the Mowat Middle School, told me, as the censorship went on, that "ten of the eleven women in the English department at its peak have bailed out." Why does she keep on? That's what she was asked by a school board member who could not understand why she kept appearing before the board to convince it to bring back *I Am the Cheese*, among other books.

"Because it's worth it," Pipkin said.

She was the school's teacher of the year in 1983. Before the place was cleaned up.

During the unsuccessful resistance of teachers and students to the purges of the school library and curriculum, the superintendent said publicly that he was very disturbed at the effect of this battle over censorship on the children.

"All this talk of their rights," he said, "has distracted them from their studies. It has confused them."

"How can I tell kids in my government class to stand up for their rights, and not stand up for mine?"

In the past, Thomas Sobol, New York State's Education Commissioner, had indicated that he agreed with Supreme Court Justice

Abe Fortas's 1969 declaration that neither "students nor teachers shed their constitutional rights to freedom of speech or expression at the schoolhouse gate."

But in the case of Thomas O'Connor, a high school teacher in Brentwood, Long Island, Sobol issued a ruling in 1989 so hostile to academic freedom that it gave license to any school board in the state to harass a teacher if he or she teaches anything "controversial."

Thomas O'Connor, the teacher whose academic freedom was shredded, had been in the profession for twenty-one years. He enjoys working with youngsters, so much so that he spends a lot of extracurricular time coaching Brentwood High School's mock trial team. He and the students travel throughout the state, and the team has won a second-place award in the statewide competitions.

O'Connor has no use for the conventional wisdom about kids that you hear in some teachers' private conversations. Like, "They couldn't care less about who's President or what's going on in Eastern Europe." O'Connor knows better—from experience. "People say," he told me, "that kids aren't really involved in public issues. But they certainly are when they're challenged."

The state Board of Regents had mandated a new course in the high schools to challenge kids. It's called Participation in Government. While teaching it, O'Connor scheduled a debate in the class. It is a senior class. The students are seventeen and eighteen years old. Bear that in mind.

The subject of the debate was: "Should There Be Censorship in School Libraries?" O'Connor insists that in preparation for a debate, his students do research with some substance to it. Not just quick copying out of an encyclopedia.

A young woman who was taking the position that there should be some censorship in school libraries brought in an article she thought would buttress her argument. She had found "Better Orgasms" in the October 1988 issue of *Essence* magazine, a magazine primarily for black readers. O'Connor read it, decided it was pertinent to the debate, and arranged to have it copied for the rest of the class.

The student who worked the copying machine inadvertently left a copy there. An alarmed secretary found it, brought it to the attention of school authorities, and Thomas O'Connor's time of troubles began.

O'Connor describes himself as a "straitlaced Irish Catholic" who is "uncomfortable talking about sex to kids." But this article was written in so clinical a style that I doubt it would raise the prurient interest of even Jesse Helms. Indeed, during the entire course of the grim investigation of Thomas O'Connor, no school official called the article obscene. Nor did Commissioner Sobol.

Written by Monique Burns, the piece ought to be made available to all high school students. Among those quoted are Dr. Gail B. Wyatt, "a black sex therapist and associate professor of medical psychology at the University of California, Los Angeles," and Dr. William M. Chavis of Wayne State University.

The approach is physiological and psychological. Emphasizing the considerable diversity of female responses during sex, the article urges men to be sensitive to, and aware of, needs other than their own.

For enabling his seventeen- and eighteen-year-olds to read this decidedly educational material, O'Connor was summoned for interrogation. The first round of the classroom debate having already taken place, there was no point in demanding the recall of the article. Its contents had already entered the minds of the students—to lodge there maybe for the rest of their lives.

However, associate principal Gary Mintz sternly told O'Connor that he certainly hoped the teacher would not—in the second round of the debate—allow his students to use such terms in the article as "orgasm" or "clitoral stimulation."

What terms would Mr. Mintz prefer? Lenny Bruce would have loved to make the acquaintance of Mr. Mintz.

After the classroom debate was over, no parent complained about the use of the article or the phrases "clitoral stimulation" and "orgasm." But Thomas O'Connor was denounced by his superiors for having shown such "poor judgment" that it "cannot go unnoticed."

A letter was put in his file. This is the way apparatchiks get their jollies. In Long John Silver's time, it was called the black spot. In modern times, a letter in your file is not an indication that you ought to pick out your headstone, but it often does presage persistent unpleasantness so long as you stay on that job. You are a marked person. Thomas O'Connor has been flagged as a person of poor judgment.

But Brentwood High School authorities had more in store for Thomas O'Connor. He was commanded by associate principal Mintz to henceforth "notify your department head, Mr. Charles McCarthy, of the dissemination of *any material likely to be considered controversial by staff, class, or community*." (Emphasis added.)

The order given to O'Connor would ineluctably lead to self-censorship on his part and on the part of any teacher who believes in challenging kids to think for themselves.

This directive, O'Connor emphasized, is dangerous to a teacher's academic freedom because it is both "vague and over-broad."

How is a teacher to know in advance what is "controversial"? And to whom? There is hardly a textbook or a school library book or a magazine article or a lecture that would not offend *somebody* in the community if he or she finds out about it.

As another teacher at Brentwood High School said in an affidavit as an appeal in O'Connor's case was on its way to the state education commissioner:

"Were I subjected to the terms of the letter which has been issued to Mr. O'Connor, I would feel constrained to cut off classroom discussion heading into a controversial area."

In September, Thomas Sobol ruled against Thomas O'Connor. The letter is to stay in the teacher's file, and the directive stands. Nothing "controversial" can be disseminated by O'Connor until he clears it with the head of his department who, presumably, might then decide to clear it all the way up the official ladder. And then we'll be in another school year.

What the education commissioner has done is tell the administration of any public school in the state that it can apply this form of prior restraint to its teachers as well. And this censorship can be based on so flimsy a rationale as whether the material is "likely to be considered controversial by staff, class, or community."

In his opinion, Thomas Sobol, in a minuet indulged in by many school administrators, tried to show himself devoted to the First Amendment while he was grinding it into submission.

School authorities, Sobol said, "have broad discretion in the management of school affairs," but this "discretion must be exercised within the confines of the First Amendment rights of teachers and students." He even had the chutzpah to quote Justice William Brennan in *Keyishian* v. *Board of Regents of the University of the State of New York* (1967): "The vigilant protection of constitutional freedoms is nowhere more vital than in the community of American schools."

However, said the commissioner, this case has nothing to do with the First Amendment. The order to get the imprimatur of higher authorities before O'Connor can teach "controversial" stuff is "simply an exercise of the district's discretion to regulate instructional content."

As for O'Connor's contention that the directive would limit his academic right of self-expression, Sobol scoffed. The directive, he says, "refers solely to the distribution to students of instructional materials."

Who the hell does Sobol think selects those materials? And to have to get approval from on high of anything that is likely to be controversial to anybody in the whole district clearly restricts the teacher's right of self-expression and academic freedom.

Then, doing a soft-shoe step, the education commissioner said solemnly that he knows there has to be a "balance" between a school district's authority and a teacher's First Amendment rights. So what is the "balance"? Well, in exercising prior review of books, articles, magazines, and so forth, "administrators may only prevent the dissemination of material which is inappropriate to children of a particular age or maturity, or material that is otherwise lacking in educational value."

The "controversial" article, "Better Orgasms," was being read and debated by seventeen- and eighteen-year-olds. Did Sobol think that sex is as abstract to them as calculus? Did he believe that this particular article was "lacking in educational value"?

"How," O'Connor said to me, "can I tell kids in my government class to stand up for their rights, and not stand up for mine?" And their own right to receive information?

So far, the most pungent press comment on the case was that of an editorial writer in *Newsday:*

"The letter should be taken out of O'Connor's file—and [Brentwood school] officials should get a D...."

And what grade would you suggest for New York State education commissioner Thomas Sobol?

Thomas O'Connor sued his school district and Thomas Sobol in state court. He lost in the state supreme court (the lowest level) and then in the appellate division. So did his students.

"What would a school day be like without the Bill of Rights?"

During the roaring sixties, when public school students were brandishing their First Amendment rights like slingshots against any and all authority, a ten-year-old on the West Side of Manhattan was distributing leaflets one day demanding the removal of the principal of his public school.

The charges—with which a good many parents in the neighborhood agreed—were that the principal was unremittingly harsh, remote, and unable to speak anything but English in this teemingly multicultural neighborhood.

Standing near the schoolhouse door, the youngster looked up to find that the principal himself was reading one of the leaflets. The principal then snatched all the rest away from the boy, who loudly proclaimed that his First Amendment rights were being trampled upon. Seeing that the principal was unmoved, the ten-year-old declared that he was imposing a citizen's arrest on the principal for violating his constitutional rights.

No one paid attention to his citizen's arrest, except to laugh at the chutzpah of the kid. I admired what he had done, or tried to do. At least he not only knew what was in the First Amendment, but he also actually believed it could work. He believed it for a time anyway.

Years later I met a teacher, Mary Maasz, in a small town in Wisconsin who was dedicated to making her students feel—as she put it—that all of the Bill of the Rights was "personal" to them, belonged to them, and could be their sword against injustices inflicted on them by any agency of the state, including their principal.

There aren't any more similarly obsessed teachers now than there were then, and so Nancy Murray, inventor and director of the Bill of Rights Education Project of the Massachusetts Civil Liberties Union, has been working to make these liberties personal to teachers and students throughout the state.

There have been conferences and institutes from which teachers bring back the incendiary word to their classes, and youngsters also take part in these seminars. On occasion, Murray proposes challenges to teachers and students. In 1991, the bicentennial year of the Bill of Rights, for instance, she suggested that students be asked to think and write about this question: "What would a school day be like without the Bill of Rights?"

At Holyoke High School, Adam Waller, trying to make this nightmare real, imagined being stopped on his way to school by a man in a three-piece suit who told him: "You know the rules; it's Monday, time for the weekly drug testing."

As soon as he gets to class, a loud voice over the intercom declares: "The dogs are going to search the lockers in five minutes." As expectant barks and yelps fill the hallway, the boy wakes from his dream, breathing a sigh of relief.

I trust that a teacher will tell Adam Waller that parts of his fantasy are quite real. Unannounced random searches of lockers and classrooms by official dogs—with no particularized suspicion, let alone probable cause, that anyone is in possession of drugs— already take place in some jurisdictions. As for weekly drug tests of schoolchildren, they are not beyond possibility in towns, cities, and states where the Bill of Rights—with regard to adults as well as children—is far less important than displaying a harder-than-nails stance against drugs.

It would be instructive to also ask adults around the country what *their* lives would be like without the Bill of Rights. In many cases, I expect, one would first have to explain just what's in the Bill of Rights.

In an editorial, the *San Diego Union* has noted that in a recent public opinion poll, "59 percent of Americans could not identify the Bill of Rights. Many pundits doubt whether the American people would even ratify those liberties if they were put to a vote today. In fact, some Americans would gladly dispense with many of the liberties contained in the Bill of Rights."

Among them would appear to be the majority of the Rehnquist Supreme Court.

As for ratification, imagine the First Amendment on the ballot. It is very doubtful whether it could be reaffirmed in many places without such qualifications as "freedom of speech, or of the press—except for racist, anti-Catholic, sexist, anti-Semitic, homophobic and any other language offensive to any ethnic or religious groups."

Epilogue

... I often wonder whether we do not rest our hopes too much upon constitutions, upon laws and upon courts. These are false hopes; believe me, these are false hopes. Liberty lies in the hearts of men and women; when it dies there, no constitution, no law, no court can save it; no constitution, no law, no court can even do much to help it. While it lies there it needs no constitution, no law, no court to save it.—LEARNED HAND

... If we forget what we did, we won't know who we are. I am warning of an eradication of that—of the American memory that could result, ultimately, in an erosion of the American spirit.—RONALD REAGAN

There are many who lust for the simple answers of doctrine or degree. They are on the left and right. They are not confined to a single part of the society. They are terrorists of the mind.—A. BARTLETT GIAMATTI

In 1791, when Vermont became the tenth state to ratify the Bill of Rights, it already had a Constitution which powerfully guaranteed that no majority could tyrannize the minority, no elected or unelected government could exercise absolute control over individuals, minorities, or controversial ideas, and no one could be held in slavery.

Vermonters in 1777 put individual rights first, and the nuts and bolts of government second in their constitution, which seems to me a better way to go about the business of *constituting* a government than to stick individual rights on as an afterthought. The first twenty-one articles of the 1777 Vermont constitution lay out the principles of individual liberty in positive terms.

For most of those who founded Vermont and the United States, protection of individual rights was the highest purpose of government, the chief reason to form a government in the first place. Our ancestors knew from bitter experience what can happen to individuals when those in power decide what is the common good, and what limits to put on individual rights.

Today... much of our society is losing its grip on the idea of freedom. We don't have the same gut understanding of the importance of liberty that our ancestors did. We think we can trade off some freedoms without losing others. We don't understand what the Bill of Rights is all about.

We all believe in free speech for *us*, but not for *them*. Holocaust survivors think anti-Semitic speech should be outlawed; Senator Jesse Helms thinks whatever he considers indecent should not be protected by the First Amendment; George Bush and a lot of others think flag-burning is an unacceptable form of expression; some women's rights advocates think any speech that degrades women ought to be outlawed; anti-choice groups think it's okay to impose their religious principles and moral values on everyone else; indulging in "hate speech" can get you thrown out of some colleges.

If all these people and others are able to make exceptions to the First Amendment, we might as well kiss free expression good-bye.

The First Amendment is not the only amendment in danger. The right to be free of unwarranted search and seizure, the right to privacy, have both been seriously eroded through what the ACLU calls the "drug exception to the Constitution."

People think they'll rid the country of drugs and crime by getting rid of some of those rules. Give the police more power, let the government steal other people's houses, cars, dignity, basic rights, the nation's heritage. You're not a criminal, you say, so it won't affect you. You think you'll be safer if someone else's rights are taken away.

The problem is: the roots of crime cannot be destroyed by burning the Bill of Rights. If we allow coerced testimony to be used in court, if we allow police to search cars without warrants and bus passengers without individual suspicion of wrongdoing; if we allow people to be kept in jail without seeing a judge for forty-eight hours (all Supreme Court decisions near and in the Bicentennial Year of the Bill of Rights), what erosion of rights will come next?

Things change in two hundred years. America was very different in 1791 when Vermont ratified the Bill of Rights, less complex, we say, less dangerous.

But I doubt that those who settled these hills would agree that life was less dangerous in 1791 than it is today, or that individual liberty is less important now than it was then.

The difference is, early Americans understood what liberty means and they defended it fiercely. They knew exactly what they were doing when they ratified the Bill of Rights....
—LESLIE WILLIAMS, EXECUTIVE DIRECTOR, THE AMERICAN CIVIL LIBERTIES UNION OF VERMONT

The Nationalist Movement, a white-supremacist organization based in Learned, Mississippi, decided to further its work during the bicentennial year of the Bill of Rights by starting a talk show on public-access cable television in Dallas. Richard Barrett, a lawyer and organizer of the Nationalist Movement, was to be the host.

Barrett expected fierce opposition in Dallas, and that would have led to more publicity for his movement and for his cable television program.

Instead, Joe Cook, president of the Dallas Civil Liberties Union, told the *Dallas Morning News*:

"Civil libertarians despise the hatred and venom these people spread about.... At the same time, these people have as much right to speak their mind, or lack of it, as anyone else does."

Then there was Giullermo Galindon, chairman of Barrios Unidos, a Mexican-American group. He had no intention of trying to prevent Barrett from spreading the noisome message of the Nationalist Movement on Dallas television. Galindon says he supports free speech, "even if it's negative and dangerous. I say let them make fools of themselves."

And a member of the City Council, Al Lipscomb, sounded like Justice Hugo Black in his approach to free speech. ("My view," said Black, "is, without deviation, without exception, without any ifs, buts or whereases, that freedom of speech means that you shall not do something to people either for the views they have or the views they express or the words they speak or write.")

Said councilman Lipscomb about the Nationalist Movement coming to town: "It is their right to that access; it is their right to attempt to recruit. And I would be completely remiss if I attempted to impede their access."

The Nationalist Movement's access to public television might well receive a reception in some other cities that would slam the First Amendment aside. Since Dallas has not been known before as a shrine of the Bill of Rights, its attitude toward hate speech merits at least some hope for the future.

To Francis Lawrence, president of Rutgers University, the need for censoring insulting speech on campus is so obvious that, he says, "it is difficult to credit the seriousness of those who assail [speech codes] as evidence of...censorship."

Accordingly, Rutgers has a stiff speech code which hauls into the dock students whose words offend on the basis of race, religion, color, ancestry, sex, handicap, marital status, and sexual orientation.

The blanket of protection would seem to omit no one, and yet there is a veritable plague of racist graffiti and other rawly offensive expressions on campus. At a meeting of more than one thousand students to discuss this subterranean defiance of the tough anti-insult policy, a student rose, angrily pointed a finger at President Lawrence and yelled: "Educate us properly and these problems will not reoccur!"

Yet colleges keep on devising these "hate speech" regulations, in a leap into faith that civility can be attained by censorship. Law professor Michael Olivas, associate dean for research at the University of Houston Law Center, keeps track of these matters and he says that as of 1992, more than three hundred institutions of higher learning punish speech either in specific speech codes or as a part of their overall rules of conduct.

Duke University, however, marches to its own drum. Its dean of student life, Sue Wasiolek, says: "Our mission is to facilitate the exchanges of differences and different opinions—not to brainwash people."

The University of Wisconsin, on the stubborn other hand, remains convinced that a court-proof speech code is the only way to insure common decency on all of its 26 campuses. In March 1992, its Board of Regents approved a new tightened set of rules that its designer, law professor Ted Finman, guarantees will sail through the courts, unlike the university's first attempt to diminish the First Amendment.

Epithets, directly addressed to a specific student or students, will be punished if they are intended to demean, or create a hostile environment. Epithets are defined as a word, phrase, or symbol that "reasonable persons recognize" will "grievously" insult or threaten persons because of their race, sex, religion, color, creed, disability, sexual orientation, national origin, ancestry, or age."

These rattlesnake epithets, moreover, must "tend to invoke an immediate violent response." When they do, they are called "fighting words." This category, as I've noted, is based on a half-century-old Supreme Court decision which says that if the speaker's offensive words result in his getting rapped in the nose by the person he is addressing, the *speaker* is guilty—even though he's the one who is being physically assaulted. The lesson to the community is that the way to get rid of offensive speech and ensure civility is to punch out the speaker.

In addition to such broad words as "grievously" and "hostile," the new Wisconsin code invites further lawsuits by saying vaguely that whether an epithet is a "fighting word" depends on the judgment of a "person of average sensibility." The same person can have quite different levels of sensibility—depending on the subject that is being festooned with epithets.

The dissenters to the University of Wisconsin's continuing folly know more about education than the institution's president, chancellor (the famed Donna Shalala), and the majority of its faculty.

An editorial by John Torinus in a conservative student newspaper, the *Badger Herald*, notes: "Most bigotry is caused by fear of the unknown and ignorance. This sorry lack of knowledge cannot be rectified by stifling debate.... By forbidding even the supremely offensive speech of bigots, the university is stripping a weapon not from racists, sexists, and ageists—but from those who are fighting bigots."

A student majoring in journalism, Scott Milfred, makes the most cogent point in all the debates around the country about speech codes: "When you tell someone you simply can't say something, that's not educating them at all." And dissenting Regent Lee Dreyfus adds: "Students will now have less freedom of speech than non-students."

Until, in June 1992, the Supreme Court—in *R.A.V.* v. *City of St. Paul*—liberated college students throughout the country from the foolishness of speech codes.

In the fall of 1991, Jamaica Kincaid, an author who is black, was talking about writing and about life to students at Dunbar High School in Washington, D.C.

As the *Washington Post* reported:

"A male student, the first to speak in this class of mostly young women, asked if Kincaid had any trouble getting strong language into her books. None, she said.

"'Express everything you like,' she declared, energized by the question. '*No* word can hurt you. *None. No* idea can hurt you. Not being able to express an idea or a word *will* hurt you much more. As much as a *bullet.*'

"A voice, hushed, said '*Wow.*'"

What about the whole question of banning speech that's offensive to women, or to other groups?

"Kincaid was angrily dismissive. 'A lot of energy is wasted on these superficial things.... I can't get upset about "offensive to women" or "offensive to blacks" or "offensive to Native Americans" or "offensive to Jews."...'Offend! I can't get worked up about it.'

"She waved a long arm at them. 'Offend,' she said again. It was an exhortation."

Index